This *Companion to Schubert* examines the career, music, and reception of one of the most popular yet most misunderstood and elusive composers. Sixteen essays by leading Schubert scholars make up three parts. The first discusses the social, cultural, and musical climate in which Schubert lived and worked, the second surveys the scope of his musical achievement, and the third charts the course of his reception from the perceptions of his contemporaries to the assessments of posterity. Myths and legends about Schubert the man are explored critically and the full range of his musical accomplishment is examined.

Cambridge Companions to Music

The Cambridge Companion to the Violin
Edited by Robin Stowell

The Cambridge Companion to the Recorder
Edited by John Thomson

The Cambridge Companion to the Clarinet
Edited by Colin Lawson

The Cambridge Companion to Chopin
Edited by Jim Samson

The Cambridge Companion to Bach
Edited by John Butt

The Cambridge Companion to Schubert

A Schubert Evening at Josef von Spaun's by Moritz von Schwind.
Bildarchiv der Österreichische Nationalbibliothek

780.92
S384F
G443c

1789
18.55

The Cambridge Companion to

SCHUBERT

Edited by Christopher H. Gibbs

CAMBRIDGE
UNIVERSITY PRESS

Christian Heritage
College Library
2100 Greenfield Dr.
El Cajon, CA 92019   79096

Published by the Press Syndicate of the University of Cambridge
The Pitt Building, Trumpington Street, Cambridge CB2 1RP
40 West 20th Street, New York, NY 10011–4211, USA
10 Stamford Road, Oakleigh, Melbourne 3166, Australia

© Cambridge University Press 1997

First published 1997

Printed in the United Kingdom at the University Press, Cambridge

A catalogue record for this book is available from the British Library

Library of Congress cataloguing in publication data
The Cambridge companion to Schubert / edited by Christopher H. Gibbs.
    p. cm. – (Cambridge companions to music)
  Includes bibliographical references and index.
  ISBN 0 521 48229 1 (hardback). – ISBN 0 521 48424 3 (paperback).
  1. Schubert, Franz, 1797–1828.   I. Gibbs, Christopher Howard.
II. Series.
ML410.S3C18   1997
780′.92–dc20   96–14260 CIP MN
 [B]

ISBN 0 521 48229 1 hardback
ISBN 0 521 48424 3 paperback

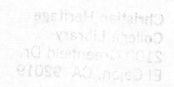

Contents

The contributors

Leon Botstein is President of Bard College, where he is Leon Levy Professor in the Arts and Humanities. He serves as the music director and principal conductor of the American Symphony Orchestra and the artistic director of the Bard Music Festival. He is editor of *The Musical Quarterly* and author of *Judentum und Modernität: Essays zur Rolle der Juden in der deutschen und österreichischen Kultur, 1848–1938* and of the forthcoming *Music and its Public: Habits of Listening and the Crisis of Musical Modernism in Vienna, 1870–1914*.

Martin Chusid is Professor of Music and Director of the American Institute for Verdi Studies at New York University. He wrote his dissertation on Schubert's chamber music, edited and wrote a monograph on the "Unfinished" Symphony, edited the string quintets and a volume of string quartets for the *Neue Schubert-Ausgabe*, and wrote numerous articles on Schubert's music. He is currently preparing a facsimile edition of Schubert's *Schwanengesang*, together with a volume of essays. He has compiled a catalogue of Verdi's operas, co-edited the *Verdi Companion*, edited *Rigoletto* for the new critical edition, and written numerous articles on the operas of Verdi, Mozart, and Dvořák.

Thomas A. Denny teaches music history at Skidmore College. He has published articles on Schubert in the *Journal of Musicology, Journal of Musicological Research, Schubert durch die Brille*, and is editing the opera *Fierrabras* for the *Neue Schubert-Ausgabe*. In 1995, in collaboration with the Westfield Center, he organized a conference on Schubert's piano music at the Smithsonian Institution in Washington, D.C.

Christopher H. Gibbs has taught music history at Columbia University, Haverford College, and currently at the State University of New York at Buffalo. He is the director of the *Schubertiade* at the 92nd Street Y in New York City. His dissertation, an examination of the reception of Schubert Lieder, won the 1992 dissertation prize of the Austrian Cultural Institute.

David Gramit is Associate Professor in music history at the University of Alberta. His essays on the social and intellectual context of Schubert's circle, Schubert reception, and the construction of musical meaning in nineteenth-century culture have appeared in *19th-Century Music, Music and Letters,* the *Journal of Musicological Research, Current Musicology,* and *Schubert durch die Brille.*

L. Michael Griffel is Professor of Music at Hunter College and the Graduate School of the City University of New York, and serves on the graduate faculty at the Mannes College of Music. A specialist in the instrumental music of Schubert, he is completing *Franz Schubert: A Guide to Research.*

Xavier Hascher teaches music theory at Strasbourg University for the Humanities and is associate researcher at the Institute for Aesthetics and Art Sciences of Paris Panthéon-Sorbonne University. He is the chairman of the French Schubert Society and editor of *Cahiers F. Schubert.* He has published *Schubert, la forme sonate et son évolution* and is preparing another book on the reception of Schubert's works in France during the nineteenth century.

William Kinderman is Professor of Music at the University of Victoria, British Columbia, and has taught extensively at the Hochschule der Künste, Berlin. He is the author of *Beethoven's Diabelli Variations, Beethoven,* and editor of *Beethoven's Compositional Process.* An accomplished pianist, he has recorded the Diabelli Variations for Hyperion.

David Montgomery is a conductor, pianist, musicologist, and editor. He received the Ph.D. from U.C.L.A. in 1987 and has since contributed to major English and American journals on the subjects of performance practice and nineteenth-century aesthetics and analysis. He has served as editor and musicologist for Sony Classical and as a historical advisor to Columbia Pictures. As a pianist David Montgomery devotes himself particularly to nineteenth-century Viennese works, and as a conductor is engaged in a series of recordings with the Jena Philharmonic for BMG's Arte Nova label. Mr Montgomery lives in Hamburg, Germany.

Kristina Muxfeldt teaches music history at Yale University. She has published on a variety of topics in early nineteenth-century social history and aesthetics.

Margaret Notley has published articles on Brahms, Bruckner, and Viennese musical life in *19th-Century Music,* the *Journal of the American Musicological Society,* and several anthologies. She is a fellow of the National Endowment for the Humanities in 1996–97.

After a successful career as a schoolmaster, as a producer and administrator in the BBC education department, **John Reed** retired to a busy life as a writer. His first book, *Schubert: The Final Years,* was noteworthy for its redating of the "Great" C Major Symphony. His most important books, however, are the critical biography of Schubert published in the "Master Musicians" series, and the *Schubert Song Companion*, which was awarded the Vincent Duckles Prize of the Music Library Association of America. He is an Honorary Member of the International Franz Schubert Institute of Vienna, and was the first Chairman of the Schubert Institute of the UK.

Charles Rosen is a pianist. Among his books are *The Classical Style, Sonata Forms, The Frontiers of Meaning: Three Informal Lectures on Music,* and *The Romantic Generation.*

Glenn Stanley is Associate Professor of Music at the University of Connecticut, Storrs, was guest editor of *Beethoven Forum III* and a contributor to the revised *Groves Dictionary of Music and Musicians.* He is the editor of the forthcoming *Cambridge Companion to Beethoven.*

Susan Youens is Professor of Musicology at the University of Notre Dame and author of *Retracing a Winter's Journey: Schubert's Winterreise, Schubert – Die schöne Müllerin, Hugo Wolf: The Vocal Music,* and *Schubert's Poets and the Making of Song.*

Chronology

1797   Born in Vienna on January 31
1806   Studies with Michael Holzer at the Liechtental church
1808   Becomes a choirboy in the Imperial Court Chapel and enters the
       Stadtkonvikt boarding school
1810   Composes the *Fantasy in D* (D1)
1811   Composes *Hagars Klage* (D5) and other songs
1812   His mother dies; writes part of *Der Spiegelritter* (D11)
1813   Leaves the Stadtkonvikt; First Symphony (D82)
1814   Successful performances of the Mass in F (D105); composes
       Gretchen am Spinnrade (D118) and nearly 150 other songs; begins
       teaching at his father's school
1815   *Erlkönig* (D328) and many other songs to Goethe poems in
       particular; completes his Second Symphony (D125) and writes his
       Third (D200); writes two Masses (D167 and 324) and four operas
       (D190, 220, 239, 326)
1816   Fourth and Fifth Symphonies (D417, 485); songs set to Goethe's
       texts are sent to the poet, but Schubert gets no response; stops
       teaching
1817   Meets Johann Michael Vogl
1818   First song printed (D586); spends the summer teaching for the
       Esterházy family in Zseliz; in the fall Schubert moves to inner city
       and lives with Johann Mayrhofer; completes Sixth Symphony
       (D589)
1819   "Trout" Quintet (D667); travels with Vogl during summer; first
       public performance of a song (D121)
1820   Arrested with his friend Johann Chrisostomus Senn; performances
       of *Die Zwillingsbrüder* (D647) at the Kärntnerthor Theater and of
       Die Zauberharfe (D644) at the Theater an der Wien; composes the
       oratorio *Lazarus* (D689)
1821   *Erlkönig* published as Op. 1; important public performances,
       publications, and reviews
1822   "Unfinished" Symphony (D759); "Wanderer" Fantasy (D760);
       completes the opera *Alfonso und Estrella* (D732)
1823   Illness; *Die schöne Müllerin* (D795); *Fierrabras* (D796); *Rosamunde*
       (D797); *Die Verschworenen* (D787)

1824   Second trip to Zseliz; Octet (D803), String Quartets in A Minor
       (D804) and D Minor (D810)
1825   Travels with Vogl to Upper Austria; begins composition of the
       "Great" C Major Symphony (D944)
1826   String Quartet in G Major (D887)
1827   Beethoven dies on March 26, Schubert is torch bearer at his
       funeral; begins the opera *Der Graf von Gleichen* (D918); completes
       Mass in A flat (D678); *Winterreise* (D911); Trio in E Flat (D929)
1828   E flat Major Mass (D950); the C Major String Quintet (D956);
       Fantasy in F Minor for piano four hands (D940); last three piano
       sonatas in C Minor, A Major, and B flat Major (D958–60);
       Schubert's public concert given on March 26; dies on November 19
1829   *Schwanengesang* (D957) published
1839   Last three piano sonatas published
       Mendelssohn premieres "Great" C Major Symphony
1853   Octet and String Quintet in C published
1863   The bodies of Schubert and Beethoven are exhumed from
       Währing Cemetery for scientific study
1865   Premiere of the "Unfinished" Symphony; publication in Vienna of
       the first extended Schubert biography
1872   Statue of Schubert is dedicated in Vienna's Stadtpark
1884   Collected edition of Schubert's works begins to appear from
       Breitkopf und Härtel (*ASA*)
1888   The bodies of Schubert and Beethoven are exhumed a second time
       and moved to Vienna's Central Cemetery
1897   Schubert Centennial, collected edition is completed

Note to the reader

Otto Erich Deutsch's invaluable collections of Schubert documents are cited within the body of the text, as well as in the notes, with the following abbreviations:

SDB   *Schubert: A Documentary Biography.* Trans. Eric Blom. London, 1946. (The American edition is entitled *The Schubert Reader: A Life of Franz Schubert in Letters and Documents* [New York, 1947].)

SMF   *Schubert: Memoirs by His Friends.* Trans. Rosamond Ley and John Nowell. London, 1958.

When necessary, full citations of the German editions of these collections are provided in the notes.

The first critical edition of Schubert's collected works (*ASA*), published by Breitkopf und Härtel (1884–97), has been superseded by a new edition – *Neue Schubert-Ausgabe* – still in progress, that will be referred to as *NSA*, followed by the series, volume, and page number.

Acknowledgments

It is a pleasure to have the opportunity to thank those people who supported in the realization of this volume. I am grateful to Walter Frisch, Ernst Hilmar, Karen Painter, and Glenn Stanley for helping to identify potential contributors and to music editor Penny Souster for her encouragement with the project.

Parts of my own chapters in this collection benefited from suggestions and readings provided by Christopher Hatch, Edward A. Lippman, Donald Wilson, Janet Johnson, Morten Solvik, David Gramit, Jane Malmo and Helena Sedláčková Gibbs.

Introduction: the elusive Schubert

Christopher H. Gibbs

WANDERER! HAST THOU HEARD SCHUBERT'S SONGS?
HERE LIES HE WHO SANG THEM.

HE WAS PLACED NEAR THE BEST ONES WHEN HE DIED, AND YET
HE WAS STILL SCARCELY HALF-WAY IN HIS CAREER.

Franz Grillparzer, Vienna's preeminent poet, sketched five epitaphs for Schubert's grave (*SDB* 899). The controversial one ultimately adopted – THE ART OF MUSIC HERE ENTOMBED A RICH POSSESSION, BUT EVEN FAR FAIRER HOPES – has been interpreted in various ways.[1] Robert Schumann, Schubert's most astute early critic, lost patience with Grillparzer: "It is pointless to guess at what more [Schubert] might have achieved. He did enough; and let them be honored who have striven and accomplished as he did."[2]

Perhaps Grillparzer's words are better viewed not as a lament over the loss of what more Schubert might have achieved had he lived longer, but rather as evidence of how the composer's genuine artistic achievement was not fully appreciated during his own time, how the true scope of his accomplishment eluded even some of his most sympathetic friends and admirers. During Schubert's lifetime, Grillparzer and the majority of his contemporaries never heard Schubert's late piano sonatas, the C Major String Quintet, the mature symphonies and operas. Many of his supreme compositions remained unknown to a Biedermeier Vienna that revered Beethoven, adored Rossini, and thrilled to Paganini.

Schubert's position, literally as well as symbolically, has changed dramatically since his death in 1828 at the age of thirty-one. Over the course of the nineteenth century, he gradually joined the elect, becoming an immortal composer: the peer of Beethoven, and superior to Rossini and Paganini. His first biographer, Heinrich Kreissle von Hellborn, wrote in 1865:

> Nowadays, when the largest part of Schubert's treasures has been revealed to us, Grillparzer's epitaph, which gave offense so many years ago, sounds to our ears still more strangely, and we may hope that over Schubert's future resting place there will be nothing carved but the name of the composer. As the simple "Beethoven" over that great man's grave, the word "Schubert" will speak volumes.[3]

Kreissle proved prescient. In 1888 Schubert's body, together with Beethoven's (buried just a few feet away), was exhumed from Währing Cemetery and moved to the "Grove of Honor" in Vienna's Central Cemetery. His new tombstone simply reads "Franz Schubert."

Masterpieces "outside" history

Among nineteenth-century composers of the highest rank, Schubert is the only one whose lifetime fame was significantly at odds with his later glory. One of the aims of this *Companion* is to explore some of the reasons for this disparity. It seeks to register the social, cultural, and musical climate in which Schubert lived and worked, to measure the scope of his musical achievement, and to chart the course of his reception from the perceptions of his contemporaries to the assessments of posterity. The volume offered here is neither an encyclopedic reference nor a comprehensive examination of Schubert's oeuvre. Rather, in keeping with the etymology of the word "companion" ("taking bread together"), *The Cambridge Companion to Schubert* is more a collection of exchanges – historical, critical, and analytical. This book explores some of the factors that have restricted the serious understanding and interpretation of Schubert, and that have made him an elusive figure to this day.

The initial neglect that Schubert's music encountered is often exaggerated. Nonetheless, certain personal, cultural, and musical factors caused an incomplete, even one-dimensional portrait of the man and his music to emerge, both during his lifetime and during the half-century that followed. Schubert's well-documented shyness and disregard for self-promotion, his lack of virtuosity as a performer, the scarcity of his own letters and writings, his untimely death, the indifference of early commentators, the biased reminiscences of certain friends – all these factors help explain why he eluded biographers.

The limited knowledge about and availability of Schubert's music during the first half of the nineteenth century also profoundly affected both critical and biographical accounts. That the public, for example, had to wait more than forty years for the première of the "Unfinished" Symphony (D759) meant that a defining work, so revealing of Schubert's artistic maturity and compositional style, remained both "outside" history and buried within it, the kernel of its eventual revision.

Indeed, for much of the nineteenth century, many of Schubert's finest compositions were unavailable, especially the large-scale instrumental works. As Schubert's oeuvre became gradually known, changes in musical culture, taste, and also production changed the context in which the music was experienced. Intimate gatherings, best known to Schubert's contemporaries, have since given way to public concerts. The vocal and dance music most familiar in his day is now largely forgotten. What commands attention today are his symphonies, chamber music, song cycles, and piano sonatas – mostly unpublished and/or unperformed publicly in the 1820s; these are the works that now define Schubert's artistic achievement and secure his stature.

By the Schubert centennial year of 1897, nearly all of his music had been published, and by the 1997 bicentennial, nearly all of it has been recorded. This broad availability allows us to explore the full range of Schubert's art and to recognize how adroitly he negotiated both the public and private spheres, combined popular and more elevated styles, and entertained Biedermeier Vienna while helping to usher in musical Romanticism.

In his own time: "favorite composer" Franz Schubert and the "highest in art"

Schubert earned his fame through his songs and dances, pieces which prompted critics to refer to him as a "favorite composer" (*beliebter Tonsetzer*).[4] Roughly 630 of his songs survive; by the end of 1828 nearly 190 were published and many others circulated in handwritten copies.[5] Schubert and his friends proved remarkably astute in choosing which ones to disseminate, perform, and publish. Those songs available and best known to his contemporaries generally remain the most prominent today. Publication triggered a self-perpetuating process: what was easily accessible became the most familiar, as well as the most frequently translated, anthologized, and arranged.

Although Schubert's Lieder enjoyed a unique position in his own time, his dances, partsongs, and keyboard music also won widespread favor, as evidenced by frequent performances, abundant publications, and substantial critical acclaim.[6] Viennese publishers released nearly 160 dances during the 1820s. These dances exhibit another important ingredient of Schubert's musical character – his conviviality – for both songs and dances were often written for, and played by, his friends and social circle. (Schubert himself never danced [*SMF* 121, 133].)

Schubert also excelled in composing partsongs, mostly for a male quartet of two tenors and two basses. About twenty were published during his lifetime, and they were publicly performed more often than his works in any other genre. Finally, Schubert was best known in his own time for his piano music. Particularly popular were piano duets, unsurpassed in this special repertory, but largely ignored today; their eclipse (as with his partsongs) was one result of the general decline in domestic music-making.[7]

Taken together, the Lieder, dances, and partsongs account for over ninety per cent of Schubert's works published during his lifetime; the rest are mostly short keyboard works for two or four hands.[8] None of Schubert's orchestral works was published during this period, nor was any of his dramatic music. Five sacred pieces appeared (one under his brother Ferdinand's name [D621]), but only one of the Masses (D452). Significant large-scale works, for keyboard or chamber ensemble, number less than a dozen publications. In contrast to the available works of Gyrowetz or Hummel, let alone Beethoven and Mozart, Schubert's publications – all from a brief seven years (1821–28) – were surprisingly numerous, but hardly representative of the scope of his art.

As is common in surveys of a composer's oeuvre, the works discussed in the second section of this book are grouped by genre and instrumentation. Such artificial divisions, however, invite duplication among chapters. Matters of style further confound tidy categories. Schubert's lyricism, for example, permeates all the genres in which he composed; the infusion of his Lieder into a wide range of instrumental works testifies to a sovereign lyric sensibility.

For the elusive Schubert, difficulties of classification are both musical and functional. Some of his most ambitious instrumental compositions are piano duets, treated in William Kinderman's discussion of the keyboard music. Much of the piano duet repertory also falls, however, under the category of social music, which Margaret Notley examines. And as Charles Rosen's commentary on some of the same pieces demonstrates, the fingerprints of Schubert's style and of his compositional innovations appear in these works just as much as in the far better known piano sonatas, chamber music, and symphonies.

Complications in classifying Schubert's work unambiguously within neatly defined categories of genre (or form), style, technical level (amateur or professional), and social function (public, semi-public, or private), begin to explain his putative neglect during his lifetime, and are consistent with an increased blurring and mixing of genres associated with musical Romanticism. The disparity between the intimate and small-scale music that defined Schubert's Viennese fame in the 1820s, and those instrumental works – the string masterpieces, late piano sonatas, symphonies – which placed him among the immortals of Western music, is a concrete manifestation of a multifaceted oeuvre that served various needs and ends, not only for Schubert and his family, friends, and critics, but also for those who listened to his works many decades later. In the first chapter, Leon Botstein examines, from a social-historical perspective, the context in which this music was first heard and warns of extracting Schubert's art from the grim realities of Viennese daily life in the 1820s.

The distinctions between amateur and professional, and between private and public (also not clear-cut), to some degree relate to other aspects of Schubert's musical character, such as his highest, most serious aspirations in certain works and a lighter, more popular sensibility found in others. Reflecting a traditional hierarchy of genres, short songs and dances had to contend with large-scale symphonies and operas.[9] Several authors in this volume refer to the famous letter Schubert wrote not long before his death to the Mainz publisher Schott in which he mentions "three operas, a Mass, and a symphony" so as to acquaint Schott with his "strivings after the highest in art" (*SDB* 740). Although the reminiscences of Schubert's friends focus mainly on the Lieder, many likewise refer to his "larger efforts" and the "highest branches of art" when discussing his big pieces. By the end of Schubert's life, critics were also getting the message. Just months before his death, the *Wiener Zeitschrift für Kunst, Literatur, Theater und Mode* wrote: "The great talent of the renowned song and romance composer is many-sided and tries itself in every branch, as do all those who possess the spirit of true and upward-striving art" (*SDB* 781).

One must be careful not to distinguish inappropriately between high and low culture, popular and serious tastes, because such lines were not drawn the same way in Schubert's time. Rossini's operas, for example, were both thoroughly professional and extraordinarily successful. And Schubert, like Rossini, remarkably mixed, even within a single composition, what we now characterize as elevated and popular styles.[10] Moreover, Schubert composed "orchestral" songs, "lyrical" symphonies, and occasionally used small Lieder as the basis for large instrumental works.[11] Still, a gap remains between the music and styles typically associated with Biedermeier music-making in Vienna and the heady cosmopolitan world of opera and symphony from which reputations – and money – traditionally came.

Schubert's music defies tidy historical boundaries and stylistic categorizations. As Charles Rosen has written about attempts to designate Schubert as a Classical, post-Classical, or Romantic composer: he "stands as an example of the resistance of the material of history to the most necessary generalization, and as a reminder of the irreducibly personal facts that underlie the history of style."[12] While he remains an elusive figure, perhaps we can appreciate that his puzzling position for nearly two centuries represents an answer more than a problem, that Schubert's multivalence partly explains his achievement and appeal.

Schubert in "the epoch of Beethoven and Rossini"

Historians would today label the period encompassing Schubert's active career, roughly from the time of the Congress of Vienna to his death in 1828, as the "Epoch of Beethoven and Schubert." Contemporaneous descriptions, however, are tellingly different. In an influential survey of music history published in 1834, Raphael Georg Kiesewetter characterized the years 1800–32 as "The Epoch of Beethoven and Rossini."[13] This description may now seem odd precisely because it reflects distinctions of genre, aesthetic ideologies, and a north–south geography that have long since ceased to matter. Kiesewetter's principal concern was with the prestigious genres of opera and instrumental music, the realm of the "highest in art," into which Schubert, as a composer most associated with social and domestic music, did not readily fit. And therefore, even though Kiesewetter himself held Schubertiades in his home,[14] he did not even mention Schubert in his book, a sign not so much of Schubert's lack of fame, or an indictment of the composer's talent, as an indication of what kinds of music mattered most. However, by the 1860s, when Vienna's preeminent music critic Eduard Hanslick wrote his still-essential *Geschichte des Concertwesens in Wien*, the period had become designated as the "Age of Beethoven and Schubert";[15] at this stage, the public recognized Schubert as one of the "immortals."

One wants to avoid uncritically perpetuating distinctions between a formidable instrumental north and a sensuous lyrical south, the "brains" of the hard-working German Beethoven as opposed to the "beauty" of the charming Italian Rossini. For one thing, the ascription of popular to Rossini and serious to Beethoven is not always clear. Rossini wrote more serious operas than comic ones, and Beethoven's most popular pieces with his own public are quite different from posterity's verdict: *Wellington's Victory*, the "Allegretto" from the Seventh Symphony, the song *Adelaide*, the Septet, and the oratorio *Christ on the Mount of Olives* were the crowd-pleasers of his day. Yet the long-standing tension between a German instrumental tradition and an Italian vocal one was much discussed in Schubert's time and forms part of many composers' own self-representations. If Rossini's later report to Wagner is accurate (and accurately reported), the topic dominated the single meeting between Rossini and Beethoven in the spring of 1822.

Where does Schubert, promoted privately by Kiesewetter in his own home yet unmentioned publicly in print, fit into this bifurcated musical culture?[16] Although Schubert yearned for success in opera and symphony, and composed prodigiously in both, he had only minimal and brief success with their public performances, all of which were early in his career. He most actively participated in a private and semi-private culture of edification and entertainment. (Where significant instrumental pieces are concerned, Schubert's greatest exposure came in presenting chamber music, largely because he had a strong and prominent advocate in the famous violinist Ignaz Schuppanzigh, a close collaborator of Beethoven.)

Beyond Kiesewetter's concern with geography and genre, his preoccupation with Beethoven and Rossini also reflects the musical culture of his time by pairing the greatest composer with the most popular one. While the venerated Beethoven claimed a new role for music among the arts, Rossini entertained and delighted. Rossini's music inundated publishers' catalogues not in complete scores, however, but rather in all manner of arrangements aimed at domestic enjoyment. Similarly, Schubert's considerable success in getting a large number of his works published came from intimate genres and from arrangements. Yet while Schubert's reputation, for all the national and institutional differences, essentially belonged to a Rossinian tradition of entertainment, albeit in a domesticated version, his creative legacy was posthumously acclaimed by many as Beethovenian in dimension.

This *Companion* helps show that both the contemporaneous and posthumous assessments of Schubert – the "favorite" composer of small pieces and the immortal genius of "heavenly length" – are sound. They are complementary, not contradictory. Historically, keyboard-dominated genres that Schubert himself cultivated during his career gave way in importance to his large-scale instrumental music; private Schubertiades opened out to public concerts. The Biedermeier Schubert known to the musical Vienna of the 1820s eventually came to be the Romantic Schubert lionized by Schumann, Mendelssohn, Liszt, and Brahms. For decades to come, Schubert's popular accessibility continued to attract listeners and win new admirers through all manner of arrangements, particularly piano transcriptions by Liszt and others. As the century progressed, Schubert was also credited with having written instrumental masterpieces, and he thereby gained new esteem.

Even as pieces representing Schubert's "highest" aspirations slowly won recognition, some of his compositional procedures and innovations continued to elude critics, and still do today. Rosen has argued recently that "the music of Beethoven is literally the origin of our conception of musical analysis, and this has unnaturally restricted analysis by limiting it almost entirely to methods of examination relevant to his music."[17] Especially when set against Beethovenian paradigms, Schubert's formal structures were often judged lacking. What the enthusiastic Schumann perceived (or perhaps excused) as "heavenly length" in Schubert, others dismissed as tedious repetition. A number of authors in this volume explore, and appreciate, how Schubert's compositional strategies and musical values differed from Beethoven's.

The complex mixture of Schubert's available and esteemed works provides a clue to the complexities of his reception – we need to grasp how he realized a lofty aesthetic realm for his music alongside a social and entertaining one. Grillparzer's notorious epitaph does not so much describe the reality of Schubert's genius as demonstrate the scope of Biedermeier awareness. Twentieth-century audiences know that the intimate Schubert, the "favorite" song and dance composer of the 1820s, had a great deal more to offer.

Schubert as "father of the Lied"

It will come as no surprise that every chapter in this book refers at some point to Schubert Lieder. For nearly two centuries Schubert's songs have resounded as the common denominator of his fame. Lieder first spread his name locally and internationally, and Lieder later secured his place in music history. While the stature of individual songs occasionally changes, *Gretchen am Spinnrade* nevertheless remains his first undisputed masterpiece, and *Erlkönig*, written shortly afterwards, one of the commanding compositions of the century.

Not since the Renaissance could masterpieces of such unassuming scale, lasting less than five minutes, so powerfully mold a career and decisively affect music history. When Schubert's fame began to flourish with the *Kunstlied*, this relatively minor artistic genre still awaited its "master." Two decades earlier, at a comparable stage in his own career, Beethoven honored his sonata-form compositions by granting them opus numbers. Schubert, in his debut publications of 1821, crowned his songs with opus numbers, signaling that they too could be significant works of substantial content.

For well over a century now, writers have hailed October 19, 1814, the date Schubert composed *Gretchen am Spinnrade*, as the "Birthday of German Song." Schubert as the "Father of the Lied" is a view all too familiar. It alarms scholars who see in this conception an implicit rejection of Schubert's predecessors and an indiscriminate use of the term "Lied" for a wide variety of pieces. Nevertheless, we must appreciate not only what Schubert took from, or how he surpassed, his models – the "real history" of the Lied in a chronological sense that Kristina Muxfeldt touches upon in her chapter – but also what prompted the perception of Schubert as the composer whose works were exemplary for this particular genre, as Beethoven's were for the symphony.[18] Earlier German Lied composers, such as Johann Rudolf Zumsteeg, Johann Friedrich Reichardt, and Carl Friedrich Zelter, composed works at the most advanced stage of the *Kunstlied*, but their efforts neither elevated the genre nor decisively rivaled, in musical quality or popular acclaim, works such as Mozart's *Das Veilchen*, K. 476, or Beethoven's *Adelaide*, Op. 46.[19]

With Schubert, the nascent Romantic Lied changed not only in musical content, but also in historical stature. As the discussion by Susan Youens demonstrates, important changes in German poetry at the turn of the century were fundamental to the new position of song. Goethe's poetry in particular inspired Schubert's earliest masterpieces. Along with this heightened literary awareness came other factors: the Romantic cultivation of small-scale forms in general, the rise of a middle-class musical culture and domestic music-making, and the new tonal qualities and technical capacities of the piano. Thrilling accompaniments of unprecedented intensity, extraordinary difficulty, and unifying power that rarely appeared in the Lieder of Schubert's contemporaries were now possible.

This constellation allowed the Lied to reach new heights in the second decade of the century. Some critics constructed elaborate historical schemes for the Lied and for Schubert's contribution to it, often in relation to the towering figure of Beethoven – for this was the one area in which Schubert surpassed the master.[20] An 1859 article in the musical journal *Signale für die musikalische Welt* presents a remarkable analogy between Schubert's Lieder and other supreme creative triumphs:

> The Schubert song is – like the Goethe poem, the Beethoven symphony, and the Shakespeare drama – a *unicum*. That is to say: the essence of the particular art form achieves its highest and purest appearance in the works of these masters. Schubert's Lieder cannot – as could Mendelssohn's, or Schumann's, or a Mozart aria – be imitated; any more than can a Beethoven symphony.[21]

By elevating, fulfilling, and therefore, in a sense, defining the *Kunstlied*, Schubert's work in this genre eclipsed his other music for decades to come. (That so much of the instrumental music went unpublished only complicated matters.) As the "Father of the Lied," Schubert was viewed not only as the preeminent composer of Lieder, but also as the one who had finally realized the potential of the genre.

The changing Schubert canon

The changes in stature of various genres, the array of venues in which Schubert's music was heard, and the growing availability of his scores help to explain the critical adjustments about what constituted the canon of Schubert's central works. While much of his dance music, and many of his partsongs, piano duets, keyboard music, and even Lieder gradually faded in popularity over the course of the century, works in other genres received increasing attention. Admittedly, however, some newly acclaimed pieces are themselves no longer much performed in the late twentieth century, including such one-time favorites as the unfinished oratorio *Lazarus* (D689) or the Singspiel *Die Verschworenen* (D787).

The popularity of specific Lieder also changed. In Schubert's time *Der Wanderer* (D489) was second in fame only to *Erlkönig*; rarely performed today, it is now associated mainly with the "Wanderer" Fantasy in C Major for piano (D760). In a letter to his parents Schubert tells how *Ellens Gesang III* (D839) genuinely moved friends (*SDB* 434–35; cf. 458). Gradually this ubiquitous song, better known as *Ave Maria*, was so egregiously misappropriated that, except in the care of the greatest interpreters, it devolved into kitsch. Many of Schubert's compositions entered the popular consciousness through myriad *fin-de-siècle* potpourris that dispensed melodious tunes from the "Unfinished" Symphony, from *Rosamunde*, and from countless songs and dances.

The chapters in the third section of this volume chart some of these changes in repertory and the role that celebrated composers and performers played in these developments. For example, while Artur Schnabel's performances and recordings are justly credited for bringing Schubert's piano sonatas into the modern concert repertory, John Reed shows that as early as 1868 Sir Charles Hallé had performed all eleven Schubert sonatas then available in print.

During the course of the twentieth century the canon has continued to evolve. For instance, while the "Arpeggione" Sonata and the "Trout" Quintet retain their popular appeal, Schubert is now most highly esteemed, and is best represented in the concert hall and on recordings, by late works such as the "Great" C Major Symphony, the C Major String Quintet, and the last three piano sonatas. Illustrative are the two Müller song cycles, both published in the 1820s and therefore known to Schubert's contemporaries. In the nineteenth century, *Die schöne Müllerin* held a prized place among Schubert's works, while after the Second World War *Winterreise* came to dominate critical and public attention. (This twentieth-century reception has vindicated Schubert who, responding to his friends' pronounced lack of enthusiasm for the latter cycle, allegedly declared, "I like these songs more than all the others, and you will come to like them too" [*SMF* 138].)

Along with these changes in canonic repertory came radically new descriptions of Schubert the man, especially in recent decades. Most significant, and widely publicized, have been Maynard Solomon's articles presenting a compelling case that Schubert probably engaged in homosexual activities.[22] But well before this claim – fiercely debated and, by some, passionately rejected – a more complex, multi-dimensional, even "neurotic" Schubert had already emerged, one more associated with a song like *Der Leiermann* than with *Das Wandern*.[23]

Paradoxically, as Schubert's own milieu recedes further into history, we continue to gain easier access to more music and more information with which to assess his artistic achievement. For generations after Schubert's death, audiences have gradually encountered the "far fairer hopes" that Grillparzer only dreamed of. The conscientious record collector can now hear more of Schubert's music than anyone ever could in Biedermeier Vienna – indeed can hear more than Schubert himself, excepting that all his music resounded in his inner ear. Listeners today could thus claim to know Schubert better than those of his own era. Yet there need be no contest as to which age knows Schubert best, most thoroughly, authentically, deeply – music transcends the time of its creation even while bearing witness to that time.[24]

Too often unacknowledged is how musical and biographical concerns alike reflect a particular historical period. Redescriptions and reassessments of Schubert will continue for as long as he is known and played. They will, ultimately, always tell us something about ourselves, as well as about the ever-elusive object of their description and regard.

PART I

Contexts: musical, political, and cultural

1 Realism transformed: Franz Schubert and Vienna

Leon Botstein

> On one very beautiful October afternoon . . . they got out at Nussdorf and
> immediately looked to see whether they could see the thick smog which
> would always hover over the city, breeding diseases – but they did not find it;
> rather on the right were beautiful green mountains and on the left beautiful
> green meadows. Above them rose a sundrenched, gray and delicately
> chiseled tower – the spire of St. Stephen's. Fashionably dressed figures
> were strolling by; carriages bearing attractive white numbers on their
> drivers' seats criss-crossed, carrying beautiful men and women seated inside.
> The coachmen's faces, owing to their especially fine appearance, betrayed
> not the slightest sign of the unhealthy air of the place.[1]

This was the way the eminent Austrian author and painter Adalbert
Stifter (1805–68), writing during the mid 1840s, recalled his first impression of Vienna. He penned this description in a thinly veiled autobio-
graphical sketch about himself and two friends who came to Vienna to
enter the university. The year was 1826. Stifter was twenty-one years old
when he arrived from Bohemia to take up the study of law. Franz
Schubert, already quite well known in the city, was twenty-nine and living
with his close companion Franz von Schober, two blocks from St.
Stephen's.

To the young Stifter – and to most other literate contemporaries of his
generation raised in the German-speaking regions of the Habsburg
Empire – Vienna was already the stuff of legend. It was a place of seductive
paradoxes and symbol of both past grandeur and modernity. Danger,
opportunity, squalor, and beauty existed side by side. Vienna with its own
uniquely alluring surface possessed (as Stifter recounted) the power to
render the ugly seemingly invisible, as if by magic. Yet the conditions of
daily life in the city during Schubert's adult life were grim if not sinister.
Vienna simultaneously ennobled and threatened the lives of those drawn
to it.

That fall, in November 1826, at the Theater in der Leopoldstadt the
wildly successful première of Ferdinand Raimund's *The Maiden from the
Fairy-World*, or *The Peasant as Millionaire*, "an original romantic-magic
fairy tale with song,"[2] took place. With Raimund a brilliant tradition of

Viennese satire began, which extended to Karl Kraus in the next century. Here was a farce marked by a trenchant seriousness: high comedy filled with fantasy and exuberance that masked a deft literary and philosophical sensibility about the ironies and sufferings of urban daily life. The uneasy and conflict-ridden interdependence between the fantastic and the ordinary that appeared on Raimund's stage was a key to its popularity among the Viennese. Likewise, the moralistically sentimental and the cruelly candid (both visible and invisible) would be combined later in Stifter's prose and pictures.[3]

The dualities that lay at the center of Raimund's and Stifter's work matched the circumstances of life in Vienna between 1815 and 1830, an era of declining living standards, deteriorating sanitary conditions, overcrowding, increased poverty, and public begging. When Schubert died in 1828, there was still no sewage system in the city. The absence of a modern water supply system was particularly devastating. No new hospital had been built since the Allgemeine Krankenhaus opened in 1784. The oft-recounted scene of Schubert becoming violently ill at a meal shortly before his death ought not to divert the attention of the modern reader from how common encounters with bad food actually were. The quality of the diet and the food was a cause of constant concern throughout Schubert's life. The "disease breeding smog" Stifter saw was not a metaphor. It pointed to dangers particular to the fast-growing city.

In the case of Schubert, posterity has been inclined to find in his music sentiments and ideas quite distant from the mundane, even when the texts of many songs deal with the everyday. As time passes, it has become increasingly hard to imagine daily life in the 1820s, particularly in Vienna. Undeterred, we locate continuities of thought and emotion in aesthetic objects from the early nineteenth century, particularly in poetry and music. This procedure is in direct conflict with the enormous discontinuities in daily life between past and present. The differences in living conditions – hygiene, health, diet, transportation, dress, the acoustic environment, and perhaps the most poorly understood of all dimensions (but yet the most crucial to music), the perception and use of time – cannot be ignored.

Given the contemporary controversy over Schubert's sexual activities and proclivities[4] (aspects of behavior easily influenced by all the mundane dimensions of life enumerated above), yet another look at the particular world inhabited by Schubert is warranted. Dying children, grave diggers, wanderers, hunters, floods, the postal service, the inn, the signpost, and the hurdy-gurdy man all meant something to Schubert's contemporaries that may elude us for no other reason than the foreignness of the past.

During Schubert's adult years a fashionable assertion and modern-sounding rhetoric of individuality became popular, only to be hounded by a seemingly unparalleled and novel consciousness of loneliness and vulnerability. Rural life was both idealized and abandoned. It became pitted against an irresistible new urban alternative. Nature took on its now all-too-familiar conceptual role as an emblem of innocence and simplicity. The urban emerged as the construct of a polar opposite: a man-made world that signaled artificiality and corruption. Commerce, industry, and the structure of society took on forms and contours understood as essential to progress and yet in conflict with common-sense mores and morality. The ambition to become rich and realize dreams of material and social advancement was dogged by the nagging sense that in the end all would be empty and destructive to any plausible notion of happiness.

The struggle with these currents and countercurrents became a hallmark of the best work done by the great Viennese artists and writers of the so-called Biedermeier and Vormärz eras.[5] The manner in which these paradoxes were dealt with set the terms of the subsequent nineteenth-century political and aesthetic struggle with modernity and its consequences. For Raimund and Stifter (and the consistently underrated Franz Grillparzer as well), who, unlike Schubert, lived into middle and old age, the severity of the artist's confrontation with reality first experienced in Vienna during the years between 1815 and 1848 left its mark. Grillparzer died in 1872 an embittered eighty-one-year-old man. Both Raimund and Stifter committed suicide.[6]

The appropriation of Schubert

Practically every biography of Franz Schubert, from Heinrich Kreissle von Hellborn (1865) to Maurice J. E. Brown (1958), has acknowledged the peculiar tradition of myth-making that has marked Schubert's posthumous reputation as man and musician. Each succeeding generation, to this day, has developed its own distinct portrait of the composer and maintained an intense psychological investment in it. The common thread, no doubt, has been the music. From Robert Schumann on, Schubert's music has inspired, perhaps on account of its undeniable susceptibility to personal and intimate appropriation, the compulsion to mold some sort of reassuring account of the composer's life and personality.[7]

The late twentieth-century debate about Schubert's sexual orientation and behavior, in this sense, might have been predicted. Despite the insights it has brought, it remains an instance of a familiar historiographical habit. The effort to pin down facts surrounding Schubert's life, following the magisterial accomplishment of Otto Erich Deutsch, continues unabated.[8] However, progress in empirical research neither dampens nor eludes the enthusiasm for ideological appropriation.

The struggle over the soul of Schubert has been most sustained and intense within Vienna, his native city. The *Schubertbund*, one of Vienna's leading choral societies, was founded in 1863 and quickly became a rallying point for schoolteachers and comparable segments of the Viennese middle class who increasingly felt themselves embattled during the Gründerzeit and the less prosperous decades that followed the Crash of May 1873.[9] The dedication of the Schubert *Denkmal* in 1872 in the Stadtpark was a major civic occasion. It was a gift to the city from the Wiener Männergesangverein, the leading male choral society of the city and an influential Viennese organization. The group performed at the dedication of the monument.[10] From the founding of the Männergesangverein in 1843, Schubert and his music were at the center of its self-image, ideology, and repertory. In 1888, the Society sponsored the transfer of Schubert's remains from the Währing Cemetery to the Central Cemetery.

During the last decades of the nineteenth century, Schubert figured prominently in the social and aesthetic split within the musical community of Vienna surrounding the parallel careers of Brahms and Bruckner. Both composers and their adherents claimed Schubert for their side, aesthetically and politically. Brahms (who edited the symphonies for the complete edition [*ASA*]), critic Robert Hirschfeld, and scholar Guido Adler stressed the Classical and universalist aspects of Schubert. Insofar as Schubert's relationship to Vienna was concerned, liberal critics understood his image as that of a populist who united all forms of music from the dance to the concert hall.

But by the end of the century, Schubert had become integral to the conservative cultural politics of Vienna's mayor Karl Lueger and the Christian Social Party.[11] In the twentieth century, Austro-fascists and Austrian Nazis extended the stance taken by pro-Bruckner conservatives at the end of the century, who espoused forms of Austro-German patriotism. Schubert fitted neatly into a chauvinist vision of a local Viennese nativist cultural tradition at odds with Jews, modernism, and cosmopolitanism.[12] By the First World War, Schubert had emerged as the quintessential emblem of an anti-modern politics of nostalgia: the symbol of a simpler, more homogeneous, and coherent Viennese world.

This Viennese obsession with Schubert ironically points to a relatively unexplored vantage point for a fuller understanding of Schubert and his music as dimensions of a history that lie outside the narrow frame of biography. The years between 1815 and 1828 – which cover most of Schubert's career as a composer – form a rich, coherent, and, above all, decisive era in the development of Viennese culture and society. Vienna, it turns out, influenced Schubert.

No doubt Schubert's status as unique and genuinely a product of the local environs – as *echt* and paradigmatically Viennese – has been exaggerated. But that overemphasis has been partly a defensive historio-graphical effort by the Viennese designed to counteract the constant and covertly disparaging reminder that Vienna's international reputation as the city of music *par excellence* was based on the accomplishments of non-Viennese figures – including Gluck, Haydn, Mozart, Beethoven, Brahms, and Bruckner – composers whose relationship to the city was often either ambivalent or detached. The canonization of Viennese Classicism within the historiography of music as the generically undis-puted foundation of a presumably universally valid system of music-making – or at least the pinnacle of the European tradition of art music – from the perspective of Viennese observers seemed implicitly, if not explicitly, to denigrate the substantive importance of the city. Soon after Schubert's death, his Viennese contemporaries took pains to locate the roots of his greatness within the city.[13] Grillparzer's great novella *Der arme Spielmann* from 1848 may be one of the first and most eloquent examples.[14]

The instinct to counteract a universalist discourse about Schubert with what, in modern terminology, would be regarded as a foray into "local knowledge"[15] – an ethnographic account and contextualization – flour-ished under the dubious patronage of pre-fascist and fascist politics in the years before 1945. However, cut off from this repugnant political agenda, the project of attempting to understand Schubert from within the seemingly narrow confines of Viennese life and culture may not be misplaced. The nasty and alluring details of the Vienna of the 1820s can go a long way in illuminating complex and hidden dimensions of Schubert's work. The end result may be a better-differentiated sense of universal aspects of Schubert's genius.

Interpretation of Schubert and his music needs to turn away from an overemphasis on psychology and personality understood as categories detached from local history. The implicitly normative psychological analysis and textual exegesis now directed at Schubert's life and work – particularly with respect to issues of sexuality – continue the tradi-tional tendency to appropriate Schubert within universalist rhetorics. This tendency led past scholars and enthusiasts astray and generated the sentimentalized and maudlin portrait popularized, for example, in the biographical sketch written by La Mara (Marie Lipsius), which first appeared in 1868.[16] That portrait properly earned the contempt of scholars.

But the effort to render Schubert polemically unrespectable *vis-à-vis* some apparently unauthentic, neo-Victorian, and haute-bourgeois criteria (as construed perhaps in the writings of Theodor W. Adorno) is as laughable as the late nineteenth-century desire to make of Schubert a naïve, lovable, lovelorn, and long-suffering romantic idol – the cherished possession of smug and sentimental culture buffs who dominated musical life in late industrial capitalist societies. Today's superficially radical views share a common heritage with the 1916 Schubert of Heinrich Berté's operetta *Dreimäderlhaus*, based on Rudolf Hans Bartsch's novel *Schwammerl* (1912).[17]

Perhaps Schubert's greatness lies in the extent to which he was unabashedly local. We seem not to object to such an admission in the cases of Stephen Foster, Duke Ellington, George Gershwin, and Béla Bartók. We accept the local circumstances of culture and society in *fin-de-siècle* Prague as crucial to an understanding of Kafka without sensing any sacrifice to our appreciation of his greatness.

Music remains a tricky aspect of cultural and social history. The narrative of music history continues to cling to an implicit social theory of *autopoiesis* and the evolutionary coherence of an autonomous system supported by a cadre of professionals and near professionals, influenced only selectively by external factors.[18] The fact that of the significant cultural residues from the Vienna of Schubert's day (with the exception of furniture design)[19] little is known, appreciated, or understood in the non-German-speaking world apart from music (e.g. Beethoven, Lanner, and the elder Johann Strauss) – including the work of Grillparzer, Raimund, and Johann Nestroy, the graphic work of Moritz von Schwind, the paintings of Ferdinand Waldmüller, and the early poetry of Nikolaus Lenau – is a disturbing symptom of how music history is usually written. Music from within the history of Vienna has been extracted and placed artificially into a European-wide story of the development of music and located out of reach of the larger and intricately intertwined matrix of its immediate environment, making music nearly impossible to approach from the perspective of contemporaneous culture.

Viennese Schubert enthusiasts have realized that there appears, by contrast, little opportunity to localize Mozart or Beethoven. The fact that Schubert might be significantly revealed by reference to his local environment itself signals what has been acknowledged by all: that in Schubert's music something entirely new and different from either Beethoven or

Mozart makes its appearance. Schubert presents a classic paradigm of how the local becomes the basis for a novel cultural formation whose transference outside of the local framework is dialectically the result of its contingency on the specifics of time and place.

The sense of the historical moment

Stifter approached Vienna knowing that it was a rapidly growing city.[20] His first impression focused on its role as a setting for intense human activity incompatibly located in the midst of a natural landscape. In the minds of Stifter and his contemporaries, the striking beauty of Vienna was associated with two moments from an irretrievable past: (1) the medieval world (idealized in the graphic work of the young Mortiz von Schwind from the 1820s and represented by St. Stephen's Cathedral); and (2) a Baroque world of architectural splendor and political greatness.[21]

Schwind's family home was adjacent to Vienna's most imposing monument of Baroque culture, Fischer von Erlach's masterpiece, the 1739 Karlskirche.[22] The gatherings by Schubert and his companions at Schwind's place were literally in the shadow of the Baroque. The Baroque implied not only the rebirth of Vienna after the defeat of the Turks in 1683, but also the subsequent exploits of Prince Eugen of Savoy and Maria Theresia. The Viennese of Schubert's day had already developed a nostalgia for the reign of Joseph II, from 1780 to 1790, which in retrospect was a unique decade of enlightened and progressive monarchical rule during which Vienna grew in stature physically, politically, and culturally.

Peter Gülke has appropriately cast doubt on the utility of the notion of historicism as a useful category for understanding the formal character and substance of Schubert's music.[23] But at the same time, Schubert came of age in a culture fascinated with the past. Schubert's contemporaries were eager to use external and recognizable hallmarks of history as frameworks in which to express contemporary aspirations.[24] Among the most visible aspects of this was the revival of interest in Greek poetry (amply reflected in Schubert Lieder), and the self-conscious interest in classicism in much of post-1815 architecture.

This cultural historicism thrived in an uneasy alliance with an ambivalent wonderment about modernity. The undeniable allure of Vienna as a center of culture and learning, of future possibilities and modern economic opportunity, persisted side by side with a profound pessimism. By the 1820s, the consequences of Napoleon's early success and ultimate defeat had become all too clear. Charles Sealsfield's notorious anonymous English-language tract *Austria as it is*, published in London in 1828, for all its reputed exaggerations, describes a world permeated by spies and repression – by corruption, deceit, and insensitivity to the plight of all but a handful. A rigid and backward-looking autocracy reigned, at whose head was a mean-spirited and willful Emperor (Franz I [1792–1835]). The guiding spirit of this regime was, of course, Clemens von Metternich.[25]

Eduard von Bauernfeld, Schubert's friend, described life in the 1820s this way in his 1872 memoir: "Today's youth cannot imagine the humiliating pressure on our creative spirits under which we, as young people – aspiring writers and artists – suffered. The police in general and censorship in particular weighed on us all like a monkey we could not get off our back."[26] The impression is not only of a police state in the sense of the application of control from above. Perhaps the crucial consequences were the deformation of personal behavior, the inability to trust, the reluctance to speak directly and honestly, and the relentless uncertainty that prevailed. One's private life could be invaded at any moment and one's sense of security undermined. Schubert himself was arrested.

But the fate of his friend Johann Senn in 1820 offers the best case in point.[27] A mixture of outward subservience, internal resentment, and self-loathing accompanied the will to survive and to avoid the heavy hand of state retribution and interference. Johann Mayrhofer, who wrote texts for forty-seven Schubert songs and with whom Schubert lived from 1818 to 1820, understandably succumbed to the temptation to acquiesce.[28] He became a censor at the end of 1820. From that point on, his relationship was no longer the same with his friends, who were able to maintain some residue of distance and resistance. After one unsuccessful attempt, Mayrhofer (who remained in the service of the state) committed suicide in 1836.[29]

The social circles in which Schubert traveled in the 1820s were the most traumatized by the politics of the era. The regime provided and controlled employment for literate and educated Viennese. Many of Schubert's friends and admirers were themselves civil servants. Rapid growth of bureaucracy in government and commerce was a hallmark of the era. Members of this "second society" were at once privileged and impotent – educated, cultivated, and also cowardly. They were, as one scholar put it, "obedient rebels," whose philosophical aspirations and everyday behavior constantly came into conflict.[30] Successful co-optation and tacit collaboration had their psychic costs.

One barometer of Viennese sensibilities with regard to the political and historical conditions of the 1820s was the striking success enjoyed by Mozart's *The Magic Flute*. Not only was the work performed often, but excerpts from it found their way into the most unusual places.[31] Until

1848, *The Magic Flute* maintained its popularity as an object of nostalgia, an innocent satirical weapon, and a screen for the oblique expression of dismay, detachment, criticism, and discontent.[32] Schubert's first dramatic essays around 1811–14, *Der Spiegelritter* (D11) and *Des Teufels Lustschloss* (D84), were "magic operas," works whose roots can be traced back to *The Magic Flute*.

In 1826, the year Stifter arrived, Grillparzer wrote a hilarious satire in response to the dissolution by the police of the *Ludlamshöhle*, a club of which Schubert may have also been a member.[33] Grillparzer's house was searched. In retaliation, he played upon the nostalgia for Joseph II and invented a "Part II" for *The Magic Flute*.[34]

But why *The Magic Flute*? It was the classic local example of serious political argument and critique masked as nearly incomprehensible childish fantasy and fairy tale. Written in German for the wider public of the Theater an der Wien rather than for the two imperial theaters – the Burgtheater and the Kärntnerthor Theater – it evoked the liberal ideas of the mid 1780s in Vienna – of Josephinism, Freemasonry, faith in reason and enlightenment, and the triumph of good over evil (symbolized in the triumph of humanist tolerance and compassion on behalf of the political community evident in the union of Tamino and Pamina). This ideological climate seemed more distant in time to the Viennese of the 1820s than the actual passage of time since the first performance might have suggested. The Metternich regime (particularly after the 1819 assassination of the writer August von Kotzebue that led to the hated Carlsbad Decrees) was in direct conflict with the claims of Emanuel Schikaneder's libretto and Mozart's idealism, so disarmingly communicated by the music. The picture *The Magic Flute* painted (most poignantly in the union of Papageno and Papagena) of the domestic harmony and personal happiness that devolved on all individuals from enlightened and benevolent government was perhaps most painful. This was the utopian symbiosis of the public and the private that Grillparzer turned on its head.

The crises of the early 1830s, which followed the July Revolution in Paris, and the March revolution of 1848 had their roots in the resentment and anger that festered in Schubert's Vienna in the 1820s. Metternich and Count Josef Sedlnitzky, the president of the Bureau of Police and Censors in Vienna from 1817 to 1848 (who perfected the system of spies, informers, and censors), understood this discontent well. He attempted to limit and control the development of *Vereine* (societies) and clubs, with the sole exception of charitable organizations dedicated to alleviating the sufferings of the poor (often through the sponsorship of benefit concerts, such as the one held on March 7, 1821, that saw the premiere of *Erlkönig*). Censorship became stricter as the 1820s wore on. Yet societies and clubs thrived. They were new social formations and the concrete evidence of change and the creation of a new kind of public realm. The state saw them as the direct heirs to the Freemasons of the late eighteenth century.[35]

Schwind's 1823 pencil drawing entitled *Loneliness* (*Einsamkeit*) appears initially as mythic and ahistorical. This eloquent expression of an interior isolation that was widely felt among Schwind's compatriots seems explicitly detached from any historical reference to the present by virtue of Schwind's generic landscape and the naked figure. Yet the image evokes a critique of the present. The figure is bent over a sword. The weapon signals both the recognition of the inherent possibility of resistance and its actual absence. The sword harks back to the Middle Ages – to the autonomy and public role associated with knighthood, a historical condition of individual self-realization inaccessible in the contemporary world to the office-holder and artist.[36] Schwind's image merits comparison to Schubert's song of the same title (D620), written in July 1818, which Schubert described as "the best I have done" (*SDB* 93).

Participation in the spread of literacy, the growth of bureaucratic functions, and the appearance of modern commerce and trade were restricted to a small segment of Viennese society. But that exclusivity only strengthened an allegiance to a central political and philosophical claim associated with the French Revolution: the legitimacy of privacy and the concept of individuality. A sense of cultural and stylistic enfranchisement was shared by Schubert's compatriots.[37] That belief stood in contradiction to the absolute power of the state to regulate life and the ongoing traditions of the high aristocracy.[38] What was most disturbing was the consciousness – in part enhanced by the growing market for books, music, amateur musical societies, and concerts – of a new public in society that was at once articulate, yet powerless and oppressed from above.

The discontent and ambivalence demonstrated by the strata of Viennese society located between the high aristocracy and the illiterate working poor took their toll in the private sphere. Much has been made of the evolution of a bourgeois ethos and morality, of a culture of respectability and domesticity in the years between 1815 and 1830. The painting and literature of the era certainly sought to portray a new urban, private, non-aristocratic world characterized by work, cultivation, marriage, and family. The self-image of the middle-class *pater familias* ensconced in his home, surrounded by wife and children – an ideal of rectitude, decency, manners, and morals – remained incomplete. However, even the notion that home and family were sacred was undermined daily by the state apparatus. The proud assertion of a distinct way of life marked by a culture that had grown up independently of inherited aristocratic status was humiliated by the monopoly of power.

In the context of political repression, the arenas for the free expression of individuality were limited. Music, the art form least susceptible to political and ideological interpretation, flourished.[39] Future generations may look back at the outings to the countryside, the gatherings in inns, the reading societies, and the Schubertiades of the 1820s with envy and nostalgia. But the romanticized picture, best exemplified by Moritz von Schwind's famous retrospective *A Schubert Evening at Josef von Spaun's*, executed nearly half a century after the fact, in 1868, tells only one part of the story. In these close-knit circles – the evenings and afternoons of song, poetry, theater, and talk – suspicion, fear, and resentment were never far from the surface. The contradictions between the divisive and tightly regulated public sphere, and claims to friendship, intimacy, and spiritual nourishment through art and culture in the private and semi-public spaces of the 1820s took their toll.[40]

Moritz von Schwind's 1822 illustrations for *Robinson Crusoe* reflect not only his affection for the book but its local popularity.[41] The attraction to the tale of the lone shipwrecked individual, creating his own world, self-reliant, in command of not only the interior of his soul but external reality, also extended to the allure that America held for Schubert and his generation. America offered a stark, distant, and fantastic alternative to the grim absence of freedom in Vienna. What books did Schubert ask for on his deathbed? The novels of James Fenimore Cooper (*SDB* 820).[42]

The urban bourgeois of the 1820s internalized the gap between appearance and reality, between aspiration and possibility, by replicating external contradictions within the home. Schubert's peers and audience became an enthusiastic market for pornography. Pornography was a sub-category of an aesthetic genre central to Schubert's aesthetic: fantasy. In a culture of rising expectations hemmed in by autocracy, the literature of fantasy became wildly popular. The limitations of reality were circumvented by reading, seeing, and listening to the patently unreal; hence we find the continuation of the model of *The Magic Flute* in the fairy tale and farce theater of Raimund and Nestroy. This form of comedy did more than elude the censors. Unlike the tradition of high-art theater, particularly the forms of tragedy pursued by Heinrich von Collin and Grillparzer, it acknowledged a deeper realism behind mere representation.[43] It also underscored the existence of an individualized and protected private realm by permitting readers, observers, and listeners an indeterminate space for their own sentiments.[44]

Since secrecy and camouflage were essential tools of survival in the public world, the audience for fantasy in both theatrical and musical settings – as well as in the visual art of the period – was asked to respond to mental acts familiar to it in daily life: the creation of secrets, communication through codes, and the conjuring up of a shielded world. Pornography offered a comparable pleasure: the expression of desire and fantasy that undermined claims of public morality and decency that seemed to thrive as helpful ideological collaborators of repression.[45]

No consideration of art, music, and literature from the Vienna of the 1820s can be complete without taking into account the peculiar intrusions of the political into the personal lives of artists. The fact that much of Schubert's music was written for use in the social settings of his own local world makes the search for precise connections between his music and the political culture especially pertinent.

Conditions of life

The urban reality of the Vienna of the 1820s did not merely inspire fear. As Stifter recounted, the city exemplified death and disease. Without ever having seen the place, Stifter recognized the terrifying danger to his life. In an 1810 tract on the "medical topography" of the city, the following assessment of Vienna was offered:

> The tall houses placed alongside narrow streets and the oppressive living quarters possess air that is essentially trapped. This is made even worse by the breathing of many people, horses, and domestic animals. Through their lack of caution and various excretions – along with the outflows of activities tied to workshops – the situation is fouled to the highest degree. And one can surmise with certainty that no one takes in air that was not shortly before in the lungs of someone else. Apparently one needs only to breathe this air four times in order to transform the most necessary life giving substance into a frightful poison.[46]

In the 1820s, air was understood as the key to health. And nowhere was air more dangerous than in the city. Fear of the spread of disease was widespread well before the cholera outbreak of 1831.[47] The poetic attachment to the natural phenomenon of wind, for example, reflected an obsession with what was considered (not entirely without reason) the bearer of both death and defense against disease. The physical development of Vienna in the 1820s only helped to deepen the linkages between putrid air, mortality, and city life. The periodic flooding reminded the Viennese of their special vulnerability to the vagaries of nature.

Between 1810 and 1820, the population of Vienna grew by nearly twenty per cent, from 224,100 to 260,225.[48] No other city in the Empire matched it in size. Despite new construction, he occupancy of buildings in the city, which had averaged thirty-two in 1810, increased to thirty-

four persons per structure. Overcrowding was a reality. At the time of
Schubert's birth in 1797 the population of Vienna was 228,279, a number
nearly comparable to the level of 1810. The years of the Napoleonic conflict interrupted a dynamic of population growth beginning in the mid
eighteenth century. However, despite the wars, as in England, improve-
ments in agriculture paralleled sustained growth in population, leading
to a drift toward the cities, particularly within the Austrian lands of the
Habsburg Monarchy in which the legal opportunity for internal migration had been liberalized after 1780. The post-1815 migration to the inner
city and its immediate suburbs was perhaps most acutely felt in the
summer, when heat exacerbated the decay of food, the stench from
sewage, and the sense – precisely in the air – of a foul place. All this was
made worse by the fact that the city was filled with animals, including
stray dogs, whose danger to humans did not go unnoticed.

Since the size of the city decreased between the years 1805 and 1810,
for Schubert's generation the growth after 1810 was even more striking.
By the time of his death, Vienna had grown to over 300,000, and the
density of occupancy had increased to thirty-eight persons per house.[49]
Most of the population growth took place in the so-called suburbs of the
old inner city, the ring of neighborhoods that are now integral parts of
modern Vienna north and west of the Ringstrasse.

If one compares a map of Vienna in 1800 with one after 1830, one can
see the gradual erosion of green areas in these suburbs. The immediate
environment around Schubert's birthplace in Himmelpfortgrund, as well
as in Rossau and Wieden where he later resided, retained many reminders
of a rural past. Throughout Schubert's lifetime the city, despite its growth,
was an unplanned and irrational mixture of the rural and the urban; the
oldest and entirely urban part, the inner city itself, was circled by a large
green area, the Glacis.

In the mid 1820s, the population (approximately 50,000) of the inner
city (where Schubert lived continuously from 1818 to 1823 and from the
autumn of 1826 to the summer of 1828) – the walled-in center of Vienna
– was segmented in the following manner: nine per cent were members of
the aristocracy and twenty per cent were servants. Forty-six per cent of
the total population were dependants, women, and children. Fifteen per
cent worked in the industrial sector, in artisan workshops, small factories,
and mills. Six per cent worked in commerce and trade. The remaining five
per cent were civil servants and professionals. Franz Schubert was part of
this five per cent.[50]

During Schubert's lifetime, the city witnessed significant changes that
clearly signaled a new age of industry and technology. Mechanized manufacture slowly made its appearance before 1830, particularly in textiles,

creating a demand for workers. The system of manufacture, however, remained in the hands of artisan guilds. Metternich was against both political and economic liberalism and condemned industrial development in Vienna to stagnation by excessive regulation designed to strengthen the guild structure.

Yet modernity made its debut. The first chain bridge, the Sophienbrucke, was erected in 1825. In 1818, the first steamship could be seen on the Danube. These modern developments helped the circulation in the city but also deepened yet another source of fear regarding accidents resulting from urban street life. Any slight wound, internal injury, fall, or dog bite was ominous. But innovations continued. In 1820, the first balloon flights took place in the Prater. Most of the buildings by the leading architect of the era, Joseph Kornhäusel, were built in the 1820s. Other important new projects, such as the Polytechnical Institute and the Veterinary Science Academy, were set in motion.[51]

Between 1809 and 1820, the mortality rate in the city declined. But after 1820, it showed a reversal resulting from the city's growth, rising steadily until the mid 1830s. The obsession with death on the part of both Schwind and Schubert was, in this sense, commonplace and predictable. In the Habsburg Monarchy during the 1820s, the death rate ranged between twenty-eight and thirty per thousand per annum. (As a point of comparison, the death rate in 1949 was twelve per thousand.) In Vienna, the death rate was even higher, ranging between forty-four and fifty per thousand in the 1820s. (Again, as a point of contrast, in Vienna in the 1890s the rate was in the low twenties per thousand per year.) Death and its ceremonial rituals – requiems, funeral processions, and burials – were a visible and regular part of daily life.[52] Schubert's death at an early age was itself not extraordinary.

Changes in the character of the diet did not help the situation. Between 1826 and 1830, the price of beef increased precipitously, nearly thirty per cent, exceeding parallel increases in wages. In the last three years of Schubert's life, rising corn prices dramatically exceeded rises in wages.[53] Taking a longer view, between the late eighteenth century and 1830, the diet of the average Viennese, in terms of poultry, bread, butter, cheese, beer, fish, and wine, deteriorated. The supply of meat in Vienna showed either stability or decline between 1816, the year after the Congress of Vienna, and 1829, the year after Schubert's death. From 1823 to 1828 the drop in the level of meat consumption was greatest.

The aesthetic idealization of the rural world was not arbitrary fantasy; neither were the aesthetization of suffering and the obsession with the fear of death. As a result, the relationship of the individual to his or her own body and to those of others was ambivalent in a quite commonsensical fashion. The body was an enemy. In a world without any relief from gastrointestinal discomfort or physical pain (with the exception of alcohol), with unequal access to clean water and rudimentary sanitation, the conception of pain and the definition of comfort or pleasure involved contrasts whose relationships to one another are different from our own. The popularity of social outings in the country among Schubert and his friends – in the open and windy air – can be explained in part by the sense that the danger of social contact was mitigated outside of the city. Both Schubert and Beethoven seized as many opportunities as possible to escape Vienna in the late spring, summer, and fall. They were conscious of desperate realities.[54]

The 1820s showed little improvement in other social conditions of life, particularly in an area dear to Schubert and his family: education. Despite formal legislation dating from 1805 requiring schooling, in part because of rapid population growth, by 1830 the situation had become intolerable. The regime was unsympathetic. The spread of even rudimentary literacy was suspect. Teachers were poorly paid and trained. The expectation for schooling, insofar as it existed, extended to only four grades. But there were few schools with four grades, and even fewer with two grades. The so-called remedial schools that were created to deal with those who did not or could not complete four grades were equally in short supply. In 1820 there were only sixty *Volksschulen*, 230 teachers, and 20,000 schoolchildren. Fifteen years later, despite a population increase of over thirty per cent, the number of schoolchildren had grown to merely 24,000, the number of teachers to 250, and the total number of schools to sixty-two.

The statistics for higher education give an even clearer picture of the extent to which the social circles in which Schubert traveled constituted a very small element of the city. In 1820, only 1400 students were in school beyond the age of twelve. The university's enrollment fluctuated during the decade of the 1820s between two and three thousand students, many of whom were not from Vienna itself.[55]

At the same time, Vienna remained impressive to its inhabitants. This unequaled urban center inspired a sense of beauty and awe. First, the attraction of the city, as Schubert expressed over and over in letters to his friends and family, was an antidote to a fear of loneliness (e.g. *SDB* 109 and 370). The city created for Schubert the unique opportunity for a social network that, despite its dangers, inspired the repression of anxiety about death and disease. Society hid from view the harsh facts and transmuted them as susceptible to both denial and aestheticization. Likewise, time – particularly in its smaller units – was precious, since a long and healthy life was never assured. The stability of personal existence that might give rise to a conception of time and expectations regarding the stages of life susceptible to rational planning and anticipation was, despite Benjamin Franklin's homespun advice, a phenomenon in Vienna, more characteristic of the mid nineteenth century after 1848.

Not surprisingly, in Schubert's Vienna, one of the most popular theories of health involved the invoking of moral standards. Luxury in diet (e.g. overeating and drinking) and clothes was suspect. Much in the spirit of Jean Jacques Rousseau's critique of progress and urban life, Viennese medical experts in Schubert's day, particularly the avid music lover Johann Peter Frank (1745–1821), cast a doubtful eye on the consequences of the so-called progress of civilization as realized in the sophisticated social character of urban life. Staying on the land and pursuing a simple life was healthy; living in the city, a modern daily existence was not. It was regarded as artificial. To live as Schubert and his companions did (e.g. diet, sleeping habits, socializing) was considered particularly dangerous in terms other than those tied to sexual behavior.[56]

But these theories contradicted the very appeal of the city. The apparent healthy appearance of Stifter's coachmen – whose employment, diet, and status made them logical victims of the unhealthy environment of the city – was evidence of the magical psychic power of the city, which resided not in the physical realities, but in the communal world and the enclaves of domestic surroundings. Stifter not only saw the hustle and bustle of happy people. He also recalled that as a student in the late 1820s he stood out in the cold gazing into the windows of the houses of members of the aristocracy and the "second society," imagining with envy the salon life to which he at that time had no access, but to which Schubert did.[57]

Furthermore, a new type of fantasy of perception and experience was inspired by the city. Stifter's young and eager visitors saw remnants of natural beauty to the right and left of the spire of St. Stephen's. What they saw were the familiar rural qualities of nature: mountains and meadows. The immediate physical impression was to surround modernity (e.g. Vienna) by representations of the absence of change. Modernity disappeared from view, shielding the danger. The threat presented by urban modernity to personal health and the world of nature – now cherished nostalgically as emblematic of things past – spurred the explosion of two forms of aesthetic expression in the 1820s: landscape painting and drawing, and fiction centered on the natural environment. The numerous contemporary depictions of natural phenomena and the prevalence of group portraiture set in the country – of the flight to the countryside to escape the stifling city – offered, through the act of viewing while trapped indoors in the city, an occasion to daydream beyond reality. Such landscapes hung in the apartments of Schubert's Viennese social equals. In their surface realism, these art works offered a psychic exit. Beneath the benign surface of repose was a longing, not only for an escape from the urban, but for an interior flight from the mundane.

Painting did not function as mere representation, but as a stimulus to personal emotion and thinking. In this sense painting was not dissimilar to music. As in the musical setting and instrumental accompaniment of an overtly bucolic narrative line in Schubert's Lieder, two levels of communication were at hand. For example, the Viennese viewers of Jakob Alt's 1836 *Blick aus dem Atelier des Künstlers* or landscapes by Thomas Benedetti or Schnorr von Carolsfeld from the 1820s – themselves migrants from villages and farms – were gazing out on a threatened, familiar world located in the past. They were reminded of the costs and broken promises of progress and the modern urban world.

Music and daily life

What has all this to do with Schubert's greatness as a composer?[58] In the first instance, one must consider the role of music-making in the political and social context of Schubert's Vienna.[59] The iconography of music-making from the visual art of the 1820s and 1830s points to three distinct but interrelated uses of music in Vienna to which Schubert responded. Music was a vehicle of a dialogue with oneself.[60] What differentiated music-making from reading was that it was not silent. Music alone retained a social character by being audible. What protected music's function as private communication, however, was its opaque meaning, particularly in its instrumental genres. Grillparzer's lone violinist in *Der arme Spielmann* or the young female at the piano were in dialogue with themselves, but at the same time were (often inadvertently) audible to others. Unpacking the meaning inherent in what was heard was as difficult as protecting the player from public exposure with respect to the expression of dangerous sentimentality.

Second (as was alluded to earlier), music functioned as the nominal and seemingly politically neutral occasion for social gatherings. One thinks not only of the Schubertiades but of the development in the late 1820s of public dancing halls.[61] Dancing, even under the repressive state apparatus, could not be eliminated. Music therefore developed as a language of social communication among contemporaries, often of covert messages at odds with surface meanings. Schubert participated in this aspect of musical life.[62] The silent moments of recognition and understanding that became part of the Viennese response to Ländler and waltzes were crucial to the popularity of dancing.

Beyond the dance, the role of music in, for example, the Schubertiades was to provide a vehicle of communication that was relatively incorruptible. In a world where one could not trust even one's friends, music offered the possibility of circumlocution and secret communication without dishonesty, something hard to achieve with ordinary language. Music provided an ideal vehicle for making a point without having to admit having made it.

In this sense, public concerts were the least significant social occasions for music. Their function in Schubert's life was marginal and limited, however much they helped to further his local professional reputation. Likewise, music contributed to the effectiveness of Viennese theater. Raimund and later Nestroy, for example, wrote with intermittent musical accompaniments in mind. Given Schubert's lack of success as a composer of music for the theater, what emerged as significant for him was his popularity in the marketplace *vis-à-vis* printed sheet music. In a world of censorship, printed music possessed advantages over other forms of printed material. It was bought and sold in a climate less characterized by fear, even though it, too, had to receive official approval.

In the close analysis of Schubert's massive output of songs, it might be helpful to apply the kind of reasoning articulated by Leo Strauss in his essay "Persecution and the Art of Writing."[63] Schubert's musical settings of texts renders them, on the one hand, more radical than their linguistic content might suggest. Texts on love and nature, which seem entirely apolitical, can assume political character by virtue of their transformation through music. Alternatively, texts with narrative content that might possess overt political significance can be rendered apparently innocent by music. Schubert's innovation in song form may constitute a complex response to the need to communicate beyond the arena of private and psychological concerns; rather, the private realm is transformed and endowed with public meaning through music.[64] In this sense, Schubert may have manipulated his remarkable genius for originality, accessibility, and simplicity in melodic invention to use those very virtues, covertly, for communicating thoughts entirely at odds with accepted verities endorsed by surface qualities.[65]

The third function of music in Schubert's age was as a dimension of intimate and domestic life. The minimal unit in this regard can be considered two people. The use of music in courtship and seduction is well documented. Perhaps one of the most popular instruments across all layers of society in Schubert's day was the guitar. Schubert's contemporaries in the 1820s recognized the fact that it was relatively inexpensive, portable and easy to maintain (by comparison to a violin). It required less skill to make it palatably usable. Error was less excruciating to the ear, yet the instrument provided a minimal harmonic accompaniment for the voice.[66]

Beyond the communication between two lovers, music created codes of friendship. The ubiquity of four-hand music and of chamber music, particularly the string quartet, mirrored the perceived importance of music as a family activity. This was especially true in Schubert's Viennese surroundings. Insofar as he was part of a culture that held to the notion of family as a sign of moral health, cultivation, and upward social mobility, one can point to the composition of Schubert's early quartets for use with his brothers and father. The borderlines between the use of music within the family and in semi-public settings and public concerts were not strict in the 1810s and 1820s. Instrumental chamber music offered the most fruitful and complex structure for protected interpersonal communication that was both direct and ambiguous.

In Schubert's lifetime, published reviews in journals of his music, particularly in Vienna, focused on three striking qualities. What observers noticed as distinctive was Schubert's capacity to use music to paint the external world and internal sensibilities with uncanny subtlety. The metaphor of painting recurs in the critical literature throughout his lifetime.[67] Second, Schubert was understood as having a penchant for extreme harmonic contrast.[68] Sudden, seemingly unprepared modulations and unexpected relationships signaling shifts in mood are described in detail. The highlighting of these two qualities by contemporaries suggests that they were aware that Schubert was reinventing the form of the song in order to expand its communicative vocabulary. The logic behind and impulse for this ambition may have been clear to Schubert's Viennese contemporaries.[69] However, reviewers from outside the context of Vienna discussed Schubert's innovativeness using a traditional framework of reference to past musical practice. Schubert's craft was deemed an aesthetic issue involving matters of comparative skill and a command of extant traditions.

A third quality noticed by Schubert's contemporaries was his use of the "fantasy" form. Insofar as formal procedures in sonata form, particularly in the use of established harmonic patterns, had become familiar through the work of Haydn, Mozart, and Beethoven and their lesser contemporaries, these procedures, by tradition, could have developed into ideological signifiers and been assumed to have comprehensible norms.[70] In Vienna, however, the breaking up of formal expectations and the use of the "fantasy" form, particularly in music for solo piano, was not understood as a phenomenon motivated by the quest for mere aesthetic originality. As the reviewer in the *Wiener Zeitung* of 1823 observed, the overt freedom of the fantasy from formal expectations mirrored the need to be "freed from the shackles" of past expectations.[71] The language of criticism took on meaning that permitted a wider ideological interpretation. The fantasy form allowed new music to elude facile linkages between music and ordinary meaning, particularly in terms of well-established norms and ideas. The need to develop a distinctive form of expression and communication, protected from the state but yet capable of illuminating the real in life, inspired Schubert to originality not only in song form but in instrumental genres as well.

The source of Schubert's extraordinary expansion of the expressive vocabulary of the song, particularly the relationship of accompaniment to the vocal line, as well as his experiments in patterns of text-setting, points to the effectiveness of the song as a means of achieving authentic musical communication within the particular circumstances of Vienna. Schubert's explicit attachment to Vienna hints at his recognition of a nexus of unique inspirations that derived from the contradictions and difficulties of existence within the city. The surface of the song in the Schubertian oeuvre lends itself to the depiction of contradictions between appearance and reality. The song form possesses natural dualities: between voice and accompaniment, between text and tonality, and contrasts between tonality and mood over time. The major–minor alternations and the parallel shifts between the real and the supernatural are perhaps the most obvious examples of Schubert's rendering of contradiction and paradox in music.

If a central issue for Schubert's generation was the tension between internal isolation and the consequences of adaptation – between past and present, rural and urban, the internalized legacy of expectations of freedom and individuality, and the external realities of autocracy – then the song, in Schubert's hands, was supremely useful and adaptable. Schubert's song literature therefore constituted a major step in the differentiation of realist strategies in the making of art. Raimund and Nestroy resorted to satire, fantasy, and farce. Stifter and Grillparzer struggled to adapt conventional prose narrative and dramatic forms. In the short form of text and music, Schubert created his own complex system of illuminating the real. The overt – the representational – was communicated as a conduit to an often contradictory underside. The experience of independent and opposing dimensions of life, perhaps possible only in music with text, fitted the real demands that emerged from daily life in the Vienna of the 1820s. Schubert invented a means of psychic and representational realism that helped to catapult music into a preeminent role, outstripping both literature and the visual arts in the culture and society of the Vienna of his time.

The chronological biographical narrative of Schubert's life can support much of this speculation. In his poem entitled "Time" written in 1813, the sixteen-year-old Schubert linked time, music, and social communication. Music is not only a conventional means for the praise of God. Music captures a fleeting moment and renders it permanent (*SDB* 31–32). In 1816, Schubert responded to Mozart's music by noting how it showed "a bright, clear, lovely distance" caught in the "darkness of this life" (*SDB* 60). In a diary entry from the same year, Schubert mused on the hypocrisy of ordinary speech. Good character is hard to reveal through speech. Speech is easily misunderstood, and often "honest language" is derided. The September 8th diary entry from 1816 is filled with reflections on how human nature carries within it seemingly contradictory qualities (*SDB* 70–71.) By 1820 Schubert asserted that music offers a "godlike" insight into the "frail and human world."[72]

The references to music throughout the 1820s by Schubert and his closest companions consistently pointed to the power of music to reveal the truth in speech; to make words function as they should, and to render genuine human communication possible. In Schubert's lost notebook from 1824 the composer credited his understanding of music to his ability to rescue good from the evils of life.[73]

By 1821, Schubert's recognition of the special function of music in maintaining friendship was firmly established. The capacity for the private and secret communication essential for friendship was best realized through music. Music was a necessity within an imperfect world, a transitional experience perhaps rendered moot by a utopia: "As brothers quietly united strive for a freer, better earth, be this my theme. The plan I cherish, which once attained, my song may perish." Music was essential in a painful and terrifying world. "Rend our ears with hideous chords; only where the tempests are raging shall we find concordant words."[74] Vienna had left its painful but redeeming mark.

2 "Poor Schubert": images and legends of the composer

Christopher H. Gibbs

"Poor Schubert." Ever since his death on November 19, 1828, this expression appears over and over again in the writings of Schubert's friends, critics, and biographers.[1] One reason, of course, is that he died so young, at the age of thirty-one. More prosaically, the adjective refers to the composer's precarious financial state throughout his life, although he was far from the destitute artist later sentimentalized in novels, operettas, and movies. The tag also conveys the sense that Schubert was neglected, that his gifts went largely unrecognized.

How and why did these recurring images of Schubert come about? Their outlines are remarkably consistent, from initial portrayals found in his friends' reminiscences, to the first entries in German encyclopedias of the 1830s, to accounts in even the *Encyclopaedia Britannica* at the turn of the century and in college textbooks today.

One can easily pick out a few more brush strokes in the established portrait: Schubert is viewed as a natural and naïve genius who wrote incomparable songs – the *Liederfürst* ("Prince of Songs"). And then there are his festive friends in the background. Even if the public at large ignored him, at least he enjoyed the loyal support of his circle. Always the best man, never the groom, Schubert is seen as unlucky in love. Early death meant that his artistic mission was left unfinished. Even with so many miserable circumstances, Schubert's music laughs through its tears, and the maudlin conflation of his life and works in myriad biographies and fictional treatments makes readers past and present weep. Poor Schubert.

Rather than rehearse once more the narrative of Schubert's life, this chapter seeks to chart its contours in relation to pervasive images and legends that adhere to that life. The discussion does not pretend to present the "true" man and composer, but rather seeks to examine critically some of the most persistent legends, and if not to reject them all out of hand, then at least to question their appeal and resiliency. After identifying the principal verbal, visual, and musical sources that inform images of Schubert, and then touching on some of the outstanding features and events of his life, the chapter will explore some of the fundamental tropes of his mythology.

"Our Schubert": sources of mythmaking

There is an intriguing psychological phenomenon whereby every listener constructs his or her own image of the composer. (In the language of psychoanalysis one might even refer to this process as something like the "transference" with the composer.) The affectionate expression "our Schubert," commonly used by Schubert's family and friends, captures a possessiveness often directed toward beloved figures, although in Schubert's case the proprietary qualities are especially pronounced.[2] The writer Heinrich Hoffmann von Fallersleben, for example, described meeting Schubert for the first time and registered his disappointment at the composer's ordinariness: Schubert "is absolutely not different from any other Viennese; he speaks Viennese, like every Viennese he has fine linen, a clean coat, a shiny hat and in his face, in his whole bearing, nothing that resembles my Schubert" (*SMF* 285; cf. 328). This remark shows that even Schubert's contemporaries sometimes conceived of him in ways at odds with "reality," and it points as well to the problematic nature of the factual sources for critical biography. Whom does one trust? Where does our knowledge of Schubert come from, and how should the evidence be weighed and balanced?

Information derives not only from written documents. To start with, posterity cares about Schubert because of the music he created, and that music powerfully informs images of its creator. One tries to envision what kind of artist would compose such pieces. As with Beethoven's image – or Bach's, Mozart's, or Wagner's – the art colors the perception of the man. Eduard Bauernfeld wrote in his memorial tribute to Schubert in 1829: "So far as it is possible to draw conclusions as to a man's character and mind from his artistic products, those will not go astray who judge Schubert from his songs to have been a man full of affection and goodness of heart" (*SMF* 31).

Visual representations complement Schubert's music by supplying concrete representations of its creator and his milieu. Some portraits of the composer were executed by artists who knew him personally,[3] and many later illustrations are based on Wilhelm August Rieder's famous watercolor, considered to be "the most like him" by Schubert's friends.[4] Schubert's affectionate nickname "Schwammerl" (often translated "Tubby," literally "little mushroom") is reinforced by the famous caricature of the diminutive composer waddling behind the towering singer Johann Michael Vogl.[5]

However powerfully music and illustrations underlie perceptions, verbal documents provide the prime information about the narrative of Schubert's life and the disposition of his character. Schubert's own writings sound initial themes that were later varied by family and friends. The first to apply the word "poor" was Schubert himself. To end his earliest surviving letter, written while away at school in 1812, the fifteen-year-old student signed: "your loving, poor, hopeful and again poor brother Franz" (*SDB* 28). Schubert's disarmingly candid letters play an essential role in defining his image, partly because of their tone, and also because of the rarity of authentic utterances. For, in contrast to the abundant letters, journals, memoirs, criticism, essays, and the like by Mozart, Beethoven, Schumann, and many other composers, fewer than a hundred Schubert letters survive, supplemented by a few pages of diary entries from 1816 and some fragments from 1824.[6] Those letters written during particularly troubled times, or the famous final communication to Franz von Schober just one week before Schubert died, therefore gain additional significance.

If Schubert's own words are rare, those of his family and friends are extensive and have proved indispensable for biographers. The "fun-loving friends," so familiar from fictional depictions, helped to establish a pattern of assessing Schubert while he was alive, and then sought to perpetuate certain views of him after his death. While the intimacy of his collaborators and champions resulted in lively, detailed accounts, many chroniclers had an interest in presenting a favorable picture of their roles. Some reports date from Schubert's lifetime, others came in memorial tributes immediately following his death, but most appeared many decades later and must be viewed especially critically. We may never know whether *Erlkönig* was written in a few hours one afternoon, as Josef von Spaun reports and posterity repeats (*SMF* 131), but this story went a long way toward establishing Schubert as a composer, like Mozart, who took divine dictation rather than as one, like Beethoven, who continually struggled over compositional problems.

As Spaun's story demonstrates, reminiscences not only purport to impart facts about Schubert's life, but also contain anecdotes that enliven simple facts. How much more effective – and memorable – is telling a story of Schubert writing his most famous song in a matter of hours than dispassionately reporting that he composed quickly.[7] The core Schubert stories remain all too familiar: his shyness made him avoid his hero Beethoven (*SMF* 66, 75, 325, 366); he wrote songs so spontaneously, on the back of menus and the like, that he would later not even recognize them (*SDB* 539; *SMF* 214, 217, 296, 302); he fell in love with Therese Grob, but she married a wealthier man (*SMF* 182). Repeated so often, these tales crystallize Schubert's personality by entering into a canon of biographical representations. History progresses through anecdote to become legend.

Some Schubert legends, of course, are true; ingredients of many others rest on solid documentation. Not only accuracy, but also interpretation are at issue. That Schubert enjoyed especially rich and significant friendships, for example, is not in doubt. More pertinent is how such facts affect posterity's views. Furthermore, it would be a mistake to discount the "aesthetic truth" of certain fictions.[8] A new anecdote about the composer often arises from, and therefore reflects, the need of a given time to create the legend in the first place. Why, for example, did it take some thirty years before anyone thought to write down the quite interesting news that Schubert visited the dying Beethoven? Probably because the incident never happened.[9] But history needed such a story by mid century. We could view this invented meeting near death as an anecdotal corollary to the exhumation of Beethoven and Schubert some decades later, and their reburial together in the "Grove of Honor" at Vienna's Central Cemetery. As Schubert's image, reputation, and music became increasingly cast in relation and opposition to Beethoven's, this reception found its poetic expression in story and legend, and ultimately in a physical transferral of their bodies in a solemn ceremony.[10]

Schubert's unknown years, first fame, and illness

Unlike the careers of famous prodigies whose activities proved sufficiently interesting to warrant early testimony – most notably the phenomenon of the *Wunderkind* Mozart – the unfolding of Schubert's less exceptional early career is not particularly well documented. He probably began composition in 1810, at the age of thirteen. The inception of Schubert's public career might be variously dated from the first performance of a significant composition (the Mass in F [D105] in October 1814), the mention of his name in the press (1817; *SDB* 68–69), or the appearance of a work in print (*Erlafsee* [D586] in 1818).[11] More decisively, it started with a highly acclaimed performance of *Erlkönig* in 1821 and the publication of the song as Op. 1 shortly thereafter. Until this point, Schubert's activities, opportunities, and reputation – although not his actual compositions – are commensurate more with a fine talent than an exceptional genius, and attracted minimal public notice.

Young Schubert had benefited from the best musical training available in Vienna after winning a position in the choir of the Imperial Court Chapel, whose ten choristers were provided with free education at the prestigious Stadtkonvikt. Report cards and testimonials attest to Schubert's general musical abilities and skill as a performer: "He shows so excellent a talent for the art of music" (*SDB* 18); but his compositional activities go unmentioned for several more years. The best anecdote distilling Schubert's early abilities is Michael Holzer's remark to Schubert's father: "If I wanted to teach him something new, he already knew it" (*SMF* 212; cf. 34). The remark may never have been uttered, but it has been recounted in nearly every biography of Schubert as evidence of his God-given gifts.[12]

The performance of his Mass in F, which occurred during the Congress of Vienna, provided some limited public exposure, as did semi-public performances of the lost cantata *Prometheus* (D451), and of a few other compositions. The critical response to these works, appearing in periodicals as well as private diaries, letters, and reminiscences, proved modestly encouraging.[13] All this, however, was provincial and preparatory. Had Schubert died before 1821, with his handful of performances and a few good reviews, but without publications, reaction would have been limited to the grief of family and friends. (The death of Mozart, Beethoven, or Liszt at a comparable age would have warranted much wider notice.) Nevertheless, during these years Schubert formed associations and friendships central to the course of his career and to the posthumous casting of his image. In addition to prominent teachers, musicians, officials, and patrons with whom Schubert came in contact, he forged close relationships with young friends who nurtured and encouraged his composing, influenced what he read and the ideas he explored, and affected his general state of well-being.

Accounts are unanimous about Schubert's lack of career cunning. Shy, humble, and modest, he enlisted friends and advocates to take on the work of promoting his career, arranging performances, approaching publishers, and so forth. Classmates from the Stadtkonvikt, such as Johann Leopold Ebner and Albert Stadler, copied as many of his songs as they could get their hands on; some Lieder survive today only through their efforts. In 1816, Schubert's lifelong friend Josef von Spaun wrote to Goethe in the hope of interesting him in an ambitious plan to publish eight volumes of songs (*SDB* 56–58). Even critics noticed his friends' ardent support. Writing about the première of the Singspiel *Die Zwillingsbrüder* (D647), one remarked: "The general verdict on Schubert can only be favorable, although not to the point to which his numerous friends endeavor to force it" (*SDB* 138–39). Others made similar observations, which echo throughout Schubert's life and after. Rarely does a composer's group of friends arouse so much comment and attention, but then the make-up, actions, and legacy of Schubert's circle are rather unusual among musicians.[14]

Schubert's career and reputation changed considerably in 1821. The first fully public performance of *Erlkönig* took place at an annual benefit concert organized by the Society of the Ladies of Nobility for the Promotion of the Good and the Useful on Ash Wednesday. The song, performed by Johann Michael Vogl with Anselm Hüttenbrenner accompanying, captivated the audience and had to be repeated. The public and critical acclaim for *Erlkönig* that evening remained unsurpassed for the rest of the composer's life. A steady stream of publications, also beginning in 1821, attracted growing interest in Vienna and slowly began to spread Schubert's name beyond Austria.

During his unknown years Schubert had written a staggering amount of music: hundreds of songs, many sonatas and string quartets, six symphonies, extensive theater and religious pieces, in all, nearly two-thirds of his entire output. (Schubert usually dated his manuscripts, which facilitates establishing their chronology.) No composer in his teens, with the exception of Mendelssohn, produced such mature masterpieces as *Gretchen am Spinnrade* or *Erlkönig*. Indeed, one is hard-pressed to think of pieces by other teenage composers as firmly established in the repertory as are many of Schubert's Lieder.

The pace of Schubert's writing had fallen off some years before his public success, and until his final two years he was far less prolific. The quantity of Lieder in particular declined dramatically, from at least 145 songs in 1815 and 112 the next year, to sixty-five in 1817, and only seventeen the following year.[15] This moderation in Schubert's creative energies, reflecting a new discrimination perhaps, roughly coincided with his emergence in the public sphere and with cautious moves toward larger-scale compositions. After the eventful winter of 1821, Schubert wrote an unfinished Symphony in E (D729), followed by the opera *Alfonso und Estrella* (D732). In the fall of 1822 he composed the "Unfinished" Symphony in B Minor (D759), then wrote the Singspiel *Die Verschworenen* (D787), and the opera *Fierrabras* (D796) the next summer. No doubt discouraged by unfinished symphonies and unperformed operas, Schubert returned in 1824 to chamber music (the Octet [D803], Quartet in A Minor [D804]), and wrote the "Grand Duo" (D812) and several piano sonatas. These were serious works intended to lead to the "grand symphony" he mentions in a letter to Leopold Kupelwieser (*SDB* 338–40).

Schubert's instrumental music thus shifted from amateur to professional, from compositions intended for the family string quartet (in which Schubert played with his father and brothers), school orchestras, and domestic dilettante ensembles, to works written for professional public performance. Schubert's letters suggest that he regarded most of his earlier large-scale works as preparatory. Asked in January 1823 to deliver a promised orchestral work for a concert, he confessed to having "nothing for full orchestra which I could send out into the world with a clear conscience," and begged forgiveness for having "accepted [the invitation] too rashly and unthinkingly" (*SDB* 265). And yet by this date Schubert had written all of his symphonies save the "Great" C Major Symphony (D944).[16]

Soon after Schubert's successful entry into the public arena through performance and publication in the early 1820s, there ensued a period of deep personal difficulties, precipitated by a serious health crisis. He was hospitalized in 1823, most likely with syphilis.[17] While the correspondence from this time testifies to widespread concern among his friends, Schubert's own comments are particularly direct and disturbing. In one of his most remarkable letters, he tells Kupelwieser in March 1824:

> I feel myself to be the most unhappy and wretched creature in the world. Imagine a man whose health will never be right again, and who in sheer despair over this ever makes things worse and worse, instead of better; imagine a man, I say, whose most brilliant hopes have perished, to whom the felicity of love and friendship have nothing to offer but pain, at best, whom enthusiasm (at least of the stimulating kind) for all things beautiful threatens to forsake, and I ask you, is he not a miserable, unhappy being?   (*SDB* 339)

In the same wrenching letter, Schubert laments the imminent dissolution of his friends' reading circle, now taken over by a "rough chorus of beer-drinkers and sausage-eaters," complains that he has no money, and bemoans the lack of interest in his most recent opera *Fierrabras* ("I seem once again to have written two operas for nothing").

Schubert's health troubles occurred around the same time as changes in the constituents and activities of his social circle. (As David Gramit has shown, the "circle" continually evolved; its most famous members never formed a contemporaneous group as depicted in later illustrations and narratives.) Some of his closest friends had left Vienna, while new personalities arrived. Spaun had long since moved to Linz, Schober was away for extended periods, and Kupelwieser was studying painting in Rome; they were replaced by "quite ordinary students and officials" (not to mention the sausage-eaters).

Restored to apparent health by 1824, Schubert reached a stage typical in venereal disease, and a new tone enters his letters. While away from Vienna that summer, he sounds a Wordsworthian note to his brother Ferdinand: "Do not think that I am not well or cheerful, just the contrary. True, it is no longer that happy time during which every object seems to us to be surrounded by a youthful gloriole, but a period of fateful recognition of a miserable reality, which I endeavor to beautify as far as possible by my imagination (thank God)" (*SDB* 363). The work he cites as proof is the magnificent "Sonata in C" for piano duet, the so-called "Grand Duo."

The progress and pacing of Schubert's professional career should be considered along with his health and social situation, and the friendships that largely determined where he lived and often the music he composed. A flood of publications and recognition had followed the winter of 1821. Even though many of the pieces published over the next few years had originated years earlier, only now was a larger public catching up with such works long familiar to Schubert's intimates. Meanwhile, although distracted by health concerns and personal despair – and possibly spurred on by these difficulties – Schubert pursued new compositional paths. In a diary from 1824 (now lost) he wrote: "What I produce is due to my understanding of music and to my sorrows; that which sorrow alone has produced seems to give least pleasure to the world" (*SDB* 336).

Late Schubert and death

To Schubert belongs the dubious distinction of being the shortest-lived composer of his stature, a situation commented upon since the day he died. Franz Grillparzer's epitaph, already discussed in the introduction, alludes to Schubert's untimely passing, as do numerous obituaries, tributes, and memorial poems from 1828–29.[18] The most common phrase in reviews, memoirs, and reference works in the decade or so after Schubert's death was a variant of the "all too young deceased composer of genius" (*zu früh verblichener geniale Tonsetzer*).

Montaigne declared that "in judging the life of another, I always observe how it ended." Remarkable circumstances surrounding death – such as suicide, murder, horrible disease, or extreme youth – typically exert an extraordinary influence on posthumous perception. The aura of incompleteness that surrounds Schubert's fame (and Mozart's) would not exist had they written the same amount of music over the lifespan allotted to Bach, Haydn, or Beethoven. (In fact, very roughly, these composers all wrote a comparable total amount of music.) The madness of Robert Schumann and of Hugo Wolf (the latter surely syphilitic) was likewise read retrospectively into their compositions.

Schubert's early death, while an indisputable reality, should not blind us to its symbolic significance. In this respect, Schubert's most popular instrumental work, the Symphony in B Minor, proves instructive on two counts. First, the première took place well over forty years after its composition. This late unveiling powerfully underscores how relatively unknown Schubert was and how unceasingly his reputation had to be reevaluated throughout the nineteenth century. Second, its nickname – the "Unfinished" Symphony – epitomizes the "unfinished" quality of Schubert's life and art, and serves as a fitting metaphor, a recurring reminder of unfulfilled promise – the theme first sounded by Grill-parzer's epitaph.[19]

It may seem odd, even inappropriate, to discuss the "late period" of an artist who died in his early thirties; yet Schubert condensed the artistic productivity of a lifetime into his remarkably brief career, and moreover persevered in his final years with the knowledge of a mortal illness. Professionally and compositionally, Schubert entered a new stage during the final two years of his life, the period, significantly, coinciding with Beethoven's final sickness and death twenty months before his own. Now thirty years old, and at the peak of his creative powers, Schubert surpassed even what Beethoven had accomplished at the same age. (Had Beethoven carried out the suicide he apparently contemplated around the time of the *Heiligenstadt Testament* [1802], in other words at the very age Schubert died, the extent of his compositional legacy would hardly match Schubert's.)

Beethoven's death in March 1827 may have spurred Schubert to new artistic heights and provided the impetus for him to seek wider public attention. As early as 1823 a "public Schubertiade" was contemplated, an *Akademie* entirely of Schubert's music (*SDB* 314). Such events were infrequent, even for Beethoven. His last, in 1824, which saw the première of the Ninth Symphony, prompted Schubert to write: "God willing, I too am thinking of giving a similar concert next year" (*SDB* 339); but nothing came of this plan until the first anniversary of Beethoven's death (March 26, 1828), just eight months before Schubert died.

Schubert's sole concert proved popularly and financially successful even though it was overshadowed by Paganini's first appearances in Vienna three days later. Publications of large-scale instrumental compositions were the essential next step in Schubert's career. With new assertiveness, Schubert now entered into protracted negotiations with prominent foreign publishers in the hope of giving his "works greater currency abroad" (*SDB* 739). The Leipzig publisher Heinrich Albert Probst met Schubert during a visit to Vienna in the spring of 1827. Writing the following February, Probst praised songs and piano compositions which "convince me more and more that it would be easy to disseminate your name throughout the rest of Germany and the North, in which I will gladly lend a hand, considering your talents" (*SDB* 735).

The Mainz firm of B. Schott's Söhne approached Schubert, claiming that it had known his works during the years when its energies were devoted to publishing Beethoven's late works (*SDB* 737). Schubert offered the Piano Trio in E flat (D929), the String Quartets in D Minor (D810) and G Major (D887), Four Impromptus (D899), the F Minor Fantasy for piano four hands (D940), the Violin Fantasy in C (D934), as well as various Lieder and partsongs. To Schott he wrote, "This is the list of my finished compositions, excepting three operas, a Mass, and a symphony. These last compositions I mention only in order to make you acquainted with my strivings after the highest in art" (*SDB* 739–40). Once again there appears Schubert's self-critical view of his earlier large-scale works. By this point he had written eight operas, five Masses, and seven (and a half) symphonies, but acknowledges far fewer compositions.

After the success of his concert, Schubert wrote with some urgency to Probst and Schott about getting works published. A letter to Schott concludes, "All I should request is publication as soon as possible" (*SDB* 764). A month later he registered his disappointment to Probst about the low fee offered for the Trio in E Flat Major, Op. 100, but accepted, adding that "to make a beginning at last, I would only ask for the speediest possible publication" (*SDB* 774). After a further delay, Probst solicited the opus number and dedication, to which Schubert responded: "The opus number of the Trio is 100. I request that the edition should be faultless and look forward to it longingly. This work is to be dedicated to nobody, save those who find pleasure in it. This is the most profitable dedication" (*SDB* 796). When the publication still had not arrived two months later, Schubert inquired yet again: "I beg to inquire when the Trio is to appear at last. Can it be that you do not know the opus number yet? It is Op. 100. I await its appearance with longing" (*SDB* 810). He probably never saw the edition, published the month he died.

Schubert's negotiations with these north-German publishers reflect his increasing fame beyond Vienna, a situation also apparent in ever more detailed and favorable reviews given his music, especially in the influential Leipzig *Allgemeine musikalische Zeitung*. The critical reception of Schubert's music is discussed in the third section of this book; suffice it to say here that the sheer number of reviews, as well as their length and import, grew dramatically in the late 1820s, and that Schubert was gradually recognized as more than just a song and dance composer. Had Schubert lived a decade longer, he would have directly benefited from the support of Robert Schumann and the *Neue Zeitschrift für Musik*, which quickly became one of Europe's commanding musical periodicals. By the late 1830s, Schumann's passionate advocacy of Schubert's cause and brilliant criticism of his music were considerably enhancing his posthumous reputation. By that time, too, Franz Liszt's celebrated piano transcriptions spread Schubert's name far and wide.

The neglected Schubert?

Although Schubert's biographers often comment that his life was "unexceptional," even "boring," that has not stopped – perhaps it has even encouraged – the mythmaking process. For example, while the true extent of his romantic relationships with women remains unclear and contested, fictional accounts delight in inventing passionate love affairs. Rather than attempt to sort out such biographical puzzles, I shall concentrate on three central tropes in the Schubert mythology: first on his putative neglect, then on his "naturalness," and finally on the air of nostalgia that permeated his life and later reception.

The idea of the unrecognized artistic genius, the artist who valiantly struggles for acceptance and yet is inexplicably ignored by the world until after his death, continues to hold a popular attraction.[20] Among nineteenth-century composers, Schubert is the only one who actually embodies (in some respects) this quintessential Romantic prototype. Unfair disregard at the hands of an ignorant public and unfailing support from a small circle of friends are central components of Schubert's popular image. Was his music indeed so neglected during his lifetime? What were the opportunities available to Schubert, the extent of his public recognition, and the standing of his fame at the time of his death?

If Schubert's early death complicated his legacy, so the unusual course of Schubert's career complicated his fame while he was alive and his posthumous fame. In his classic history of Viennese concert life (1869), Eduard Hanslick offers the following concise assessment of Schubert's position in the 1820s: "There is, of course, nothing favorable to report concerning Schubert's artistic career in Vienna. Its significance was discovered only after his death." But he urges his readers to remember "two important mitigating circumstances":

> The time-span of Schubert's public career was extremely short – it lasted
> from the appearance of his first works (1821) to his death (1828) – not more
> than seven years. The young composer was even on his way to winning a
> large public for himself in Vienna, after he had pleased and won such favor
> among family circles, when death snatched him in the first bloom of
> manhood. Second, it should not be forgotten that Schubert began his career
> and achieved his best work in a musical genre which at that time had still
> not been taken up in public concert life: the Lied.[21]

As Hanslick rightly notes, Schubert's initial fame was limited primarily to the still relatively insignificant genre of the Lied, to which one might add other genres that did even less to enhance his stature: partsongs, dances, and short piano pieces. With this intimate music, mainly for voice and/or piano, Schubert was one of the most widely performed and published composers in Vienna during the 1820s.[22] His instrumental music – symphonic, chamber, and keyboard – that predominates in modern concert halls, recording studios, and radio programs was unknown beyond Vienna. Such a dramatic dichotomy between a composer's lifetime fame and his later stature is unusual. True, only a few of Mozart's symphonies and concertos, and comparatively little of his chamber, dramatic, and religious music, were readily available and regularly performed before the first collected edition of his works. But Mozart was widely regarded as a genius who excelled in all these areas, whereas the reception of Schubert in his own time, and for decades to follow, was far less balanced and well informed. Long after Schubert's death, his compositions continued to be discovered, then performed, published, and discussed for the first time. Only with the publication of a complete thematic catalogue of his works (1874) and the first collected edition (1884–97) did the entire scope of Schubert's oeuvre become known and his scores become available.[23]

Reading standard accounts of Schubert's life gives one the sense that many biographers emphasize the negative aspects. The quantity of Schubert's music published during his lifetime is extremely large, but his difficulties with publishers receive far more attention. The same phenomenon recurs with Schubert's critical reception: most reviews of his music were supportive, often enthusiastic, but more often biographers emphasize the exceptional unfavorable review. Schubert himself sometimes complained of not getting certain compositions published, broke off relations with Anton Diabelli for some years, grumbled about critics, and expressed disappointment that his dramatic and symphonic music went unperformed. Yet he does not seem to have viewed himself as "neglected." Perhaps "struggling" would more appropriately describe Schubert's situation in the 1820s, as he tried to establish a freelance career in a time of widespread inflation, censorship, and rampant trivial music. (Even Beethoven, twenty-seven years Schubert's senior and recognized as the greatest living composer, encountered trouble with Viennese cultural and political forces during the same years.) According to Spaun, one of Schubert's most reliable chroniclers, all the "unfavorable circumstances which surrounded Schubert's life, were utterly unable to break his spirit ... great as was the discrepancy between achievement and recognition and reward, he was, nevertheless, far removed from all bitterness" (*SMF* 24–25).

It is precisely reminiscences like this, however, that have been read to make Schubert out to be more neglected and financially impoverished than he actually was. Schubert's level of income in his maturity far exceeded what would be expected given his humble family origins. (It is another matter that Schubert, like Mozart, could be irresponsible spending his money.) Publications, performances, dedications, teaching, and occasional patronage yielded a respectable level of income. Although the publications earned far more for the publishers than for Schubert, the quantity of works issued is large. This availability, together with the large number of public performances of his works, mainly Lieder and part-songs, belies the notion of crushing neglect.

Schubert's slow achievement of public awareness can be partly explained by his not being a virtuoso performer, by the intimate genres he cultivated, and by the limited opportunities Vienna's concert life afforded, specifically the absence of a public concert hall before the 1830s and the lack of professional orchestras beyond those associated with theaters.[24] Yet in just seven years the quantity of publications is most impressive for a young composer who was by all accounts shy and reluctant to promote himself. The list of the composer's compositions published during his lifetime points concretely to the paradox of Schubert's coexisting fame and neglect: although Schubert was widely performed and published, recognition came only in certain areas. For the rest of his music, much of which won Schubert's posthumous immortality, "neglected" is not the best word; the better term is "undiscovered."

The "natural" Schubert and the "mighty" Beethoven

The legend of Schubert's neglect points to a putative marginality and vulnerability that emerge in other ways as well, as in the idea of Schubert the "natural" artist. Even some of his friends and champions helped to establish Schubert as a vessel of the muses; as an inspired young composer, mainly of Lieder, who wrote remarkably quickly; as one who was undervalued by publishers and the general public alike, and yet who enjoyed the constant support of devoted friends. The underlying message, that Schubert's music, however brilliant, is still somehow artistically flawed, endorses a fault-finding that is another consistent feature of Schubert's image.[25]

Patronizing remarks about Schubert's music already surfaced in reviews during his lifetime. For instance, an otherwise sympathetic critic in the Frankfurt *Allgemeiner musikalischer Anzeiger* chided Schubert's notational spelling mistakes and "other inconveniences" in the Op. 52 Lieder (*SDB* 538; cf. 513). The poet Johann Mayrhofer, with whom Schubert lived for some years, wrote: "Devoid of a more profound knowledge of texture and thorough-bass, he truly remained a natural artist"

(*SDB* 861; *SMF* 13). Josef von Spaun concurred: "For all the admiration I have given the dear departed for years, I still feel that we shall never make a Mozart or a Haydn of him in instrumental and church composition, whereas in song he is unsurpassed. . . . I think, therefore, that Schubert should be treated as a song composer by his biographers" (*SMF* 30). And such was Schubert's fate for decades to come.

The emphasis on Schubert's "natural" talent often implies or explicitly invokes a lack of formal training and discipline. Johann Friedrich Rochlitz, former editor of the *AmZ*, confessed in a letter to Ignaz von Mosel that "several new compositions by your Schubert have won my interest and affection," but opined that the "highly gifted artist needs only a scientifically trained friend to enlighten him gently about himself" (*SDB* 523). Such comments come even from Schubert's staunchest supporters. Leopold von Sonnleithner, in his biographical obituary that amounts to the "official" view of Schubert in 1829, regretted that Schubert never had an appropriate mentor to guide his early artistic development,[26] and he identified another concern: his friends were, by training and inclination, more literary and artistic than musical; their preoccupation was with Lieder, and some of them little appreciated Schubert's larger and more purely musical accomplishments.

The notion of Schubert as a "natural artist," drawing strength from Schubert's friends, circulated widely in criticism, lexicons, histories, and biographies. The first entries about Schubert in encyclopedias of the 1830s, for example, where one turns in the hope of finding more objective information, presented the following:

> Unfortunately [Schubert's] studies remained unregulated in that he did not study the basics with a master of the art, but made his way more through his own experiments and through the imitation of his predecessors.[27]

And:

> This splendid young composer provides further proof that a profound natural talent can overcome all the hindrances of trouble and need, and can obtain perfection even without instruction, but also that this great and continuous effort kills the corporeal existence too soon.[28]

The anecdotal trace of Schubert's "natural" artistic gifts, unencumbered by learning, is found in his decision shortly before he died to undertake counterpoint lessons with the prominent theorist Simon Sechter (*SMF* 106). Their sole lesson together later received far more attention than warranted (both Sonnleithner and Mayrhofer mentioned the instruction in their 1829 memorials).[29] A mid-century article in the popular press shows the consequences of presenting Schubert as an untutored natural: "History is unanimous that, apart from his classic songs, Schubert neither did, nor could, achieve anything outstanding, whether in the field of dramatic, oratorio or chamber music, for he was a natural composer; he himself was only too well aware of this and even in the last years of his life endeavored to acquire the knowledge he lacked in the theory of composition" (*SMF* 424–25). This passage is remarkable for its conflation of legends and clichés: Schubert as the natural composer, not adept in large-scale forms, but gifted in song, who recognized his own limitations and wisely sought academic counsel shortly before his death.

Schubert may himself be responsible for some of these reactions, partly because of his humility, and because he highlighted the speed with which he composed. He documented sometimes writing seven or eight songs in a single day, and occasionally indicated how many hours it took to compose a piece. But I think there is more to the perception of Schubert as a "natural" composer, and here Beethoven enters the picture.

Much of Schubert's image was created in counterpoint to Beethoven's. While in the literature on Beethoven, Schubert is usually referred to only in passing, or goes entirely unmentioned, there is no biographical study of Schubert in which Beethoven does not play a role. The two are opposed in terms of a supposed "work ethic" and characteristic genres (Lied versus symphony), as well as in fame, personality, lifespan, and so on. Schubert's effortless spinning forth of immortal melodic miniatures is contrasted with Beethoven's endless scribbling of sketches for monumental instrumental masterpieces.

By the mid nineteenth century, a shy, natural, feminine Schubert was increasingly being cast against a mighty, solitary, and masculine Beethoven. One should not underestimate how even some of Schubert's closest friends and supporters helped to establish his fame as an inspired composer who tossed off lyrical gems without heroic Beethovenian struggles. The leading Schubert singer of the day, Johann Michael Vogl, referred to Schubert's compositions as coming "into existence during a state of clairvoyance or somnambulism, without any conscious action on the part of the composer, but inevitably, by an act of providence and inspiration," and described a "second way of composing through will-power, reflection, effort, knowledge," a clear allusion to Beethoven.[30] The Lied is the genre ideally suited for a natural genius because of its small scope, intimacy, and more obvious melodic, rather than structural, character. A Lied can be dashed off on the back of a menu perhaps, but a symphony cannot.

The identification of Beethoven with symphonic masterpieces and of Schubert with intimate genres of modest proportions further promotes the image of Schubert the "natural" through associations with women, nature, and the home.[31] The poet Nikolaus Lenau remarked in 1839 that

"Schubert's compositions are wearing thin. There is a certain coquetry, an effeminate weakness about them" (*SMF* 248). Robert Schumann had been more specific about the gendered opposition between a masculine Beethoven and feminine Schubert the year before in his review of Schubert's "Grand Duo":

> Compared with Beethoven, Schubert is a feminine character, much more
> voluble, softer and broader; or a guileless child romping among giants. Such
> is the relationship of these symphonic movements to those of Beethoven.
> Their intimacy is purely Schubertian. They have their robust moments, to be
> sure, and marshal formidable forces. But Schubert conducts himself as
> wife to husband, the one giving orders, the other relying upon pleas and
> persuasion.[32]

One of the most remarkably gendered comparisons came in 1863 with the first exhumation of Schubert's and Beethoven's bodies from Vienna's Währing Cemetery.[33] Gerhard von Breuning, who had known both composers, observed the event and remarked, "it was extremely interesting physiologically to compare the compact thickness of Beethoven's skull and the fine, almost feminine thinness of Schubert's, and to relate them, almost directly, to the character of their music."[34] This comparison became well known because of its inclusion in the first substantial biography of Schubert, which appeared in 1865, written by Heinrich Kreissle von Hellborn. Confronting Schubert's well-preserved skull, the "doctors and hospital attendants who were present were astonished at its delicate, almost womanly organization."[35]

Kreissle's book served as the basis for writings about Schubert for the latter half of the nineteenth century, despite its many weaknesses and its recourse to hearsay and gossip. At one point Kreissle, too, weighs in with a comparison between Beethoven and Schubert. While more coded, the feminine and masculine traits of the childlike Schubert and powerful, intellectual Beethoven – heart versus brain – are still clearly in evidence:

> Their two natures were essentially distinct and different. If Schubert's easy
> disposition, his childish naïveté, his guilelessness in the ordinary dealings
> of life, his delight in a glass of wine and sociable habits, his sincerity, and a
> good mixture of Viennese geniality, remind one of Mozart's character, these
> very qualities essentially contrasted with and distinguished him from the
> somewhat capricious, mistrustful, sarcastic, and haughty Beethoven, whose
> depth of intellect and greatness of soul, coupled with his vast Classical range
> and versatility of power, enabled him to tower, in many respects, above
> both Mozart and Schubert.[36]

The comparisons to Beethoven, both the musician and the man, continue to this day and have taken a somewhat different turn with recent investigations of Schubert's possible homosexuality and the implications for musical analysis. In some ways these contemporary dialogues resound long-standing themes. Beethoven is still crucial to the discussions – even when he goes unmentioned – because he continues to serve significantly as Schubert's "Other."

Nostalgia

The theme of nostalgia also has its origins in the composer's own time, which is somewhat surprising given that it would seem to require some temporal mediation. The nostalgia that colors Schubert's posthumous reception – references to lost youth and to a golden past – already begins to punctuate the letters and journals of Schubert's closest friends in the early 1820s (e.g. *SDB* 351, 405, 476), and reappears for the rest of his life. (Given Schubert's precarious medical condition, his own laments may also represent a "hymn to lost health" [e.g. *SDB* 374].) Bauernfeld captured this nostalgia in his diary after a reunion with Schubert, Schwind, and Schober during the summer of 1826: "According to the old custom, we all spent the night together, and how much we had to tell! Poetry is over, the prose of life begins anew" (*SDB* 545).

The air of nostalgia comes not only from verbal accounts but maybe even more strongly from visual images, from Schubert's own wistful music, and especially from later arrangements of it. Visually, depictions of joyous music-making and carefree socializing are central to posterity's conception of Schubert and his environment.[37] The most famous scene, *A Schubert Evening at Josef von Spaun's*, dates from the 1860s; its creator was one of the composer's closest friends, Moritz von Schwind (1804–71), an important artist whose images of Schubert span many decades.[38] Remembering the brief time they lived together Schwind reportedly told composer Ferdinand Hiller: "There could be no happier existence. Each morning he composed something beautiful and each evening he found the most enthusiastic admirers. We gathered in his room – he played and sang to us – we were enthusiastic and afterwards we went to the tavern. We hadn't a penny but were blissfully happy" (*SMF* 283; cf. 213). Nearly forty years after leaving Vienna, Schwind created the *Schubert Evening at Spaun's* and wrote to the poet Eduard Mörike: "I have begun to work at something which I feel I owe the intellectual part of Germany – my admirable friend Schubert at the piano, surrounded by his circle of listeners. I know all the people by heart."[39]

Schwind portrays the Schubertiade as a sanctuary and haven – a charmed place where Schubert might accompany Vogl singing that ode to

their art, *An die Musik* (D547), which sets Franz von Schober's sentimental words.[40] Despite Schwind's immersion in this milieu during the 1820s,
the captivating image he created decades later may distort as well as
enlighten; as with lively anecdotes, compelling illustrations enshrine pervasive legends. Schwind offers a Vienna devoid of disease, political repression, and the hardships of everyday life. Such a cozy picture of Schubert's
circumstances, a nostalgia for an "Alt Wien" that had long passed – and
that in any case never quite existed as later imagined – found complementary musical expression in the countless reworkings of Schubert's
melodies. Franz Liszt's popular *Soirées de Vienne* evokes just such an
idealized past. In word, image, and music, the Schubert circle increasingly
came to represent a carefree bygone Vienna, in which – despite
Metternich's repressive regime, limited professional opportunities, and a
rapidly declining standard of living – good, simple, and happy times still
prevailed. (Leon Botstein explores some of these issues in the preceding
chapter.)

Soon after Schubert's death, Spaun, Sonnleithner, Bauernfeld,
Mayrhofer, Ferdinand Schubert, and others published tributes, reminiscences, and writings that are the foundation of all later biographical
work.[41] Unlike their unfortunate friend, many of his acquaintances lived
long lives, continuing to reminisce (nostalgically) in old age. The popular
image of Schubert, distilled from their writings, spread widely in sentimental biographies and novels,[42] in theater pieces,[43] and eventually in
films.[44] Centenaries in 1897 and 1928 saw an extraordinary flood of such
materials, the nostalgia now expressed not by those who had known
Schubert personally, but by later generations that yearned for simpler
times. If biographers had complained that Schubert's actual life was
uneventful, more creative adapters evidently found attractive raw
material in it to fire their fantasies.

The most influential force in Schubert's popularization was Heinrich
Berté's phenomenally successful operetta *Das Dreimäderlhaus*, which
premiered at Vienna's Raimundtheater on January 15, 1916. It proved one
of the most profitable works of musical theater ever written.[45] Derived
from Rudolf Hans Bartsch's extremely popular Schubert novel
Schwammerl (1912), the plot tells of the hopes and dreams of Schubert
and his friends Schober, Schwind, Vogl, and Kupelwieser. Terribly shy,
Schubert courts Hannerl, the youngest of three sisters (Haiderl, Hederl,
and Hannerl); through a series of confusions, Hannerl ends up with "the
poet" Schober, while Schubert, unrequited in love, is left alone with his
music. The score consists solely of adaptations of Schubert's music,
mostly drawn from dance and keyboard compositions. In popularizing a
composer's life on stage or screen, a potentially powerful ingredient is the

use of his own art as subliminal accompaniment. Schubert's music becomes the soundtrack for mythological narratives of his life. As listeners have become less musically literate, extramusical crutches, often biographical rather than hermeneutic, provide the point of entry to the music and give it meaning.

What might be called the "SchuBerté phenomenon" would seem to mark the nadir of the representation of Schubert's life and music. In Berté's operetta, Schubert's music is fragmented, melodies are fetishized, and his personality, friendships, lovelife, and daily circumstances distorted. The personal nostalgia of Schubert and his friends devolves into sentimental kitsch. And yet Berté captures a side of Schubert – his music as unsurpassed melody and popular entertainment – that had gradually become overshadowed in the nineteenth century as his more substantial works – and structures – gained recognition. Paradoxically, even as Berté trivialized Schubert's life and work, he resurrected the Biedermeier composer whose small-scale songs and dances first delighted Viennese audiences of the 1820s.

Schubert today

As the twentieth century is drawing to a close, Schubert's image is once again changing, most noticeably between the 1978 sesquicentennial of his death and the 1997 bicentennial of his birth. The canon of Schubert's most highly valued compositions continues to shift, so that *Winterreise* (D911), for example, with its existential despair, now eclipses the less disturbing *Die schöne Müllerin* (D795).

An example of the evolving image of Schubert is a painting acquired in 1991 by Vienna's Kunsthistorisches Museum. It is a handsome portrait, unsigned, of a young man seated at a piano; a pencil on the instrument suggests a composer. In a recent monograph on the work, Rita Steblin argues that it depicts Schubert around the age of seventeen and was perhaps commissioned after his first success with the Mass in F in 1814.[46] Both the identification of Schubert and the attribution to the Viennese painter Josef Abel have been questioned,[47] but the image is being disseminated all the same, appearing on record covers, in program books, and in the popular press.[48]

Fritz Lehner's gripping film *Mit meinen heissen Tränen* (1986) introduced a darker Schubert – not simply suffering, but alienated, ill, and isolated even among family and friends.[49] While Lehner's film was creating a considerable stir in Europe, Maynard Solomon's investigations of Schubert's "possible homosexual orientation" and "compulsive hedonism" preoccupied the attention of English-speaking countries.[50] The exceptionally intense reactions his articles provoked, responses and counter-responses that often carry not so hidden personal and political agendas, further underscore the "transferential" relations that are possible with "our Schubert."[51]

As with other components of Schubert's legacy, one hopes further documentation will someday appear and help to clarify the truth. But truth is left behind once an image – Schubert and his merry friends cavorting in Berté's operetta, a beguiling painting of a young composer, a challenging biographical conception of Schubert as womanizer, homosexual, or hedonist – enters the popular imagination. Incontrovertible facts, untrustworthy legends, symbolic anecdotes, and simple mistakes all affect perceptions of Schubert and prove difficult, sometimes impossible, to dispel. Although the popular image of Schubert rests largely on anecdotes, most colorfully promoted in novels, operettas, and films, more sober and objective studies often project essentially the same view. Scholarly discussions of Schubert's casual compositional methods or loose formal structures merely put a scientific spin on popular anecdotes that have Schubert composing songs on any scrap of paper and then forgetting about them.

The image of Schubert changes in response to the culture that perceives him. The Biedermeier Schubert, the Romantic Schubert, and now a Postmodern Schubert are creations of periods that approach historical documents and musical compositions with changing expectations, seeking new information, and asking different questions. We must resist the nostalgic fallacy that the past understood Schubert best because of a closer proximity to him, just as we must resist the danger of thinking that present-day views penetrate deepest simply because they draw upon a wider range of documentation and music. The sentimental distortions of Schubert's life and music on stage and screen at least reflect something of the playfulness and Biedermeier conviviality that have increasingly been displaced, in the Postmodern era, by a more complex image of a suffering and neurotic "poor" Schubert.

3 "The passion for friendship": music, cultivation, and identity in Schubert's circle

David Gramit

What was Schubert's circle?

To frame this chapter by means of such an apparently straightforward question may seem simplistic. If we take it seriously, however, it leads to an approach to Schubert's immediate context considerably different than the catalogues of Schubert's friends, their idiosyncrasies, and their accomplishments that have been a mainstay of Schubert scholarship. Both idiosyncrasies and accomplishments, admittedly, were considerable, and such anecdotes can provide entertaining reading as well as accurate information; however, not only are several accounts of this type already available,[1] but a focus on the *who* of Schubert's circle also implies that the nature of that group is self-evident.

A moment's reflection suggests otherwise: why should Schubert have been associated from the earliest studies and accounts with a circle of friends, to the extent that "Schubert's circle" (or the equivalent *Schubertkreis*) has achieved the status of a standard formula? "Bach's circle," or "Mozart's," for instance, have nothing approaching such currency in their respective fields.[2] No one would suggest that these earlier composers had had no friends or associates, so what is it about Schubert's friends – or our perception of them – that has made them indispensable in Schubert studies, to the extent that Newman Flower, whose 1928 biography focused perhaps more single-mindedly on the circle than any other, could write: "the passion for friendship lived in Schubert. He could not exist without friends"?[3]

The easy familiarity of such assertions and the approachability they imply reduce a crucial shift in the social position of composers to an individual personality trait and fold Schubert's culture into our own by failing to question the meaning of such basic concepts as friendship in Schubert's context. The following considerations seek to avoid these pitfalls by providing not a biographical collection, nor even a record of the self-perceptions of Schubert's associates, but rather an interpretation of the nature and significance of that group within its culture from the perspective of our own.

Friendship, cultivation, and social class

Our knowledge of Schubert's friendships begins with his schooling, and so any account of Schubert's circle that goes beyond his immediate family takes as its starting point Schubert's appointment as a boy soprano in the Imperial Court Chapel in 1808. Although Schubert received musical training as a result of this position, his appointment also gave him access to something that few earlier musicians would have known: an education in the Vienna Stadtkonvikt, a boarding school whose student body consisted primarily of boys and young men from families of considerably higher social standing than Schubert's. The lists compiled many years later by Albert Stadler, one of Schubert's school friends, make the point unintentionally but clearly:

> Among our fellow pupils were: Michael Rueskäfer (Deputy to the Finance Minister, Excellency, etc.), Franz von Schlechta (now Freiherr and head of a department at the Finance Ministry), Franz Kindinger (Councillor at the Ministry of Justice), Josef Kleindl (*Justiz-Hofrat*), Josef Kenner (Upper Austrian *Statthaltereirat*, retired, poet of "Der Liedler"), Franz Werner (legal adviser to the General Staff), Josef Beskiba (Deputy-Director at the Technical High School), Benedikt Randhartinger (Court *Kapellmeister*). . . . Every evening there was an orchestral practice with full orchestra. . . . The Court organist, Wenzel Ruzicka, conducted on the violin and, in his absence, our Schubert, who played the violin very nicely, took over. . . . As second violin [former student] Josef von Spaun (Court Councillor, but in those days still a junior) very often helped us as a visitor. Cellos were Anton Holzapfel (. . . Vienna Borough Councillor, now retired and living at Aistersheim near Wels), a thoroughly trained musician and a special friend of Schubert's; – Max von Spaun (*Kammeralrat* in Laibach); violins, Anton Hauer (President of the High Court of Justice in Linz) and Leopold Ebner (*Kammeralrat* in Innsbruck); first flute, Franz Eckel (Director of the Institute of Veterinary Surgery . . .); first clarinet, Josef Kleindl; timpani, Randhartinger; all seminary pupils at the time, and others I no longer remember.[4]

Stadler's parentheses served simply to specify the location and later position of his fellows (and, perhaps, to suggest some prestige – ne'er-do-wells are conspicuously absent) and likely seemed unremarkable at the time, but the overwhelming preponderance of government officials and bureaucrats they reveal is a clue to one of the distinctive features of Schubert's cultural milieu. This administrative/professional middle class made up a tiny portion of Vienna's population, but together with the (even less numerous) aristocracy and professional musicians themselves, they made up the bulk of the musically literate Viennese public, a group of only a few thousand in a city whose population numbered some 300,000 in 1827.[5]

That Schubert's Stadtkonvikt education brought him into contact with such men begins to suggest the contingency of many of the contexts with which Schubert is associated: the bourgeois salon, the Schubertiade, the cultured cluster of friends. None could reasonably have been extrapolated from the circumstances of Schubert's birth as the son of a primary school teacher in one of Vienna's poorer districts. These, however, are precisely the contexts that his fellow students had been raised to value above all others, for the primarily bureaucratic middle-class culture of Austria and Germany was one in which *Bildung* – intellectual, spiritual, and emotional cultivation as a lifelong pursuit – had become both a cherished value and evidence of suitability for membership in an administrative/cultural elite. In the words of Wilhelm von Humboldt, the Prussian civil service reformer of the turn of the eighteenth century: "Nothing is so important in a high-level official of the state as the complete conception he has of mankind and as the degree of intellectual clarity with which he ponders these questions and responds to them emotionally. . . . There is nothing so important as his interpretation of the idea of *Bildung*."[6]

Recognizing the centrality of this phenomenon to Schubert's intellectual and aesthetic context begins to explain the tenacity of Schubert's circle as a topos. Earlier composers, whatever their private relationships, had had their status defined not by those relationships but by their (often hereditary) calling, their relations to their patrons, or beginning in the late eighteenth century, to a growing music-buying, concert-going public. By contrast, Schubert could be seen – despite income from music sales during the latter part of his life – to have lived almost exclusively in relation to his friends; whatever more formal positions might later have materialized were prevented by his early death. This friend-dominated life was lent plausibility by anecdotes stressing Bohemian poverty and dependence on those friends even for such professional necessities as staff paper. Schubert appeared, then, not as a hereditary craftsman, but as an artist in, if not entirely of, the middle class, and this status brought with it the kind of personal associations familiar to and cherished by the bourgeois audience for music. Further, the pathos of Schubert's humble origins and continuing poverty, regardless of their basis in fact, could only reflect favorably on his subsequent admirers: their appreciation put them in a position analogous to the anecdotally immortalized early friends whose acts of kindness had nurtured a young genius.

The prominent role of anecdote in these considerations leads to another observation on the place of the circle in the historiography of Schubert. Because of Schubert's early death and the substantial gap between that death and the first full biographical study, published in 1865,[7] posthumously collected anecdotes have come to play an enormous role in establishing our image of the composer and his context. The bulk of these anecdotes derive either from obituary notices or from responses to inquiries by would-be biographers. Inevitably, Schubert assumes a centrality in both instances that has more to do with the purpose of the document than with the writer's experience during Schubert's life. The result has often been a conflation of posthumous fame and contemporary circumstance that constructs a circle with Schubert himself firmly at its center, surrounded by perceptive but fundamentally inferior admirers drawn only by Schubert himself. Once again, Flower's biography sets the familiar tone: "Without Schubert, most of these people would not have been in common touch. . . . It was the extraordinary personality of Schubert that blended them. The richness of his mental gifts adorned his poverty, but it was the secret lodestone of his heart that brought these friends together and held them."[8] Against this image we may place the descriptions of two of Schubert's friends, one of whom knew Schubert at the beginning and one at the end of the composer's career. First, consider the account of Johann Senn, an early friend exiled for politically suspect activities in 1821:

> The German struggles for liberation, from 1813 to 1815, had left in their wake a significant spiritual upheaval in Austria too. Among other things, there was gathered in Vienna at that time, as it were by instinct and not as the result of any intention, a splendid, companionable circle of young writers, poets, artists and cultured people generally, such as the Imperial City had scarcely ever seen hitherto and which, after it was disbanded, sowed seeds for the future in every direction.   (*SMF* 334)[9]

Eduard von Bauernfeld, who met Schubert only after Senn's departure, wrote independently in quite similar terms:

> At the time Schubert came out into the world several young men in his native city, mostly poets and painters . . . , gathered together, whom genuine striving after art and similarity of views soon united in sincere friendship, and into whose circle Schubert too was drawn. The mutual communication between these youths and their artistic conversations had a great effect on him and stimulated him, if not so much to talk, at any rate to the most varied musical productivity. . . . He often expressed regret . . . that the friendly union of so many worthy young men, as will happen, became disrupted by their pursuing different careers and by other chances.[10]

In both accounts, Schubert is part of an active group of varied composition, but even in Bauernfeld's memorial tribute he is neither the sole center of attention nor the reason for the group's existence.

Literary activity in Schubert's circle

The regret that Bauernfeld reports Schubert to have felt at the transitory nature of the circle is plausible, for the context of relationships in which Schubert lived was indeed constantly changing. Of the school companions mentioned by Stadler, only Josef von Spaun remained close to Schubert until his death. Career and family considerations, as well as occasional personal differences, drew friends apart both geographically and personally; a few examples must suffice. Schubert met the poet Johann Mayrhofer through Spaun in 1815; they grew increasingly close until the early 1820s, after which there is virtually no evidence of personal interaction, let alone intimacy.[11] The painter Leopold Kupelwieser had become a close friend by the time of Mayrhofer's withdrawal; in 1823, however, he began an extended trip to Italy, and despite correspondence with Schubert during his absence, he too is far less prominent among Schubert's friends after his return. By the end of Schubert's life, in addition to his long-time friends Spaun and Schober – both of whom had also at various times left Vienna for extended periods – Moritz von Schwind and Eduard von Bauernfeld were among those closest to Schubert. The former he had most likely met in 1821, the latter only in 1825. Although the image of a circle, with its associations of fixity and completeness and its long history, going back to Schubert and his friends themselves, is unlikely to be replaced, a loose and constantly shifting web of relationships offers a more apt metaphor.

Whatever this group is called, however, one of its primary values is both obvious and constant: a seriously pursued interest in the arts, including but by no means limited to music. This variety of interests has fueled a recurrent criticism of Schubert, equating excessive traffic with practitioners of other arts with a betrayal of disciplinary integrity; a betrayal confirmed by what has been perceived as the insufficiently disciplined form of Schubert's larger works. As early as February 1829, Leopold von Sonnleithner wrote in the monthly report of the Gesellschaft der Musikfreunde:

> It is much to be regretted that, especially in his earlier days, Schubert chose scarcely a single musical artist for his closest and most intimate relationships, but for the most part only artistic practitioners in other branches, who could indeed pay homage to his genius, but were incapable of leading it. An excellent, experienced composer would probably have guided Schubert towards even more works of the larger kind and have stood by him as adviser in matters of outward form, well-planned disposition and large-scale effect.   (SDB 856)

From the standpoint of bourgeois self-cultivation, however, such a variety of contacts bespoke well-roundedness rather than amateurishness, and it is that context that defines the literary and aesthetic values of Schubert's friends.

The future bureaucrats of the Stadtkonvikt are thus once again relevant, particularly a single group with whose members Schubert had continued interaction throughout his life. Josef von Spaun, Josef Kenner, Johann Mayrhofer, Franz von Schober, as well as Schubert's later friends the Hartmann brothers, Franz and Friedrich (Fritz), and a number of more peripheral friends including Spaun's brothers Anton and Max, and Anton Ottenwalt, all shared common ties to Upper Austria, primarily to Linz; many also had in common schooling at the monasteries of St. Florian and Kremsmünster. The older members of this group, particularly Anton von Spaun and Ottenwalt, adopted an educational ideal based on moralistically oriented studies of the classics as well as of recent German literature.[12] Similar ideals had been advocated by educational reformers such as Herder and Humboldt, but had not yet had significant impact on Austrian schools;[13] accordingly, the friends resolved independently to cultivate both themselves and those whom they could influence. Their zeal, their means, and the role of the arts in the process are suggested in the following excerpts from letters written by Anton von Spaun to Schober, whom the elder friends found a perpetual challenge to their ideals of moderation and self-discipline:

> Feeling and thinking – in them is higher existence. From both proceeds action – but what shall we act upon? We cannot depose tyrants, live for the world in death for the Fatherland, we cannot teach wisdom to youth in the columned corridors of Athens, nor struggle on behalf of oppressed innocence – but we can still act and achieve true greatness. It's not true when someone says: the world is as it is, the individual can do nothing against it, it's foolishness to want to protest against the spirit of the age. Just to be better than our times is already a great deal, and it's even better to pull others out of their tumult – and because it would be bad not to practice in life what one realizes is good, you, I, and all who are inspired by like convictions will hold firmly to them and sow them everywhere we find unspoiled character and receptivity to them.
>
> *
>
> We must study humanity, and all ages, and what the best people of the past did and thought, and how one thing leads to another, and how one thing follows out of another, so that we can understand clearly and have a positive influence on the people we love, on our brothers. Beauty too influences human hearts powerfully, refreshingly, and upliftingly, and the sounds of music, a madonna by Raphael, an Apollo, the song of a divinely

inspired poet, all pull heavenwards with an unknown power; therefore let us too dedicate our lives and flee nothing so much as an excess of destructive passions and the deficiency and emptiness of an indolent spirit.[14]

In many such letters, which scholars have only recently begun to reconsider, a record of the reading and discussion that these values implied has been preserved. They are evident as well in much of Mayrhofer's classicizing poetry and in the pages of the two volumes of the *Beyträge zur Bildung für Jünglinge* (Contributions to the Cultivation of Youth) on which several of the friends collaborated in 1817 and 1818. From our perspective, such idealism can seem naïve and resolutely unconnected to the political cynicism of Restoration Austria, but – perhaps precisely because of that – their program provided not only a prominent place for the arts, but also a basis for judging them: "every art worthy of humans has as its goal the betterment of our circumstances – directly or indirectly serving our perfection or ennoblement."[15] The friends looked to classical models and revered artists and authors (most prominently Goethe and Schiller) who could be seen to follow those models. A corollary of this stance was an attitude toward Romanticism that ranged from suspicion to outright rejection. Thus Mayrhofer contrasted the "distortions and blunders of the German school" of artists to the "canon of the beautiful and truthful, in a word, the classical," which had been lost since the fall of Rome; Anton von Spaun criticized the "completely incoherent, chaotic longing of the heart" characteristic of modern poetry; and Anton Ottenwalt castigated critics who "most often lead a petty, perhaps perverted life, let history count for nothing, know of nothing but the dreary night of the absolute everything-and-nothing doctrine, over which the will-o'-the-wisps and spooks of Romanticism hover."[16]

The extent to which this circle and its views overlapped with Schubert's deserves careful consideration, particularly since the passages just cited contrast so markedly with the conventional portrait of Schubert the Romantic. There can be no question of Mayrhofer's long and intense contact with Schubert, but Anton von Spaun and Ottenwalt only visited Vienna during Schubert's lifetime; those in Vienna most closely associated with Schubert – including Josef von Spaun, Mayrhofer, and Schober – never matched their counterparts in Linz in their overt pedagogical zeal.[17] They did, however, share not only their passion for literature and the arts, but also the habit of formally established meetings to encounter and discuss those arts. So, for instance, Johanna Lutz wrote to her fiancé Leopold Kupelwieser on November 18, 1823, that "last Saturday there was a meeting at Mohn's, where the readings were fixed for Mondays and Thursdays" (*SDB* 392). In Kupelwieser's and Schober's absence, these meetings eventually broke up, but on his return, Schober organized another reading group, frequently reported in the diaries of the Hartmann brothers.

With the passage of time, though, *what* was read around Schubert was changing as well. Schubert's own occupation with song texts by such poets as Novalis and Friedrich and August Wilhelm Schlegel in 1819 and thereafter, along with a concomitant decline in the quantity of texts by Goethe and Schiller, parallels a significant change in the group's literary horizon, corresponding as well to the increasing prominence of younger men among Schubert's closest friends. Although the fluid nature of the circle precludes setting rigid boundaries, Senn's arrest and exile, as the most dramatic and abrupt event in which Schubert was involved, offers a useful marker. Senn (*b.* 1795) and the friends associated with him and Schubert before 1820 were virtually all of Schubert's age or older, for example Josef von Spaun (*b.* 1788), Mayrhofer (*b.* 1787), Kenner (*b.* 1794), Schober (*b.* 1796), and the brothers Anselm and Josef Hütten-brenner (*b.* 1794 and 1796, respectively). Schubert remained in contact with some of these older friends throughout his life, despite extended separations from most for a variety of personal and professional reasons; Kupelwieser (*b.* 1796) and Franz von Bruchmann (*b.* 1798) – both promi-nent in the early 1820s but more distant by the end of Schubert's life – were also near-exact contemporaries. After 1820, however, most of Schubert's close associates were notably younger: Eduard von Bauernfeld (*b.* 1802), Benedikt Randhartinger (*b.* 1802), and Franz Lachner (*b.* 1803) – the latter two, as active professional musicians, exceptional among Schubert's close friends – Moritz von Schwind (*b.* 1804), Fritz von Hartmann (*b.* 1805), Ernst von Feuchtersleben (*b.* 1806), and Franz von Hartmann (*b.* 1808). Although as intensely interested in literature as the older group, this younger one was not only more sympathetic to such cur-rents as the Romanticism of Schlegel and Hoffmann and the cynicism of Heine or Kleist, but also considerably more eclectic in its taste.[18]

Even this brief overview of literary taste begins to suggest something that has long been recognized about the role of Schubert's circle, particu-larly in relation to his vocal music: its members both provided song texts and collaborated on operatic projects (as did Mayrhofer, Schober, Bruchmann, Senn, and Kenner) and introduced Schubert to the poetry of their own acquaintances (as Josef von Spaun did in the case of Mayrhofer and Bruchmann did for August von Platen). Even more importantly, they mediated his introduction to an extraordinarily broad corpus of poetry, the product of a culture in which the writing of poetry was simply a part of being an educated person. It is less easy to dismiss the phenomenon of poet-officials if one remembers that not only the likes of Kenner and

Mayrhofer, but also Goethe and Grillparzer (who moved in many of the same Viennese social circles and was an acquaintance of Schubert's later years) exemplify it. In any case, Schubert's exposure to the latter two figures was due in large part to his close contact with those like the former.

Cultivating connections: Schubert's circle in society

While the literary relevance of Schubert's circle may be obvious, and the short-sightedness of some of its members concerning Schubert's instrumental music is easily ridiculed,[19] their role in facilitating his activity both within and outside the realm of Lieder was also considerable. Simply put, their social connections were far more powerful than his own, and they willingly exploited them to his benefit, making crucial introductions, providing performance opportunities, and facilitating the publication of his music. Most obviously, through his early friends, Schubert established his ties to Johann Michael Vogl, the retired court opera singer who became Schubert's friend, a mentor of sorts, and a staunch advocate. Vogl, another Upper Austrian, also shared the Linz circle's dedication to classical-humanistic moral cultivation to the extent that it is difficult to distinguish his ideals and influence from their own.[20]

In a society in which the administration and often the performance of serious music was still to a great degree the domain of the same cultivated amateur class that was vital to literary culture, the friends' ties to those outside the world of professional musicians were perhaps even more significant. Thus, Josef von Spaun's friend, the lawyer Josef Wilhelm Witteczek, collected Schubert's songs in manuscript and sponsored musical evenings dedicated to Schubert's music. Through Spaun's cousin, the poet and philosophy professor Matthäus von Collin, he encountered not only literary figures like the pioneering orientalist Josef von Hammer-Purgstall, Johann Ladislaus Pyrker (the Patriarch of Venice and poet of two of Schubert's songs), and Karoline Pichler (who presided over one of Vienna's leading literary salons), but also significant figures in the Viennese musical world, including Count Moritz von Dietrichstein (administrative head of music at the imperial court) and Ignaz Franz von Mosel (who along with others of Schubert's social contacts, including the Sonnleithner family and Raphael Georg Kiesewetter, was a leading figure in the Gesellschaft der Musikfreunde, founded in 1814 and central to the promotion of serious musical taste in Vienna).

Both close friends and these more influential acquaintances came to be participants in the Schubertiades, evenings devoted to performances of

Schubert's music and to social interaction of those for whom that music was culturally meaningful. This formulation may seem needlessly circuitous, but it is necessary to encompass the range of events to which the term referred. Its original sense, specifying one aspect of the literary and musical activities of Schubert's circle, is suggested in Schubert's own letter of December 7, 1822, to Josef von Spaun: "Our life together [*Zusammenleben*] in Vienna is quite agreeable now. We hold readings at Schober's three times a week, and one Schubertiade."[21] Within a few years, however, Schubert's growing reputation – itself partially a result of advocacy by his friends – had changed the connotations of the term. The change appears clearly in the diary entry of Franz von Hartmann, a younger friend of the late 1820s, for December 15, 1826:

> I went to Spaun's, where there was a big, big Schubertiade.... There was a huge gathering. The Arneth, Witteczek, Kurzrock and Pompe couples, the mother-in-law of Witteczek: Dr. Watteroth's widow, Betty Wanderer, and the painter Kupelwieser with his wife, Grillparzer, Schober, Schwind, Mayrhofer and his landlord Huber, the tall Huber, Derffel, Bauernfeld, Gahy (who played gloriously *à quatre mains* with Schubert) and Vogl, who sang almost 30 splendid songs. Baron Schlechta and other court probationers and secretaries were also there. I was moved almost to tears.... When the music was done there was grand feeding and then dancing.   (*SDB* 571–72)

At such events, Schubert's immediate circle and the broader society of similar interests came together, strengthening their sense of shared culture through conversation and dancing, as well as through a serious interest in music. In music, as in literature, promotion of that serious taste was crucially bound up not only with defining and advocating that taste, but also with thereby defining one's self and one's associates – and excluding other tastes from those associations. Serious art requires serious contemplation, and the contemplator must be appropriately cultivated to appreciate the unspoken significance that lies beyond mere recreation.[22] The cultivated bureaucrat and the artist are thus united; the socially marked rift lay not between bourgeois and Bohemian but rather common and cultivated. In this context, statements that might be read to mark off the artist resonate differently, as when Schober wrote to Schubert on December 2, 1824, "are we not precisely those who have found our life in art, while others found only entertainment in it?" (*SDB* 385) or when Bruchmann wrote to Platen on June 20, 1823, "life here is so miserable that the artist is the only person with whom a cheerful, beautiful life is still possible."[23] Schubert's own letter to Schober of November 30, 1823, differentiates even more explicitly, not between artist and other, but between cultivated and crude:

> Our circle, as indeed I had expected, has lost its central focus without you.... True, as a substitute for you and Kupelwieser we received four individuals: the Hungarian Mayer, Hönig, Smetana and Steiger, but the majority of such individuals make the society only more insignificant instead of better. What is the good of a lot of quite ordinary students and officials to us? If Bruchmann is not there ... we go on for hours under the supreme direction of Mohn hearing nothing but eternal talk about riding, fencing, horses and hounds. If it is to go on like this, I don't suppose I shall stand it for long among them.   (*SDB* 300–301)

The material implications of this split for Schubert as a composer were considerable. In a society where the musical public itself was small, the potential market for serious music (as Schubert himself seems to have conceived it) was frustratingly limited, as Schubert's letter to Schober of September 21, 1824, suggests: "with [music publisher Maximilian Josef] Leidesdorff things have gone badly so far: he cannot pay, nor does a single soul buy anything, either my things or any others, except wretched fashionable stuff" (*SDB* 375). Nor was this attitude limited to composers; long after Schubert's death, his friends still opposed elite and popular taste in socio-economic terms. Josef Kenner made the tart observation that "today publishers with their reprints, and biographers are living on [Schubert's] tardily appreciated posthumous works, now that Liszt's conjuring tricks have made him palatable to the public" (*SMF* 82); and Josef von Spaun, whose obituary article had noted that "success and money never served [Schubert] as incentives in the dedication of his life to art," later opined that "Schubert did not get the recognition he deserved in Vienna. The great majority of people remained, and still remain, uninterested. The blame for this does not lie with the lovely songs; the public that is enthusiastic over *Rigoletto* and finds [Gluck's] *Iphigénie* boring cannot be Schubert's public."[24]

I have so far discussed only men within Schubert's circle, for there is little verifiable evidence of Schubert's interacting with women with anything like the degree of intimacy that can easily be documented with many men. This is not, however, to deny that women played significant roles in Schubert's life. Some supposed connections, like the anecdotally reported liaisons with Therese Grob and Caroline Esterházy, are never likely to be disproven to an extent that will disabuse those who believe them, nor established with a degree of certainty that will convert skeptics. But Schubert's work with the singer Anna Milder, or with Wilhelmine von Chézy, the author of *Rosamunde*, and his social interaction with women like the extraordinarily musical Fröhlich sisters, or Marie Pachler, his hostess for an 1827 stay in Graz, are undeniable. Since Schubert's interaction with women has recently played a role in a controversy over his sexual orientation, and since both issues relate directly to the nature of Schubert's circle, the subject warrants closer examination.

Maynard Solomon raised the issue of Schubert's sexuality in two articles, the second of which achieved a notoriety that has spread well beyond the confines of the musicological community.[25] Drawing on a wide variety of evidence, including allusions by Schubert's friends to questionable morality on the part of the composer, passages in correspondence that can be interpreted as veiled references to same-sex activity, and the preponderance of intense male friendships among Schubert and his close friends, Solomon cautiously hypothesized that "although I cannot be certain that some of the evidence . . . may not be wide of the mark, I believe it is reasonably probable that [the] primary orientation [of the members of Schubert's circle] was a homosexual one."[26] Despite detailed – and considerably less cautious – attempts at rebuttal, there seems no convincing reason to deny the probability of Solomon's proposal, while remembering as well his caution: coded references to forbidden practices can hardly be expected to yield entirely unambiguous interpretations.[27] Still, it is difficult to interpret passages like this one, from an unpublished letter of August 8, 1825, written by Antonio Mayer to Schober, as referring to anything but sexual activity that must not be discussed openly:

> I am the happiest of men . . . – I have a three-coloured cat! . . . Since you have gone, I have relied much more on cats; it's better than going to the dogs. I have made the acquaintance of two slender, one imposing, one curious, and two hardworking cats. I could tell you a lot about that, but since I don't know if my friends are also yours, it would be doubly indiscreet to talk about it, first because it could bore you, and second because I could compromise my cats.[28]

In short, Solomon's interpretation provides a background to much of the activity of Schubert's circle more plausible than either Anselm Hüttenbrenner's claim that Schubert had a "dominating aversion to the daughters of Eve" (*SMF* 70) or the mildly – but conventionally – adventurous Schubert proposed by Solomon's opponents.

Schubert's connection to the Linz circle of the Spauns, Kenner, and Ottenwalt should be recalled in this context, for although it seems unlikely that this circle had an explicitly homosexual orientation – Ottenwalt had, after all, given perversion as one of the faults of Romantic critics, and Kenner's evaluations of Schubert's later life are the most vehement[29] – the powerfully charged relationships between young men that the friends encouraged had strong affective and physical, if not explicitly sexual, components. An unpublished letter by Ottenwalt to Schober of January 1, 1816, sets this tone and reveals the role that music could play in it:

Anton sat at the piano in Frau von Brandt's room, and while darkness fell
he played his variations on the Almerlied, the new ones on the Russian
folksong, the theme of which I love so, because it is in the minor, and the
melancholy Traunerlieder and some others. The tones carried me away. . . .
Suddenly I realized that the Kremsmünster students would have to leave the
next day; I was driven to them . . . . Then I remained standing there between
them, gave friend Kahl my right hand and put my left around our beloved
Ferdinand, who sat arm in arm with Kenner. He drew me closer with his
right arm, and as the tones thus spoke directly into the soul, I felt the gentle,
fervent press of their hands, and I had to look back and forth into their faces
and their beloved eyes. They sat so still, pleasantly moved by the music, but
yet so peaceful and cheerful, and I gazed at them so, thinking: oh, you good
souls, you are indeed happy in your innocence. Music makes you gentler, but
not sad, not upset; what your heart desires you grasp in the hand of a friend,
and you know no other wishes, you whom the melody gives only loftier
waves.[30]

The distinction between such physical and emotional expressions of
same-sex friendship and activity we would define as homosexual can be
totally unambiguous only if homosexuality is defined with a focus on
genital activity that would never be acceptable in the case of heterosexual-
ity.

Again, although one student of Spaun's circle noted with palpable
embarrassment the "fast mädchenhaft" tone of such passages,[31] women
themselves are conspicuously absent. In this respect, the issue extends
beyond sexual orientation to encompass the link between gender definition and the high culture that so fascinated Schubert's circle. In this
society of cultivated bureaucrats, artists, and artist-bureaucrats, cultivation was a sign of belonging to the class cultivated to serve society and the
state; women, who could have no such expectation of official service, also
had no overt incentive to participate in such cultivating circles, nor were
they encouraged to do so.

This is not to deny the role of the arts as pre-marital feminine
"accomplishments," nor to suggest that no women achieved cultivation
or artistic prominence, despite social disincentives. One such exceptional
case from Schubert's circle is instructive. Johanna Lutz, who wrote faith-
fully to Leopold Kupelwieser during his Italian journey, is one of the principal witnesses to the reading society of 1823–24 mentioned above; she
was involved enough to relay on relatively detailed reports.[32] When
reporting on that society, however, despite her own apparent involvement, she mentions only men. Her letters also contain numerous reports
of women, often in interaction with Schubert and his friends, but the
reading group, excepting herself, seems to have been entirely male. Far
from being "mädchenhaft," such groups were a largely masculine affair; in

terms of gender construction, their precise position on a continuum of homosocial relationships ranging from the promotion of mutual interests through friendship to active homosexuality is less crucial than the interpersonal bonds they established and the emotional and artistic sensitivity they cultivated, all of which prepared their members to participate in and so continue the (male-dominated) society to which they belonged.[33]

Refuge or training ground? The practice of art in everyday life

There is a tension between this alignment of Schubert's circle with the values of a cultural elite and Solomon's proposal that Schubert belonged to a repressed homosexual subculture. The tension – but also the potential for explanation – is clearest in Solomon's account of what Schubert gained from his surroundings:

> There were, however, compensations for Schubert's concealment within the hermetic and self-sustaining world of his own subculture. Through his homosexuality Schubert left a realm of compulsion and entered what – at least momentarily – appeared to be a realm of freedom. To its members, the bohemian-homosexual community represented freedom from the restraints of family and the state, freedom from the compulsions of society and the straitjackets of heterosexuality, freedom from the imperative to raise a family and to make a living in a routine job – in short, freedom to ignore the reality principle in favor of the pursuit of beauty and pleasure. These were temporarily adequate, if ultimately insufficient, indemnities for a precarious existence on the margins of society.[34]

That Schubert's friends at times perceived themselves as threatened by oppressive powers is beyond question, and as Kristina Muxfeldt has pointed out, sexual and political liberty – and crime – were at best incompletely distinguished by the law.[35] By becoming government officials, teachers at state-supported institutions, and the like, however, most of Schubert's friends also were or eventually became part of the same repressive apparatus whose incursions they resented; it will not do to imagine a band of revolutionaries confronting the state at every turn. The character of Mayrhofer, freedom-loving poet and dutiful book-censor, is the most extreme example, but beyond individual idiosyncrasies, we encounter what John Reed terms "the curiously schizophrenic character of Viennese society at the time, on the one hand a huge but inefficient bureaucracy, and on the other a civilized and tolerant middle class devoted to artistic pursuits."[36]

The split Reed notes is indeed significant, albeit less of an aberrant curiosity than of a strategy of coping that has significant ramifications for the arts. As Anton von Spaun's letters, rejecting the deposition of tyrants in favor of selective reading, suggest, the turn to self-cultivation seemed self-evident; there was no viable alternative. Nor was seeking refuge from a hostile society through aesthetic activity limited to marginal sub-cultures. Rather, it was characteristic of the domesticated, self-limiting, and extremely widespread art and literature of the Biedermeier; indeed, in the words of one literary scholar, "the central concern of the period seems to be how to preserve the hope for a regenerative change in history while taking into account defeat and limitation."[37] Such art can be dismissed as inferior to a Classic–Romantic "mainstream" only at the cost of distorting the place of the arts during this period.[38]

The question of the marginality or centrality of Schubert's circle, then, yields no straightforward answer. The freedom and artistic pursuits that Schubert and his friends valued indeed placed them in opposition to the authorities of Restoration Austria, threatened by overt expressions of freedom of any kind. Furthermore, many viewed the bureaucratic positions they eventually assumed as tedious and deadening.[39] But yet, not only could the demands of the state ultimately not be evaded, self-cultivation itself proved admirable preparation for state service, and not only in theory, as the later success of many of Schubert's associates testifies.

Art too played a conflicted role. As a realm in which free thought could find expression, in which the "Hoffnungspflanzen, Tatenfluten" ("plants of hope, floods of deeds") that Mayrhofer described in *Heliopolis 2* (D753) could thrive, it was carefully watched over by the state. But that freedom was circumscribed not only by overt restriction but also by awareness of that restriction and the resultant self-limitation: no one could object to art that merely provided refuge in "gray hours," to quote Schober's *An die Musik* (D547). This effectively eliminated any possibility that the "floods of deeds" art might generate would be anything but meta-phorical, but if change was impossible, the blending of art and life at least made the inevitable tolerable.

Bauernfeld suggested one means by which this was possible in a letter to Schober of October 1826; wit and irony, two central concepts of Romantic aesthetics, appear not as tools of art criticism, but as tactics for everyday life:

> The human being is a serious beast, says Schlegel, and I add to that: it is
> really our duty to work against this bestiality. No one would deny that the
> essence of today's world is gratification – but how a poor devil can maintain
> himself among all these gratifiers [*Geniessenden*] and authorities
> [*Machthabenden*] other than through irony, I don't know.[40]

Mayrhofer's 1836 suicide is only the most dramatic evidence that the aestheticizing solution was ultimately a makeshift; it could make life more liveable by creating an interior space immune to repression, but the tension between that space and the hierarchy of power outside it remained unresolved.[41]

Mayrhofer's fate, however tragic, can be dismissed as irrelevant to autonomous art, just as Bauernfeld's comments could be seen as trivializing great Romantic themes. Similarly, Schubert himself can be considered apart from his context and his music isolated from its surroundings. The result is music heard as pure sound or the expression of eternal aesthetic laws, or, less extremely, as a corpus of masterworks of Romantic (or Classical) style. Such a segregation of art and ideas from the circumstances of life is well suited to the concert hall and its ideal of aesthetic autonomy, but to listen to such "pure" music is also to silence the voices that once surrounded it and gave it meaning.

An alternative hearing recognizes that art – not only the relatively small-scale genres (song, partsong, dance, piano music) for which Schubert was known during his life, but also the more prestigious genres of chamber music, symphony, and opera through which he hoped to establish his name as a serious composer – takes on meaning not only through aesthetic contemplation but also through other, less rarefied associations. To acknowledge this is, after all, only to take Schubert himself seriously: in his letter to his brother Ferdinand of July 1824, he wrote of his "fateful recognition of a miserable reality, which I endeavor to beautify as far as possible by my imagination [*Phantasie*] (thank God)" (*SDB* 363). Brought into relation to such texts – and Schubert's circle, stripped of its sentimental veneer, provides them in rich variety – Schubert's music gives up its splendid isolation, but in doing so reveals a very human voice both threatened by and embedded in structures of power, making do in part by making music. The recovery and continued survival of such a voice, I would argue, will be ample compensation for the loss of an eternal but neutralized cultural monument.

4 Schubert's inflections of Classical form

Charles Rosen

The mimetic elements of *Gretchen am Spinnrade* (D118) have always been easily identified, and they are amazingly specific: the right-hand *sempre ligato* represents the turning wheel; in the left, the tenor *sempre staccato* imitates the continuous clicking sound of the spinning, and the bass (particularly in measures 4 and 6) the occasional impulse that the spinner's foot must give to the pedal. These elements dominate the opening of Schubert's first acknowledged masterpiece of October 19, 1814 (see Ex. 4.1, measures 1–16). And every music student knows that the imitation gives the basic structure of the song at its climax: as Gretchen remembers Faust's kiss, the wheel ceases to spin, only to start up again as she returns to the contemplation of her sorrow and her despair.

Mimesis determines the song in other ways as well, one aspect already revealed in the first sixteen measures. First, however, we should remark the faulty declamation. The meaning of the opening lines demands accents on "hin" and "schwer." However, my *peace* is gone, my *heart* is heavy, is Schubert's odd emphasis, which goes against the sense, as if another state of mind could be gone, some other organ heavy. But it makes a better sound: "Ruh" has a more beautiful and agreeable vowel for singing than "hin," and it is clear that musical considerations take priority over meaning and prosody for Schubert, and they continue to do so until the end of his life. (Also active is a persistence of Monteverdi's aesthetic, in which it is the individual words and not the phrase which are expressed – "Ruh" and "Herz" are weightier in expressive value than "hin" and "schwer.")

Most remarkable about this opening page is the transition to the second stanza, measures 11 to 14 – or, rather, how unremarkable, unassuming is the return to the tonic after the C major half-cadence on V of III. A swift dominant–tonic cadence is all that is needed. The second important cadence in the song is similar (see Ex. 4.1, measures 13–32). After this full close on III, the return to the tonic is almost identical to the first return, equally unobtrusive, even perfunctory. The music modestly returns to the opening and starts again. This time, however, the return is from a greater distance: Schubert has set stanzas two and three without pause as if they were one – correctly following his text here, as the third stanza continues and parallels the structure of the second (in Schubert's manuscript, stanza two has only a comma at the end and moves directly into the next verse). The harmony has moved further afield, with a modulation to ii (E minor) and then to A minor before settling on F major with a chromatic plagal cadence. The increase of passion is in the words as well as in the music ("Where I do not have him is the grave to me"). The unemphatic simplicity of the return to the tonic that follows is therefore all the more striking.

The construction is unprecedented: instead of a Classical opposition of two harmonic fields and its resolution into the primary harmony, we have here what we may call a wave form. The music starts in the tonic, moves away and then returns, starts again and moves further away, and then returns and starts again. After this, the next departure has even greater power. The first stanza is repeated with its half close on V of III, the music turns with the fifth stanza forcefully to the dominant minor with a cadence that is performed twice, and then moves directly from A minor to F major and into the sixth stanza with no pause (see Ex. 4.1, measures 37–54). In the sixth stanza starting at measure 51 we arrive at the first radical change of texture. The wheel continues to spin, but the clicking sound has disappeared, and the foot no longer gives its impulse to the spinning-wheel.

That is, our consciousness of the spinning – or, rather, Gretchen's – recedes into the background as the memories of Faust grow more vivid. At this point, Gretchen begins to remember Faust physically: his proud manner of holding himself, his noble form, the smile of his mouth, the power of his eyes, the enchanting flow of his speech, the press of his hand – and then with the memory of his kiss, the wheel stops altogether. And after the accelerated excitement of a continuously rising series of harmonies (F major, G minor, A flat major, B flat major) the stopping of the wheel calls back the reality of the tonic D minor with a dominant-ninth chord (see Ex. 4.1, measures 55–73). The wheel starts up again with difficulty and then goes smoothly back to the opening. Once again the first stanza is repeated, to be followed by a new wave of excitement. The harmonic form, although again over a rising bass, now at last moves steadily towards resolution with a full tonic cadence emphatically repeated, but the tessitura goes into the singer's highest range and stays there until the final phrase. It is Schubert who adds the opening two lines of the poem at the end, returning with the same simplicity to the beginning (see Ex. 4.1, measures 108–15).

The originality of the conception lies not only in the series of waves that persistently drop back into the tonic and start up again until the passion has exhausted itself, but also in the idea of representing the

Example 4.1 *Gretchen am Spinnrade* (D118)

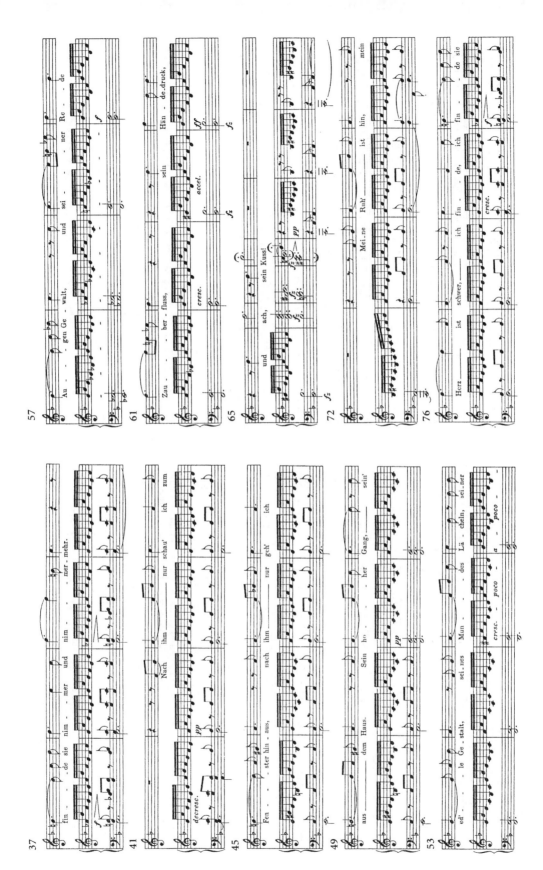

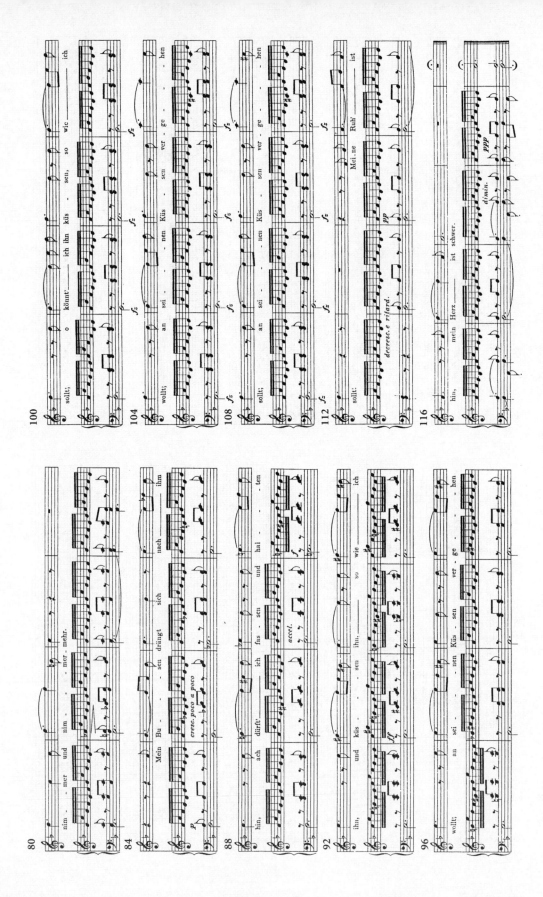

poetry phenomenologically – that is, through Gretchen's sense both of the present reality of the spinning and of the memories of the past, the gradual disappearance of her awareness of the present action. We must emphasize that it is not the spinning that is objectively imitated by Schubert but Gretchen's consciousness of it. This is the first song in which Schubert was able to represent a double time-scale, a relationship so crucial to Romantic poetry, both the sense of the immediate present and the power of past memory and how they interact with each other. The stroke of genius is the way the present action of spinning recedes only gradually from consciousness as the memories become more poignant, more physically present. To accomplish this Schubert needed a new type of structure in which the articulation of harmony imposed by the cadences is not exploited; the full articulated opposition that was traditional had to be evaded. The radical musical conception of wave-like motion was to have an influence that can hardly by overestimated on the composers that followed Schubert.

Selige Welt (D743), a later song of 1822, literally represents the dashing of waves against the earth ("wo sich Wasser an Erde bricht") (see Ex. 4.2). The chief element of mimesis is the motif of the opening measure, but it imposes its significance only gradually through the rhythmic treatment as the song develops, and the motif overlaps with itself. We can see this initially in measures 4 and 5 as the element is displaced from the opening of the measure to the center. In measures 7 through 10 the overlapping is more intricate, starting with a secondary motif displaced over the bar-line as the boat goes to and fro (*hin und her*), and then returning to the principal motif, also displaced over the bar-line with a spectacular stretto effect, *fortissimo*.

The initial harmonic movement is fairly conventional – A flat major, A flat minor, and C flat major – but what follows is more idiosyncratically Schubertian, basically a half-step move from C flat major to C minor, prepared by straying through the harmonies of G major and E minor ("the madman seeks his fortunate island"). Is it fanciful to remark that the will-power of the madman who seeks in vain to direct his boat toward a definite goal is portrayed by a much more symmetrically organized and steady rhythm and yet by a harmony that is errant and unpredictable? In measure 17, the return to the A flat major tonic is extraordinarily laconic, a single unharmonized E♭ *fortissimo*. The crashing chords that end each of the opening phrases and also the return of the first phrase at the end are exhilarating. The poetic celebration of unplanned, irresponsible liberty "as the wind blows" inspired this most dramatic of all Schubert's brief songs. The contemporary political implication of the poem is reflected in the triumphal ending,[1] and Schubert was able to seize all the ironic

Example 4.2 *Selige Welt* (D743)

enthusiasm of the lines. There is a conventional Classical opposition at the center of two tonal areas, A flat and C flat, but the resolution is surprising, essentially purely linear, as the C flat moves to C natural. This was a technique to which Schubert often turned in his later years.

The half-step shift may be conceived as a large-scale generalization of Schubert's constant delight in moving between major and minor modes (a change of mode essentially, after all, a displacement of a half step in a perfect triad). The large-scale shifts are sometimes remarkable for their simple brutality. In the last of the Six Grandes Marches for piano four hands, Op. 40 (D819), probably written in 1824, the end of the first section leads by a crashing accent from E major to F major:

Example 4.3 Six Grandes Marches, Op. 40 No. 6 (D819), mm. 8–18

In order to achieve this effect, Schubert must revoke his conventional modulation from the tonic E to the dominant B major and return to E major. This inspires a coda at the end of the second section where Schubert can repeat the half-step movement but transfer it to the dominant (and he prepares the passage with the traditional allusion to the subdominant that was almost obligatory in a recapitulation in Viennese Classicism):

Example 4.4 Six Grandes Marches, Op. 40 No. 6 (D819), mm. 46–53

A similar shift – from A to B flat – with an equal absence of subtlety may be found in the fifth of these Marches, and even more spectacularly in the second of the Two Characteristic Marches for four hands in C Major (D968b), where the recapitulation begins in B major for eight measures and then simply moves back to the tonic without interruption.

In 1824, the same year that the Grandes Marches were composed, the shift of a half step became the major structural principle of one of Schubert's largest works, the "Grand Duo" for piano four hands (D812). It plays an important role in all of the movements except the scherzo. In the first movement the shift is prepared with unusual power; it arises from the chromatic details of the opening phrases:

Example 4.5 "Grand Duo" (D812), first movement, mm. 1–18

The motif that is the principal agent of the harmonic structure appears in measures 9 (G-G#-E) and 11 (transposed A-A#-F#), but the groundwork for its peculiar sonority is laid with the chromaticism already found in the previous phrase. The motif takes on a dynamic energy in measures 28 to 34, and alters the harmony with a sudden *fortissimo* from C major to C sharp minor:

Example 4.6 "Grand Duo" (D812), first movement, mm. 28–57

This enables Schubert to begin a lyrical "second subject" in A flat major. After sixteen measures of this he moves sequentially to G major, so reversing the original upward shift down to the more conventional dominant.

This three-key exposition (C major, A flat major, G major) uses the submediant in a way that is very different from Beethoven's employment of mediant relationships. When Beethoven polarizes tonic and mediant (or submediant), he prepares the opposition through the dominant of the new key exactly as he normally prepared the more conventional dominant by the dominant of the dominant. Schubert escapes this polarization. He does not contrast C major and A flat, and he does not insist on the dominant of the new key – the preparation is almost entirely plagal with a dominant only at the last moment. This gives him not only the apparently uncomplicated surface of the new theme, but also the equally relaxed lyricism of the transition. The dramatic change is not from C major to A flat major (or to its E flat dominant), but from C major to C sharp minor, and it arrives swiftly. Once this is accomplished, the tapering-off and the diffusion of tension is leisurely, extended over almost sixteen measures. Just as Schubert in *Gretchen am Spinnrade* developed an original harmonic structure by refusing to exploit the contrast of harmony at the cadences, he now uses an analogous procedure to revolutionize sonata technique. He eliminates the dramatic contrast of key area, and substitutes a dramatic contrast of chromatic alterations. The dramatic power is focused upon moments of transition which seem to explode briefly almost without warning, but the large-scale harmonic structure is no longer burdened with the standard articulated tensions of tonic–dominant relationships, and can achieve lyric continuity and breadth. This new relaxed grandeur is reflected by the number of important opening movements by Schubert marked Allegro moderato or Molto moderato. (The last Piano Sonata in B flat Major [D960] uses a harmonic structure similar to the "Grand Duo" [B flat, F sharp minor, and F major], and the arrival at the dominant is divested of its normal force, and takes second place in intensity as well as drama to the preceding F sharp.)

Shortly after the opening of the development section of the "Grand Duo" a long and insistent build-up on a dominant seventh of B major (similar in character although not in motivic structure to the passage that prepared the move up a half step to C sharp minor in the exposition) is startlingly resolved a half step downward to a $^6_4$ triad of B flat minor (turning to the major at once). The short development section begins and ends in E, which makes this enormous and lengthy climax on B flat very radical with its relation of an augmented fourth:

Example 4.7 "Grand Duo" (D812), first movement, mm. 125–41

The return of the modulatory passage in the recapitulation is completely transformed, but what Schubert does with it there reveals the nature and the significance of these modulations for him. It is approached – quite properly for a recapitulation – through the subdominant:

Example 4.8 "Grand Duo" (D812), first movement, mm. 202–50

(continued)

Example 4.8 (*cont.*)

The harmonic progression here is perhaps even more astonishing than the original one in the exposition. The natural purpose is to lead the harmony from F sharp minor back to C major. A parallel with the exposition would go through D flat major. However, the new harmonies added by Schubert to the passage would, if things now continued as they were before, lead through the subdominant minor to a playing of the "second theme" in the subdominant F major, a traditional way of arriving at the tonic by Classical conventions. But instead, the modulation veers back to the tonic, and when it is reached, the mode still remains minor. In fact, the "second theme" which appeared in A flat major is never recapitulated in its full form in the major, but is played twice in C minor. (We should also remark on the insistent presence in this replaying of the harmonies of A flat major.) A theme in the major mode recapitulated only in the minor is, I believe, unprecedented in a sonata.

The reappearance of material in the recapitulation is essentially one of equivalence in Classical form, intended to balance the expository form and to resolve it. That is why a glance at the subdominant traditionally balances some of the tonic–dominant presentation in late eighteenth-century theory and practice, and why Beethoven invariably balances a mediant in the exposition with a submediant in the recapitulation (Opp. 31 No. 1; 53; 127; 130; 132) or the submediant with the flatted submediant (Op. 106). However, for Schubert here in the "Grand Duo," the disequilibrium of the flatted submediant in the exposition is restored in the recapitulation by the minor mode of the tonic. A flat major is balanced by C *minor*, as if the A flat had implied a change of mode as well as tonal center. Schubert is moving toward a treatment of harmony that we find even more systematically in the generation that followed, where Chopin and Schumann often regard mediant relationships as changes of mode, as if they were major and minor forms of the same tonality – or, rather, of the same tonal area. The Classical force of the subdominant is largely lost for these later composers, and only partially reconstituted by Brahms. It still has its power for Schubert, however, as we can see from this passage.

We can also grasp, therefore, that the three-key exposition for Schubert is not the interplay of three equivalent tonalities, but that the second key is largely a contrast of mode. In the Quintet in C Major of 1828 (D956), for example, the E flat major passage that stands between the tonic and the dominant is approached through the tonic minor, and keeps returning to the tonic minor – it is, in fact, only a way of suspending the tonic minor until the music can affirm the dominant.[2] On the return, the passage is approached, as we might expect, through the subdominant minor and repeated almost literally. Like the A flat major of the "Grand

Duo," the E flat major of the Quintet's exposition is an extension of Schubert's beloved hovering between major and minor modes.

In the "Grand Duo" and the Quintet, producing the "second subject" in a manner that allows it to function as a minor mode of the original tonic instead of affirming the dominant clearly downgrades the polar opposition of tonic and dominant. In both cases, as well, the postponed arrival of the dominant is not given greater tension but is heard as a lyric extension and prolongation of the previous theme. To go from A flat major to G major, as in the Duo, allows the music to settle gracefully into the end of the exposition. In the Quintet, where the E flat is basically a form of the tonic minor, the G major dominant is established by a large plagal cadence which attenuates the power of its own dominant. In spite of all of Schubert's enormous debt to Mozart and Beethoven, we can see that his forms are no longer theirs.

The exposition of the Andante of the "Grand Duo" (in A flat major) places its most explosive climax on a change from E flat major to E major (naturally repeated later going from A flat major to A major), but the finale returns in the coda to the opening movement's juxtaposition of C major and C sharp minor for its most remarkable passage:

Example 4.9 "Grand Duo" (D812), fourth movement, mm. 394–437

Example 4.9 (*cont.*)

Once again, we can observe that Schubert's shifts of a half step generally illustrate his most uncompromising display of power in which single
harmonies are simply repeated at great length. (The *più lento* in this
passage inspired Brahms to an imitation in the finale of his Quintet in F
Minor for piano and strings, Op. 34.)

The reduction of large-scale tension in favor of a more even lyric tone
enabled Schubert to concentrate the tension into local explosions which
have often seemed to musicians to be insufficiently prepared or even

unjustified (Alfred Brendel, for example, refuses to perform the first ending of the exposition of the Sonata in B flat Major, where the important motif of the low trill is heard for the first and only time *fortissimo*). However, Schubert was often able to combine his un-Classical sensibility with an extraordinarily skillful manipulation of Classical conventions. His use of the shift of a half step in the Sonata in A Major (D959) shows both his handling of tradition and his successful integration of stylistic ideals that might appear incompatible. The development section of the first movement begins with an oscillation between C major and B major which has no precedent in Classical practice. The development is introduced by a cadential phrase in E major which repeats a B over and over in the highest voice. Without warning the B is suddenly moved up a half step to a C♯ with a paradoxical effect of resolution; like Beethoven, Schubert knew that insistent repetition gives the eventual change a semblance of resolution (see Ex. 4.10). In what follows, a new melody based on the preceding cadential phrase swings from C to B and back again three times in a series of five-measure phrases.[3] The combination of this static harmonic structure with the irregular regularity of a five-measure period is

Example 4.10 Piano Sonata in A Major (D959), mm. 126–62

(continued)

Example 4.10 (*cont.*)

beautifully calculated. The continuous swing back and forth between two neighboring pitches weakens the sense of direction. The odd-numbered grouping of five blurs the traditional alternation between strongly and weakly accented measures. The two procedures act together to suspend momentum. At the end of the development the music goes from C minor to A minor, and then develops the most powerful of all Schubert's preparations for the return to the tonic with a long dominant pedal. It might be objected that since the music has already reached the tonic, a preparation for a tonic return is not necessary, but this would be to misunderstand the importance of mode for Schubert. It is not the return to the tonic but the return to the major mode that is prepared with such force.

This development uses Classical form for entirely new purposes. The traditional driving force of a development is suspended: in place of the energetic sequential movement that had once seemed essential and that we expect from a development, Schubert creates lyric sequences that have no direction, but rock back and forth. It is true that Beethoven had himself experimented with moments of stasis in a development, notably the first movement of the Quartet in B flat Major, Op. 130, but in his work these moments are integrated into a dynamic harmonic movement. In Schubert's A Major Sonata the excitement of a triumphal return to the tonic with the reappearance of the opening material, a device that Beethoven had taken from Haydn and Mozart but made so much more forceful, is transformed by Schubert. The reappearance of A major is anticipated by eight measures of A minor and becomes a return to the major mode. It is clear that Schubert can handle a Classical preparation of a return by a dominant pedal with great skill, but he does not want it to have the same significance in his forms that it had in the work of previous generations.

It is also clear that Schubert generally preferred melodic structures that do not lend themselves easily to the techniques of motivic development that he learned from Mozart and Beethoven, although he was capable of using these techniques with great mastery when he wanted (see the treatment of the opening notes of the Sonata in A Major). He often concentrated, not on the motif, but on the space outlined by the motif, rearranging the elements within that space in different permutations, and putting the expressive weight on the expansion of the initial space. An extraordinary example[4] of this technique is the violincello melody from the slow movement of the Trio for Piano and Strings in E flat Major, Op. 100 (D929):

Example 4.11 Piano Trio in E flat, Op. 100 (D929), second movement, mm. 1–21

Example 4.11 (*cont.*)

In this wonderful slow Hungarian march, cousin to the slow movement of the C Major Symphony, the first three phrases outline a sixth from G to E♭. The second phrase (measures 7–10) rearranges the elements but repeats the motif of the second half of the opening phrase. The third phrase (11–14), however, retains mainly the profile of the space outlined by the opening phrases, sharpens the A♭ to an A♮, and seems like a free cancrizan of the original shape. The last phrase (17–21), after a written-out fermata on the dominant, enlarges the sixth to a tenth from E♭ down to the C – or to an octave and a sixth if one is sensitive to the upbeat to the phrase from the low G. The motif of the rising sixth is replaced by a falling sixth, introduced by an accented descending third.

Only this descending third and the rising sixths are used later for traditional development. They form a second theme in which Schubert exploits the popular yodel association of the rising sixth that remains only latent in the opening measures (see Ex. 4.12). This is more open and expansive, while the intensity of the opening measures depend on Schubert's technique of concentration on a limited space, the permutation of the elements within, and the expressive expansion that follows. I

Example 4.12 Piano Trio in E flat, Op 100 (D929), second movement, mm. 41–49

Example 4.13 *Nachtviolen* (D752)

think that Schubert derived the technique from song-writing, where he often exploits just a few notes of the singer's range. Schubert's invention could encompass traditional melodic forms very close to Mozart's or Beethoven's, but this was a melodic form that he made his own.

The small range made for a peculiar intensity, and the rearrangements of the elements within that range caused the original form of the motif in the opening measures to lose some of its identity: the listener's interest is focused on the expansion of the range that will follow. One of the most famous of Schubert's songs, *Nachtviolen* (D752) of 1822, starts with the narrow interval of a fourth, and dwells on it relentlessly before expanding it upwards to a sixth and then a seventh (see Ex. 4.13, measures 1–15). It is in the nature of this type of melody to render feeling obsessively, and the music responds here to the rhythm of the poem as much as to its content and provides a depth of emotion only hinted at by the text. The second stanza begins with the same interval of a fourth with a different arrangement of the elements. It uses much the same pitches as the first stanza, and the reordering now implies a dominant harmony in place of the tonic (see Ex. 4.13, measures 16–28). If we compare Schubert's insistence on a few notes with Beethoven's (the slow movement of the A Major Symphony, for example), we can see that Beethoven's motifs retain their integrity as the melody proceeds, while in Schubert the original form dissolves into its constituent elements and presents new and original shapes.

Similarly in *Nacht und Träume* (D827) of 1825, for example, the opening motif – D#–A#–B – gives a frame of a fourth, and the second part of the phrase enlarges the space to a sixth and then an octave. The initial fourth is expanded in the phrases that follow to a fifth and then to a seventh (D# down to G#, and F# up to E), but basically these phrases are devoted to filling up the space of the fourth from A# to D# in different ways. Measures 12 and 13 recall the end of the first phrase, with the elements permuted, but the motif itself as such receives no further development, expressive as it is, and as stimulating as it would have been to composers from Haydn to Beethoven:

Example 4.14 *Nacht und Träume* (D827), mm. 5–14

This lack of Classical motivic treatment gives great intensity in a way that may appear at first sight to be compatible only with small forms, although Schubert was able to use the technique for extremely grand effect at the opening of works like the Piano Sonata in B flat Major and the "Great" Symphony in C Major (D944).

To see how radically different Beethoven and Schubert were, we may take the use of a similar motif in both where the function of the motif appears in fact to be structurally identical (I am not interested here in claiming that Schubert borrowed from Beethoven). Both motifs outline a half step, and the well-known works are the opening movements of the "Appassionata" and of the Sonata in B flat Major:

Example 4.15 (a) Beethoven, Piano Sonata in F Minor, Op. 57, "Appassionata," first movement, m. 10, beats 2 and 3

(b) Schubert, Piano Sonata in B flat (D960), first movement, m. 8

Both motifs appear at the same points:

(1)   At the end of the first statements of the main theme. In Beethoven in measure 10, Schubert in measure 8. In Beethoven it is echoed at once, in Schubert it comes back transposed after the second phrase. *Pianissimo* in both composers.

(2)   At the end of the development: *ff* in Beethoven, *ppp* in Schubert.

(3)   At the same point of the recapitulation as its appearance in the exposition.

(4)   In the coda. In Beethoven at the end of the first section of the coda, just before the last page; in Schubert at the end. Diminuendo to *pianissimo* in Beethoven, *ppp* in Schubert.

(5)   These are the only places where the motif is heard in its integrity in both composers, except for the first ending of Schubert's exposition, here for the only time *fortissimo*.

The motifs are essentially dissonant, but in spite of the coincidence of appearance in both works, the use and effect is very different. In Beethoven the motif is related to the basic harmonic structure of the movement which contrasts the Neapolitan with the tonic, and echoes of the motif augmented are heard throughout even if the only integral replayings are at the points already mentioned. It even inspires the famous dominant pedal on a $^6_4$ chord at the opening of the recapitulation. In Schubert it serves in the harmonic plan to initiate the chromatic move to G flat major and its register is evoked by the modulation to F sharp minor, but its role is both less dynamic and more coloristic.

Beethoven's *fortissimo* explosion of unprecedented violence at the end of the development has no parallel in Schubert (unless the first ending of the exposition is such an attempt). The last appearance of the motif in Beethoven's coda is resolved for the first time in the piece, and with extreme violence. There is no need for this in Schubert, and the appearances of the motif at the end of the development are not in fact dissonant except for the last one. In Beethoven the sonority is relatively neutral and essentially malleable; Schubert exploits the delicate sonority throughout his movement, which is why his one Beethovenian explosion at the first ending of the exposition has aroused such distaste – a feeling that it is unSchubertian. We may say that Schubert's trill creates a sense of distance by its sonority: in this case the motif retains its integrity as in Beethoven, but it also – and this is not the case with Beethoven – conserves the integrity of its specific texture, its aural quality. The rhythm of Beethoven's motif is imitated through all the registers, while Schubert's remains only in the lowest part of the bass (except for one appearance at the end of the development, where its register is still relatively low). When Schubert uses a technique largely associated with Beethoven, he employs it to very different effect. For Schubert, the essence of the motif is only partly its pitch content but even more its contrast of register and its sonority.

Both the half-step shift of the harmonic field and the technique of using the space outlined by the motif as basic rather than its interior shape work toward the same end: they diffuse the urgent rhythmic impetus implied by motivic or harmonic structure and turn the music inward into more intense but less focused effects of contemplation. They reduce the impression of directed will-power and unremitting control implied by the musical language we call Classical. One final example from Schubert's latest style should make this clear. The astonishing move from C sharp minor to C major in the slow movement of the Sonata in B flat Major briefly suspends the traditional drive towards resolution of this recapitulation by a harmony so distant as to appear initially to deflect the movement toward the tonic. It makes the tension more diffuse by appearing to resolve, but in a manner so paradoxical that it creates a shock and sustains the drama at what is only apparently a lower level of intensity but is actually a subtle and breathtaking postponement. The *pianissimo* and the uninterrupted rhythm do the rest, and the page needs no further commentary:

Example 4.16 Piano Sonata in B flat (D960), second movement, mm. 98–107

5 Schubert and his poets: issues and conundrums

Susan Youens

Lieder begin with words; they are born when a composer encounters poetry. If the statement seems obvious, it is not reflected in writings on music, which tend to "skip over" the literary surroundings in order to arrive more swiftly at musical matters. Considerations of historical context are customarily confined to discussions of the composer and the music rather than the poet and the poetry, even in those instances where the poet and composer knew one another. Although scholars have, on occasion, probed questions of transmission – how a composer found a particular poetic repertory and, more commonly, Schubert's "reading" of those poems he set to music – many issues remain tantalizingly fertile areas for investigation. There are even basic enigmas of identification yet to solve – who was "A. Pollak," whose name appears on the title page of the late song *Frühlingslied* (D919). Who wrote the texts for *Auf den Sieg der Deutschen* (D81) or the beloved *Wiegenlied* (D498)? Song composers tend to search a variety of sources for new and old poetry to convert into Lieder; if they do so in special ways and for specialized reasons, they are nonetheless active participants in the literary milieu of their day.

The gravitational forces that draw a composer to a particular poet, poetic circle, or specific anthology are multitudinous and shift into new configurations at each encounter with a body of poetry. Proximity to local writers, access to poetic works from Germany as well as Austria, friends with wide-ranging philosophical and literary interests, literary fads and fashions (the Walter Scott craze, the Ossian enthusiasm, and the like), and various crises in life all play a part in Schubert's adoption of a poem for musical purposes – as long as the poem had music in it, *his* music. This evocative phrase, difficult to define, is at the heart of the songwriting enterprise and is one of its most intriguing mysteries. What constitutes music-in-poetry for this composer? Why did Schubert find music in certain poems by Goethe, to cite only one example, and reject far more as not "komponabel"? Did he not encounter the poetry of Joseph von Eichendorff and the anthology *Des Knaben Wunderhorn*, or did he not like them? In other words, why are certain staples of early nineteenth-century

German song composers not to be found in this Austrian composer's repertory? As Schubert's musical development proceeded, his tastes in poetry altered – in what ways and at what times? How did Schubert feel entitled or emboldened to emend the poetry he selected? Who were his poets? What gave rise to their poetry? What standing did they have in the literary community of their day and place? What might be the political backdrop to certain poetic sources in an age of anti-liberalism, censorship, and police spying on the citizenry? What circumstances conspired to bring these poets and this composer together? How did Schubert come by poems not published in his lifetime and written by non-Viennese poets (the Pomeranian schoolmaster Karl Lappe's *Im Abendrot* [D799] and *Der Einsame* [D800], for example)? Why did Schubert gravitate to particular poems at particular times in his compositional life?

If the number and variety of issues at stake seem overwhelming, so does the roll-call of Schubert poets: there are some 110 of them, ranging from the eighteenth-century provider of operatic poetry, Pietro Metastasio (1698–1782), to Heinrich Heine, with occasional forays into a more distant past represented by translations of Petrarch, Shakespeare, and the Greeks; Franz von Bruchmann's poem *An die Leyer* (D737) is a free paraphrase of a work attributed to the sixth-century B.C. poet Anacreon, and a Viennese Shakespeare edition of 1825 (translations by August Wilhelm von Schlegel, supplemented by Eduard von Bauernfeld and Ferdinand Mayerhofer) provided Schubert with the texts for the *Trinklied* (D888), *Ständchen* (D889), and *An Sylvia* (D891). Surveying the list of authors, one can detect certain patterns, whatever the influence of fortuitous circumstance or the composer's love of experiment. In numerous instances, Schubert set only one or two poems by a given poet (unlike his later successor Hugo Wolf's practice of setting numerous texts from a few poetic sources): *Frühlingsglaube* (D686) is Schubert's single solo Lied to a text by Ludwig Uhland, and there are only two songs to texts by Karl August Graf von Platen-Hallermünde, both masterpieces (*Die Liebe hat gelogen* and *Du liebst mich nicht*, D751 and 756 respectively). Friedrich Kind, Friedrich Wilhelm Gotter, Karoline Louise von Klenke, Johann Nepomuk Ritter von Kalchberg, Georg Friedrich von Gerstenberg, Johann Ludwig Ferdinand von Deinhardstein, Josef Karl Bernard, Karl August Engelhardt, Josef Franz von Ratschky, Friedrich von Köpken, Count Johann Majléth, Michael Lubi, Christian Ludwig Reissig, Gottlieb Conrad Pfeffel, and Gottlieb von Leon are numbered among those who provided Schubert with only a single song text. There are relatively few poets represented by ten or more songs, sometimes clustered together chronologically (twenty-two of the twenty-three songs to poems by Ludwig Hölty belong to 1815–16, and twenty of the twenty-one songs to texts by Ludwig Theobul Kosegarten were composed in 1815), sometimes more widely distributed over a period of several years. Notably, it is the better poets – Goethe, Schiller, and Schubert's friend Johann Mayrhofer – whom Schubert revisited at different times in his brief compositional life.

It is evident from the dispatch with which Schubert discovered poetic sources that he and his friends looked assiduously for new poetic wellsprings from which to create Lieder. For example, the songs *Abendbilder* (D650), and *Himmelsfunken* (D651) of February 1819 are settings of poems by Johann Peter Silbert, a professor of French at the Vienna Polytechnic Institute, whose poetic anthology *Die heilige Lyra* was published that same year by the Viennese firm Strauß – did Schubert receive the poems in manuscript before publication or seize immediately upon a newly published source? As a result of the quest for new poetry, those German and Austrian poets now relegated to second-class status or worse but who enjoyed a season in the sun during Schubert's lifetime are amply represented in his songs. For example, the *Poetisches Tagebuch* (Poetic Diary) of Ernst Konrad Friedrich Schulze (1789–1817) was highly praised in its day, and Schubert chose ten poems from it in 1825–26, only two years after the diary was published posthumously in 1823; the exquisite *Im Frühling* (D882) and the powerful *Über Wildemann* (D884) seem in retrospect as foreshadowings of *Winterreise* in 1827. The fact that song composition is dependent upon the existence of bodies of lyric poetry, that the Lied springs from the renaissance of lyricism in the eighteenth and nineteenth centuries, is crystal-clear in Schubert's oeuvre.[1]

The issue of literary discrimination and "bad poetry"

Disparagement of Schubert's taste in poetry-for-music is a commonplace nowadays, but it was not always so: critics in the 1820s and 1830s often praised Schubert's choice of poetry and his ability to "translate" his chosen poems into music. The composer's first biographer, Heinrich Kreissle von Hellborn, pointed out that Schubert first gravitated to the "sweetly sentimental" poetry of Hölty, Matthisson, Salis-Seewis, and Kosegarten because those poets were much loved at the time, but that his friends Johann Mayrhofer, Franz von Schober, and Johann Michael Vogl then "worked on his choice of poems," and he thereafter favored texts by authors such as Goethe and Schiller.[2] Later scholars, less impressed with the composer's taste in texts, have simultaneously "explained" the phenomenon of so much mediocre poetry in the Schubert song corpus and apologized for it by observing that poetry apt for music and poetry destined for literary greatness are not necessarily one and the same. Schubert himself would seem to affirm the assertion when he fashions a beautiful song from Franz von Schober's *An die Musik* (D547) – purest cotton candy in verse, but it summed up a central fact of Schubert's existence and therefore appealed to his musical imagination. Eduard von Bauernfeld (1802–90), a later member of the Schubert circle and a professional writer himself, vigorously refuted Kreissle's charge that the composer was undiscriminating in his choice of poetry:

> Moreover in literature, too, he was anything but unversed and the way he understood how to interpret, with inventiveness and vitality, the different poetic individualities, like Goethe, Schiller, Wilhelm Müller, J[ohann] G[abriel] Seidl, Mayrhofer, Walter Scott and Heine, how to transform them into new flesh and blood and how to render faithfully the nature of each one by beautiful and noble musical characterization – these recreations in song should alone be sufficient to demonstrate, merely by their own existence and without any further proof, from how deep a nature, from how sensitive a soul these creations sprang. A man who so understands the poets is himself a poet.   (*SMF* 230)

In his reminiscences of Schubert, Anselm Hüttenbrenner recalls Schubert saying on one occasion when Hüttenbrenner had praised a newly composed song (which one, we do not know): "Yes, there you have a good poem; then one immediately gets a good idea; melodies pour in so that it is a real joy. With a bad poem one can't make any headway; one torments oneself over it and nothing comes of it but boring rubbish. I have already refused many poems which have been pressed on me" (*SMF* 182–83). "There is nothing of music in this poem" (again, we do not know which one), Schubert once complained to Johann Gabriel Seidl (1804–75), a popular Austrian poet whose verse this composer discovered immediately upon its publication in 1826 (although he did set eleven poems by Seidl in the last years of his life, including *Das Zügenglöcklein* [D871], *Bei dir allein* [D866, 2], *Der Wanderer an den Mond* [D870], *Die Taubenpost* in *Schwanengesang* [D957, 14], and the beautiful *Im Freien* [D880]). Schubert also refused poems by Friedrich Rochlitz and Joseph Freiherr von Zedlitz, and he found little to suit his taste in the poetry of such well-known providers of texts for song composers as Friedrich Baron de La Motte-Fouqué. What a composer chose *not* to set from among the repertories current and fashionable at the time is as revealing as the texts he found of worth. For instance, given the keen interest in folk poetry in the late eighteenth and early nineteenth centuries, and the premium placed on *Volkstümlichkeit* (folksong style) and *Sangbarkeit* (singability) by the Berlin song composers of the preceding generation, Schubert's lack of attraction to this popular body of verse is all the more notable. One looks in vain for a single setting from Achim von Arnim's and Clemens Brentano's anthology *Des Knaben Wunderhorn* (1806–08). It was not until 1827 that he set Johann Gottfried Herder's translation of the Scottish ballad *Edward* from the *Stimmen der Völker in Gesang* in a homorhythmic, chordal style which demonstrates his knowledge of the conventions of *Volkstümlichkeit* (D923); even so, one observes the repeated unharmonized D's in measures 1–2 of the piano introduction and the mediant relationship of tonic G minor and the B flat minor to which Schubert turns in mid-strophe and hears *echt* Schubert. For his exercises in folksong transmogrified into art song, he preferred the artistry of Goethe, Wilhelm Müller, and Mozart *imitating* and trans-forming folk poetry and folk melodies to the real thing, as in *Heidenröslein* (D257); even his near-hundred strophic songs composed between 1814 and mid-1816 are settings of Goethe, Matthisson, and Hölty, not of folk poetry. Schubert, it seems, not only exercised literary discrimination, but was conscious of doing so and prided himself on it.

Where Schubert's poetic source was an entire large anthology of one poet's verses, it is interesting to notice both how choosy the composer was and how his choices changed over time when he revisited a former source. For example, in 1815, Schubert selected three specimens of late eighteenth-century nature poetry from the works of Friedrich Leopold Graf zu Stolberg-Stolberg (*Morgenlied*, D266; *Abendlied*, D276; and *An die Natur*, D372); when he went back to the same well the next year, he set four poems about love (the unfinished ballad *Romanze*, D144; *Daphne am Bach*, D411; *Stimme der Liebe*, D412; and *Lied in der Abwesenheit*, D416). On his final visit to this poet's works in 1823, he chose two poems on death, including the exquisite *Auf dem Wasser zu singen* (D774) – it was in the summer of 1823, one recalls, that a gravely ill Schubert was hospitalized for the syphilis diagnosed in late 1822 or early 1823. Further examples of Schubert's careful choices of poetry from a larger collection include Schulze's *Poetisches Tagebuch*, containing a hundred poems, from which Schubert chose ten of the best. (Another issue that comes to the surface in this case is the way in which the composer's knowledge of the larger body of poetry colors his approach to the individual specimens. Schulze was mentally disturbed, obsessed with love for two women who did not return his love, and the poetic diary is the record of that obses-sion, however altered by its conversion into art. Schubert, I believe, incor-porates his awareness of the pathology unfurled throughout the entire diary into his Schulze songs.[3])

One must always keep in mind the literary situation of the day, includ-ing what was praised at the time. Posterity may have condemned the likes of Ernst Schulze, the Collin brothers, Ladislaus Pyrker, and many other

Schubert poets to obscurity or outright oblivion, but in their own day, they won considerable local acclaim because their poems addressed then-current literary and other issues, whether in Vienna alone, other areas of Austria, or the wider German-speaking world.[4] Schubert may have realized that Karl Gottfried von Leitner or Johann Georg Jacobi were no match for the likes of Goethe, but Leitner was well regarded in the early 1820s by those with influence on Schubert, and the result was a group of remarkable songs composed in late 1827 and early 1828 (including *Der Kreuzzug*, D932; *Des Fischers Liebesglück*, D933; *Der Winterabend*, D938; and *Die Sterne*, D939). Ewan West has observed that the major Austrian writers were more devoted to the theater than to lyric verse (Franz Grillparzer exemplifies the phenomenon) and that the local lyrical tradition was of uneven quality, with only Nikolaus Lenau's reputation surviving intact to the present day.[5] Nonetheless, Austrian poets such as Seidl were often lauded at the time in terms worthy of Goethe or Schiller, as many reviews confirm. Composers might naturally be influenced by such praise. The brothers Heinrich and Matthäus von Collin, both Schubert poets, exemplify all of the phenomena West discusses: they were highly regarded in their own day as dramatic poets, their lyric output small by comparison but significant for Schubert, whose settings of Matthäus von Collin's *Der Zwerg* (D771), *Wehmut* (D772), and *Nacht und Träume* (D827) are among his beautiful Lieder. Similarly, Caroline Pichler (1769–1843, the poet of *Der Sänger am Felsen*, D482; *Lied* [*Ferne von der grossen Stadt*], D483; and *Der Unglückliche*, D713) is little known now outside of Austria and seldom read, except by scholars, but in her day she was a significant literary lioness in Vienna.[6] Schubert was among the visitors to her salon in the early 1820s – did he, one wonders, know the full context of *Der Unglückliche* in her novel *Olivier?*[7]

A case-history of changing tastes: the poets of Schubert's youth

Schubert's tastes, not surprisingly, changed as he grew older, as he met writers and read newly published works, and as different compositional issues engaged his attention. He began his prodigious song oeuvre by inheriting Mozart's poetic sources – Gabriele von Baumberg (1766–1839), known as the "Sappho of Vienna," was the poet of Mozart's Lied *Als Luise die Briefe ihres unvertrauten Liebhabers verbrannt*, K. 520 – and the pre-Romantic and early Romantic poets of the late eighteenth century, such as the pietistic Ludwig Theobul Kosegarten (1758–1818), mentor to the artists Philipp Otto Runge and Caspar David Friedrich. Kosegarten was a favorite with Austrian and Prussian song composers, and Schubert joined the long procession of Kosegarten composers with twenty strophic songs composed between June and October 1815, plus a final, more complex creation two years later in May 1817, *An die untergehende Sonne* (D457). The lyric verse of Friedrich Gottlieb Klopstock (1742–1803), who spellbound an entire generation of writers by making, in Schiller's phrase, "everything lead up to the infinite," was also a source for thirteen Schubert songs in 1815–16, including *Das Rosenband* (D280), a lovely specimen of Anacreontic lyricism, and the dialogue-song *Hermann und Thusnelda* (D322). The latter is notable for the foreshadowing in the accompaniment to measures 84–111 of the principal accompanimental figure in *Ellens Gesang I*, both songs poetic celebrations by fictive women of heroic male exploits (the poets are male and so is the point of view), and for the exquisite A flat major cantilena "Ruh' hier, ruh' hier, dass ich den Schweiss von der Stirn' abtrockne und der Wange das Blut!" ("Rest here, that I may wipe the sweat from your brow and the blood from your cheeks"). "Hermann" is Arminius, the hero of the battle of the Teutoberger Wald in 9 A.D.; he became the archetypal German hero, and Schubert's choice of such texts as *Hermann und Thusnelda*, reflects the fervent nationalism of the day.

Composers always respond to other composers, and Schubert therefore gravitated to two related late eighteenth-century – early nineteenth-century poetic repertories popular with other song composers: the poetry of Friedrich von Matthisson (1761–1831) and Johann Gaudenz Freiherr von Salis-Seewis (1762–1834). (One of Beethoven's most popular works was his song *Adelaide*, Op. 46, to a poem by Matthisson, and Schubert too composed a setting of this famous text, D95, in 1814, despite fears that he would "have to write it exactly as Beethoven did" [*SMF* 77].) Matthisson was also a favorite of Schubert's song-writing predecessor Johann Rudolf Zumsteeg (the teenage Schubert immersed himself in Zumsteeg's ballads and songs and announced his intent to modernize the model inherited from that composer),[8] and twenty-seven of Schubert's twenty-nine Matthisson songs belong to the early years 1812–16. Salis-Seewis's single volume of verse, first printed in 1793, was reprinted in Vienna in 1815; the very next year, Schubert began setting his poems to music, culminating in the masterpiece *Der Jüngling an der Quelle* (D300) (this song also exemplifies Schubert's willingness to emend his chosen poems, as Salis-Seewis's final line "Elisa! mir zu" becomes Schubert's haunting "Louise, dir nach," its liquid -l, open -a vowel, comparative lack of consonantal emphasis, and contrasting dark-bright vowels [-ou followed by -i] more "musical" than the original).[9]

Still another instance of Schubert's early reliance on the literary enthusiasms of an older generation is the group of nine Ossian settings, composed between June 1815 and February 1816. The Ossian poems, one of the most notorious of all literary frauds, were the creation of James MacPherson (1736–96), a Scotsman obsessed with Scottish nationalism who invented a Gaelic Homer[10] – the blind and elderly bard Ossian who sings massive, mournful verse-tales of the battles of his father, King Fingal of Morven (north-west Scotland), of his own dead son Oscar, and of past glory – and insisted upon its "authenticity" in the teeth of doubts raised almost immediately by skeptics. The litany of exotic names that ring throughout the ballads – Cuthullin, Trenar, Dermid, Caruth, Branno, Gormur – do not ultimately disguise their creation by an eighteenth-century pre-Romantic sensibility, but the night mists, moonlight, and ghosts of MacPherson's imagination enflamed all of Europe for a time, with Napoleon among the devotees of Ossian. In 1815, when Schubert composed six of his Ossian ballads (*Kolmas Klage, Ossians Lied nach dem Falle Nathos, Das Mädchen von Inistore, Cronnan, Shilrik und Vinvela*, and the first version of *Lorma*, D217, 278, 281, 282, 293, and 327, respectively), he was both still attracted to the large-scale ballad composition of his earliest youth and had rediscovered Goethe, whose Werther is passionate about Ossian. The popularity of this poetry was still so great in the late 1820s and 1830s that Anton Diabelli began the publication by installments (*Lieferungen*) of the Schubert *Nachlass* in July 1830 with the Ossian ballads.

The young Schubert and his circle of friends were devoted with particular intensity to the two giants of the era, Johann Wolfgang von Goethe (1749–1832) and Friedrich Schiller (1759–1805): there are seventy-four Goethe Lieder – more than any other poet – and forty-four Schiller Lieder. David Gramit has even speculated convincingly that the Dioscurii, or twin stars, in Mayrhofer's poem "Schiffers Nachtlied" (Schubert set it to music as *Lied eines Schiffers an die Dioskuren*, D360) are Goethe and Schiller, gods to whom the reverent sailor dedicates the rudder by which he steers his course.[11] Of the two bodies of song, the Schiller repertory begins earlier, with Schubert's first setting of *Des Mädchens Klage* (D6) in 1811 (two other settings would follow, D191 of 1815 and D389 of 1816); Schiller at the time was even more respected in the conservative Viennese literary community than Goethe. Schiller's mammoth ballads, such as *Der Taucher* (D77), and small, insouciant "Come and kiss me, sweet-and-twenty" spring songs, such as *An den Frühling* (D283 and 587), were the composer's most frequent choices from the poetry of a writer whose aesthetic philosophy was the pole star of the youthful Schubert circle. If Schubert had his manifest difficulties with Schiller's poetry and therefore set many of the Schiller poems two and three times in an attempt to capture "the right tone" (for example, *Der Jüngling am Bache* [D30] of September 1812, was recast three days later and then again seven years later, in 1819),[12] he also had wonderful successes, such as *Die Götter Griechenlands* (D677) and *Gruppe aus dem Tartarus* (D583; first attempted in 1816, the second version completed in 1817).[13]

Goethe, in his magnitude and multiplicity, was even more a catalyst for stylistic experiment on Schubert's part; it is, after all, with *Gretchen am Spinnrade* (D118) and *Erlkönig* (D328) that a hitherto unprecedented power appears in German song. This poet, who fittingly coined the word "Weltliteratur" ("world literature"), wrote poetry that ranges from dithyrambic odes to the distilled perfection of the *Roman Elegies*, from the Baroque richness of *Faust* to mastery of the short lyric, from Anacreontic playfulness to the furies of the *Sturm und Drang*, from reflective classicism to, at last, a symbolism which unites all of his earlier tendencies.[14] It is his incomparable achievement to have imposed the unity of dominant concerns on a massive body of work so heterogeneous in style and form, to have found a way of experiencing and writing in which the thing experienced is always interfused with the emotions of the experiencing subject and is therefore rendered symbolic. But curiously, Schubert's engagement with Goethe's poetry has not yet received the scholarly attention it deserves; even the Goethe songbooks now in the Vienna City Library and the Paris Conservatoire collection merit renewed study. What of Goethe's lyric repertory did Schubert choose and what did he shun? How and why did the composer's youthful obsession with Goethe dwindle over the years? What are the possible correlations between the choice of certain Goethe poems and the compositional, or even biographical, issues at that time in Schubert's life? (For example, Schubert set *Ganymed*, D544, in 1817 at a point when he was most interested in composing tonally progressive songs. He was also at the time in close contact with his friend Johann Mayrhofer [1787–1836], who was a student of the Greek classics, who venerated Goethe and was, perhaps, homosexual; personal resonances might well cluster about this song of a youth beloved by Zeus.) What more should be said of Schubert's long struggle with the Harper's and Mignon's songs in *Wilhelm Meisters Lehrjahre*? An entire book on the topic of Schubert and Goethe is surely overdue.[15]

And so too is consideration of other aspects of Schubert's tastes in poetry once youth was behind him. To which poets did Schubert turn in 1816–17 (among them, Christian Friedrich Schubart, Matthias Claudius, second settings of previous Schiller poems, and Mayrhofer) and why? When Schubert returned in 1816 to Hölty's poems, after the ten Hölty songs of 1815, can one trace differences in his musical approach to the same poet? What was the effect of Schubert's using the "emended" 1804 edition of Hölty's poems by Johann Heinrich Voss? What is the story of Schubert's involvement with the Viennese Romantics and the circle around Friedrich Schlegel? To these questions, one could add many others.

Poesia per musica and the issue of taste, part 2: Schubert and his friends

The circle of Schubert's close friends, despite changes over the years, always included writers, and Schubert immortalized several of those associations by setting his friends' poetry to music. Because most of his versifying companions were amateurs (in a city which made much of amateur performance) and cannot claim Goethean powers, this fact has lent additional credence to the charge that Schubert was undiscriminating in his choice of verse. However, his friends on occasion both introduced him to the works of better-quality poets the composer might otherwise not have known (it was through Franz von Bruchmann that Schubert discovered Friedrich Rückert's *Östliche Rosen* of 1821, from which the composer took texts for six songs) and themselves provided poetry undeniably not of the highest calibre but apt for Schubert's music. The Burgtheater actor Johann Anton Friedrich Reil's *Das Lied im Grünen* (D917 of June 1827), is an example of the phenomenon – Schubert's turn to D minor at the words "grünt einst uns das Leben nicht fürder," followed by the courageous rejection of minor-mode pessimism, is unforgettable – and there are others as well.

It is, however, possible to defend at least one of Schubert's friends against the accusation of poetic feebleness. Johann Mayrhofer was, in Brahms's words, the "ernsthafteste" ("the most serious") member of the *Schubertkreis*, the poet of forty-seven Schubert songs. Mayrhofer, who was a boyhood friend of Joseph von Spaun in Linz, met Schubert through Spaun in 1814 and subsequently became one of the dominant influences on Schubert's thought during the crucial years 1817–20. An unexplained rift between the erstwhile companions in late 1820 (was it due to Mayrhofer's temperament, difficult to endure at close range? His acceptance in 1820 of a position as a censor, contrary to his own and to Schubert's ideals? His putative homosexuality? All of the above? – no one knows) put an end to their close association. In Mayrhofer's poetry, one finds a synthesis of themes from antiquity, the yearning for an unattainable ideal realm modeled after the Platonic "heaven" of Ideas and pure Spirit, and a distinctive pitch-black pessimism born of ineradicable psychological distress; to this is added experimental poetic forms and near-expressionistic verbal gestures. Drawn to Stoic philosophy from youth, he fought his chronic depression with considerable strength of will but could not ultimately master it, even through the poetry that, along with delight in nature, were his sole consolations for existence. He committed suicide in 1836.

One can also cite the Mayrhofer songs as an interesting example of the confluence of circumstance, poetry, and compositional imperatives; that is, a composer may well be drawn to a particular repertory at a particular time because of a correspondence with his own musical development. The Mayrhofer Lieder run the gamut from gigantic ballad-cantatas (*Uraniens Flucht*, D554) to tiny strophic songs (*Alte Liebe rostet nie*, D477), from grandiose mythological subjects through gloomy personal meditations to tender musings and more, but despite this variety, one can see, especially in the twenty songs of 1817, a certain strain of radical experimentation. Progressive tonality appears in the magnificent *Auf der Donau* (D553) – a masterpiece which should be better known than it is – and astonishing chromaticism in *Freiwilliges Versinken* (D700). Mayrhofer's complexities thus elicited musical complexities; well before Wagner, Schubert in the Mayrhofer songs anticipated tonal maneuvers that would not become commonplace until the end of the century.

Although none of his other friends provided him with quite so rich a source of poetry as Mayrhofer, they are nevertheless a significant presence in the roster of Schubert poets. Franz von Bruchmann (1798–1867), the son of a wealthy merchant, provided the composer with five song texts (*An die Leyer*, D737; *Im Haine*, D738; the exquisite *Am See*, D746; *Schwestergruß*, D762; and *Der zürnende Barde*, D785) – inferior poetry, but Schubert forged masterpieces from it in 1822–23, when everything he touched turned to gold; Bruchmann's Lon Chaney-style graveyard mists and chromo-lithographed piety in *Schwestergruß* are enveloped in some of Schubert's best music. Franz von Schober (1796–1882), a wealthy and somewhat dissolute dilettante (his habit of becoming engaged briefly and unsuccessfully to his friends' sisters, only to be warned away, is but one indication of a questionable character) who was a massive presence in Schubert's life, wrote gushing claptrap, but *Am Bach im Frühling* (D361), *Todesmusik* (D758), *Schatzgräbers Begehr* (D761), and, above all, *An die Musik*, are extremely fine songs nonetheless. Franz Xaver von Wssehrd Schlechta (1796–1875), a government employee and occasional poet, was a loyal admirer of the composer, one whose poetry is more original and more substantive than Schober's: of the seven Schlechta songs, *Fischerweise* (D881), *Widerschein* (D639), and *Totengräber-Weise* (D869) are especially notable.

Personal ties to a poet were, on occasion, augmented by other factors as well, such as the influence of other song composers. In 1812, Schubert met Theodor Körner (1791–1813), recently arrived in Vienna and already garnering fame as a playwright for the Burgtheater; the young, enthusiastic, and charming Saxon poet made a great impression upon the Schubert circle, on Spaun and Mayrhofer in particular. On August 26th of the following year, Körner, who had joined a German volunteer regiment fighting in the War of Liberation, was killed in a skirmish at Gadebusch, and a volume of his patriotic poems, published under the title *Leyer und Schwert*, became a best-seller. But when Schubert in 1815, the year of the Congress of Vienna and a time when memorials to Vienna's adopted son were rife, set eleven Körner poems, he may also have been responding to settings of Körner's poems by the Viennese composer Stephan Franz, whose *Sechs Gedichte von Theodor Körner*, Op. 10, were published in 1814, as well as to memories of someone he knew personally and to the historical ferment of the day. Both Schubert and Franz evoke Mozart in their Körner settings: the beginning of Franz's *Sängers Morgenlied* recalls Mozart's *Abendempfindung an Laura*, K. 523, and Schubert's songs too seem like *hommages à Mozart*.

Several of Schubert's friendships with amateur writers deserve closer investigation so that we might come to know the poet as well as the songs. Johann Ladislaus Pyrker (1772–1847), the poet of *Das Heimweh* (D851) and *Die Allmacht* (D852), led an interesting life, recounted in a lively autobiography; at different times Patriarch of Venice and Archbishop of Erlau, he wrote a considerable quantity of verse. And knowledge of the poets surely includes knowledge of their other poetic works: one can better understand Matthäus von Collin's *Der Zwerg* if one realizes that he wrote at least one other poem about sexual obsession and death. Just as songs belong within the context of an entire oeuvre, so do poems.

Lieder and life: the biographical bridge

While verse by someone else does not originate from the composer's life and creative endeavors, Schubert, I would suppose, was intermittently drawn to poetry on particular subjects because those poems addressed his most pressing concerns at the time. While the dangers of speculating about such biographical issues should be obvious, adolescents and young adults, including artists in their youth, often seek a mirror of themselves in art. Schubert's first extant song-fragment is a gigantic unfinished sketch, possibly from early 1810, of an even more gigantic poem, "Lebenstraum," by Gabriele von Baumberg; it is possible that his attention was drawn to her because of a scandal the preceding year in which Gabriele's husband, the political revolutionary Janos Batsányi, fled into Parisian exile one step ahead of the State police, thus reviving her name in Viennese circles, and because the poem asserts a woman's right to Parnassian artistry. Schubert, already in contention with his father about a vocation, may have found in Gabriele's poem confirmation of his own belief that he was destined to be a composer. If a woman could make such a claim, so could he (or so one imagines a possible scenario); this is also an early demonstration, however inept and unfinished, of his musical sympathies for female poetic personae.[16] The same classic adolescent struggle may have fueled his settings of Gottlieb Conrad Pfeffel's *Der Vatermörder* (D10), and Schiller's *Leichenfantasie* (D7), the latter an almost comic – were it not so true to the hurt feelings of adolescent parent-and-child misunderstandings – portrayal of the commonplace teenage fantasy that a father only realizes his son's glorious gifts after the youth has died. Graveside remorse is vividly depicted in harmonies already radical for 1811.

Adolescent self-dramatization is one thing, adult experience another. But it is difficult to imagine that the choice of poetry is entirely disinterested at all times in adulthood, that personality and circumstances do not at times direct the choice of poetry. We do not know precisely when or how Schubert discovered the *Siebenundsiebzig Gedichte aus den hinterlassenen Papieren eines reisenden Waldhornisten* (Seven-and-Seventy Poems from the Posthumous Papers of a Journeying Horn-Player, published in Dessau in 1821) by Wilhelm Müller, an anthology which begins with the lyric monodrama *Die schöne Müllerin*, but we do know that the composition of this, Schubert's first song cycle to poetry by a fine and undervalued poet, coincides with the composer's discovery of a fatal venereal disease, with the quarantine customary for syphilitics in the initial contagious stage and the first serious medical crisis brought on by the disease. Schubert would have known that there was no cure and that his malady often culminated in horrifying paralysis or madness. That he should be drawn to a large and ambitious work in which a youth dies as a consequence of sex (whether from disease or from shock and despair is of less import than the termination in death) seems somehow logical. Four years later, he would return to the second volume of the same poet's verses for *Winterreise*, D911 (the poet's title is "Die Winterreise"), an even more bitter exploration of love, alienation, and living death. That he might have seen in Müller's numbed, paralysed hurdy-gurdy player a premonition of his own possible fate seems all too likely; that he confronted it and turned it into music of such unflinching, austere beauty seems nothing short of heroic.[17]

Speculations about biographical connections are possible in other instances as well, although the paucity of the Schubert documentation makes such guesswork an uncertain enterprise. It cannot presently be determined whether Schubert and the Romantic philosopher–poet–novelist Friedrich Schlegel ever met, but their groups of friends certainly overlapped. One of the sixteen songs on texts by Schlegel (and Schubert is one of the few composers to have set Schlegel's lyric poetry to music), *Fülle der Liebe* (D854), may, according to the research of Lisa Feurzeig, be Schubert's "last word" on his connection with the circle around Schlegel, in particular, its numerous amorous complications and involvement with magnetic healing. The slightly overblown grandiosity of this 1825 song, hints at a critique of pretentiousness, as well as the musical recognition of great beauty and grief.

Schubert as poet's editor

The case of Schubert's setting of Matthäus von Collin's *Nacht und Träume* highlights several recurring challenges of Schubert song scholarship: what precisely was the textual source, and did Schubert make emendations to the poem? The matter is all the more intriguingly complex when the poet himself was prone to revision and the composer felt free to make still more alterations *en route* to the finished Lied. Schubert's song text is as follows:

> Heil'ge Nacht, du sinkest nieder;
> Nieder wallen auch die Träume,
> Wie dein Mondlicht durch die Räume,
> Durch der Menschen stille Brust.
> Die belauschen sie mit Lust;
> Rufen, wenn der Tag erwacht:
> Kehre wieder, heil'ge Nacht!
> Holde Träume, kehret wieder!

> Holy night, you sink down;
> Dreams too float down
> like your moonlight through space,
> through the silent hearts of men.
> They listen with delight,
> cry out when day awakes:
> Come back, holy night!
> Fair dreams, come back!

In Collin's *Nachgelassene Gedichte* (Posthumous Poems), published in 1827, his friend the famous Orientalist Joseph von Hammer-Purgstall includes two poems entitled "Nacht und Träume" and "Nachtfeyer" ("Celebration of Night"), poems which are actually variations of the same work. "Nacht und Träume" was perhaps written in 1813, certainly by 1814, as it appeared in Johann Erichson's *Musen-Almanach für das Jahr 1814.*[18]

Nacht und Träume

Nacht! verschwiegne, sankst du nieder?
Nieder durch die dunklen Räume
Wallen heimlich jetzt die Träume
In der Menschen stille Brust,
Die belauschen sie mit Lust;
Rufen, wenn der Tag erwacht:
Kehre wieder heil'ge Nacht!
Holde Träume, kehret wieder.

Night and Dreams

Night! quiet one, did you sink down?
Down through the dark spaces,
dreams secretly now float down
through the silent hearts of men.
They listen with delight,
cry out when day awakes:
Come back, holy night!
Fair dreams, come back!

"Nachtfeyer," which appears for the first time in the *Nachgelassene Gedichte* (was "Nachtfeyer" Collin's title or Hammer's?), differs from Schubert's text only in lines 3–4: "Wie dein Licht durch diese Bäume, / Lieblich durch der Menschen Brust." There are several possible scenarios to explain the existence of three different versions of the same poem. When Schubert composed his setting sometime before June 4, 1823, when Anton von Spaun wrote to Schober that he had heard Vogl sing *Der Zwerg, Greisengesang,* and *Nacht und Träume,* he could have taken the poet's two existing versions – if one postulates that both versions existed at the time – and conflated them, replacing the dramatic, exclamatory–questioning beginning of "Nacht und Träume" with the quieter, awe-struck exhalation of both the song text and "Nachtfeyer"; perhaps he might have done so because he could find the stuff of music in images of motion, in night's descent, but not in silence, hence the deletion of the word "verschwiegne." Furthermore, he might have replaced Collin's "dein Licht" with "dein *Mond*licht," thereby darkening the vowel sounds and rendering more gentle Collin's succession of short words. In still another scenario, Schubert might have conferred with Collin on emendations to the published version of "Nacht und Träume," the result the song text which Collin then varied still further, at some unknown time, as "Nachtfeyer." All such speculation aside, we do not know how the textual discrepancies in "Nacht und Träume" came into being, only that they exist. The problem resurfaces elsewhere in the Schubert song oeuvre as well: was it Schubert who eliminated two-thirds of Mayrhofer's published text for *Erlafsee* (D586), or did the composer use an earlier version without the mystico-symbolic enigmas one finds in the printed poem? We do not know. The poem in its printed version is filled with an anguished symbolism that seems private and hence beyond absolute decoding.

Schubert *did* on occasion alter the poetic texts he set to music, the emendations running the gamut from slight to drastic; Kristina Muxfeldt, for example, discusses Schubert's alterations to published poetic sources, with *Nachtviolen* (D752), *Greisengesang* and *Versunken* (D715) as specific instances.[19] Schubert did so, one can speculate, for a variety of reasons, ranging from replacement of the poet's language for better-sounding, more singable words through changes for the sake of a specific musical idea to large-scale disagreements with something in the poetic content. In Müller's "Letzte Hoffnung" from *Winterreise*, Schubert changed the poet's initial two lines, "Hier und da ist an den Bäumen / Noch ein buntes Blatt zu sehn" ("Here and there, yet a colored leaf can still be seen on the trees") to the song text "Hie und da ist an den Bäumen / Manches bunte Blatt zu sehn" ("Here and there on the trees, many a colored leaf can still be seen"), to remove the "r" which interrupts and darkens the initial words "Hier und da" and to alter the singular ("Noch ein buntes Blatt") to the many ("Manches bunte Blatt") in accord – I believe – with his conception of many falling intervals in the piano intro-duction. Four years earlier, he had done something far more radical to *Die schöne Müllerin*: he eliminated not only Müller's prologue and epilogue but three entire poems from the body of the narrative ("Das Mühlenleben," "Erster Schmerz, letzter Scherz," and "Blümlein Vergi-ßmein"). When he did so, it was not because those poems were incidental to the tale and easily dispensable; in fact, what happens in the last of those omitted poems drives the miller lad to suicide. We cannot know for a cer-tainty why Schubert deleted those poems, but elsewhere I have suggested that he did not want *his* protagonist to suffer the degrading experience Müller's lad undergoes. Schubert not only excised three poems but also "rewrote" the poetry he did set by overwhelming the poetic indices of delusion, frenzy, and near-insanity with brighter, more buoyant music: Müller's poem "Mein!" is "wahres Rasen" ("truly raving"), according to the famous nineteenth-century singer Julius Stockhausen, but Schubert's setting is all symmetry and joy, with only a few quickly suppressed hints of disturbance.[20]

Striking it right: Schubert and multiple versions

Over and over throughout his brief life, Schubert made a practice of returning to a poem he had already set to music and setting it again, sometimes at a distance of a few hours or a day, sometimes years later. In certain instances, the changes are relatively minor, and in others, Schubert re-reads the poem from a different musical stance altogether and invents entirely new music; for this reason above all others, it is difficult to determine an exact "count" of Schubert's songs. The ubiquitous habit of producing versions (which Maurice Brown defines as entirely fresh settings of a poem, such as the two settings of Goethe's *An den Mond*, D259 and 296) or variants (defined as alterations to an existing song, the altered work written as a separate manuscript)[21] of a single poem tells of poetry's multiplicity – just as a poem unlocks a variety of associations in readers' minds, so too does it impel varying musical gestures in composers' minds – and Schubert's perfectionism, of dissatisfaction with something in the first conception and a determination to try again, to wrest still more music from the poet's images.

It was a habit begun early. Where the composer was, conjecturally, too displeased with the setting even to finish it, he abandoned it, left it as a fragment, and started afresh. (But how revealing it is that he kept these uncompleted youthful ruins, long after what led him to the song in the first place had vanished.) For example, Schubert made his first attempt to set Friedrich von Matthisson's *Der Geistertanz* (D15) sometime around 1812, devising fifty-one measures of episodic-sectional, mock-horror music after the model of Zumsteeg; unhappy with the results, he tried again on a grander scale that same year (or so the Deutsch cataloguers suggest), the music replete with *Schauerballade* effects (D15A). This too failed to pass muster with the self-critical composer, and Schubert dropped the project altogether until October 14, 1814. The third time was truly the charm (D116), the composer discovering both his own sense of humor and that of the frisking ghosts. (Schubert returned to the text again in 1816 and set it as a male partsong [D494; TTBBB].)

In another example of "Schubert revising Schubert,"[22] this time a study in opposites, Schubert first set Körner's *Sängers Morgenlied* (D163) on February 27, 1815, then again (D165) on March 1, a few days later. For the initial version, Schubert took his point of departure from the first stanza of Körner's six and created a buoyant greeting to the sun in G major, with energetic melismas propelling the vocal line along at strategic points. One notes in particular the unison setting of the words "mit geheimnissvollen Worten" ("with secret words") in measures 9–10 and the chromatic neighbor-notes on either side of the dominant pitch – Schubert would later signify the secretive nature of the wanderer's thoughts in *Letzte Hoffnung* from *Winterreise* in a similar way, a gesture with antecedents in his youth. But the word "Ach" ("Ah") at the beginning of stanza two of *Sängers Morgenlied* is the signal for a change of tone, for greater gravity. Schubert did more than merely ignore the *Sehnsucht* ("yearning") awakened by the arrival of day in the February 27 version – he set it to the merry strains of the first verse, sound and sense thus at odds throughout the last half of the song.

> Süßes Licht! Aus goldnen Pforten
> Brichst du siegend durch die Nacht.
> Schöner Tag! Du bist erwacht.
> Mit geheimnisvollen Worten,
> In melodischen Akkorden
> Grüß' ich deine Rosenpracht!
>
> Ach! der Liebe sanftes Wehen
> Schwellt mir das bewegte Herz,
> Sanft, wie ein geliebter Schmerz.
> Dürft' ich nur auf goldnen Höhen
> Mich im Morgenduft ergehen!
> Sehnsucht zieht mich himmelwärts.
>
> Sweet light! Through golden portals
> You break victoriously through the night.
> Beautiful day! You are awake.
> With mysterious words
> And melodious sounds,
> I greet your roseate splendor!
>
> Ah, the soft breath of love
> Swells my moved heart
> As softly as a beloved pain.
> If only I could wander on golden heights
> In the fragrant morning!
> Yearning draws me heavenwards.

Presumably disturbed by the discrepancy, Schubert returned to the poem two days later in order to compose a setting whose atmosphere derives from the *second* stanza, not the first, and is therefore reflective of the bulk of the poem. This second version, marked "Langsam" and in a far more reverential mood, entirely devoid of the gaiety of the first version, is a foreshadowing of measures 16–21 of *Morgengruß* from *Die schöne Müllerin* of 1823, at the words "So muß ich wieder gehen" ("So I must go away"). The morning *mise-en-scène* and the shared yearning, albeit for different objects, might well have impelled the harmonic, motivic, figurational, and rhythmic resemblances eight years later. (One poet's words can on occasion recall to life the music first devised to another poet's words, as when Schubert based his setting of Matthias Claudius's *An die Nachtigall*, D497, on his prior setting of Josef Ludwig Stoll's *An die Geliebte*, D303.[23])

Much more remains to be brought to light regarding Schubert's literary world, and these few pages exist more to point out issues than to provide conclusions; if some of the plethora of questions raised here cannot be fully answered, others can. When scholars approach Lieder, Schubert's or anyone else's, from the vantage point of curiosity about its origins in language and explore the poet and the literary tradition as well as the musical context, there is much, I believe, to be gained.

PART II

Schubert's music: style and genre

6 Schubert's songs: the transformation of a genre

Kristina Muxfeldt

In the late eighteenth century the composition of Lieder was principally an amateur pursuit, taken up by composers who concentrated their efforts on this genre alone. Composers of the more acclaimed public genres, whether instrumental music or opera, only occasionally turned to song as a diversion, which explains why there are so few truly distinguished songs by Mozart and Beethoven. Even the most memorable of their songs only marginally challenge the amateur status of the genre, or else, like Beethoven's *Adelaide*, they resemble Italian aria more than the simple folk manner of the German Lied. Beethoven's *An die ferne Geliebte*, Op. 98, is the only attempt by a composer of stature to compose a more ambitious work from songs so deeply invested in the *Volkston*. Yet significantly, the immediate roots of Beethoven's only song cycle lie much less in the tradition of the north-German Lied, with which he had had contact from his earliest years in Bonn, than in his extensive confrontation with British folksong resulting from the arrangements he was commissioned to provide for the popular series of Irish, Scotch, and Welsh folksongs issued by the English publisher George Thomson.[1] (Haydn, too, had been enlisted in this enterprise.) The deep association of Lied with the naïve and heartfelt expression of folksong must have served as a form of restraint as well as inspiration for Beethoven, defining both the character and the outer limits of the genre.

The songs that would eventually be published by Franz Schubert as his Opus 1 and Opus 2, *Erlkönig* (D328) and *Gretchen am Spinnrade* (D118), had already been composed when Beethoven's cycle went to press in 1816. While both composers lived and worked in Vienna at the same time, they were of different generations, different national origin, and brought up in somewhat different musical environments. Beethoven was forty-six when he wrote *An die ferne Geliebte*, an isolated work in his career, Schubert only seventeen when he composed *Erlkönig* and *Gretchen am Spinnrade*, the works with which he would launch his reputation, and it is Schubert's songs, not Beethoven's, that have been credited with elevating the stature of the genre.

Although by the later eighteenth century it was instrumental music that was celebrated as the highest form of musical art by avant-garde critics, the public vocal genres of opera, and to a lesser extent Mass, never really lost their former prestige. The Lied, on the other hand, suffered from being understood as amateur *Hausmusik*, a status fostered by the eighteenth-century ideal of strophic song which held musical invention to a modest scope, giving priority to the expressive powers of the singer over those of the composer. It is significant that Schubert's debut works are both very dramatic in character: neither Goethe's ballad "Erlkönig" nor Gretchen's song from *Faust* lent themselves to the contained forms of strophic Lied. This is not to say that Schubert avoided strophic settings, but the ideals of *Volkston* and strophic song were not for him aesthetic constraints as they so often were for Beethoven, rather only one option among many expressive possibilities (an option he would continue to draw on whenever it suited his purpose for the rest of his career). Interestingly, when Josef Hüttenbrenner reviewed *Gretchen am Spinnrade* for the *Sammler* in May of 1821 he was concerned to establish that Schubert's song was *equally* as original as Beethoven's *Adelaide* and Mozart's *An Chloe* and *Abendempfindung*. It was these composers he hoped to align Schubert with, not the *Liederkomponisten* like Johann Rudolf Zumsteeg or Johann Friedrich Reichardt, many of whose works had served Schubert as direct models (*SDB* 177).

Numerous compositional models for Schubert's earliest songs have long been recognized and documented. There are the big dramatic *scenas* of Zumsteeg (their reputation forever fixed as "songs that influenced Schubert" by Eusebius Mandyczewski's decision to reproduce them in an appendix to the Schubert song volumes of the old Breitkopf und Härtel edition [*ASA*]); the strophic folk-like songs in the tradition of Reichardt and Carl Friedrich Zelter; the ballads, and modest dialogue songs, usually involving an opposition of major and minor for the two characters, abundantly represented among the Lieder of Zumsteeg. The proliferation of songs that behave as recognizable types – whether or not we can identify specific models for them – continued for quite a number of years, even after the composition of songs as original in formal and harmonic innovation as *Gretchen am Spinnrade*, *Erlkönig*, *Rastlose Liebe* (D138), and *Nähe des Geliebten* (D162), all written by 1815. (Can it be coincidence that so many of the most original early songs are settings of Goethe?)

Yet the recognition that the genre itself was undergoing a radical transformation must have come fairly early. Robert Schumann not only acknowledged it but located the development after Beethoven when he observed that the only genre to have made true progress since Beethoven was song.[2] Today it is above all the two song cycles to texts by Wilhelm

Müller, *Die schöne Müllerin* (D795) and *Winterreise* (D911), that are celebrated as Schubert's greatest achievement. We must remember, however, that in Schubert's day these songs were more frequently performed individually than as complete cycles – at least in public. While there is no doubt that Schubert performed the cycles in entirety for the circle of friends who always served as his first audience (such a performance of *Winterreise* is documented), the first complete public performance of *Die schöne Müllerin* did not take place until 1856.[3] Even at its publication in 1824, the work was released in multiple volumes issued months apart. Unlike either *An die ferne Geliebte,* or the later song cycles of Schumann, all of the songs in the Schubert cycles can stand as independent songs on the basis of their structure and formal closure, although only relatively few are actually effective performed alone. Schubert's transformation of the Lied began with the individually composed song and this remained the basis of his conception even in the song cycles.

Like many other early nineteenth-century composers of Lieder, Schubert devoted considerable practice to inventing memorable melodies and discovering ways to emphasize the meaning of striking images in a poem through expressive changes in declamatory style, texture, figuration, or harmony. Leafing through the earliest song volumes of the old Breitkopf edition[4] can seem like browsing through a lexicon of expressive devices cued to poetically charged images. The music responds with infinite inventiveness to each new image or mood. At the other extreme, it is also true that some of Schubert's most frequently performed songs do not exceed the expectations of even the most modest parlor song: with all its naïve charm and memorability, the lovely *Heidenröslein* (D257), also to a poem by Goethe, stays entirely within the bounds of an amateur aesthetic.

However, the most ambitious of the early songs show that the impressive large-scale continuity of ideas that would eventually lead Schubert to the sustained expression of the two great Müller cycles was already at his command at the age of seventeen – even if inconsistently. As is well known, Schubert sometimes set the same poem more than once over a distance of some years. The multiple settings of the Mignon and Harper songs from Goethe's *Wilhelm Meister* register Schubert's shifting and increasingly personal conception of the genre. Even more stark is the difference in compositional strategy between the two settings of *Am Flusse* (D160 and D766, a Goethe text composed in 1815 and again in 1822), where what we might call an additive effort to mimic textual images in striking harmonic and textural changes in the earlier setting (two measures of arpeggiated chordal accompaniment at "you [my songs] sang only of my love," answered by two measures of operatic pathos – "but she now scorns my constancy" – and, later, bitter recitative – "you were inscribed in water, so flow away with the stream") gives way to a long-range cumulative conception that allows poetic nuance to be registered without interrupting the larger sweep. In the later song, the sustained figuration in the piano evokes the continuously flowing river, its motion subtly modulated by the two swerves to a distant tonic which dissipate before they resolve ("Flow away, beloved songs, *into the sea of oblivion*"; "*You were inscribed in water*, so flow away with the stream") and the unsymmetrical wave-like phrase structure that gives musical expression to Goethe's symbolic image of the poet's songs dissolving into oblivion. The perpetual motion of the river's flow is the background image that pervades the poet's reflection. Schubert has conceived an analogous musical flow, a symbol that fuses the river with the poet's songs "inscribed in water." In the greatest of the early songs hints of this latter technique are already very much in evidence. (For a discussion of *Gretchen am Spinnrade*, perhaps the most masterful early example, see Charles Rosen's chapter "Schubert's inflections of Classical form" in this volume.)

Indeed, Schubert's control in the most impressive of the early songs already extended to a remarkable range of compositional parameters that had never before been turned with such concentration to the modest genre of song (and which he himself would not master with the same success in purely instrumental genres for several years to come). The command of harmonic implication in *Nähe des Geliebten*, for example, in which G flat, so remote from the opening harmony, is gradually revealed as tonic, is hardly less sophisticated than the carefully directed root motion by fifths that underlies the dissonant surface of the opening phrase of *Dass sie hier gewesen* (D775), progressing inexorably toward the dominant of the pure C major that will sound in the refrain (see Exx. 6.1 and 6.2).[5] One of the most concentrated and exotic-sounding songs Schubert ever wrote, the Rückert song was composed some seven years after *Nähe des Geliebten*, in 1822. In both songs the focused progression from a remote point to a sharply defined tonic through a mass of surface dissonance is used to capture a similar poetic idea: the mental act of conjuring a beloved – distant in *Nähe des Geliebten*, near enough to have left behind a scent on the breeze and to induce a lover's tears in *Dass sie hier gewesen* – into a vivid and sensual presence.[6]

The imagination with which Schubert was able to conceive and control musical motions that would stimulate an analogy with some physical or mental act was unmatched by any of his contemporaries (although others before him had experimented with some of the requisite techniques, including the perpetual motion figurations so characteristic of Schubert's most famous songs).[7] Schubert's harmonic ambition and originality in

Example 6.1 *Nähe des Geliebten* (D165), mm. 1–5

Example 6.2 *Dass sie hier gewesen* (D775), mm. 1–18

the songs was remarked from the moment they first began to appear in print in the early 1820s – admittedly, not always with admiration.[8] (Only about a third of the roughly six hundred songs ever made it into print during Schubert's lifetime.) The rich palette and extreme economy of Schubert's modulatory technique allowed him to register minute nuances of feeling without breaking up the larger flow of events. Whether in the fluid modulations of the Friedrich Schlegel setting *Die Gebüsche* (D646), a song which seems designed to test how far the pull of a tonic can extend, or in the frequent shifts in mode in *Winterreise*, carefully calibrated to distinguish events as the wanderer's memories, fantasies, or present experience, modulation through tonal space is used with unparalleled effect to mimic the movements of inner experience. We shall want to return to this point presently.

But first, another technical innovation of Schubert's songs – the originality of his placement of the voice in the texture – deserves a separate discussion. In contrast to the folksong-based style that even Beethoven rarely exceeded in his songs – in which the singer's melody dominates and the piano is largely given the role of accompaniment, often doubling the melody in the right hand – Schubert's songs are full of remarkable inventiveness in the positioning of the voice within the texture. (Again, we may discover occasional earlier precedents for Schubert's departure from the rigid identification of the vocal line with the melody: the pedal G sustained by the singer while the piano has the tune in *Wo die Berge so Blau*, the second song in *An die ferne Geliebte*, is a rare exception for Beethoven, for which an even earlier model may be found in Reichardt's *Erlkönig*.) Schubert frequently delighted in exploiting the restless and uncanny effect of a vocal line treated as a functional bass, sometimes doubling it in the left hand to create a more hollow sonority. The technique is sustained through the entire first stanza of the exquisite *Der Wanderer* (D649), on a text of Friedrich Schlegel, in which the moonlight advises the wanderer always to stay on the move, never to seek a home: "Ever onward to others you shall pass, you shall wander, nimbly escaping all complaints." The stable chorale-style counterpoint of the introduction is suspended the moment the singer enters – a wanderer whose path is guided by the bright light of the moon. The feeling that the harmony is ungrounded comes from a combination of the unusually high register of the bass line and the avoidance of contrary motion between the outer voices, so fundamental to a perception of harmonic stability: even when the singer and left hand supply the bass notes it sounds as if the true bass has dropped out (see Ex. 6.3).

In the expansive and marvelously original *Im Walde* (D708), based on a poem by Schlegel celebrating imagination and creativity, a similar device emerges without preparation from a more typical accompanimental texture and is used in conjunction with a series of fluid modulations marked *ppp*, to seize a mysterious image in the poem: the gentle sound of the rushing streams that transform pain into creative blossoms. The harmony just prior to the textural change is inflected expressively up a half step from the tonic E major to F. Suddenly the left hand leaps up into the tenor register where it takes command of the harmony, staking

Example 6.3 *Der Wanderer* (D649), mm. 1–7

out a path to the leading tone of C major. The broken chords in the right hand oblige with a protracted dominant seventh before the voice re-enters in C, mysteriously doubling the left hand's false bass line beneath the continued broken chords in the right for a full seven measures. Exquisitely beautiful, the passage is also painfully unstable. The magical transformation is completed when the singer again splits off from the left-hand tenor, and the true bass gradually returns (see Ex. 6.4).

Later in the same song the poet's powerful image of creative energy as a breeze that courses through the soul ("Schöpferische Lüfte Wehen fühlt man durch die Seele gehen") is rendered in another series of astonishingly free harmonic turns governed by the tenor. This time singer and left hand work together in contrary motion, but it is the tenor seizing control of the harmonic direction through a series of chromatic descents beneath the rapid figuration in the right hand that allows for the fluid modulations – from A flat to C flat to D in the space of ten measures. While the bass does not actually drop out this time, with each repetition of the phrase it merely doubles the harmonic initiative of the tenor line. Metaphysical states are represented in so many of these songs by a sudden loss of the true bass, the voice that grounds the harmony.

There are many subtle examples of left hand and singer working together in the song cycles, often doubling each other's lines for significant stretches, as for example in the songs *Auf dem Flusse* and *Die Krähe* from *Winterreise*. In the former, the expressive power of the melodic doubling of the voice in the left hand turns on an extraordinary sensitivity to

Example 6.4 *Im Walde* (D708), mm. 68–83

Example 6.5 *Auf dem Flusse* (D991, 7), mm. 1–12

Example 6.6 *Auf dem Flusse* (D991, 7), mm. 41–47

the register in which the doubling sounds. The heart-stopping effect of the hushed drop of the harmonic foundation down a half step to D sharp minor at "wie still bist du geworden" ("how still you have become") is reinforced by the dramatic drop of the left hand into the lower octave. At the rhyming phrase "erkennst du nun dein Bild?" ("do you now recognize your image?") the effect is magnified as the bass drops still another octave while the singer pushes upward to make an emotional cadence an octave above the earlier phrase (see Exx. 6.5 and 6.6).

One of the most celebrated instances of a vocal line departing from its conventional role as melody-bearer occurs in *Die liebe Farbe* from *Die schöne Müllerin* where the interaction between singer and left hand beneath the pulsing F♯'s in the right hand is poignantly expressive: the vocal line begins by providing the functional bass, with the left hand outlining the same contour mostly in thirds above; after the first phrase the

Example 6.7 *Die liebe Farbe* (D795, 16), mm. 1–11

two lines cross, allowing left hand and singer to exchange positions. As the left hand descends below the voice into the true bass register in preparation for the first cadence, nostalgic horn-fifths are created between the two, a musical reminder of the distant beloved, tinged with the painful (if only half conscious) memory of the hunter's disturbing presence ("Mein Schatz hat's grün so gern") (see Ex. 6.7).

There are equally striking examples in which it is the right hand that interacts with the vocal melody in ways that depart from the normative model of simple melodic doubling. In the exquisite *Nachtviolen* (D752), on a poem of Johann Mayrhofer, the interaction of the upper voices is controlled with remarkable subtlety. The right hand traces the outlines of the melody slightly out of phase with the voice, reaching above the vocal line at the expressive cadences at "into the velvety blue," where the two voices momentarily intertwine. (For the text and a translation of the poem see Table 6.1.) The unsynchronized doubling is brought to an extraordinary heterophonic climax on the final line of text, "and in silent nights the sacred union flowers forth": left and right hands, both in treble clef, sound rhythmically varied versions of the same melody an octave apart; the singer is sandwiched between them, a vibrant inner voice singing an outline of the same melody with added upward reaches that negotiate the space between the two hands (see Ex. 4.13, pp. 000–00). (Sung by a tenor rather than a soprano the earlier voice-crossings are less acute but the resonance created by variants of the same tune replicated in three octaves at the climax is even more remarkable.) The originality of

Example 6.8 *Sehnsucht* (D516), mm. 6–9

Der Ler - - che wol - - - ken - na - - - he Lie - der er - schmet - tern zu _____ des

Win - - - ters Flucht, _____

the invention lends the intimate imagery of the text a surprisingly personal stamp. We shall see later that this device is part of a much larger compositional conception, for Schubert almost certainly also had a hand in fashioning the text.

Yet another form of interaction between upper voices is developed in an earlier song *Sehnsucht* (D516), also on a Mayrhofer poem. The lark's ornate song, entering half a measure behind the voice in the upper register of the right hand, is a continuation of the nocturne-like tune initiated by the singer, displaced into the bird's octave; when the lark enters the singer becomes a subsidiary inner voice. The actual melody is neatly divided between singer and the right-hand lark, its continuity masked by the registral leaps (see Ex. 6.8). (In Schubert's composition autograph both voices are notated on a single staff so that even the page gives the appearance of a single voice splitting into two with each interjection of the lark.)

One of the most characteristically Schubertian strategies from the earliest songs to some of the latest is the representation of an inner experience through an analogy with some outward physical motion or sound. There are countless familiar examples: Gretchen's increasing distraction from her activity as she remembers Faust is given a measurable presence through the astonishingly realistic representation of the action of the spinning wheel, ceasing to spin at her climactic memory of his kiss. In *Gute Nacht*, as elsewhere in *Winterreise*, the plodding steps of the poet-wanderer, called up by the insistently plodding rhythm, force the events of the cycle into the present, heightening the emotional force of his departure from the town by defining it as an intense recollection: when the song begins, the protagonist has long left behind the house and the gate he paints so vividly. The brook's final song in *Die schöne Müllerin* is conceived as a monotonous lullaby that blends the soothing lapping of water with tolling bells and distant horn calls in a harmonic setting completely devoid of all tension. The earlier poems – and songs – have all been sung from the perspective of the miller and, indeed, it is the virtual identification between brook and miller reinforced in Schubert's setting that makes this final song so intensely moving: at the close of the cycle, miller and brook have quite literally merged into a single indistinguishable voice. Each of these songs draws on the imitation of an outside physical movement or sound to create the effect of immediate, present experience, and in each of them the core of that experience consists in a powerful act of imagination or memory. The literal actions of the present moment – the spinning, the walking, the gently lapping water – become a continuously evolving symbol through which the interior life finds expression.

The early Goethe setting *Rastlose Liebe*, from 1815, is an especially revealing example of this Schubertian tendency to create an experiential perspective because both the persona and the action of the poem are conceived in greater abstraction. In *Gretchen am Spinnrade* we are drawn into Gretchen's fantasy through the motion of the wheel; in *Erlkönig* it is, as Donald Francis Tovey perceptively observed, the boy's terror during the gallop through the night that is captured in Schubert's setting (not the father's, as in Carl Loewe's setting);[9] in *Winterreise* we experience events as if through the wanderer's psyche as he plods through the landscape. The situation in *Rastlose Liebe* is more complicated in that no lyric subject is defined for the entire first stanza. We come upon an experience already underway, as if we had walked in late on a film screening, suddenly finding ourselves surrounded by violent storms with no characters in sight: we enter upon the scene as if this were our own experience. The poem opens with a rapid succession of images of stormy weather landscapes, formulated to give a vivid impression of a subject moving through them with great determination and force:

Dem Schnee, Dem Regen	Through snow, through wind
Dem Wind entgegen,	Headlong into winds,
Im Dampf der Klüfte,	Into steamy ravines,
Durch Nebeldüfte,	Through fragrant mists,
Immerzu! Immerzu!	Ever on! Ever on!
Ohne Rast und Ruh!	Without halt or rest.
Lieber durch Leiden,	Rather through suffering
Wollt' ich mich schlagen	Would I battle,

Als so viel Freuden	Than to endure
Des Lebens ertragen.	Such of life's pleasures.
Alle das Neigen	All this inclining
Von Herzen zu Herzen,	From heart to heart,
Ach, wie so eigen	Oh, how singularly
Schaffet es Schmerzen!	It brings about pain.
Wie, soll ich fliehen?	How shall I flee?
Wälderwärts ziehen?	Dash for the forest?
Alles vergebens!	All for nothing!
Krone des Lebens,	Pinnacle of life,
Glück ohne Ruh,	Happiness without rest,
Liebe bist du!	Love, art thou.

Everything in the opening lines unites to drive to the end of the stanza: the enumeration of harsh elements, the relentless rhythm of the first four lines, the quickened pace and emphatic repetition at "Immerzu, Immerzu" and, above all, the withholding, even to the end, of subject and verb. Who is it who passes through this kaleidoscopic array of landscapes?

We learn in time, through the ironic reflections in the second stanza, then more explicitly in the last, that this vivid series of stormy landscapes is neither the representation of a direct present action nor a powerful memory, but an elaborate simile for the turbulence aroused by passionate love. Goethe's scene shifts back and forth between the storms the poet creates as outward images of inner life and his reflections on those scenes. The persona of the poem is revealed as a poet – the poet? – engaged in vivid imagination. The immediacy of the image encourages our identification with it.

Schubert's *Rastlose Liebe* seizes upon and sustains the impulsive, driving motion of Goethe's first stanza with only a slight slackening of pace in the middle. The song drives to the ecstatic celebration of love that spans the final twenty-seven of the singer's measures. A pounding anapestic rhythmic figure in the left hand enters together with the singer, comes into sharp relief at "Immerzu, immerzu," then continues to pulsate through to the end of the song. At the same time, a long harmonic sweep reinforces the effect of the rhythmic pulsing, sustaining tension through to the exuberantly set final lines: the broad wash of tonic harmony at the opening, tinged with the minor mode through the poignant inflection of minor ninths (at "Regen" and "Klüfte"), drives to a firm cadence in the dominant at the end of the first stanza; that arrival is almost immediately left behind by a wonderfully Schubertian turn of harmony to the flat mediant on the ironic "Freuden"; this in turn sets up the rising sequence on the following couplet (the phrase is merely wrenched up a half step, a simple but powerful device for creating a feeling of urgency), which leads, again just a few measures later, to the dramatic cadence to the relative minor at "alles vergebens!" The return to the tonic in the ensuing measures comes like a great sigh, and the remainder of the song is given to a lengthy celebration – in an unambivalent *major* tonic – of Goethe's laconic conclusion: "Krone des Lebens, Glück ohne Ruh, Liebe bist du!" The weight of the entire song is thrown to the end. It was clearly something in the idea of Goethe's opening lines, the powerful evocation of inner movement through an imprecise but suggestive parallel with powerful external manifestations of nature's turbulence, that fired Schubert's imagination.[10] Other aspects of the poem, while not ignored, are subsumed in the larger vision.

This conception, highly personal almost to the point of obscuring a crucial aspect of Goethe's poem, reveals a good deal about Schubert's own compositional disposition. For unlike Schubert's *Rastlose Liebe*, Goethe's poem does not sustain the impression of driving motion through to the final lines. Instead, it modulates between two distinct lyric temperaments – or voices. The one, impassioned and restless, is written as if in the midst of the experience. It spans the entire first stanza, as we have noted, disappears during the middle couplets, then resurfaces at "Wie soll ich flieh'n? Wälderwärts zieh'n?" and in the feigned exasperation of "alles vergebens!" The posture of the second voice is distant and removed: a poet surveying the scene, commenting ironically on the events called up in the active lines. While the first couplet of the middle stanza, "Lieber durch Leiden wollt' ich mich schlagen, als so viel Freuden des Lebens ertragen," can perhaps still be understood to grow out of the breathless passion of the moment (despite its artfully constructed inversion of affect), the second couplet surely cannot. With a sophisticated ambivalence the lyric persona in these lines universalizes his sentiment, casting it in the language of a naïvely simple, folklike maxim: "Alle das neigen von Herzen zu Herzen, Ach! wie so eigen schaffet es Schmerzen!" The self-consciously distant poet stands detached from the passionately engaged images of the first stanza, drawing a lesson in the universality of human experience from his position of remove. He is interrupted once again by the impassioned voice at "Wie soll ich flieh'n?" but the universalizing poet has the final say, abstracting from his individual experience a proverbial truth about the nature of love.

Schubert's setting gives dramatic continuity to Goethe's conflicting voices, subordinating the reflective, universalizing lines to the sweeping motion of the passionately engaged persona. The uninterrupted focus for him is on the restless movement, culminating in an affirmation of love that explodes Goethe's ironic closing formulation into some thirty measures of impassioned experience.[11]

The effort to convey an impression of immediate experience through music is, as we have remarked, a pervasive characteristic of Schubert's style over much of his career. The extent to which this was a matter of calculated compositional choice becomes even more apparent when we examine the poetic texts of some of the songs that differ significantly from the poems on which they are based. When textual revisions attributable to Schubert go beyond small changes undertaken for metric considerations or minor alterations that may be explained as slips of the pen or memory, encompassing the excision of entire lines or stanzas or even the rewriting of portions of text, they shed considerable light on the impulses governing Schubert's compositional decisions.

A particularly revealing example, worth examining in some detail, involves Schubert's revisions to *Nachtviolen*, a song touched upon earlier. *Nachtviolen* was composed in April 1822, to a poem by Schubert's friend, Johann Mayrhofer. The song was never published during Schubert's lifetime, but it has survived in an autograph manuscript with a text that diverges significantly from two extant versions of the poem by Mayrhofer,[12] the earlier in a hand-written collection of poems entitled *Heliopolis*, dated in the manuscript September and October of 1821.[13] A heavily revised version was published in a larger collection of Mayrhofer's poems by Friedrich Volke in Vienna in 1824, well after Schubert's setting. Table 6.1 shows the variants between the versions.

A comparison of Mayrhofer's published text with the poems as they appear in the poet's autograph manuscript reveals that *his* revisions, although numerous, do not radically alter the poems. For the most part, we find Mayrhofer laboring over the right word: there is some waffling between dative and accusative cases in the last line of the first stanza; in the second verse, "blicket" is replaced with "schauet"; "schweigend" becomes "ahnend" (roughly equivalent to a change from "look" to "gaze" in the first instance and "silently" to "knowingly" in the latter); and the mild spring air becomes summer air. The most substantial revision is Mayrhofer's replacement of the apocalyptic, not entirely coherent, image in the final line, "Und die Welt erbleicht und sinkt" ("And the world pales and sinks") with "Und die Welt erreicht sie nicht" ("And the world can reach it not"), a more firmly rational, if considerably blander, formulation, but one which nonetheless barely alters the effect of the line. Both versions entail a sudden shift in perspective, serving to distance the outside world from the central experience of the poem.

The text of Schubert's song agrees with Mayrhofer's autograph manuscript in all of these discrepancies in wording, and, with one minor exception ("versinken" instead of "vertiefen" in the third line), it is true to Mayrhofer's manuscript text in every detail. However, several additional

Table 6.1. *The poetic transmission of "Nachtviolen"*

Mayrhofer manuscript *Heliopolis*, Sept./Oct. 1821	*Gedichte von Johann Mayrhofer*, Vienna: Bey Freidrich Volke, 1824 *Nachtviolenlied*	Schubert, D752; manuscript [April 1822]	Schubert's text in translation†
Nachtviolen, Nachtviolen! Dunkle Augen, Seelenvolle, – Selig ist es sich vertiefen In dem sammtnen Blau.	Nachtviolen, Nachtviolen! Dunkle Augen, Seelenvolle, – Selig ist es sich vertiefen In **das sammtnen Blau.**	Nachtviolen, Nachtviolen! Dunkle Augen, Seelenvolle, – Selig ist es sich **versinken*** In dem sammtnen Blau.	Nightviolets, Nightviolets!†† dark eyes, soulful ones, – How blissful to immerse oneself In the velvety blue.
Grüne Blätter streben freudig Euch zu hellen, euch zu schmücken; Doch ihr blicket ernst und schweigend In die laue Frühlingsluft.	Grüne Blätter streben freudig Euch zu hellen, euch zu schmücken; Doch ihr **shauet** ernst und **ahnend** In die laue **Sommerluft.**	Grüne Blätter streben freudig Euch zu hellen, euch zu schmücken; Doch ihr blicket ernst und schweigend In die laue Frühlingsluft.	Green leaves seek cheerily To illuminate you, to adorn you. Yet you gaze earnestly and in silence Into the mild spring air.
Ja, so fesselt ihr den Dichter Mit erhabnem Wehmuthsstrahle Trafet ihr sein treues Herz.	Ja, so fesselt ihr **den Dichter:** Mit erhab**nem Wehmuthsstrahlen** Trafet ihr sein treues Herz.	Mit erhabnem Wehmuthsstrahle** Trafet ihr **mein** treues Herz.	With a sublime ray of melancholy You have struck my faithful heart.
Und nun blüht in stummen Nächten Fort die heilige Verbindung: Unaussprechlich, unbegriffen, – Und die Welt erbleicht und sinkt.	Und **so** blüht in stummen Nächten Fort die heilige Verbindung; Unaussprechlich, unbegriffen, **Und die Welt erreicht sie nicht.**	Und nun blüht in stummen Nächten Fort die heilige Verbindung.	And now, in silent nights, The sacred union flowers forth.

* "versenken" in the posthumous publication issued by Gotthard in 1872 (where the song appears in A♭).

** "Mit erhab'nen Wehmuthstrahlen" in Gotthard's publication.

† The three lines omitted by Schubert might be rendered "Yes, you thus captivate the poet" and "Inexpressible, uncomprehended – And the world pales and sinks," the final line replaced in Mayrhofer's 1824 edition with "And the world can touch it not."

†† Properly "Dame's violet" in English but the literal name is central to the meaning of the poem.

revisions of an entirely different nature have been made. As none of them are reflected in Mayrhofer's later publication (and none of the poet's later revisions are reflected in Schubert's text) we may infer that they are almost certainly Schubert's own modifications. Three entire lines of Mayrhofer's poem – the first line of the third stanza, and the final two lines of the poem – have been omitted from the setting, and the remaining pairs of lines in the third and fourth stanzas are treated as a single new stanza. In accordance with the first cut, the pronoun "sein" has been changed to "mein." The result is a very different poem. What Schubert's text omits are lines which, in one way or another, create a sense of distance from the intimate experience related in the poem. The directness of expression is considerably heightened by the change of the pronoun to the first person: it is no longer the third-person *Dichter* who loses himself in the dark violets and who later stops to reflect on the world's reaction to this association, but the poetic "I" whose heart has been captured and who revels in the immediate experience – or, better, in the vivid memory – of their union. Never mind Mayrhofer's veiled circumscriptions about the nature of the relationship – "inexpressible, uncomprehended" – and never mind the world's response, or inability to respond: Schubert was interested purely in a representation of the experience itself.[14] His focus on this experience is what generates the obsessive motif that pervades the song: the concentrated establishment of a stable identity, an obsessively repeated motif sounding within a restricted range, prepares the expressive explosion of texture and register in the climactic final lines. To set Mayrhofer's full text would have meant destroying the vividness of the experience.

We have come to recognize something peculiarly Schubertian in this approach to music and experience. Robert Schumann would later learn how to conjure complex emotion in a song by exploiting harmonic ambiguity, or to trigger sentiment by invoking musical styles laden with associations – a sudden outburst of waltz music, distorted *stile antico* counterpoint – but no other composer of song has ever surpassed (or even demonstrated the ambition to match) Schubert's ability to represent the inner movement of experience in sound. Schumann's language is that of an ironist, Schubert's profoundly, if sometimes deceptively, naïve. Is this what has drawn so many critics in recent years to try and discern in his music a trace of the composer's own experience?

7 Schubert's social music: the "forgotten genres"

Margaret Notley

The conviviality of Schubert's milieu thoroughly colors our image of him. It seems fitting that his contemporaries should have known him best not only for his Lieder but also for his work in other genres conducive to friendly music-making by amateurs. This social music included part-songs and dances for solo piano, as well as pieces for two pianists at one instrument – a medium, Alfred Einstein noted, that is "symbolic of friendship."[1] Because they suited the tastes of the rising middle classes and the configuration of the Viennese music world, many such compositions by Schubert were published and performed during his lifetime, yet they are often overlooked today. Even in his Vienna, sociability would not usually have been considered an elevated attribute, and each genre had further limitations. Despite the popularity of the social music, it could never have ranked high in the system of genres.[2]

Einstein, for one, was bothered by the "sociable" Schubert, in particular the composer of the four-hand music, whom he set in opposition to the "deeply serious Schubert," the "real and great Schubert" of the later string quartets and piano sonatas.[3] The implicit standard to which he held Schubert was, of course, Beethoven, the master of the string quartet and piano sonata who expended little effort on his work in the lesser genres.[4] Although their careers overlapped, the two men had come of age as composers in different circumstances: Schubert did not compose for the aristocracy as Beethoven had. If he sometimes wrote with publishers (as opposed to patrons) in mind, Schubert for the most part did not regard his social pieces as mere potboilers. He had, in the words of Alice Hanson, "amateur yet discerning audiences";[5] he made his way in the world with this music, and it was in his interest to compose it well. As Einstein surely recognized, Schubert could be "sociable" and "deeply serious" at the same time.

This particular mixing of categories may also reflect the character of musical life in Vienna at a time when distinctions between private and public, amateur and professional, social event and concert did not always hold. Because no concert hall yet existed,[6] there were few fully public performances; the city's musical life revolved instead around private and semi-public events. At some soirées, accomplished Viennese musicians who did not necessarily make their living as performers played and sang with professionals. The stated purposes of the "Evening Entertainments" (*Abendunterhaltungen*), the semi-public concerts of the Gesellschaft der Musikfreunde, included "musical activity and pleasure," but also "the promotion of conviviality among the music lovers of our city of residence."[7]

While this environment for a time gave importance to music that facilitated social intercourse, these genres eventually merged with others or faded into obscurity. Schubert did not manage to change their standing. Still, he composed some of his most vivid, inspired music in these "forgotten genres." What possibilities did he find in them, and how did he work around the aesthetic tone and other compositional features that defined and limited them? How compromised was each kind of music by its social function? In what ways do these compositions relate to his works in the higher genres? Since the answers differ for his dances, piano duets, and partsongs, each requires a separate story.

Schubert's dances for piano solo

The passion for dancing in Biedermeier Vienna made publishers especially receptive to Schubert's dances for solo piano. His first instrumental compositions to appear in print were the *Originaltänze* (D365), published as Op. 9 in 1821. Seven more collections came out between 1823 and his death in 1828; additional dances appeared in anthologies.[8] Publishers rushed all of this music into the market for *Fasching*, the climax of the dancing season in Catholic Vienna.

Schubert composed examples of most of the dances popular at the time. In his early years, he wrote a number of minuets and, in the 1820s, one cotillion and two galops. Throughout his life, he cultivated the écossaise, a duple country-dance imported from Great Britain. His triple-meter waltzes, Ländler, and German dances, however, sound most characteristically Schubertian and inspired a host of later composers; I will therefore focus on them here. Schubert himself almost invariably referred to these as "Ländler" or "Deutsche Tänze" – only on one extant manuscript, apparently, does he call a dance a "Walzer" – but his publishers most often preferred to issue them as waltzes.[9]

Schubert's dances, which number approximately five hundred, would seem to epitomize the ephemerality of most social music. According to the reports of his friends, he improvised these minuscule pieces for their dancing and listening pleasure in the evening, and on the following morning sometimes wrote down those that he liked (*SMF* 121). Since they appear to have a place somewhere between compositions and recorded improvisations, how seriously should we take them?[10] He composed functional rather than stylized dances, so he worked under clear technical constraints, four- or eight-measure phrases and small forms with two sections, each to be repeated. While Maurice J. E. Brown deemed "Schubert's elevation of the short dance ... comparable to his elevation of the Lied,"[11] he believed these restrictions made the first genre intrinsically insignificant, whether improvised or not. Brown nevertheless stressed the fascination of Schubert's dances as "notes" in a kind of musical "journal" – this would apply especially, of course, to the dances as they appear in the manuscripts – and he traced the transformation of one Ländler into a section of the Scherzo in the D Minor String Quartet, "Death and the Maiden" (D810).[12]

Brown also raised the possibility, although he gave no examples, that these improvised "jottings" might give us a glimpse of Schubert trying out particular compositional and instrumental techniques. A group of Ländler within the *Walzer, Ländler, und Ecossaisen*, Op. 18 (D145, numbers 4, 6, 7, 8, 9, and 12), all in D flat major and taken from one autograph, seem to do just that. (Brown compiled a catalogue of Schubert's dance manuscripts, in which this one, containing altogether eight Ländler, is number 38.[13]) In this set the composer embroidered plain harmonies arranged in repetitive patterns, using a variety of pianistic effects: striking articulations and shifting between registers, along with trills and other kinds of figuration. If a continuum between improvisation and work is hypothesized, these dances probably lie close to the first category.

A group from the next manuscript (Brown's MS 39) show a different kind of preoccupation. Schubert entered these five dances as F sharp major "Deutsche Tänze" in his autograph, but they came out as F major waltzes in the *Originaltänze* (numbers 32–36). The dances, which bear the date March 8, 1821,[14] play with the possibilities of modal mixture, in other words, of borrowing (flatted) notes and chords from the parallel minor key. In each the chromatic inflections underpin his interpretation of the genre's even phrases and divided form.

The division in the middle of the dances works as a signal for change.[15] In numbers 32 and 34, for example, the section before the double bar is tonally closed; the flatted notes do not enter until after that cadence. Schubert built the two openings in otherwise contrasting ways, and this influenced what happens thereafter. Like many additional dances by him, number 32 does not begin on the tonic. This gives an extra lilt to the initial eight measures, a period or pair of balanced four-measure phrases.

A more subdued period, self-enclosed in D flat major after the double bar, acts as a foil (see Ex. 7.1).

Schubert constructed the opening eight measures of number 34 in the less balanced form of a sentence: the second four-measure phrase seems to move more rapidly than the first.[16] A dissonant (German-sixth) harmony helps maintain the quicker pace after the double bar, in a prolongation of the dominant ($D\flat$ – C – B – C in the bass) that lasts until the final measure. All five dances let us see the composer linking modal mixture with nuances in his handling of the form – do they document his first inspirations?

Certain other dances unequivocally are works rather than improvisations. The thirteenth of the *Valses sentimentales*, Op. 50 (D779), stands out for the originality of its form, the continuous two-part writing in the right hand, and even the marking "zart" ("tenderly") – exceptional in this repertory by Schubert. Although the beauty of most of these dances lies in fleeting subtleties that resist analysis, the intricacy of this one invites it (see Ex. 7.2).

This waltz opens, as did the previously discussed dance, with a two-measure introduction: the piece in effect begins in measure 3, on the supertonic. Series of suspensions draw the first phrase out into an indissoluble eight-measure span. A new motif (mm. 16–17) in the second phrase must break the whirling pattern to bring the section to a close. When this cadential motif reappears twice after the double bar in a bright C sharp major (mm. 22–23, 26–27), its new placement in each four-measure phrase entails yet another such phrase, in which the motif completes itself and the C sharp major triad resolves by chromatic magic to an A^7 (m. 29), thus preparing the off-tonic reentry of the original melody and, with the syncopated phrase rhythm, creating an elegant dovetailing in the form.

This waltz holds its own as an "autonomous" aesthetic object. But does it make more sense in general to consider the possibility of dance *collections* as works? In a few manuscripts, certainly, a closed key-scheme or a coda indicates that Schubert conceived a group as a cycle, just as these same features serve to unify some of the published sets.[17] The twelve *Valses nobles*, Op. 77 (D969), for example, are organized around C major in this pattern: C–A–C–G–C–C–E–A–A minor–F–C–C. The character of these waltzes may also mark them as a cycle, for they are the most extroverted collection, as well as pianistically the most difficult because of the many passages in octaves.

In a recent article, David Brodbeck has pointed out that at least one group of dances was unlikely to have had its origins in improvisation at a party: Schubert wrote them while receiving treatment for syphilis,

Example 7.1 *Originaltänze*, Op. 9 Nos. 32 and 34 (D365)

possibly while in the hospital.[18] With Einstein and Brown,[19] Brodbeck notes the unvarying high quality of the Ländler in this manuscript (Brown's MS 47), none of which appeared in print during Schubert's life-time. These dances were finally published in 1864 in an anonymous edition (Op. Post. 171, D790) by Johannes Brahms, who had become an ardent collector of Schubert autographs during his first years in Vienna.

Example 7.2 *Valses sentimentales,* Op. 50 No. 13 (D779)

No doubt because he recognized the fineness of all twelve Ländler, Brahms chose to maintain the integrity of Schubert's manuscript. Yet the set begins and ends in different keys, and there are no other overall unifying features. Five years later Brahms selected Ländler from several sources, much as publishers during Schubert's lifetime had done, to make a companion volume of twenty dances.[20] He carefully ordered the chosen Ländler, but he did not try to make a cycle.

For the most part Schubert's sets do seem to be loosely strung gems. When other composers fell under their spell, though, they responded by creating more tightly organized collections, in this way solving the problem of the brief forms. In a rapturous review, Robert Schumann made the *Deutsche Tänze* from Schubert's Op. 33 (D783) whole in his own imagination by transforming them into a ballroom scene.[21] He went on to write dramatized sets of his own, including *Papillons* (Op. 2, 1829–31) and *Carnaval* (Op. 9, composed in 1833–35). While *Carnaval* contains a *Valse noble* that at least initially follows the style of Schubert's collection, the earlier *Papillons* seem more continuously indebted to him. To unify this piece, Schumann opened and closed in D major, bringing back the first waltz during the finale in a programmatic fade-out. Maurice Ravel's homage to Schubert, the *Valses nobles et sentimentales* (composed in 1911), likewise centers around his own version of G major; during the last dance, fragments from all but one of the seven earlier waltzes reappear. In the *Soirées de Vienne* (published in 1851), Franz Liszt used actual dances by Schubert as the basis for nine concert pieces, providing introductions, elaborations, transitions, and codas around and between unadorned appearances of the original dances.

Already in 1821, Carl Maria von Weber had published a glittering concert piece with a programmatic introduction, the famous *Aufforderung zum Tanz*. There is no evidence that Schubert aspired to compose a similar kind of work or even to have his dances performed outside the home. His constant cultivation of the genre did, however, leave its traces in his larger compositions: in his waltz- or Ländler-like "minuets" and "scherzos" – especially in their trios – and in the rhythmic character of passages like the second theme of the "Unfinished" Symphony (D759).

Compositions for piano, four hands

Domestic performances have always provided the only natural venue for piano duets. Because private music-making was centrally important and, too, because an increasing number of middle-class families could afford to buy pianos, the market for four-hand music flourished in Vienna in the 1820s.[22] Many of Schubert's piano duets date from his Hungarian sojourns in 1818 and 1824 as the musician-in-residence of the Esterházy family in Zseliz; he may well have written others specifically for publication. During his lifetime, a higher proportion of his compositions in this genre than in any other appeared in print, and with good reason: he was the greatest of all composers of four-hand music.

If the unstylized condition and brevity of the form limited Schubert's dances for piano solo, the unfortunate, homebound medium itself kept his four-hand music from rising in the hierarchy of genres. But do piano duets constitute a genre after all? Carl Dahlhaus observed that most musical genres are defined by a number of separate attributes: thus, the string quartet of the late eighteenth and nineteenth centuries is distinguished by its formal layout and sophisticated tone as well as by the group of players that give it its name; while a fugue, characterized only by a compositional procedure, is "underdetermined" as a genre.[23] Is four-hand music more than a medium? Can we speak of Schubert's piano duets as a genre within at least his own output?

If we exclude three of his piano duets from consideration, patterns of manner and affect, if not of form, do seem to mark Schubert's four-hand music as a genre. The works that do not fit are the sonatas composed in the summers at Zseliz, the B flat Sonata (D617) from 1818 and the "Grand Duo" (D812) from 1824, along with the Fugue in E Minor (D952) from 1828. In its form, naturally, but also its almost consistently elevated style, the "Grand Duo" in particular resembles the later solo sonatas rather than the other duets: it would have fallen into Einstein's category of the "deeply serious Schubert," if he had allowed any four-hand piece to do so. The fugue, which reflects an intensified interest in counterpoint in the final months of his life, stands outside the mainstream of his work altogether.

Einstein shrewdly observed that the "Grand Duo" could not be an arrangement of a symphony, as Robert Schumann and Joseph Joachim (among others) had suspected, because "Schubert, as a symphonist, would have limited himself to a quite different range of modulations."[24] He was similarly aware of an essential stylistic difference between the piano sonatas and most of the four-hand music, but the pejorative cast of his comments marred his insight. Despite his enthusiasm for many of the piano duets, he valorized the later piano sonatas and string quartets at their expense, focusing his criticism of the composer's "sociable" side on an easygoing manner and, especially, a tendency toward facile brilliance.

No piano duet by Schubert is more "easygoing" yet eloquent than the A Major Rondo (D951) from 1828, "the apotheosis of all Schubert's compositions for four hands."[25] After a thirty-two-measure refrain, the first episode moves to the key of the dominant with a melodious absence of drama, arriving at the official second theme – this is a sonata-rondo – only in measure 69. Schubert's leisurely approach works because he handles the internal rhythms of individual phrases and larger sections with consummate skill. This understated mastery and the tasteful ornamentation throughout the composition make it sound unfailingly gracious; only at the end of the recapitulation, in the passage beginning with a deceptive cadence to ♭VI in measure 241, does suppressed yearning break through the good manners (the outburst in the central episode is more predictable).

Characterizing the four-hand style as "sociable" seems appropriate, but that quality should not be underrated. The function of this music was, indeed, to promote pleasant social relations. To fulfill this role, Schubert accommodated a variety of musical tastes. For example, while he rarely used imitative counterpoint in the solo sonatas, he lavished it on the piano duets. The four-hand works also emphasize less complicated attractions: instrumental brilliance, as well as picturesque rhythms and sonorities presented for their own sake. An impulse to provide entertainment becomes evident in the kinds of compositions represented. With the B flat Sonata, the seventeen duets published through 1828 included six individual marches or collections of them, four sets of themes and variations, two groups of polonaises, two rondos, a single overture and divertissement.[26] When one publisher solicited a piano duet, he specified "a fairly brilliant work of not too large dimensions, such as a grand polonaise or rondo with an introduction, &c., or a fantasy" (*SDB* 439).

The *Divertissement à l'hongroise* (D818), as befits its name, may offer the most extreme example of the "divertimento aesthetic" in Schubert's piano duets. In this work, he surrendered to the considerable delights of an exotic primitivism. By itself, the first of the three movements features virtually the entire array of effects that make up the *style hongrois*: short phrases, dotted rhythms, drone fifths (mm. 71–72), melodic augmented seconds (mm. 81 and 136–37), imitation of the cimbalon (e.g., in mm. 15 and 20), heavy encrustation with grace notes and other embellishments.[27] This movement, moreover, forgoes almost any semblance of development or, at times, even large-scale harmonic direction. The lengthy section between measures 93 and 123, for instance, comprises a number of short repeating strains that veer between B flat major and D minor, in a manner that seems more wayward than intentionally ambiguous, before finally heading back toward the tonic, G minor, after measure 124. (On another level, of course, Schubert deliberately chose to compose primitivistically.) Although the remaining two movements maintain the colorful style, they adhere more closely to formal and harmonic norms of Western Classical music from this period. The second movement, with its spondaic rhythms and air of relentless melancholy, anticipates the opening of the Andante in the "Great" C Major Symphony (D944), but Schubert designed it as a conventional march – albeit a Hungarian one in C minor – with trio (in A flat major). And while the rondo-finale displays the folkloric traits of the opening movement, Schubert organized it around a harmonically focused refrain in rounded binary form.

Schubert's piano duets inhabit the same expressive universe as his chamber music with piano.[28] The two genres, furthermore, have a technical feature in common. A pianistic texture in the "Trout" Quintet (D667) and both piano trios derives from the four-hand practice of doubling a melody at the octave in the two hands of the primo player.[29] (See, for instance, mm. 26 ff. in the first movement of the B flat Trio, Op. 99 (D898); mm. 23–41 in the Andante con moto of the E flat Trio, Op. 100 (D929); and the first variation of the "Trout" Quintet.) Unlike most chamber music, though, Schubert's piano duets often do not bother to pretend that the players are equal individuals.

What, then, does the symbiotic relationship between the duo-pianists have to offer? Because the form of theme and variations emphasizes differences in texture, Schubert's four-hand sets demonstrate the compositional possibilities most clearly. Each of the summers in Zseliz produced not only a sonata, but also a set of variations for piano duet. The *Variationen über ein französischen Lied* from the summer of 1818, Op. 10 (D624), were Schubert's first published four-hand work (which he dedicated to Beethoven). As in the chamber movements based on *Die Forelle* (D667/iv), the operatic duet "Gelagert unter'm hellen Dach der Bäume" (D803/iv), and *Der Tod und das Mädchen* (D810/ii), most of these variations retain the melody of the theme, usually doubled in the two hands of the primo player, although sometimes divided between the two pianists (for example, in the sixth variation). An even finer piece, the *Andantino varié* published in 1827, Op. 84 No. 1 (D823), includes more learned and more ethereal four-hand textures. In the third variation, the primo left hand has the melody, as the two right hands engage in imitation at the distance of a half-measure. And in the fourth variation, the primo right hand plays high, delicate figuration, while the secondo right hand and primo left hand share the melody; in the first half of measures 99 and 100, it is clear only to the players which one has it. Schubert's late variations on a theme from Hérold's *Marie* (D908, published as Op. 82 in 1827), in contrast, show the noisy excitement possible in four ostinato patterns layered on a piano. This set enjoyed considerable success, prompting one publishing firm to ask him twice for similar duets "which, without sacrificing any of your individuality, are yet not difficult to grasp" (*SDB* 735; also, 814).

Schubert's greatest set of variations may be the four-hand *Variations sur un thème original* in A flat (D813), composed during his second summer in Zseliz and subsequently performed to appreciative audiences on several occasions (*SDB* 363, 370, 401). This work, too, is distinguished by felicitous imitative counterpoint, with the lines divided variously between the two players, as in the second variation, or the two hands of the primo pianist, as in the third. The seventh variation stands out as most remarkable for its deliberately ambiguous chromaticism: it hovers between F minor and C minor before finally moving to the dominant of

A flat in preparation for the last variation. Diversion of any ordinary sort is hardly the point here, but the set does conclude on a much lighter note; when Schubert aimed at a loftier style in his four-hand music, it rarely remained unmixed with simpler pleasures.

Schubert juxtaposed the elevated and the entertaining most starkly in the Allegro in A Minor (D947) from 1828, which came out posthumously under the spurious title "Storms of Life" ("Lebensstürme"). This sonata-form movement opens in a forceful Beethovenian vein with the quasi-orchestral massiveness possible in the four-hand medium. The thematic restatement that begins in measure 37 would typically merge with a form-defining modulation. Schubert makes this second statement harmonically richer than the original, yet it leads only to an arpeggiation, in low octaves, of the dominant-seventh chord (mm. 81–88). At this point, he creates one of his most miraculous moments: from the dominant seventh he takes the leading-tone, the tensest note in tonal music, with no mediation as a secondary tonic (m. 89). A new theme is presented in A flat major, after which the piece shifts by another common-tone modulation to the orthodox key of the relative major (C). The unstable, visionary effect is maintained through a diaphanous texture characteristic of the medium: the primo right hand plays high figuration against a repetition of the new theme in the middle register and low octaves in the secondo left hand. After the heroic beginning and otherworldly second group, the exposition changes stylistic gears, becoming in a lengthy closing section conventionally – sociably – brilliant.

The partsongs

Like the other genres considered in this chapter, Schubert's partsongs had their roots in gregarious music-making. The Austrian traditions that he received remain murky, but most scholars agree on a few points. Although his partsongs became staples of the choral repertory later in the century, he wrote them in what appears to have been the Austrian custom of one singer to a part.[30] While he composed for both mixed (SATB) and unmixed male and female voices, male songs predominated in his work, as in that of his predecessors: all but one of the nineteen partsongs published before his death were for male voices only.[31] Whatever the particular medium, the partsong as he inherited it seems to have provided less an aesthetic than a convivial experience. An anecdote by Anselm Hüttenbrenner suggests the casualness, in particular, of many of the male songs – the Biedermeier equivalent of the barbershop quartet. Hüttenbrenner related that Schubert and he would get together with two other students every Thursday to sight-read new vocal quartets by each of them, and he recalled that once, having forgotten to write a quartet beforehand, Schubert composed one on the spot (*SMF* 179). He later (1818) wrote a piece for mixed voices actually entitled *Die Geselligkeit* (D609) – "conviviality" – and he produced *Trinklieder* throughout his life.

Unlike his four-hand music, Schubert's partsongs proved able to bridge the gap, admittedly sometimes blurred, between domestic and concert performance. In the *Abendunterhaltungen* presented by the Gesellschaft der Musikfreunde in the 1820s, a vocal quartet by Schubert often ended an entertainment that had opened with a string quartet.[32] These partsongs also appeared on programs in public spaces like the Kärntnerthor Theater. Even before they were performed publicly, he had begun to try out new compositional possibilities that pushed at the limits of the genre, writing exquisite but small-scale works, presumably for the pleasure of just a few close friends and himself. Later, however, he *redefined* the partsong to make it more fully worthy of performance in the largest halls. The upward mobility of the genre had a predictable effect on him: he became ambitious for it.

In contrast to both the dances and the four-hand music, it is possible to chart a clear development in the partsongs. I will therefore discuss Schubert's work in this genre chronologically, beginning with his student years. As part of his lessons with Antonio Salieri, he most likely set German as well as Italian texts in three- and four-voice textures of various kinds.[33] After completing his studies, he initially preferred the chordal textures and strophic settings of the popular idiom. He appears to have first experimented with innovative approaches in two partsongs from 1817. In *Lied im Freien* (TTBB, Salis-Seewis, D572) he set the stanzas in contrasting textures and keys, using vaguely illustrative figuration. In the fourth stanza ("There dip and rise"), for example, repetitive oscillating figures within a meandering movement from B flat minor to B major evoke simultaneously gleams of light on a brook and the flickering consciousness of the observer. Madrigalesque tendencies stand out even more in his first partsong setting of Goethe's *Gesang der Geister über den Wassern* (TTBBB, D538).[34] Schubert broke this sublime poem into small grammatical units; inevitably, the meaning of the whole got lost in the proliferation of cadences and musical images. In later partsongs, he was to create more economical sign-systems in the service of high-minded themes: for example, the merging of subject and object (Nature with a capital N), barely suggested in these works. And in a number of these later compositions, the return of the opening, a feature of both settings from 1817, would become an event of great significance; he began to compose three-part forms in which what happens in the middle transforms the reappearance of the first section, itself now made longer and weightier.

These trends came into focus in two works from April 1819. Schubert's setting of Goethe's *Nur wer die Sehnsucht kennt* (TTBBB, D656), the fourth of six essays at Mignon's song, demonstrates his ever-widening conception of what could be treated as a partsong: a girl's lyric sung by five men! Here he relied almost totally on harmonic effects, lush even by his standards, using figuration only at the rhetorical break in the poem: "Es schwindelt mir, es brennt mein Eingeweide."[35] In *Ruhe, schönstes Glück der Erde* (TTBB, unknown poet, D657), Schubert used three rhythmic signs as imagery. The first stanza, set in a rocking 6/8 meter, apostrophizes "Rest," comparing its blessed calm to "a grave among flowers." After the middle stanza has introduced a dotted rhythm to represent "the storms of the heart," the lullaby rhythm returns at the words "are quiet" and "rock to sleep." With "as they grow, as they increase," the hemiola version of 6/8 comes in as a second sign for unrest. The third and final stanza begins as a beautifully varied version of the opening, but the hemiolas reappear briefly when the poet speaks of the soul "rising from the grave." The ending suggests that the desired "rest" is the union of the soul with Nature in death.

In December 1820 Schubert set Moses Mendelssohn's translation of the *Twenty-third Psalm* (SSAA with piano) for his new friend Anna Fröhlich, who taught at the Vienna Conservatory. This celebrated setting received many performances by her pupils over the years, from a semi-public examination concert in 1821 under the auspices of the Gesellschaft der Musikfreunde to a "Grand Pupils' Concert" in 1828 at the Kärntnerthor Theater. Fröhlich also commissioned several other works for her students, including one of his late masterpieces.[36] An account of Schubert's partsongs is, however, largely a chronicle of his works for male voices.[37]

The concert of March 7, 1821, at the Kärntnerthor Theater that featured *Erlkönig* marked Schubert's first breakthrough with the Viennese public. Also on the program were the partsongs *Das Dörfchen* (TTBB, Gottfried August Bürger, D598) and the final version of *Gesang der Geister über den Wassern* (D714). These represent the poles of his mature work in the genre: the former, his unpretentious, genial vein; the latter – for the unusual medium of four tenors and four basses with instrumental accompaniment by two violas, two cellos, and a double bass – his aspiration to compose an artistically ambitious concert piece. Yet *Das Dörfchen* was an outstanding success – the audience demanded it be repeated – while *Gesang der Geister* failed utterly.

Schubert had sketched *Das Dörfchen* in December 1817 and completed it in 1818; he composed it even as he tried out radically new possibilities in other partsongs. In this one, though, he had come up with a formula that worked over and over with both audiences and critics: a sentimental text set for male voices in square-cut phrases and conventional harmonic progressions, mostly homophonic but with a simple canon toward the end. The mutability of taste becomes an issue in Schubert's social music only in trying to account for the popularity of this composition and its successors. What did they hear in *Das Dörfchen* that we do not? And how could they not have recognized the genius of his Goethe-setting?

Most likely Schubert composed the new version of *Gesang der Geister* expressly for the concert at the Kärntnerthor Theater. He began working with the text again during the eventful month of December 1820 – writing first for two tenors and two basses with piano accompaniment before settling on the larger ensemble – and he finished in February, shortly before the concert. The instrumental accompaniment permitted transitions to bind together the various sections of the poem, thus avoiding the fragmentation of the earlier version. In this final setting, he put much greater weight on the overtly symbolic first and final stanzas than on the pictorial center. The conceit that frames Goethe's poem in the outer stanzas compares the human soul to water, while the middle develops the image of a waterfall: hitting against cliffs on its way into a chasm; gliding through a valley; and, finally, being stirred up by its "lover," the wind. Schubert opposed the higher and lower registers in his gloriously dark sound-world to suggest both the vastness of the waterfall and the loftiness of Goethe's symbolism. Most of the time his devices, like dividing the eight voices into tenors versus basses, do not serve precise mimetic purposes (see, for example, measures 19–22 and 27–30). When they do, the effect is astounding, as in measures 97–100, where the change in register and dynamics portrays the cascade's fall into the abyss (with the double bass at the bottom) after its "angry, stepwise foaming" against the cliffs (see Ex. 7.3).

Walter Dürr and Dietrich Berke have argued persuasively that an undated letter from Schubert to Leopold Sonnleithner, in which he declined an offer from the Gesellschaft der Musikfreunde to perform a partsong, can only refer to the debacle of *Gesang der Geister*:

> You know yourself how the later quartets were received: people have had enough of them. True, I might succeed in inventing some new form, but one may not count with certainty on anything of the kind. But as my future fate greatly concerns me after all, you, who take your share in this, as I flatter myself, will yourself admit that I must go forward cautiously.   (*SDB* 264)[38]

Schubert had created a "new form," but the audience had not accepted his attempt to transmute this social genre. During the next few years he

Example 7.3 *Gesang der Geister über den Wassern* (D714), mm. 94–102

made an artistic retreat in it, composing only what he knew the public wanted. In 1822–23, three sets of partsongs appeared in print, two of them with *ad libitum* piano or guitar accompaniments.[39] In *Die Nacht* (D983C) from the third set (Op. 17), all short and unaccompanied, he carefully paced the words, working sensitively with a chordal texture and a restricted range of harmonies. Most of the partsongs from this period, however, have lost the appeal that they obviously had then.

Of more interest are Schubert's settings in 1825 of texts from Sir Walter Scott's *Lady of the Lake*, which included, with five Lieder, two strophic partsongs: *Coronach* for female voices (SSA with piano, D836) and *Bootgesang* for male voices (TTBB with piano, D835). Schubert seems to have intended these seven pieces, published as Op. 52 the following year, to be sung as a cycle. With *Der Gondelfahrer* (TTBB with piano, D809) in 1824, and then *Wehmuth* (TTBB, D825) and *Mondenschein* (TTBBB, D875) in 1826, he resumed the imaginative imagery and flexible three-part forms of the earlier years.[40] This new surge of creativity – or faith in the audience for this genre – reached a climax in three late works: *Grab und Mond* (TTBB, D893) and *Nachthelle* (T, TBBB with piano, D892), both to texts by Johann Seidl and dated September 1826, and *Ständchen* (A, SSAA with piano, Franz Grillparzer, D920) from July 1827. The dialogue between grave and moon, two stanzas with a free line in the middle, gave rise to an idiosyncratic two-section form. Schubert conveyed the poem's eeriness through deliberate solecisms in the part-writing: incomplete chords with peculiar doublings. *Grab und Mond* appeared with the more conventional *Wein und Liebe* (D901) in an anthology of works aimed at amateur male singing groups, and received critical praise for its outstanding originality in a part of the repertory usually dedicated to mediocrity (*SDB* 763–64).

Schubert wrote *Nachthelle* and *Ständchen*, on the other hand, as concert pieces. His ambitiousness comes through with special force in the Seidl setting; it is evident even in the range of dynamics: from *ppp* (at the end of the first section) to *fff* (at the end of the middle section). High, portato chords in the right hand of the pianist set the scene: stars and moonlight glistening over a group of houses. In the central stanzas, the poetic subject welcomes the radiance into the "house" of his heart, as he imagines the boundaries between what he sees and himself breaking. A traditionally bright modulation from E flat to C major in a piano interlude prepares the transfigured return of the opening.

Ständchen, like such earlier partsongs as *Gebet* (SATB, D815) and *Des Tages Weihe* (SATB, D763), was an occasional work, in this case a birthday present from Anna Fröhlich to one of her young pupils, but it forms a companion piece to *Nachthelle*. In both compositions, Schubert made effective use of a solo versus tutti texture to spin out phrases and create sections on a grand scale; in other respects, they complement rather than resemble each other. Each work has three clear sections. The tonal scheme overflows the borders of the sections in *Nachthelle*, with a modulation early in the first and no return to the tonic until well in the third. In keeping with his altogether more moderate conception in *Ständchen*, the first and third sections are self-contained. For while the text of *Nachthelle* and its setting portray an intense subjectivity, the subject-matter of *Ständchen* connects it to the partsong tradition of conviviality: this serenade celebrates friendship. *Ständchen* received its first performance at a birthday party in a private garden. Fröhlich's students later sang it at an "Evening Entertainment," and Schubert chose it for the concert of his compositions on March 26, 1828. His work in the social genres culminates fittingly in *Ständchen*: a piece suitable for performance in all the available venues, and a delicately witty paean to the pleasures of being with other people.

Schubert composed this music with the audiences of his time, not an abstract ideal listener, in mind. While certain partsongs may best be regarded as artifacts of social history, the success of most of this repertory speaks well for those audiences and his understanding of their tastes. The rejection of the somber *Gesang der Geister* represents the only significant failure. Perhaps he miscalculated a new audience in his first public concert, since we know that a slightly later private performance did succeed (*SMF* 375–76). Maybe, also, Einstein was only partially wrong when he asserted that "Schubert is more popular in his 'sociable' and easy-going guise than when he is uncompromising and great" – wrong because he placed sociability and greatness in opposition. *Gesang der Geister* can no more be classified as social music than can the C Major String Quintet (D956). Nor did Schubert compose the "Grand Duo" and *Nachthelle* in his sociable manner. But *Ständchen* with, among other works, the four-hand Rondo in A and the thirteenth *Valse sentimentale* represent summits in that style. More temperate than "uncompromising," these masterpieces of subtle phrase rhythms, too, are the great Schubert.

8 Schubert's piano music: probing the human condition

William Kinderman

FOR ALFRED BRENDEL ON HIS 65TH BIRTHDAY

Long underestimated, Schubert's compositions for piano have recently begun to assume their rightful place beside Beethoven's legacy as works of almost unparalleled expressive range and depth. Several factors contributed to their neglect: the fact that much of this music remained unpublished during Schubert's lifetime; the dominance, in these works, of musical expression over technical virtuosity; and the overpowering influence of Beethoven, whose works set standards that are not directly applicable to Schubert. Complaints of an alleged looseness of organization in Schubert's music, as expressed by critics like Theodor W. Adorno, who once described Schubert's thematic structure as a "pot-pourri," have often arisen from an inadequate understanding of the aesthetic idiom of these works.[1] Schubert's music is less deterministic than Beethoven's in that it does not present a self-sufficient sequence of events; it seems that the music could have taken a different turn at many points. Yet these very shifts in perspective are often exploited by Schubert as structural elements in the musical form, and they also embody a latent psychological symbolism. A key to this symbolism is found in Schubert's songs, in which the protagonist, or Romantic wanderer – who assumes the role of the lyrical subject – is so often confronted by an indifferent or hostile reality. Musically, Schubert uses a combination of heightened thematic contrast, juxtaposition of major and minor keys, and abrupt modulation to reflect this duality between internal and external experience, or imagination and perception – between the beautiful, bright dreams of the protagonist, on the one hand, and a bleak external reality, on the other. Beginning around 1820, analogous procedures of thematic contrast appear in Schubert's instrumental music, and these devices contribute to the remarkable development in his musical style, culminating in the three profound sonatas of 1828 (D958–60). Our discussion will focus first on the solo sonatas and then on the most important pieces in other forms, including music for piano duet.

The sonatas

Schubert's output of sonatas embraces twenty works, of which several are incomplete, including the impressive C Major Sonata of 1825 (D840), the so-called "Reliquie" Sonata. Some authors count as many as twenty-four, but three of these – in E Major (D154), in C sharp Minor (D655), and in E Minor (D769A) – are too fragmentary to be effectively performed, whereas the Sonata in E flat Major (D568) is a transposed and elaborated version of the Sonata in D flat Major (D567).[2] Least familiar are the first eleven sonatas, from the years 1815–18. This group of works became more accessible with the publication in 1976 of the third volume of sonatas in the Henle edition.[3] Basic uncertainties remain concerning these early sonatas: some movements were left incomplete; some sonatas lack finales; and suspicions that certain movements belong together as parts of the same sonata are in some cases unavoidably speculative.[4] Because of such uncertainties, András Schiff included only complete movements in his recent comprehensive recording of the sonatas, apart from the first movements of D571 in F sharp Minor and D625 in F Minor, which he describes as "fragments of such extraordinary musical quality that their exclusion would mean a major loss."[5]

Schubert of course left fragmentary masterpieces in other genres, most notably the *Quartettsatz* in C Minor of 1820 (D703) and the "Unfinished" Symphony in B Minor of 1822 (D759). When viewed in the aesthetic context of early Romanticism, his inspired sonata fragments can be distanced from the odium of failure and valued in terms of what Friedrich Schlegel described as a "futuristic" quality. The artistic fragment is thereby conceived as "the subjective core of an object of becoming, the preparation of a desired synthesis. [It] is no longer seen as something not achieved, as a remnant, but instead as a foreshadowing, a promise."[6] Yet Schubert's critical judgment in aborting unpromising later movements to masterly torsos deserves respect.[7] His struggle to sustain the level of artistic accomplishment is reflected in the sonata fragments, which occupy a significant place in his creative development. A piece like the opening Allegro moderato of the F sharp Minor Sonata (D571) from 1817, as Dieter Schnebel has observed, already displays that uncanny suspension of sound and time so characteristic of many later Schubertian works.[8] Here soft rising arpeggiations of the left-hand accompaniment open a tonal space filled out by the main theme, which yields in turn to a thematic variant of the accompaniment figure. As the bleak melancholy of F sharp minor gives way to the brighter tonal sphere of D major, the flowing figuration and subtle harmonic nuances enhance the change, elaborating the sound as if in resistance to the inevitable passage of time or the transience of life itself.

Schubert's fragmentary piano sonatas of earlier years often reflect a tension between Classical models and his own distinctive evolving style. The influence of Beethoven's sonatas tends to surface in Schubert's works in the corresponding keys: D279 in C Major shows the impact of the "Waldstein" Sonata, Op. 53, whereas the Rondo in E Major (D506) was evidently inspired by that of Beethoven's Op. 90: a lyrical rondo in the major mode follows a terse opening movement in E minor. Among the most impressive of these early pieces is the F Minor Sonata (D625/505) from 1818, whose opening Allegro of D625 shows a complex affinity to Beethoven's "Appassionata" Sonata, Op. 57, in the same key.[9] In this F Minor Sonata, though not in all of its companions, the young Schubert breaks free of the burden and anxiety of influence. His resourceful reinterpretation of such compositional models became an abiding trait, which reached its culmination only in 1828, in works like the rondo finale of the A Major Sonata (D959).

In the earlier A Major Sonata (D664), a lyrical Allegro moderato and a meditative slow movement are joined to a vivacious, waltz-like finale – a movement which may have helped inspire the finale of Schumann's Piano Concerto, Op. 54. This sonata was written in Steyr during the summer of 1819, when Schubert also composed his popular "Trout" Quintet (D667) in the same key. The three movements of D664 are linked through a subtle network of motivic relations. The appoggiatura B–A from the end of the first movement becomes the basic motif of the ensuing Andante, where it is varied and reharmonized: at the reprise this figure is treated in dialogue between the hands, and in the coda Schubert darkens the inflection to B♭–A, thereby setting into relief the descending scale from B which launches the exuberant finale. That falling scale, in turn, balances the ascending scalar passagework from the opening movement, as is first heard at the close of the lyrical opening period of this Allegro moderato. This delightfully intimate sonata is not untouched by darker shadows, but it displays little of the dramatic contrasts and formal expansiveness characteristic of later sonatas.

Since so many of Schubert's works remained unpublished during his lifetime, their opus numbers usually lack any chronological significance. Although a relatively early work, the A Major Sonata (D664) bears the posthumous opus number 120. Even more misleading are the opus numbers of Schubert's three sonatas in the key of A minor. The A Minor Sonata (D784) from 1823, for instance, received opus number 143, yet it was composed two years earlier than the four-movement Sonata Op. 42 (D845) – the first of the three sonatas published during Schubert's lifetime. Like his still earlier A Minor Sonata of 1817 (which was posthumously published with the still higher opus number of 164) Op. 143

Example 8.1 Sonata in A Minor, Op. 42 (D845), first movement, mm. 1–8

contains only three movements and lacks a scherzo or minuet preceding the finale. This is an unusually concentrated work characterized by a somber "orchestral" coloring: the bass accompaniment of the principal theme of the first movement suggests drum rolls and the accents of trombones. As Alfred Einstein has pointed out, the second subjects of the outer movements stand apart, like "visions of paradise" in the major mode;[10] like the wanderer's dreams and recollections of his first lost love in Schubert's song cycle *Winterreise* (D911), these lyrical visions are fragile and transitory, and are dispelled by the return of forceful accents and turbulent music in the minor.

A pair of works from 1825 – the fragmentary C Major Sonata (D840), and the big Sonata in A Minor, Op. 42 (D845) – mark a new stage in Schubert's resourceful treatment of thematic contrast and development within the sonata design. Like all the later sonatas, D845 has a four-movement design. The beginning of the opening Moderato presents a quiet, mysterious, unharmonized motif outlining the tonic triad, followed by a series of chords with a descending bass line (see Ex. 8.1). In measures 4–6, this motif is restated one pitch higher, so that the accented highest tone is F, corresponding to the E of measure 1. This rising step E–F and its transpositions pervade all of the subsequent themes of the movement, and often seem even to control the direction of the harmonic progressions and changes in key. Repeatedly, the vigorous flow of the other themes is interrupted by reappearances of this unison motif in the minor mode from the outset of the work. This motif assumes thereby the character of a motto, or seminal element, out of which the piece evolves through thematic development and variation, and to which it suddenly and repeatedly returns. It is as if this musical material represented an object of contemplation, whose subsequent appearances arrest the action of the more dynamic themes of the sonata form, the underlying substance of which is all prefigured in the opening motto. Such is the nature of Schubert's musical form that the appearances of an important theme or motif can seem spontaneous and surprising, while possessing at the same time a quality of inevitability. In the A Minor Sonata, the return of the original form of the thematic motto at the end of the development is presented in a wonderfully subtle series of modulations, which conceal the

Example 8.2 Sonata in C Major (D840), first movement, mm. 114–18

exact beginning of the recapitulation. The coda, on the other hand, begins with an astonishing and unexpected, yet eminently logical, reinterpretation and enlargement of the rising motivic step E–F as a gateway to a new key area, F major. Relationships such as these are readily heard by the sensitive listener, and it does not require much technical knowledge of music to begin to appreciate them.

As John Reed has pointed out, the expressive associations of this initial unharmonized thematic material in the A Minor Sonata are clarified by its use in a song which is exactly contemporary, *Totengräbers Heimwehe* (D842).[11] Its sinister implications are confirmed here by the words the music is used to accompany: "Abandoned by all, cousin only to death, I wait at the brink, staring longingly into the grave." The A Minor Sonata is only one of a number of important instrumental works by Schubert associated with death, including the D Minor Quartet (D810, with its use of Schubert's song *Der Tod und das Mädchen* [D531]), the Fantasy in F Minor for piano duet, Op. 103 (D940), and the C Minor Piano Sonata from 1828 (D958).

The companion work to D845 is the C Major Sonata (D840) from early 1825 in two movements, the minuet and finale having been left incomplete. This piece is missing from many older editions of Schubert's sonatas. Its opening movement, marked Moderato, is related thematically to the A Minor Sonata, Op. 42, and displays the same close motivic network linking the second subject to the principal theme. The tonal plan is wide ranging: the second subject begins in the remote key of the leading tone, B minor, and the beginning of the recapitulation is here once again merged with the end of the development by an effective series of modulations. The development is forcefully dramatic in character, its climax leading again to B minor, and relies heavily on rhythmic diminution of the opening motif comprising six beats, which are compressed into a figure of triplet eighth notes (see Ex. 8.2). Towards the end of the movement, a powerful chordal passage leads to an emphatic C major cadence but fails to achieve finality, and the Moderato ends quietly, with chords derived from the opening theme. The following slow movement is tragic in character, and it too is linked thematically to the opening subject of the first movement. This unfinished Sonata in C Major is a worthy counterpart among the sonatas to Schubert's "Unfinished" Symphony, and should receive more attention.

The D Major Sonata, Op. 53 (D850), dates from later in 1825, and was written at Gastein in the Austrian Alps, just after Schubert's main period of work on the "Great" C Major Symphony (D944). This was the second sonata published during the composer's lifetime. The work is unusual in the swift and ardent character of the opening Allegro vivace, which demands considerable virtuosity, and in the air of *naïveté* of the rondo finale, which perplexed Robert Schumann.[12] The first movement opens with an emphatic tonic chord, followed by a motif of repeated chords treated in rising sequences. This material assumes a majestic and almost orchestral character at the beginning of the development. The bold and extensive second movement, marked Con moto, also requires a faster tempo than most of Schubert's other slow movements. Its continuity springs from two initial rhythmic motifs permeating the principal and subsidiary themes respectively. The formal plan is that of a rondo, in which the rhythmic motif of the subsidiary theme is combined with – and for a brief, climactic moment overshadows – the final presentation of the principal theme near the conclusion. The scherzo of this sonata is symphonic in scope and character, and introduces rhythmic complications involving a combination of 3/4 and 3/2 meters. The lively and forceful character of the music later gives way to softer passages containing a charming counterpoint of rhythms, in which every second measure contains accents on each beat of music, divided between the hands, and it is with this material that the scherzo quietly ends. In the rondo finale, the appearances of the main theme in the high upper register are increasingly decorated through melodic ornamentation, and are effectively set into relief by the two contrasting episodes, especially the second episode with its turbulent middle section in G minor.

The third and last of the sonatas published in Schubert's lifetime is the Sonata in G Major, Op. 78 (D894), which was written in the fall of 1826, several months after his string quartet in the same key. Older editions of this sonata contain the title "Fantasie" for the first movement.[13] The mood of lyric serenity in which this work begins seems to recall the opening of Beethoven's Fourth Piano Concerto in G Major, Op. 58, especially since the initial, sustained sonorities of the two pieces are virtually identical. In both works, the opening G major chord – with B as the highest pitch – is magically transformed by a later shift into the tonality of the mediant, B major, a goal which in Schubert's sonata is reached through B minor, a key more closely related to the tonic. The second subject of this movement comprises a playful, dance-like theme subsequently elaborated in an ornamental variation. In the development, abbreviated but emphatic statements of the opening subject – dramatized by use of the minor mode and the high upper register of the piano in the right hand, as well as by an intensification in dynamics to *fff* – are juxtaposed with similarly shortened but ornamented appearances of the dance-like theme in the major. This juxtaposition of contrasting themes is thus used as a structural device, and as a means for building to the expressive climax of the musical form. At the same time, it evokes musically the dichotomy of harsh reality and beautiful dreams familiar from the world of Schubert's Lieder.

The second movement is an Andante, in which appearances of a calm lyrical theme are separated by two turbulent episodes in minor keys. As in Schubert's other slow movements of this type, some of the rhythmic animation of the first episode is carried into the subsequent return of the principal theme, while at the end of the movement, this theme is recalled in its initial simplicity. The last two movements, a Menuetto and rondo finale, are linked rhythmically through their persistent use of an upbeat figure of four rapidly repeated chords or octaves. Another rhythmic figure outlining a turn connects the minuet to its trio, which is a trans-figured Austrian Ländler of the utmost quietude and delicacy.

The three sonatas completed in September 1828 each contain reminiscences of Beethoven, who had died in March 1827, and whom Schubert was to survive by only twenty months. The influence of Beethoven's 32 Variations in C Minor, WoO 80, on the opening theme of Schubert's C Minor Sonata, D958, is obvious and striking, but still more significant is the manner in which Schubert departs from his model, extending the progression into a lengthy opening period of vehement and tragic character. Especially impressive in this movement are the mysterious, chromatically veiled passages of the development. The second movement contains a hymn-like theme in A flat major, which returns in variation after dramatic episodes in other keys, in a manner not unlike the slow movement of Beethoven's *Sonate pathétique*, Op. 13, in the same key. At the end of this movement, a remarkably subtle passage restates and concisely summarizes the entire modulatory plan, utilizing surprising enharmonic shifts in tonality. Following the scherzo in C minor is a weighty finale based on a persistent tarantella rhythm comparable to the finales of Beethoven's E flat Major Sonata Op. 31 No. 3 or Schubert's own D Minor Quartet. In this rondo-sonata movement, however, the poetic evocation is perhaps less of a dance than of a ride on horseback, thrilling and yet strangely ominous. The obsessive, driven character of the music shifts focus in the central episode in B major, which presents a seductive, cajoling vision reminiscent of the Erlking.

That Schubert's last three sonatas are intimately connected through motivic and tonal means has received increased recognition since Alfred Brendel's detailed analytical study and most recent recordings.[14] The evidence of Schubert's surviving compositional drafts and autograph scores shows that this interconnected sonata trilogy emerged only gradually, after he had begun work on the final Sonata in B flat, the genesis of which overlapped with that of the preceding Sonata in A Major. On the other hand, the parallel at the outset of the first sonata to Beethoven's C Minor Variations, WoO 80, was originally even more literal, as Hans-Joachim Hinrichsen has pointed out.[15] In the end, the first movement of the C Minor Sonata offered a rich quarry of musical relationships which Schubert utilized in each of the two succeeding works.

In the A Major Sonata (D959) the influence of Beethoven is felt most in the impressive finale, which was modeled on the finale of Beethoven's Sonata in G Major, Op. 31 No. 1, as both Charles Rosen and Edward T. Cone have shown.[16] Rosen also pointed out that Schubert surpassed his model, and this is nowhere clearer than in the elaborate coda, in which phrases from the principal theme are broken off into silence, and reharmonized in unexpected keys. Just as the thread seems to be regained, we plunge into a whirlwind Presto, which is itself interrupted by a resumption of the reprise of the theme, leading to an allusion, in the final measures, to the principal theme of the *first* movement. This first-movement theme also forms the basis for the coda of that movement, where it is presented in a texture and articulation unmistakably suggesting chamber music for strings, reminding us thereby of Schubert's other major compositional preoccupation during these last months of his life, his great C Major String Quintet (D956).

The center of gravity of the A Major Sonata lies in the extraordinary slow movement in F sharp minor, marked Andantino. The almost hypnotic effect of its main theme recalls several of the Heine Songs and *Der Leiermann* from *Winterreise* (D911, 24). Some indication of its expressive associations may be gained from analogy to the song *Pilgerweise* (D789), where similar music in F sharp minor is set to the text "I am a pilgrim on the earth, and pass silently from house to house. . ." The controlled melodic repetitions of this theme stress a few important pitches in a narrow register, and create an atmosphere of melancholic contemplation, or obsession. The almost static quality of this music is also connected to its structural role in the movement as a whole, however. Nowhere else did Schubert employ such an extreme contrast as in this Andantino, where the music of the following middle section seems to unleash not just turbulence and foreboding, but chaotic violence. Here, as so often in Schubert, the contrasting sections are complementary, and need to be heard in relationship to one another. The outer sections of this ternary

Example 8.3 Sonata in A Major (D959), second movement, mm. 120–31

musical form thus embody the reflective mode of the lyrical subject, but the music of the contrasting middle section annihilates this frame of reference. Descending sequences of amorphous passagework reach C minor, the most remote of key-relations from the tonic, and the music continues to build relentlessly, exploiting the most extreme registers and a structural use of trills as a means of sustaining the tension of the musical lines at fixed levels of pitch. The approach to C sharp minor at the climax is achieved in a passage of savage intensity. Following this climax, a fragile recitative appears, only to be broken off repeatedly by massive accented chords (see Ex. 8.3).

In this movement, as Alfred Brendel has observed, one can sense an affinity between Schubert and his great artistic contemporary, the aging Francisco Goya, who in his etchings and paintings of war left a damning indictment of human cruelty, and of the fragile vulnerability of individual human beings confronted by power. In this sense, the Andantino of Schubert's A Major Sonata bears comparison with a painting such as Goya's *The Third of May, 1808*, which is based on the contrast between the hard, inhuman brutality of the soldiers making up the firing squad, and the soft, defenseless, and crumbling human targets. The nineteenth-century myth of Schubert's easy-going *naïveté* dies hard, and few artists have probed so deeply into the tragic aspects of the human condition.

In the last two movements of the A Major Sonata, Schubert offers more positive perspectives on the music of the Andantino. In perhaps no other work is the network of thematic correspondences between movements so far-reaching as here. The brilliant arpeggiated chords that open the scherzo reshape the dark arpeggiated sonorities that had closed the Andantino, for instance, whereas the trio reincarnates the opening motto theme of the first movement. Schubert reworked the main subject of the rondo-sonata finale from the slow-movement theme of his earlier Sonata in A Minor (D537) from 1817, and Charles Fisk has suggested that this preexisting theme must have served as Schubert's point of departure and even "as the source of the sonata's principal motives."[17] In the finale, a window on the Andantino opens at the culmination of the developmental central episode leading to the reprise. This massive passage rests not on the dominant of the tonic A major but instead on C sharp, dominant of the F sharp major with which the recapitulation begins. Broken chords in the middle register alternate between chords of C sharp major and F sharp minor, stressing the same pitches as in the main theme of the Andantino, and Schubert heightens the characteristic semitone tension from that movement by pitting the minor ninth D in the high register against its resolution C# several octaves below. The exquisite F sharp major texture with which the reprise begins is no mere "false" recapitulation: it absorbs a transfigured vision of the key of the tragic slow movement glimpsed through the veil of the rondo theme.

Like its companion works in C Minor and A Major, the final Sonata in B flat Major (D960) is representative of Schubert's finest and most advanced style, and combines lyrical charm, structural grandeur, and a daring but controlled treatment of key-relations. The first movement begins, in the words of Donald Francis Tovey, with a "sublime theme of the utmost calmness and breadth,"[18] whose first half ends mysteriously in a long, low trill on G♭. Following the second phrase of the theme, the trill is heard on B♭, but it soon unfolds downwards to initiate the sustained pedal point on G♭ that controls a restatement of the main theme in that key. As is characteristic of Schubert, the exposition incorporates three main keys and thematic areas, the second of which – in F sharp minor – may be linked to the mysterious trill as well as to the Andantino of the preceding sonata.

The development section is based largely on the third thematic area from the exposition, with its dactylic rhythm and similarity to Schubert's song *Der Wanderer* (D489), and modulates widely before building to a great climax in D minor. In the ethereal passage which follows, the sublime opening theme, now preceded by its trill, is stated softly in the high upper register. As Tovey and others have observed, this recall of the main theme is delicately poised, not "in" but "on" the tonic key, as if contemplated from a vast distance. After two further appearances of the trill on G♭, the ensuing recapitulation assumes a character of overwhelming immediacy and inwardness. As in the finale of the A Major Sonata, Schubert enhances the return of his main theme through a subtle wealth of thematic allusion and an impressive mastery of tonal perspective.

The slow movement in C sharp (D flat) minor, marked Andante

sostenuto, assumes an almost static character due to a recurring accompanimental figure which ranges a span of four octaves under and over the melody. The contrasting middle section of this movement is suggestive of a song, and combines a lyrical melody with an accompaniment in rapid notes, and an active bass line. The playful gaiety of the following scherzo movement is enhanced by its effective changes from major to minor, and its wide tonal range. Particularly striking is the manner in which Schubert approaches the reprise of the scherzo theme in B flat major from the remote but adjacent key of A major. Harmonic subtleties are even more conspicuous in the finale, which opens with a call to attention: a G octave in the left hand appended to a theme which persistently begins in the "wrong" key, C minor, instead of B flat major. This striking gesture may be connected not only to the opening of the finale of Beethoven's string quartet in this key, Op. 130, but also at least distantly to the mysterious trill on the minor submediant in Schubert's first movement. Only with its final appearance in this rondo-sonata movement is this material explained and completely resolved: the octave call-note descends by semitones through Gb to F, the dominant note of B flat, and a brilliant coda caps Schubert's very last composition for the piano.

Fantasies, *Moments musicaux*, Impromptus, and *Klavierstücke* (D946)

Many of Schubert's piano works other than sonatas consist of short pieces grouped into collections, such as the *Moments musicaux*, Op. 94 (D780), the Impromptus, Opp. 90 and 142 (D899 and 935), and the *Klavierstücke* (D946), not to mention the numerous collections of dances. Another genre that occupied the young Schubert was the fantasy; his very earliest compositional efforts include several such works. His first outstanding composition in this vein is the "Wanderer" Fantasy in C Major, Op. 15 (D760) of 1822. The "Wanderer" Fantasy consists of four movements – an Allegro, Adagio, scherzo, and finale employing fugue – which are closely interrelated thematically, and performed continuously, without pauses between the movements. The basic unifying element is a dactylic rhythm linking the outer movements with the focal point of the whole work, a self-quotation from Schubert's song *Der Wanderer* in the theme of the slow variation movement. The relationship of these movements also suggests an open-ended sonata form, with the Allegro comprising the exposition and the Adagio standing in place of a development section. This structural plan of interconnected movements broke new ground, and provided an important model for the new genre of the symphonic

Example 8.4 *Moment musical* No. 6 in A flat Major, Op. 94 (D780), mm. 61–77

poem as cultivated by Franz Liszt in the 1850s, and many other composers in the last decades of the nineteenth century.[19] The special popularity
of this technically difficult work owes much to Liszt, in fact, who not only
played it in an arrangement for piano and orchestra but also offered a solo
version which for once makes portions of the piece easier to play.

Schubert's Impromptus and *Moments musicaux* develop a tradition of
characteristic piano pieces stemming from the Bohemian composer
Václav Tomášek, and transmitted to Vienna by his pupil Jan Voříšek, who
took up residence there in 1818. Most of these pieces were apparently
written in the last two years of Schubert's life, but some date from earlier
years. The Allegretto in A flat comprising the last of the *Moments musicaux* was actually one of Schubert's first published examples, since it originally appeared as an independent piece, entitled "Plaintes d'un
Troubadour," in December 1824. (The third one had been published the
year before as "Air russe.") Like many of this type, it is in ternary form,
with a trio in D flat major serving as the contrasting section. In the main
section of the piece, the music is inexorably drawn from within into the
tonal sphere of the foreign key of the flat sixth, F flat, spelled enharmon-
ically as E major. This gravitation toward E major begins insidiously, as
melodic stress on E or F♭, and gradually gains strength through repetition
until it usurps the tonality, creating a sudden shift in the key perspective.
Even near the end of the piece, after the tonic A flat major has been
reestablished in a reprise of the opening, the tell-tale F♭ returns, and the
music veers dramatically away from the tonic (see Ex. 8.4). The final
cadence is shadowed by this conflict in key perspective, and the music
resolves precariously to an unharmonized A♭, doubled in octaves, in the
closing measures.

The second and fourth of the *Moments musicaux* contain internal contrasting sections, while the third and fifth pieces, both in F minor, are tightly unified by their unbroken rhythmic movement. The main theme of the second piece in A flat major is somewhat reminiscent of the beginning of the G Major Sonata in its rhythm, broad choral texture, and serene character, while the two episodes present a haunting melody in F sharp minor, accompanied by triplets in the left hand. In the fourth piece, the expressive contrast of the principal sections is striking: a *moto perpetuo* in C sharp minor in a stratified Baroque texture is interrupted by a soft, ethereal theme in the major reminiscent of a dance, which recurs fleetingly before the conclusion. The first of the *Moments musicaux*, in C major, is also in ternary form, but with a less pronounced contrast between the principal sections. This piece begins with a summons: a unison triadic fanfare motif which later returns in imitation, in several voices.

The first of the Impromptus, Op. 90, also opens with an arresting introductory gesture: sustained octaves on G, marked *fortissimo*. This gesture sets into relief the quiet, declamatory phrases of the main theme in C minor, which at first appear harmonized. The rhythm is processional, and the atmosphere is that of a narrative, evoking the landscape of ceaseless wandering familiar from Schubert's song cycles. This narrative quality is sustained through repetition of the theme against a changing harmonic background, as well as through motivic relationships linking the main theme to the secondary theme, beginning in A flat major. The secondary theme, in turn, lends its accompaniment in triplets to subsequent appearances of the main theme, and the resources of modulation and modal contrast are effectively exploited. Near the end, the triplets disappear, the initial declamatory phrases are sounded together with subdued references to the octaves on G from the outset of the work, and the music concludes movingly in C major.

The second and fourth impromptus of Op. 90 are in ternary form, and display similarities in character and structure. In both, rapid passagework based on descending scales or arpeggios dominates the outer sections, whereas the inner section or trio contains more declamatory or lyrical material in the minor. The contrast between these sections is most pronounced in the second impromptu, where appearances of an etude-like *moto perpetuo* in E flat major enclose a central episode *all'ongarese* in B minor. In the coda, the music of the episode returns, initially in that key, before being diverted to E flat minor. The trio of the fourth impromptu is passionately lyrical, with a beatific glimpse of C sharp major in its second part. Unlike these two pieces, the third impromptu in G flat major is completely unified in mood and texture. This is a broadly lyrical and meditative work, which Einstein described as a "pre-Mendelssohn 'Song without Words.'"[20]

In the *Moments musicaux* and Op. 90 Impromptus, the individual pieces are admirably contrasted in an open-ended sequence, with the last piece in a different key from the first. The tighter design of the four Impromptus, Op. 142, led Schumann to believe that parts of this opus originally belonged to a sonata.[21] The first section of the opening piece, an Allegro moderato in F minor, is indeed structured much like a sonata exposition, but this is not true of the middle section based on an expressive dialogue between treble and bass accompanied by arpeggios in the middle register. After a full recapitulation of the opening section, mainly in F major, the music from the middle section returns, first in the tonic minor, then in the brightness of the major. In the closing moments, F minor is reaffirmed in a terse statement of the opening theme, with a new cadence.

The second impromptu is a dance-like Allegretto in A flat major, with a trio in D flat major employing arpeggiated textures. The basic rhythm of both sections stresses the normally weak second beat of the triple meter. The third piece is a charming set of five variations in B flat major, on a theme Schubert had used twice before: in the incidental music to *Rosamunde* (D797), and the slow movement of the A Minor String Quartet (D804).

The fourth impromptu of Op. 142 is one of Schubert's most brilliant works. The enormous rhythmic vitality of the outer sections derives in part from unpredictable accentuation, and alternations of duple and triple meter. The cadential trills are emphasized by syncopated accents, generating energy which is released in rapid scale passages. In the contrasting middle section, the climax is reached in scale passages for both hands, culminating in a swift, four-octave descent in A major across the entire keyboard. Other passages in this impromptu suggest the influence of Hungarian rhythms. Especially impressive is the conclusion: a quiet, mysterious passage is broken off by a powerful and virtuosic coda employing octaves in both hands. Just as the final cadence in F minor is affirmed in the highest register, Schubert recalls the rhythm from the middle section in chords in the left hand, while resolving the climax of that section to the tonic in a dramatic and astonishing scalar descent of six octaves through the entire tonal space.

The three *Klavierstücke* (D946) were not arranged as a set by Schubert, but were assembled by Johannes Brahms, who prepared the first edition of these pieces for publication in 1868. The third piece may predate the first two, which were composed in May 1828. In character and form, these works resemble the Impromptus, though there is an *al fresco* quality entirely their own. The autographs of these pieces are probably not complete in every respect as they stand, and certain tempo markings, such as in the internal episode of the third piece, for instance, appear to be missing. The strength of the internal contrasts is greater than in the Impromptus. The first piece juxtaposes a turbulent Allegro assai in E flat minor with an elaborate lyrical episode in B major in a slower tempo; Schubert wrote down a second slow episode in A flat major, but canceled the passage in the autograph score. The third piece employs a ternary design in which music of a lively and cheerful Bohemian flavor foreshadowing Smetana encloses an extended episode characterized by an almost hypnotic immobility, owing to its static and repetitive rhythmic patterns. In the second piece, on the other hand, the relationship of the contrasting sections is reversed, inasmuch as the opening material is idyllic in character, and the two episodes are more dramatic or agitated. The opening lyrical theme of this Allegretto in E flat major was adapted from the chorus beginning Act III of Schubert's opera *Fierrabras* from 1823, as John Reed has pointed out.[22] Like the canceled episode from the first of the *Klavierstücke*, this theme is reminiscent of a Venetian barcarole in its rhythm and flowing texture, and its frequent melodic parallel thirds are also Italianate in character. Each of the two contrasting sections – in C minor and A flat minor/B minor respectively – introduce smaller note values which reflect an inner agitation in the music. The climax of the first episode is reached when the music turns unexpectedly to C major, with the theme heard in a high register. Use of the high upper register assumes even more importance in the second episode in A flat major, where the music evokes a remarkable quality of yearning, foreboding, and poetic sadness.

Music for piano duet

Our survey of the piano works would remain seriously incomplete without mention of Schubert's music for piano duet, which includes the Sonatas in B flat Major (D617) and in C Major "Grand Duo" (D812), and three compositions composed in 1828: the Allegro in A Minor "Lebensstürme" (D947), the Rondo in A Major (D951), and the Fantasy in F Minor (D940). The Fantasy is one of Schubert's most outstanding pieces, and shows a remarkable treatment of thematic, tonal, and modal contrast, which we shall examine in some detail. While clearly indebted to the model of his songs, this composition goes far beyond them in exploring the structural and expressive possibilities inherent in the controlled juxtaposition of strongly contrasting themes. Like the earlier "Wanderer" Fantasy, the F Minor Fantasy consists of four interrelated movements performed without a break.[23] In both works, an opening Allegro is followed

Example 8.5 Fantasy in F Minor, Op. 103 (D940), mm. 37–52

by a slow movement, scherzo, and final movement employing fugue. The thematic treatment in the duet fantasy, however, has no parallel in the earlier work, and involves a particularly close relation between the outer movements of the cyclic form.

The lyrical opening theme of the F Minor Fantasy bears some affinity to the processional themes of pieces like the Andante of the "Great" C Major Symphony, and *Gute Nacht* and *Wegweiser* from *Winterreise*. Its processional character derives from a regularity of rhythmic pulse in duple meter and the steady octaves in the bass, repeated twice per measure. As Eric Sams has pointed out, the melody itself has an insistent conversational character, suggesting the rhythm and intonation of speech.[24] The overall quality of the theme is narrative; it seems to evoke the landscape of ceaseless wandering familiar from the two Müller song cycles.

After the repetition of the initial thematic statement, the music shifts into A flat major, and the lyrical melody passes to the bass. This section represents the middle part of a ternary thematic construction. The opening theme returns, however, in F major, and the brighter sound of the major mode is enhanced by richer harmonies in the bass and the emphasis on A in the melody (see Ex. 8.5). Schubert also exploits the high upper register of the piano in the last phrases before the melody cadences in the tonic.

That cadence brings a shock – a contrasting second theme in F minor,

| Lyrical theme | F minor |
| Melody passes to bass | A flat major, modulates to V/F minor |

| Lyrical theme restated | F major |
| Second theme, funereal rhythm | F minor, modulates to |

| Lyrical theme | D flat minor, modulates to |
| Second theme, funereal rhythm | A minor modulates to |

| Lyrical theme | F minor |
| Second theme, funereal rhythm | F major (leads to second movement) |

NOTE: Thematic juxtaposition is shown by boxes.

Figure 8.1 Fantasy in F Minor, first movement: the tonal plan

which is utterly opposed to the opening theme in affective character. The menacing character of the new theme is due to its stress on D♭, the dissonant minor second above the dominant note, its pointed accents, and its funereal rhythm. This rhythm, first announced in the bass, consists of the pattern ♩. ♪♩♩, representing a related but more energetic form of the rhythm ♩♩♩ associated by Schubert with death in the song *Der Tod und das Mädchen*.

By analogy with Schubert's songs, the statement of the first lyrical theme in major assumes an air of unreality, of illusion. The illusion is rudely shattered by the plunge into minor and the threatening second theme. This drastic thematic juxtaposition then serves as the structural basis for the rest of the first movement. After the initial statement of the second theme, the lyrical theme returns in D flat minor, closing with a cadence in A minor, where it is once again juxtaposed with the theme in funereal rhythm. A last statement of the opening theme in F minor completes the series of modulations through a circle of descending major thirds, F–D flat–A–F. This appearance too is juxtaposed with the second theme, which, in a reversal of roles, now appears transformed – *pianissimo*, *legato*, and in major. The statement of the second theme in major has a resolving effect, serving to round off the first movement before the dramatic opening of the Largo in F sharp minor. The tonal and thematic plan of the first movement is shown in Figure 8.1.

The dual perspective of the F Minor Fantasy reaches its culmination only in the last measures of the entire work. The last movement represents a recapitulation and development of the first movement. After a sudden modulation from the key of the scherzo, F sharp minor, the lyrical theme returns in F minor. The entire opening section is then restated, in somewhat condensed form, up to the crucial passage in which the lyrical

Example 8.6 Fantasy in F Minor, Op. 103 (D940), mm. 550–70

theme appears in the major mode. From this point, the work takes a new course.

The dark-hued second subject now becomes the basis for an extended fugue. In the latter part of the fugue, the principal rhythmic motif undergoes a series of canonic imitations, while its free inversion is worked into the rhythmic accompaniment as triplets in the bass. The music then builds toward a tonic cadence in F minor, which is twice avoided before it appears at the final statement of the fugal theme in the lowest register. Again the music comes to a climax on a series of diminished-seventh chords, with the expectation of a cadence in the tonic. This time, however, the cadence is denied: the fugue simply breaks off on the dominant (see Ex. 8.6).

The conclusion of the Fantasy after this dramatic silence is one of the most extraordinary passages in Schubert's works. It begins by recalling the plaintive lyrical theme from the outset of the work, but the reminiscence lasts only a few measures. The last measures, rising in sequence, already pick up the darker coloring of the second theme; then, ten measures before the close, Schubert steps from one theme into the other through a subtle transformation of his material. The closing eight-measure statement is a development of the second theme, employing not only the funereal rhythm, but the melodic stress on D♭; the descending triplets in the bass are derived from the fugue. In these final measures, the dark-hued second theme supersedes the lyrical theme to provide the cadence and resolution of the whole work.

This cadence owes much of its power to the fact that it serves as the true conclusion of the fugue, after the abrupt interruption and the reminiscence of the lyrical theme. The actual cadential progression refers back to several cadential passages in the fugue, in which the dotted rhythmic motif of the subject is extended by a series of quarter notes. This time the progression is strengthened by the presence of a descending chromatic line, doubled in octaves, that highlights the dissonant semitone D♭–C in the last two chords. The chromatic line, beginning on F, passes through E, E♭, and D, reaching D♭ in the penultimate chord, which is emphasized dynamically. Schubert's omission of the implied dominant chord at the cadence results in a kind of enhanced subdominant cadence in which two crucial motivic elements of the work are combined: the D♭–C semitone relationship in the treble and the fourth in the bass, the thematic hallmark of the opening theme.

The overall scheme based on the relationship of these two evocative themes suggests a tragic symbolism analogous to that of *Winterreise*, and reminds us once more of the close kinship between Schubert's vocal music and his works for piano. Like the song cycle, the F Minor Fantasy is haunted by a sense of progress toward an inescapable destiny, an idea tied to the universal human theme of mortality. In a sense, the very structure of the Fantasy is posited on this appropriation of poetic content from the world of Schubert's Lieder. In this remarkable composition, the expressive content of the wanderer's tragic journey is transformed, as it were, into a purely musical structure, absorbed into the sphere of instrumental music.

Schubert's F Minor Fantasy, *Klavierstücke*, Impromptus and *Moments musicaux* as well as the "Wanderer" Fantasy and the later sonatas reflect an almost unfailing consistency of accomplishment. A combination of directness and intimacy of expression, poetic sensitiveness, and structural control and grandeur is characteristic of Schubert's mature musical style. His departures from Beethoven's more deterministic approach are not in themselves a shortcoming, for they are very often inseparable from his basic artistic quest to explore the qualities of experience, as seen from a vantage point whose divided perspective encompasses both external perception and the inward imagination.

9 Schubert's chamber music: before and after Beethoven

Martin Chusid

Secretly, in my heart of hearts, I still hope to be able to make something of myself, but who can do anything after Beethoven?

Schubert to Josef von Spaun (SMF 128)

Schubert was not born into a family of professional musicians, as were Bach, Mozart, and Beethoven. As a result, he was never expected to become a virtuoso, never wrote a full-fledged concerto, and showed relatively little interest in composing for virtuosos.[1] Instead his family made music together; and for much of his life Schubert's compositions (songs, dances, four-hand piano music, but also most of his chamber and orchestral music) were written for *Liebhaber*, lovers of music, amateurs. When, near the end of his life, he was asked by the publisher of his E flat Piano Trio, Op. 100 (D929), to name a dedicatee, his response was: "This work is dedicated to nobody, save those who find pleasure in it" (*SDB* 796). Nor did he consort with the best musicians of his day, those at the cutting edge of contemporary music (i.e. the players promoting the music of Beethoven) until relatively late in his career. When he did, the result was a series of masterpieces: his last three string quartets, the Octet, the Piano Trios in B flat and E flat, and the String Quintet in C Major, to name only the chamber works of his last five years (1824–28).

But these impressive compositions rest on a considerable body of earlier chamber music, and to understand the mature Schubert, it is vital to recognize that before he wrote his first large group of successful songs (1814–16) he had already completed at least twelve string quartets and a string quintet. A case can be made that Schubert, the master of the Lied, was as indebted to his experience with instrumental music as was Mozart, the master of opera, to his experience writing instrumental compositions.

Schubert's chamber music for strings

Schubert's early interest in string music was a natural one. Before he sang or played a keyboard instrument, he received violin lessons from his father; and when quite young he joined the family string quartet.[2] It is safe to say that most of his string quartets as well as the string trios and the early string quintet were written for this group, perhaps augmented by other players. Since music for strings comprises the largest share of Schubert's chamber music, it will be discussed first in this chapter.

From 1808 to 1813 Schubert, as a singer in the Royal Chapel Choir, attended and lived at the Vienna City Seminary. This meant that every evening he played in the Seminary orchestra, and at some point became *Kapelldiener* (assistant to the orchestra's musical director) caring for the music, instruments, stands, candles, etc. He also led the orchestra, no doubt from the principal violinist's chair, whenever the director, Wenzel Ruzicka, played at the court opera. The repertory of this group, a symphony and one or two overtures every evening, is important for our discussion.

Schubert's experience with orchestral music, however, was not limited to the Seminary orchestra. There are reports that friends and neighbors joined the family group and it grew into a small orchestra.[3] Christa Landon, one of the original chief editors of the *Neue Schubert-Ausgabe*, found arrangements of orchestral works by Haydn and Mozart for string quartet and quintet with the name of Schubert's father at the top.[4] These obviously formed part of the family music library. Furthermore, although they are not directly linked to the Schubert family, there are also printed arrangements for string quartet of overtures by Antonio Salieri, Schubert's teacher.[5] These arrangements may explain one of the most unusual of Schubert's chamber works, an original Overture for String Quintet (D8), his earliest dated chamber composition (June 29, 1811), a piece he also adapted for string quartet (D8A). His model was an orchestral work by Luigi Cherubini, the overture to *Faniska*.[6] A similar work, an Overture for String Quartet in B flat (D20), was lost after the editors of the old Complete Edition (*ASA*) decided not to publish it.[7]

There are a number of other indications of the influence of orchestral music in Schubert's early chamber music for strings. For example, he modeled the finale of his String Quartet in C Major (D32) on the first movement of Haydn's Symphony No. 78 in C Minor; and there are also relationships between Schubert's own early orchestral music and his string quartets.[8] This tendency culminates in the String Quartet in D Major (D74) whose slow movement and finale are close enough to be considered a kind of sketch for the parallel movements of his First Symphony (D82), also in D major, completed October 28, 1813, about a month after the Quartet. Furthermore, the form of the first movement of the Quartet in D is that of a majority of opera overtures of the time: a sonata form without a development section or repeat signs after the exposition. Well-known examples that Schubert knew of this form include the overtures to Gluck's *Alceste*, Mozart's *Figaro*, Beethoven's *Prometheus*, and several by Rossini. Not surprisingly, almost all of Schubert's own overtures use this form. When the recapitulations do not begin in the tonic key (e.g. those by Gluck and Salieri), the structure resembles the older bipartite sonata form, although without the repetition of either part. The bipartite principle is a most important one for Schubert, and explains many of the unusual formal procedures to be found in his larger instrumental works; and not only in the first movements. In addition to formal approach, it is the style of Schubert's early string writing that shows orchestral influence: excited string tremolos, doublings at the octave; double, triple, and even quadruple stops; as well as melodic ideas that at times suggest orchestral brass (e.g. fanfares). A striking example of the latter occurs in the opening movement of the String Quartet in B flat (D36) which introduces a repeated trumpet-like fanfare at the same structural position, the end of the development section, as the trumpet call in Beethoven's *Leonore* Overture No. 3.[9] Interestingly enough, once the First Symphony was completed, subsequent string quartets by Schubert begin to sound less orchestral. But the tendency recurs in his last quartets, especially the D Minor "Death and the Maiden" (D810) and the G Major (D887).

Between November 1813 and the latter part of 1816, that is after Schubert left the City Seminary and returned home, he wrote five string quartets of which four are extant in a completed state (D87 in E flat, Op. 125 No. 1; D112 in B flat, Op. 168; D173 in G Minor; and D353 in E Major, Op. 125 No. 2).[10] Undoubtedly also written for the family quartet, each has considerable musical value; but the B flat (D112) is the most beautiful. Perhaps because he began the piece as a string trio, there is a sense of intimacy lacking in most of the earlier quartets.[11]

The description of tripartite sonata form (i.e. with exposition, development, and recapitulation) by Carl Czerny, a pupil of Beethoven, is useful in understanding the spacious first-movement forms of Schubert and particularly the Allegro ma non troppo of D112. Czerny's account divides the form into two parts, the first of which corresponds to the exposition and is in turn subdivided into five sections: (1) "principal subject" (2) "its continuation and amplification, together with a modulation into the nearest related key" (3) "the middle subject [second theme] in this new key" (4) "new continuation of this middle subject" (5) "a final melody [closing theme] closes in the new key in order that the repetition may ... follow unconstrainedly."[12]

The implicit alternation of tonally stable sections (1, 3, and 5) and unstable, that is modulatory or at least harmonically more active, passages, (2 and 4) suits well Schubert's penchant for tonal movement and interesting harmony. In the exposition of D112, first movement, the longest and most important passage corresponds to Czerny's section 2, for which Schubert writes a new melody from which he derives all his subsequent thematic material. But it is his tonal movement in this passage that is especially noteworthy. Whereas in the music of his predecessors this section is primarily devoted to establishing a new key, often by way of its dominant, Schubert prefers a deliberately round-about approach; and he almost never stresses the new key's dominant. In this movement, for example, he begins section 2 in G minor (mm. 35ff.), returns to B flat (mm. 72ff.), then moves to E flat (mm. 81ff.), and briefly tonicizes G minor again (mm. 93–95). After sixty measures he is back where he began! He doesn't establish F major, the key of the middle subject, until two measures before that subject (mm. 101–02).

The analogous passage continuing the middle subject (Czerny's section 4) is equally exciting but much shorter. It consists of a sequence in three ascending stages, each modulatory (mm. 124–36). Czerny continues his description of first-movement form as follows:

> The second part . . . commences with a development of the principal subject, or of the middle subject, or even of a new idea, passing through several keys, and returning again to the original key. Then follows the principal subject and its amplification, but usually in an abridged shape, so modulating that the middle subject may likewise reappear entire, though in the original key; after which, all that follows the middle subject in the first part, is here repeated in the original key.

When hearing the relatively short development section of D112, the listener may feel that it lacks the excitement of the exposition. In fact, until the time of the "Unfinished" Symphony (D759, fall 1822), Schubert's greatest problem with sonata form is his inability to construct development sections that can serve as the climax of the movement, as Beethoven's so often do. In the recapitulation Schubert reveals his priorities clearly, namely his need to retain the tonal variety of his exposition. Often, as here, he increases the length of his principal subject area by introducing new tonal movement (mm. 217–42). This allows the same degree of modulation in sections 2 to 5 of the reprise; and yet the movement will close in satisfying fashion in the tonic key.

To organize the slow movement and finale of the B flat Quartet, for the first time in his career he selects another traditional form: the rondo with its alternation of refrains and episodes. But here too Schubert reveals his predilection for more harmonic motion than his predecessors. During the slow movement, for example, the second of the three refrains is in the key of the dominant rather than the usual tonic. Furthermore, in both movements Schubert prefers a single, lengthy modulating episode that returns, naturally with a different tonal orientation, instead of two or more different episodes. When Mozart or Beethoven, Schubert's principal models at this time, contrived a return of an episode, invariably the first, it was always *after* they had presented a second (different) episode; and that return would always be in the tonic key. This portion of the movement would then resemble a recapitulation of a second group in sonata form. As a result the form is often referred to as a sonata-rondo. Schubert's returning episode, on the other hand, retains the modulatory quality of the original episode, even as it concludes in the tonic. Finally, and again unlike his predecessors, the harmonically adventurous Schubert writes both Scherzo and Trio of D112 in a key other than his tonic. Here it is the subdominant, E flat.

In December of 1820 Schubert wrote the *Quartettsatz* ("quartet movement") in C Minor (D703), his only incomplete chamber work regularly performed today. In this regard it resembles his "Unfinished" Symphony, another composition dating from a period in the composer's career sometimes referred to as his "Years of Crisis" (1818–23).[13] This is an apt description, especially for his larger instrumental works, fewer of which were written at that time than either before or after, and with a far higher percentage of incomplete compositions than at any other stage in his career.

One of the striking features of the *Quartettsatz* is the greater participation of the cello. This reflects, perhaps, the fact that Schubert was no longer living at home and writing for the family quartet. His father, the cellist, appears to have had modest performing skills. Most importantly, for the first time in his string chamber music Schubert seems to have come to grips with Beethoven's awesome achievements. This meant instrumental compositions on a large scale with a wide range of emotional states, works which present the composer with the problem of unification. Failure to find a solution for that problem may have contributed to Schubert's abandoning the fine beginning (41 measures) of a slow movement in A flat major intended to follow the completed Allegro assai. The fragment breaks off as Schubert was modulating back to the tonic from an effective contrasting passage in the distant key of F sharp minor. The editors of the old Complete Edition – and Johannes Brahms was a particularly influential member of that group – compare the quality of the fragment with that of the completed movements of the "Unfinished" Symphony and regret Schubert's failure to finish the work.[14]

The structure of the completed movement has often puzzled commentators who for the most part fail to recognize the young composer's predilection for bipartite form. In bipartite movements only the thematic ideas heard in the final section of the first part need recur in the tonic key during the latter portion of the movement. And this is the situation in the *Quartettsatz*. The principal subject returns only in the brief coda; the continuation of that subject never returns; and the soaring middle subject, originally in A flat, is now heard in two keys, B flat and E flat, neither of which is the tonic. Only the unusually extensive closing section, originally in G major, the opposite mode of the dominant and *not* a usual contrasting area for movements in minor, returns in the tonic, C, but in major. The coda is the only section in the second part that is in C minor, the key in which the movement began.

Two broadly conceived symphonic fragments, the completely sketched but never fully orchestrated Symphony in E of 1821 (D729) and the "Unfinished" Symphony of the following year, suggest Schubert's increasing preoccupation with Beethoven after the *Quartettsatz*. But it is only in the winter of 1823–24 that Schubert began to interact on a regular basis with musicians of Beethoven's circle. Most importantly, he became friendly with the violinist Ignaz Schuppanzigh, leader of the first professional string quartet, and recognized as the most influential and successful proponent of Beethoven's music in Vienna. Schuppanzigh, who had been absent from the Austrian capital for a number of years, regularly promoted a subscription concert series, and was the leader from the concertmaster's chair of the orchestra for the first performances of many of Beethoven's major orchestral works, including the Ninth Symphony. Preparations for that event occasioned a touching letter from Schubert dated March 31, 1824, to his friend Leopold Kupelwieser suggesting how strongly he felt the need to emulate Beethoven:

> Of songs I have not written many new ones, but I have tried my hand at several instrumental works, for I wrote two Quartets for violins, viola and violoncello and an Octet, and I want to write another quartet, in fact I intend to pave my way towards grand symphony in that manner. – The latest in Vienna is that Beethoven is to give a concert at which he is to produce his new Symphony, three movements from the new Mass and a new Overture. – God willing, I too am thinking of giving a similar concert next year.
>
> (*SDB* 339)

Perhaps more than anything else, two aspects of Beethoven's achievements seemed to preoccupy Schubert in 1824. One of them was cyclic unification,[15] and the other was the older composer's success with variation form. It can hardly be coincidental that in April 1822 Schubert dedicated his "Variations on a French Song," Op. 10 (D624), for piano duet to Beethoven with "veneration and admiration," or that during the year

1824 he composed the largest number of variation sets of any period in his life. These include the weak set on his fine song *Trockne Blumen* for flute and piano (D802) in E, the same key as his more successful variations on a passage from his song *Der Wanderer* (D489), the slow section of the Fantasy for Piano in C Major, Op. 15 (D760, November 1822). Also composed in 1824 were the variations for Piano Duet in A flat, Op. 35 (D813), and two sets for chamber works: the Andante from the Octet (D803), which has elements in common with Beethoven's Septet, Op. 20, as well as the finest set of variations Schubert ever wrote, the slow movement of his String Quartet in D Minor (D810). The Quartet is named for his song *Der Tod und das Mädchen* (D531), from which the theme of his variations derives. Of his sixteen variation sets, five were written in the year 1824.[16]

In an age when variations were popular – Carl Czerny is reputed to have written 500 sets – one might wonder why the usually prolific Schubert did not write more of them. The answer may relate to the tonal and harmonic restrictions inherent in the form. In sets of ten variations or less, normally the variations remain in the same key with one in the opposite mode. Occasionally, as in the Andante from the Octet, there is an additional variation in another key. But even Beethoven, who experimented once with each variation in a different key in his piano set, Op. 34, never did so again, and they are far from his most successful variations. It seems clear that for Schubert the form limited his normally fertile harmonic imagination. It is unfortunate that he never felt free enough to combine groups of variations with other formal approaches, as Beethoven did magnificently in the slow movements of the Fifth and Seventh symphonies.

The three string quartets mentioned in the letter to Kupelwieser (the A Minor, D Minor, and G Major), Schubert's most impressive contribution to the genre, were originally intended to be published as a set of three, perhaps in emulation of Beethoven's Op. 59, the Razumovsky Quartets. But Schubert's third, the G Major (D887), was not written until 1826 and only the first, the A Minor (D804), was actually printed during his lifetime. It appeared in September of 1824 as Op. 29 No. 1, "Trois Quatuors . . . composés et dediés à son ami Ignaz Schuppanzigh . . . par François Schubert de Vienne." The first performance had taken place on March 14 of that year in the subscription series mounted by Schuppanzigh with the violinist leading his quartet. On the same program was Beethoven's Septet.

As the letter suggests, Schubert must have composed the D Minor Quartet in close proximity to the A Minor, and they have much in common. Both are in minor keys with effective use made of the contrast between minor and major; in addition, both are cyclic, that is the individual movements are linked motivically.[17] There is also a striking similarity in the dependence of both slow movements, as well as the Minuet (D804) and Scherzo (D810), on previously composed compositions by Schubert. The sources of the slow movements are well known: the principal theme of the Andante of the A Minor derives from the section in major of the *entr'acte* following Act III of his incidental music to *Rosamunde* (D797).[18]

The Minuet was the best-received movement of the A Minor Quartet at the first performance; and it is perhaps the finest, certainly the most poignant, dance movement in Schubert's larger instrumental works. The arresting beginning in the cello and the transition to the Trio derive from his song *Die Götter Griechenlands* ("The Gods of Greece," D677, November 1819) set to a text by Schiller beginning "Schöne Welt, wo bist du?" ("Beautiful world, where are you?"). The striking contrast of A minor and A major, so important for the song, is also crucial for the Minuet and the quartet as a whole; and the tonalities of both song and quartet are the same, A. The key of the song *Death and the Maiden*, D minor, is also that of the quartet, although the theme is transposed to G minor for the slow movement

Less well known is the fact that the Scherzo of the D Minor Quartet is derived from a previously composed dance, arguably one of Schubert's greatest, the G sharp Minor Ländler (D790, 6; May 1823). (It forms part of a splendid set of twelve German dances first edited by Brahms and published as Op. 171 in 1868.) Since the dance is relatively short, to achieve the proportions of a scherzo in a multi-movement composition Schubert expanded the piece considerably. Despite the additions, the substantive relationship will be clear from a comparison of measures 1–6 of the dance and measures 9–14 of the Scherzo (see Ex. 9.1).[19]

The two figures, marked 'x' and 'y' on the example of the Scherzo (Ex. 9.1b), are important throughout the quartet as cyclic elements. The first, a short scale, is already present in the Ländler, but the second, the repeated notes (figure 'y'), is not. The rhythm of figure 'y' is a triple-meter version of the dactylic pattern associated with "Death" in the song. That this rhythm was not present in the dance, but added consistently to the Scherzo and its Trio, is a strong indication that the cyclic element was quite intentional on Schubert's part.

Schubert wrote once to Leopold von Sonnleithner that a composer cannot always count on finding the right structure for a composition (*SDB* 265). But he found just such a structure for the slow movement and finale of the A Minor Quartet. It was an unusual type of rondo in which the refrain appears twice rather than the three times considered definitive for the form. Schubert's structure is A B A C B Coda, in which A is the

Example 9.1a and 9.1b

G♯ Minor Ländler (D790, 6), mm. 1–8

D Minor String Quartet (D810), third movement, mm. 1–22

refrain, B and C are episodes differing from one another, and the coda, taking the place of the final refrain, is derived from refrain material. The young composer appears to have derived this approach, which he subsequently used for other movements as well, from the finale of Mozart's String Quintet in C Major (K. 515).[20] Schubert knew the work as he had borrowed the Mozart quintets from a friend previously.[21]

Schubert wrote the last, and in many ways the most original, of his string quartets, the G Major, in 1826. By this time he is no longer particularly concerned with writing variations, nor does he use short motifs cyclically to relate movements. Instead there is a complex web of connections, some obvious, others less so. The most important of these is modal contrast, the alternation of major and minor on several levels. The first movement begins with a juxtaposition of the tonic (G major) triad with its parallel triad (G minor), an idea he almost immediately repeats on the dominant (mm. 6–10). During the recapitulation (mm. 278ff.) he reverses the procedure; now the minor triad is first. In the quartet's finale, a quick and extended sonata-rondo in 6/8 meter much like that of the D Minor Quartet, each time the refrain occurs there is a descending tonic minor triad followed by an ascending G major scale. Both the rondo slow movement and the highly imaginative Scherzo, a kind of miniature sonata form, also make important use of modal contrast.

Schubert's String Quintet in C Major, for string quartet and a second cello (D956, summer or early fall 1828), is generally recognized as one of the finest chamber works of the nineteenth century, a fitting successor to Mozart's string quintets. One reason for Schubert's choice of two cellos may have been modesty, to avoid a direct comparison with Mozart who preferred two violas in his quintets. Another, probably stronger, reason was the richer sonorities offered by the cellos.

Spaciousness, a quality also present in the first movement of the G Major Quartet, characterizes the Quintet. The tone is set by the slow moving, even static harmonic progression with which the first movement opens. Unlike Schubert's normal inclination to initiate a movement with a march-like or even dance-like rhythm, both here and in the opening of the G Major Quartet he presents his harmonies – rather than a memorable, well-contoured melody – without a regular rhythmic pulse. As a result, the Quintet opening contrasts powerfully with the surging rhythmic momentum generated during the continuation of the principal subject. In Beethoven's conversation books Schubert is reported to have assiduously attended the first performances of all the older master's late quartets (*SDB* 536). One of the lessons he seems to have learned was the effectiveness of powerful, sometimes unexpected, contrasts. His own contributions in the Quintet are the rich sonorities, the way he balances the five instruments in varied groups, and the incredible beauty of the modulating middle theme. Particularly noteworthy is the way Schubert constructs the development section in the first movement. He devises an extended sequence consisting of three long, highly modulatory stages, a compositional technique he developed near the end of his career.[22] Shortly before the recapitulation (mm. 262ff.), Schubert introduces an ascending arpeggio in the first violin reminiscent of the principal theme in the first movement of Mozart's C Major Quintet.

The sublime slow movement, one of Schubert's relatively few Adagios, is in three parts. The principal theme of the first moves effortlessly and without pause for twenty-eight measures, a *tour de force* of continuity suggesting music of much later composers. The key is E major, one he likes for elegiac settings, witness the slow movement of the "Unfinished" Symphony. The strong contrast with the second part of the movement, a passionate outburst in F minor, is typical of the Quintet. The tonal relationship of lowered second degree to the tonic of the movement, F minor to E, is important elsewhere in the composition.

The Scherzo, an expansive movement whose proportions and tonal variety bring it closer to sonata than to dance form, has a Trio which is surely the most unusual Schubert ever wrote. Following Beethoven's lead in the Trio of the Scherzo in the Ninth Symphony, Schubert abandons the usual triple meter for common time. Furthermore, in place of the extremely rapid Presto – the Scherzo is the quickest movement in the Quintet – he substitutes an Andante sostenuto. There is also a highly unusual key-scheme. This parallels the slow movement whose central portion was also designed to provide maximum contrast. In the Trio, as in the second part of the slow movement, Schubert moves a half step higher, from C to D flat major. To make the relationship with the slow movement even stronger, he begins the Trio with four measures of an unaccompanied melodic line suggesting F minor. The impression of the Trio as a whole is that of a funeral march, not unlike the slow movement of the "Eroica" Symphony with which it shares an important melodic element (see Ex 9.2).

The energetic and, for Schubert, relatively concise finale is another sonata-rondo employing the form of the finale of Mozart's C Major Quintet (A B A C B Coda). It is the only movement in which the tonic minor plays a role as important as that of the tonic major.[23] Schubert's close, with a sustained trill in the cellos on D♭ recalls the trills and half-step relationship in the slow movement, and especially the D flat Trio where trills were also important. The range of contrasting moods successfully encompassed by Schubert in the quintet as a whole is quite remarkable and ultimately deeply satisfying.

Schubert's chamber music with piano

Schubert began to write chamber music with piano relatively late in his career. In 1816, a year in which the influence of Mozart reached its peak, Schubert wrote three short but attractive sonatas for piano "with the accompaniment of the violin," published posthumously by Diabelli as "Three Sonatinas" (Op. 137). The first of the three, in D Major (D384),

Example 9.2a and 9.2b

Beethoven, "Eroica" Symphony, Op. 55, second movement, mm. 1–5

String Quintet in C Major (D956), third movement, mm. 1–8

owes much to the first movement of Mozart's E Minor Piano and Violin Sonata (K. 304), especially in the opening and closing sections of the respective expositions. The lovely E major Trio of Mozart's second movement, a Tempo di Menuetto, must have deeply impressed Schubert, foreshadowing as it does his own tenderest dances.

That same year he wrote an Adagio and Rondo Concertante for Piano Quartet (piano, violin, viola, and cello; D487), another work influenced by Mozart. It was composed for a choir director, Heinrich Grob, brother of the soprano Therese Grob toward whom Schubert was romantically inclined for several years. Not especially demanding of the pianist, the piece falls into that category of early chamber works that can be performed with additional string instruments, perhaps even a small orchestra.[24] As is often true of Schubert's lesser instrumental works, the most interesting passages are to be found in the slow section, the Adagio.

During the year 1818 Schubert wrote his first significant group of four-hand compositions, an activity that left an indelible impression on the scoring for piano of such works as the A Major "Trout" Quintet for piano, violin, viola, cello, and contrabass (D667). One of Schubert's most popular instrumental compositions, it appears to have been written for a wealthy music patron and amateur cellist, Sylvester Paumgartner, of Steyr in Upper Austria. He is said to have suggested that Schubert include a set of variations on the composer's song *Die Forelle* (D550). As no autograph exists, the date of composition is uncertain; but Schubert visited Steyr during the summers of 1819, 1823, and 1825. Otto Erich Deutsch suggested fall 1819, which is supported by three pieces of musical evidence. First, most writers on Schubert's instrumental music have remarked on the number of sonata-form movements in which the recapitulation begins in the key of the subdominant; but they generally fail to notice that he did so only in works dating from 1814 through 1819. Since the recapitulation of the first movement of the "Trout" Quintet begins in the subdominant, this would seem to rule out the later years of 1823 or 1825. Secondly, Schubert wrote five slightly different versions of the song *Die Forelle*. The theme of the variation movement in the Quintet most closely resembles the version written in 1818. And, finally, Schubert chooses for the finale of the quintet a bipartite form in which the second part quite literally repeats the first, except for the sequence of keys. In other words, the second part is virtually a transposed version of the first. The second movement, the Andante, is similar but with a somewhat more interesting progression of tonalities. None of Schubert's larger instrumental movements of the 1820s is written in such a mechanical fashion.

To provide a unifying thread for much of the Quintet, Schubert adopts the sextuplets of the song's accompaniment and writes related figures in four of the five movements – all but the Scherzo. As in the song, the figure generally has a subordinate function; the piano usually introduces it; and, except for the slow movement, the figure ascends, as in the song. The feature suggesting four-hand writing consists in both hands playing exactly the same notes an octave apart. While passages of this sort occur elsewhere in Schubert's chamber music for piano, they do so far less often than here.

Schubert completed his two masterpieces for piano, violin, and cello, the Trios in B flat Major, Op. 99 (D898) and E flat Major, Op. 100 (D929), during the last twelve or thirteen months of his life, together with a less effective Adagio for Piano Trio in E flat (D897) called "Notturno" and generally believed to be a discarded slow movement for the B flat Trio. Considering the quality of the two completed trios, it is startling to realize that Schubert's only prior experience of writing for this instrumental combination was a single weak movement in B flat major written some fifteen years earlier (D28, 1812) and called by the young musician "Sonate."[25]

There is no extant manuscript for the late B flat Trio and, therefore, no firm date of composition. But the untitled and equally undated manuscript of the "Notturno," its presumed original slow movement, is of the same paper type as that of the E flat Trio whose manuscripts (including a sketch) are dated November 1827. Since Schubert apparently bought this paper sometime after September 24, 1827, and used it until April 1828[26] at least three movements of the B flat Trio would seem to have been written within months of the E flat Trio. But, in view of the fact that the new slow movement for Op. 99 is tripartite, a form Schubert used for slow movements of his larger instrumental works primarily at the end of his life, that (replacement?) movement may have been written during the summer or fall of 1828. If so, this might explain the publication of Op. 99 after Op. 100, even though it was given (by Schubert?) an earlier opus number.

Whatever their order of composition, the piano trios have much in common. In both there is the extended four-movement design favored by Beethoven with three movements in the tonic key.[27] Both slow movements begin with cello solos and each is in a key closely related to the tonic of the composition. Both Scherzos are elegantly contrapuntal, although the E flat Scherzo is more obviously so. It begins with a canon lasting twenty-seven measures. Was the model the fugato passages in the Trio of the Scherzo in Beethoven's "Archduke" Trio, Op. 97?[28] Each Scherzo has a more homophonic Trio in the subdominant. But it is the finales that have the most in common. Each is of considerable length and essentially bipartite in form, despite the title "Rondo" in Op. 99. Both are in duple meter – 2/4 for Op. 99, 6/8 for Op. 100 – with a vital rhythmic shift during the contrasting sections. In the B flat Trio there is a striking displacement as Schubert substitutes 3/2 meter for 2/4 at three points in the movement. In the finale of the E flat Trio the duple compound meter (6/8) gives way to an *alla breve* which is still duple, but with a simple subdivision of the beat (¢). This occurs at no less than five points in the movement. As the *alla breve* comes to the fore, there is an increased number of impacts per beat (four in place of three) and, consequently, an increase in excitement that helps propel the music forward.

Although not obviously, Schubert prepares for the repeated notes of the *alla breve* passage by introducing groups of repeated notes increasingly in his opening section. Initially these occupy subordinate roles; later, however, they assume thematic importance. See the cadence at measures 15–16 and especially the long upbeat to the contrasting idea of the first group treated imitatively (mm. 33–34). The repeated notes, however, not only provide coherence in the finale. They are part of a larger design, one in which all the movements of the trio are unified. Observers always point to the effective return twice of the principal theme of the slow movement in the finale (mm. 273ff. and mm. 693ff.) Unnoticed is the presence of themes – in the Andante con moto it is the introductory chords – with four repeated notes or sonorities in each movement. During the opening Allegro it is the modulating middle subject beginning in B minor (mm. 48ff.), a theme similar to the main idea of the Minuet in Schubert's G Major Sonata, Op. 78 (D894), also in B minor. In the slow movement it is the march-like chords introducing the main melody, said to be derived from a Swedish folk song. The four repeated notes are built into the canonic theme of the Scherzo as well as the lovely derived subject of the E major section (mm. 30ff.) In the Trio there is a double reference: the repeated quarter notes of the Scherzo are introduced by the original figure from the first movement (♩♫♫). This idea is then treated contrapuntally for twelve measures. Since Schubert closes both the first and last movements with the repeated-note figure, it is clear he wanted to emphasize the cyclic element.

Another relationship exists between the Minuet of the G Major Piano Sonata and, in this case, the B flat Trio. Schubert (subconsciously?) inverted the transition and first measures of the Minuet's Trio to shape his principal subject of the Scherzo in the B flat Trio (see Ex. 9.3).

Schubert's Octet and closing remarks

Schubert's Octet in F Major (D803) was completed March 1, 1824, for Ferdinand, Count Troyer, a clarinettist and Chief Steward of Archduke Rudolf, a composer who studied with Beethoven and to whom both the "Archduke" Trio and Schubert's A Minor Piano Sonata, Op. 42 (D845), were dedicated. Troyer is reported to have asked Schubert to write a composition resembling Beethoven's Septet.

Schubert fulfilled the commission, and a private performance of the Octet took place that year at the Count's home. In addition to Troyer, the performers once more included Schuppanzigh as first violinist and most of the players who took part in the premiere of Beethoven's Septet, in his

Example 9.3a and 9.3b

G Major Sonata, Op. 78 (D894), third movement, mm. 53–58

Piano Trio in B flat, Op. 99 (D898), third movement, mm. 1–8

lifetime the most popular of all his works.[29] The first public performance of the Octet took place on April 16, 1827, again at a concert organized by Schuppanzigh and with most of the same players as in 1824, with the exception of the clarinettist.[30] What may have brought the Septet to Troyer's attention was the fact that Schuppanzigh had scheduled its performance at the concert of March 14, 1824, together with Schubert's A Minor Quartet.

The correspondences between the Septet and the Octet are considerable. Schubert followed Beethoven's instrumentation (violin, viola, cello, contrabass, clarinet, bassoon, and horn) with the addition of a second violin. In the tradition of outdoor music suggested by the presence of three wind instruments, there are six rather than four movements, and for the most part a cheerful, relaxed mood. Beethoven wrote a Scherzo and a Minuet; and so did Schubert, except that he reversed their order. The older composer wrote a theme and variations in the key of the dominant and in duple meter as his fourth movement; and so did the younger. Although Schubert did not choose Beethoven's principal key, E flat major – he chose F major instead[31] – Schubert did follow closely the relationships of the individual movements to the respective principal keys. The only exceptions are the Trios to Scherzo and Minuet which Beethoven retained in the tonic; Schubert did not. Beethoven composed slow introductions to both quick movements (i.e. the first and last) and so did Schubert. Furthermore the lengths of those introductions are almost identical. Both Adagio movements begin softly with a clarinet solo and are in a compound meter. And, finally, the composer of each finale interrupts the flow of his movement at exactly the same point, the joint between development section and recapitulation. Beethoven introduces a cadenza at measure 135; Schubert reintroduces a portion of his slow introduction at measure 370.

Most of this information is common knowledge. Less often remarked is the cyclic element that Schubert introduced into each of his movements, a short dotted figure dominating the first movement. As in the D Minor Quartet, also written in early 1824, there are both rhythmic and melodic elements at play. In addition to dotted or double-dotted patterns, sometimes accentuated by an additional short upbeat, there is also melodic motion by step in either direction. Once the step-wise motion has been established, however, Schubert allows himself leeway; he stretches the interval, sometimes as much as an octave. Again as in the D Minor Quartet, the direction of the melodic component may vary. As with most motifs, it is the rhythmic aspect that is least mutable. Schubert may have received the stimulus for the rhythmic component and repeated pitches of his cyclic figure from the double-dotted repeated notes in the introduction to the last movement of Beethoven's Septet.

The cyclic motif has been traced throughout the Octet elsewhere[32] and I need only mention here the source of the theme Schubert adapted for his variation set: a duet, "Gelagert unterm hellen Dach," from the second act of his Singspiel, *Die Freunde von Salamanka* (D326, 1815). At several points Schubert introduces the cyclic figure into the instrumental version of the melody, a strong indication of his cyclic intent.

Before concluding, I should like to discuss briefly the musical factor that most impressed – in some cases disturbed – his contemporaries: Schubert's imaginative harmony. His propensity for rich, often dissonant sonorities and the frequency of unexpected harmonic progressions or tonal sequences is audible in his very first compositions. During the finale of the String Quartet in Mixed Keys (D18, 1810 or 1811), probably his earliest extant chamber work, the young musician increases the dissonant force of an already dissonant augmented-sixth chord by simultaneously sustaining its tone of resolution in the cello. To highlight this unusual sonority, Schubert calls for a *forzando*, writes the three upper strings in what amounts to an excited string tremolo (repeated sixteenth notes at a presto tempo), and then repeats the progression immediately (see Ex. 9.4).

In his earliest works Schubert's harmonic exploits are not always con-

Example 9.4 String Quartet in Mixed Keys (D18), fourth movement, mm. 28–31

vincing. But they are later. The exposition of the first movement in his last string quartet, the G Major, provides a stunning example of Schubert's modulatory imagination and control. As noted earlier, the contrasting and juxtaposition of tonic major and minor is crucial for the entire composition. During the exposition of the first movement, Schubert takes advantage of the fact that his first group (principal subject) contains passages in both tonic major and minor to compose a remarkable modulatory contrasting region. The passage (middle subject) begins with D major, the expected dominant of G major. But Schubert then uses the importance of the tonic minor to introduce two additional tonal areas, the dominant and relative of G minor (D minor at m. 104 and B flat major at m. 110). Since the passages in D major and B flat major also tonicize momentarily other scale degrees, the effect is tonally kaleidoscopic. The closing section includes scales of D melodic minor (i.e. with lowered sixth and seventh degrees) alternating with a syncopated thematic idea in D major derived from the middle subject. The exposition and a slightly abbreviated recapitulation are, from the tonal point of view, incredibly rich; but they are also thoroughly convincing. The point to be made from this admittedly extreme instance is that in Schubert's extended forms modulation provides more than a path to, or a preparation for, the next tonally stable passage. But if there is so much tonal movement in the expositions and recapitulations of his sonata-form movements, what can Schubert do in his development sections? For some possible answers we might return briefly to the first movements of his piano trios.

At the end of the development section of the first movement of the B flat Trio, there is an oft-remarked and quite startling turn to G flat major (m. 187). It is startling because there were twenty-six measures of dominant preparation for B flat (the expected tonic) comprising the end of the development section (mm. 160–85). To be sure, earlier in the movement Schubert wrote a low G♭ trill at the cadence of the principal subject (m. 9).[33] He also introduced, more thematically, bass G♭'s in his closing section (mm. 101, 105, and 109), as well as similar bass G♭'s during the dominant preparation just mentioned (mm. 176 and 180). Ornamental elaborations of F, either as dominant or temporary tonic, they only partially prepare the ear for a recapitulation on G flat. I believe Schubert wants us to hear the event as a surprising one, a momentary tonal obfuscation, clarified almost immediately by a modulation to the expected key at the continuation of the principal subject (m. 211).

This and other late recapitulations in keys other than the tonic (e.g. in the finale of the "Great" C Major Symphony [D944]) differ considerably from the dominant and subdominant recapitulations of Schubert's earlier years. Those keys were usually prepared; they emerge naturally from their (generally shorter) development sections; and the overall effect is often of a bipartite rather than tripartite sonata form. Two aspects are of importance: the length and relative significance of the development section, and the impact at the point of recapitulation. As suggested earlier, it is only from the time of the "Unfinished" Symphony and its first movement that Schubert is able to handle extended developments. One of the ways he does so, and I think successfully, is with sequences, each of whose stages is of substantial length and modulates (i.e. within the stage itself). We saw an example in the String Quintet's first movement. There is an equally extended sequence forming the body of the development section of the first movement of the E flat Piano Trio.[34] This is a single extremely long sequence with three stages (cf. mm. 195–246, mm. 247–98, and mm. 299ff.) More often, Schubert writes several shorter sequences, as in the first-movement development sections of the last three string quartets.

Did Schubert find this particular approach to organizing development sections on his own? Perhaps. But there is a model, and he could hardly avoid knowing it. The composer? Not much of a riddle. The piece? The first movement of the "Pastoral" Symphony.

10 Schubert's orchestral music: "strivings after the highest in art"

L. Michael Griffel

Schubert inherited the attitude from the end of the eighteenth century that to succeed as a composer – both commercially and artistically – one had to write good operas and symphonies. Throughout his life he turned and returned to these two genres, despite his realization that no throng of listeners, not even his most ardent fans and friends, requested such compositions of him. Schubert felt that he needed to go beyond the confines of the song, piano piece, and chamber work in order to link his name to those of Haydn, Mozart, and, especially, his greatest contemporary, Beethoven.[1] In February 1828, just nine months before his death, Schubert informed the publisher B. Schott's Söhne of his available compositions. In this letter he lists various chamber compositions, works for piano solo and duet, songs for one or more voices, and choral works. After all this, however, he reveals his creed as a composer: "This is the list of my finished compositions, excepting three operas, a Mass and a symphony. These last compositions I mention only in order to make you acquainted with my strivings after the highest in art" (*SDB* 739–40).

It was rare for Schubert to discuss his symphonies in his correspondence. One senses that, although his aims may have been pragmatic in the case of opera, they were idealistic in connection with the symphony, and that, perhaps, his most important artistic goal was to compose a remarkably fine symphony – a great symphony – to match the symphonic accomplishments of Beethoven. Whether or not one believes this goal was met, few would refute the position that Schubert left us some of the most moving and uplifting symphonic music of the nineteenth century.

Schubert's orchestral works comprise seven completed symphonies, one symphony left unfinished after the completion of two movements, five unfinished (sketched or fragmentary) symphonies without any completed movement, seven finished overtures, one fragment of an overture, and three other unfinished (sketched or fragmentary) movements. Table 10.1 presents these works in chronological order of composition.

Schubert first tried his hand at symphonic composition around 1811, at the age of fourteen. Two fragments in D major survive in the University

Table 10.1. *Chronological list of the orchestral works**

Overture in D Major, D2A (fragment in orchestral score, 1811?)
Symphony in D Major, D2B (fragment of one movement in orchestral score, 1811?)
Overture in D Major, D12 (1811/1812)
Overture in D Major, D26 (1812)
Fragments of an orchestral work in D Major, D71C (in orchestral score, 1813)
Symphony No. 1 in D Major, D82 (1813)
Fragment of an orchestral work in B flat Major, D94A (in orchestral score, 1814?)
Symphony No. 2 in B flat Major, D125 (1814–15)
Symphony No. 3 in D Major, D200 (1815)
Symphony No. 4 in C Minor, D417, *Tragic* (1816)
Overture in B flat Major, D470 (1816)
Symphony No. 5 in B flat Major, D485 (1816)
Overture in D Major, D556 (1817)
Overture *in the Italian Style* in D Major, D590 (1817)
Overture *in the Italian Style* in C Major, D591 (1817)
Symphony No. 6 in C Major, D589 (1817–18)
Symphony in D Major, D615 (fragments of two movements in piano sketches, 1818)
Overture in E Minor, D648 (1819)
Fragmentary sketches for an orchestral work in A Major, D966B (piano sketches, after 1819)
Symphony in D Major, D708A (fragments of four movements in piano sketches, 1820–21)
Symphony [No. 7] in E Major, D729 ("Sketch," four movements sketched on orchestral score
    paper, 1821)
Symphony [No. 8] in B Minor, D759 ("Unfinished," full score of two completed movements plus
    the two pages of the unfinished scherzo; also a piano sketch of the scherzo and part of the
    trio, 1822)
Symphony [No. 9] in C Major, D944 ("Great," 1825–26)
Symphony in D Major, D936A (piano sketches of three movements, 1828)

Note:
*Not included in this Table are D4, D812, and D849, for the following reasons: D4 (1812?), the
Overture to J. F. E. Albrecht's comedy *Der Teufel als Hydraulicus*, falls outside the domain of
music for concert orchestra; it belongs with Schubert's other overtures for staged dramatic
works. D812, the Sonata in C Major for Piano Four Hands (the "Grand Duo," 1824), was
thought by Robert Schumann to be the piano arrangement or reduction of a symphony;
however, Schubert clearly marked it as *Sonate*, and, despite the work's occasional orchestral
texture, there is no documentary evidence whatsoever to support Schumann's view. D849,
the mythical "Lost" Symphony, remains only a wish of ardent Schubert lovers.

Library in Lund, Sweden. An overture (D2A) and the first movement of a
symphony (D2B), both containing a completed "Adagio" introduction in
3/4 time and an incomplete "Allegro" ("con moto" in the symphony) in
common time, disclose a schoolboy taking his first steps in orchestral
composition. In these twin efforts, employing practically the same thematic material, the handwriting is large, neat, and easily read; the bar-
lines are ruled; and the musical ideas are formulistic. The symphonic
autograph also gives evidence of the youngster's inexperience with the
rhythmic and orchestrational conventions of the time.

The two completed overtures written while Schubert was a student at Vienna's Stadtkonvikt, D12 and D26, were most likely seen and refined by Antonio Salieri, Schubert's composition teacher there. The first is constructed like D2A, whereas the second breaks this pattern and begins directly with an "Allegro spiritoso." Although no record exists of public performances of these overtures during Schubert's lifetime, there is every reason to believe that the school orchestra played them and that, in fact, Schubert composed them for the school body. These four earliest efforts show that the young Schubert did not differentiate generically between the overture and the symphonic first movement.[2] Furthermore, he restricted himself to D major, because that was the easiest key for orchestral musicians to negotiate during the early nineteenth century.[3]

It was not until two years later that Schubert finished his first symphony, but then he produced five more within five years (1813–18). Each of these six works is modeled on the symphonic style of Schubert's immediate predecessors: primarily Haydn, Mozart, Beethoven, and Rossini. We recognize in Schubert's early scores many of the favorite melodic motifs, harmonic progressions, and organizing principles of these previous composers; and the historical evidence surrounding Schubert's first six symphonies suggests that he was gaining experience as a symphonist by building upon their strengths. It would have been senseless for a Viennese teenager to have proceeded otherwise, especially with Beethoven at the height of his own compositional career in Vienna, awaiting the first performances of his Seventh and Eighth Symphonies (in 1813 and 1814, respectively), and with Rossini's operas taking Vienna by storm as early as 1816. And so Schubert produced the kinds of symphony that his school orchestra and amateur neighborhood orchestras were accustomed to read through without much difficulty.[4]

In 1816 Vienna's Gesellschaft der Musikfreunde launched a series of orchestral concerts, which must have given Schubert a new impetus to compose a symphony worthy of public performance. With his ongoing exposure to wonderful symphonies and overtures (primarily to operas) by such composers as Gluck, Haydn, Mozart, Beethoven, Spontini, and Cherubini – and with, one can assume, the goal of a Gesellschaft performance – Schubert could not resist writing orchestral works of his own. Why would he have? The way to fame and fortune in the Beethoven–Rossini era was as a writer of symphonies and operas, and Schubert craved success at both.

Although Schubert never gained renown as an orchestral composer during his own time, even his first six symphonies have come to be greatly admired. Considering the period 1800–20, with the exception of Beethoven, one cannot name successful competitors to Schubert as symphonist: there are impressive contributions by Tomášek, E. T. A. Hoffmann, Weber, Méhul, Gossec, Spohr, Clementi, and Cherubini (roughly in that chronological order), but Schubert's six as a group command more attention today than the symphonic output of any composer in the above list. In 1813–18, however, Schubert could only have dreamed of sharing the public's attention with the likes of Hoffmann, Weber, or Spohr, not to mention Beethoven.

From his studies and observations, Schubert was familiar with the Austro-Italian symphonic format of his era: many scalar and triadic themes, plenty of tuneful melodies, tonic and dominant tensions and relaxations, crescendos and sforzandos, repeated tones and expectant pauses, diminished-seventh chords and suspensions, lilting trios and whirlwind finales, adagio introductions and ABA andantes. Especially from Mozart he picked up ideas about tuneful melodies, balanced orchestral forces, and subtlety of phrasing. Yet, the symphonies of Beethoven ultimately weighed most heavily upon Schubert's mind, with their large dimensions, resulting length, refocusing of tonal relationships, cyclical structure, resolution-finales, and ventures into the extramusical.

When Schubert subtitled his Fourth Symphony (D417) the *Tragic*, he must have been influenced by Beethoven's Fifth. As Schubert's only completed symphony in the minor mode, this C minor work is also the most agitated and dramatic among his first six. The choppy, driving rhythm of Schubert's opening theme is significantly similar to many a theme in Beethoven's C minor works. But already in Schubert's Symphony No. 1 (D82), there are references to Beethoven. The second theme of the first movement (at m. 78), for instance, is a variation of the *Prometheus* theme in Beethoven's "Eroica" Symphony (first performed in 1805), as is the second theme of Schubert's finale (at m. 86; see Ex. 10.1). Schubert's First is also closely tied to Mozart's Symphony No. 38 in D Major, the "Prague" (1786), in that their slow movements have striking similarities: both "Andantes" are G major movements in D major symphonies, are in 6/8 time, and begin with the strings presenting the main theme over a long-held tonic pedal point.

Schubert's Fifth Symphony (D485), like its partner Overture in B flat (D470) of the same time, also owes much to Mozart. Schubert's Minuet begins with a theme that is confusingly similar to the minuet theme in Mozart's Symphony No. 40 in G Minor (1788), greatly admired by Schubert at the time.[5] The Sixth Symphony (D589) is in an undeniably Rossinian style, and Schubert seems to have prepared himself for it by writing three overtures, D556 and the two Overtures "in the Italian style" (D590 and D591), a short time earlier.[6]

None of Schubert's symphonies was, in any event, played in a public

Example 10.1a, b and c

(a) Beethoven, Symphony No. 3, Op. 55, fourth movement, mm. 75–83

(b) Schubert, Symphony No. 1 (D82), first movement, mm. 78–86

(c) Schubert, Symphony No. 1 (D82), fourth movement, mm. 85–93

concert during his lifetime. Coupling this fact with an awareness of his remarkable originality in composing Lieder, Schubert came to disavow his efforts as a symphonist (*SDB* 265). He sensed the dependence of his early symphonies on older models, and took no steps to have them performed for a public audience. In refining his instrumental style, Schubert became increasingly aware that his youthful pieces fell far short of the new symphonic standards established by Beethoven. The maturing Schubert recognized some of the peculiarities of form, repetitiousness, and superficiality in his early symphonies.[7]

In any event, as a fast-rising independent musician, Schubert kept these works out of the public arena and reserved them for informal, social, salon-style performances. This is confirmed by contemporaneous hand-copied orchestral parts in the Gesellschaft archives for five of the first six symphonies, with watermarks and paper dating from Schubert's lifetime and with at least one correction in the composer's own handwriting for a first-violin part of Symphony No. 1. Since Schubert seems not to have intended to publish these works, the care he took to correct the violin part suggests only that he was preparing the piece for performances, such as those in the Viennese merchant Otto Hatwig's house. Hatwig's orchestra numbered thirty-six players by the spring of 1818: seven first violins, six seconds, three violas, three cellos, two double basses, two flutes, two oboes, three clarinets, three bassoons, two horns, two trumpets, and one pair of timpani.[8] Schubert himself played viola in this orchestra, as he had in the Schubert family string quartet from at least 1812 on.

Schubert had been dependent on the financial support of his friends since 1816. Starting in 1818, however, when he permanently resigned from teaching at his father's school, Schubert determined to live on his earnings as a composer. With renewed ambition, he set about writing symphonies again, but ran into trouble. In May 1818, two months after working up the courage to apply for membership in the Gesellschaft (denied until 1821), he sketched two movements for a Symphony in D Major (D615). These piano sketches occur on two folios and contain several indications of orchestration, but both movements are cut short, the first after 119 measures and the second after 120. The first movement's slow introduction contains motifs that govern the ensuing sonata form, and the second movement is in a Haydnesque mood.[9]

With the success of *Erlkönig* at the Kärntnerthor Theater on March 7, 1821, the Viennese public began to take greater notice of the young man, and publication of his shorter works commenced in 1821 (in the next seven years more than 120 of Schubert's compositions would be issued). Quickly he rose to an exalted position among the living composers in Vienna, as his Lieder, piano pieces, dance music, and sacred works were performed steadily. Yet throughout this period, the symphony – that exalted, "Beethovenian" genre – remained on his mind.

Most likely in a mood of self-confidence and optimism, Schubert again prepared piano sketches for a Symphony in D Major (D708A) in May and June of 1821. This time he sketched portions for all four movements, as the five extant folios indicate, but again he left all the movements stranded, after writing 178, 72, 146, and 227 measures, respectively. Also as before, he cued in a few indications of the instrumentation. Of primary interest in these sketches are the avoidance of a slow introduction in the first movement, the D major–A flat major diminished-fifth relationship between the first and second themes in the opening exposition, the exciting scherzo with an opening rhythm that prefigures the scherzo movement in Schubert's "Great" Symphony, and the Rossinian tarantella-like rondo finale.

Not long after these 1821 piano sketches, Schubert went a great deal further toward completing another symphony. In August 1821 he sketched a Symphony in E Major (D729) in an orchestral-score format. In fact, he even went so far as to orchestrate, that is, to complete, the thirty-four measures of the first movement's "Adagio" introduction (in E minor) and the first seventy-six measures of the ensuing "Allegro." The rest of that movement (298 more measures) remained a skeleton, as did all of the "Andante" (117 mm.), the Scherzo ("Allegro") (122 mm.) with Trio (70 mm.), and the "Allegro giusto" finale (623 mm.). But Schubert's sketch in this instance shows clearly the motivic and thematic progression of the piece, its structure, much of its orchestration, dynamics, expression, and some of its harmonies. Yet, attempts to complete the work by such musicians as John Barnett in 1883, Felix Weingartner in 1934 (published by Universal), and Brian Newbould in 1977–78 (published by The University of Hull Press in 1992) have shown that without Schubert's own harmonic and timbral manipulations the music does not quite sound like Schubert. Nonetheless, even in these versions one senses Schubert's gradual separation from the Classical symphonic style.

The sketched score of D729 reveals that in 1821 Schubert conceived of the symphony as a long, expansive work, with outer movements in some type of sonata form, a tuneful Andante, and a busy Scherzo. The opening measures of the symphony would contain the seeds of the entire first movement and even, perhaps, of the whole work. The tonal system would favor bass motion by thirds, and the texture would depend at times on linear contrapuntal interplay among the several lines. In the orchestra the woodwinds (especially oboes and clarinets) would sing more and more of the thematic ingredients, and the brasses, including three trombones, would share in the melodic work. Interestingly, as on other occasions, Schubert seems to have prepared himself for this work by first writing an overture; however, in this instance the time lag was two and a half years. The Overture in E Minor (D648) of 1819 is a harbinger of Schubert's mature symphonic style, including the use of three trombones and wonderful woodwind dialogues.

So, from May 1818 to August 1821 Schubert had sketched ten symphonic movements but abandoned them all. Then came the fateful year of 1822 in which he contracted the syphilis which eventually led to his death six years later. This disease caused Schubert to withdraw from society for over a year. A letter from him to his friend Franz von Schober, dated August 14, 1823, includes the comment: "I . . . am fairly well. Whether I shall ever recover I am inclined to doubt" (*SDB* 286). Tragically, this illness marred the remaining six years of Schubert's life, which from 1822 on shows otherwise inexplicable periods of withdrawal, apathy, depression, and sickness. It may be this disease which prompted Schubert's abandonment of his next symphony, his best-known and best-loved, the "Unfinished" Symphony in B Minor (D759), dated October 30, 1822. Though not a very poetic reason for leaving the piece unfinished, Schubert's possible mental association of the symphony with his devastating disease would help explain not only why he ceased to work on it but also why in 1823 he sent the manuscript to his friend Anselm Hüttenbrenner in Graz, probably to repay a debt. In any event, after completing the first two movements and twenty measures of the third, Schubert abandoned the rest of the Scherzo. Piano sketches for that movement are complete for the Scherzo section (112 mm) and fragmentary for the Trio section (16 mm). A fourth movement was not even sketched.[10] Hüttenbrenner kept the manuscript to himself until 1865, when he yielded it to Johann Herbeck, the conductor of the concerts of the Gesellschaft der Musikfreunde in Vienna, for a performance by that group in December.

Had Schubert written just this one symphony, unfinished though it may be, his place in any account of the history of the symphony would still be secure. In the hyperbolic but commonly held view of Sir George Grove, the "Unfinished" abounds in: ". . . imagination in its grandest, and wildest, and most delicate flights; tenderness to a degree which no poet or composer ever surpassed; . . . melodies such as few musicians have been gifted with; facility and power of expression which Mozart himself might have envied."[11] Grove was perceptive to mention wildness, because the thematic transformations and rhetorical *coups de théâtre* residing in this composition are no less astonishing, no less original than the shocking events in such a contemporaneous work as Mary Shelley's *Frankenstein* (1818).

If syphilis was, at least partially, responsible for the banishment to Graz of Schubert's most unusual symphony, a far more pervasive problem seems to have been at the root of Schubert's long-lasting incompatibility with the symphonic genre. And that problem was having to contend with the overwhelming presence of Ludwig van Beethoven and his already well-known Symphonies Nos. 1 through 8, all written by 1812, performed by 1814, and published by 1817. Having outgrown his anti-Napoleonic period of hostility toward the revolutionary and eccentric Beethoven, Schubert, by 1822, openly adored that god among symphonists and, perhaps more secretly, envied and feared him. On April 19, 1822, Schubert dedicated his "Variations on a French Song" (D624) for piano four-hands, Op. 10, to Beethoven, with the unusually obsequious wording: "To Ludwig van Beethoven by his Worshipper and Admirer Franz Schubert."[12] On August 14th of the same year Joseph Hüttenbrenner, Schubert's factotum and Anselm Hüttenbrenner's brother, wrote to the publisher C. F. Peters that among the many Viennese who admired Schubert was, in fact, Beethoven. Said Hüttenbrenner of Schubert: "In short, and without exaggeration, we may speak of 'a second Beethoven.' Indeed that immortal man says of him: 'This one will surpass me'"(*SDB* 232). Whether or not Beethoven really said anything of the kind, Schubert must have thought he did, for Hüttenbrenner would in all likelihood have repeated to Schubert whatever he had told the publisher. At the age of twenty-five, then, Schubert faced the challenge of writing a symphony that would be as convincing as Beethoven's without sounding like a copy of the great master. Despite the wonders of the "Unfinished" Symphony, Schubert was not satisfied with it, could not complete it, shipped it off to Graz, and agonized over the immediate problem of his illness. Schubert was consciously or subconsciously postponing the publication of a first symphony and the inevitable comparisons with Beethoven that would result.[13] One should, furthermore, keep in mind that Beethoven was, on the whole, brash and unafraid, whereas Schubert was modest and somewhat timorous, and that by the age at which Schubert died, with seven and a half symphonies to his credit, Beethoven had composed just his first two symphonies.

We thus find Schubert in 1822 reluctant to give up the sure successes of more Lieder and other short pieces for the risky and frightening business of writing a symphony that could stand up to Beethoven's. In an 1823 letter to Josef Peitl, a teacher at Schubert's old school, who had requested an orchestral work for the student orchestra to play, Schubert stated: "Since I have nothing for full orchestra which I could send out into the world with a clear conscience, and there are so many pieces by great masters, as for instance Beethoven's Overture to 'Prometheus,' 'Egmont,' 'Coriolanus,' &c. &c. &c., I must very cordially ask your pardon for not being able to oblige you on this occasion, seeing that it would be much to my disadvantage to appear with a mediocre work" (*SDB* 265). The proximity of Beethoven's name to Schubert's confession of mediocrity reveals the standard by which Schubert was judging his own symphonies; by 1823 he did not consider them worthy even for a student performance. The Beethoven challenge left Schubert no peace of mind, and on March 31, 1824, in a letter to a friend, the painter Leopold Kupelwieser, we find more confessions and the revelation of Schubert's secret plan:

> Of songs I have not written many new ones, but I have tried my hand at several instrumental works, for I wrote two Quartets for violins, viola and violoncello and an Octet, and I want to write another quartet, in fact I intend to pave my way towards a grand symphony in that manner. – The latest in Vienna is that Beethoven is to give a concert at which he is to produce his new Symphony, three movements from the new Mass and a new Overture. – God willing, I too am thinking of giving a similar concert next year.   (*SDB* 339)

"Grand symphony" and "Beethoven" were linked in Schubert's mind. He wanted to write a *grand* symphony, that is, a long, large-scale dramatic orchestral work, one that might tax the capabilities of players and listeners alike *and* overwhelm them with its largeness, importance, and effectiveness – just as Beethoven's "Eroica," Fifth, and Seventh Symphonies had done. The next Schubert symphony would have to be as good as any of Beethoven's, and Schubert was, as he himself said, paving his way toward the writing of such a work by leading up to it, by "practicing," with string quartets (the A Minor, D804, and D Minor, D810, masterpieces) and an octet (another of Schubert's finest chamber works, D803, modeled on Beethoven's Septet, Op. 20). The ultimate goal was the writing of a great symphony, as great as Beethoven's, one that might lead to an all-Schubert concert, status equal to Beethoven's, and the end of Schubert's symphonic hang-up.

In addition to Schubert's letter to Kupelwieser, several other letters written and comments made by Schubert's friends attest to the fact that in 1824 the composer was planning a symphony and that in 1825 he was working on it. No symphony, however, dated 1824 or 1825 is extant. In fact, after the "Unfinished" Symphony of 1822 the next dated symphony is the big C Major, known as the "Great" (D944), whose autograph is dated March 1828. This puzzling situation gave birth to the notion of a so-called "Lost" Symphony, an idea proposed most forcefully by Grove. The "Lost" Symphony, still listed in the newest (1978) edition of the Schubert thematic catalogue as D849, is also called the "Gmunden" Symphony, the "Gastein" Symphony, and the "Gmunden-Gastein" Symphony, because it was in the Austrian towns of Gmunden and Bad Gastein, where Schubert spent most of the period from May to October of 1825, that he allegedly wrote his new symphony.[14]

Evidence suggests, however, that the "Lost" or "Gastein" Symphony is none other than the "Great" C Major Symphony, with its puzzling date of March 1828 in Schubert's handwriting on the autograph score. Examinations of the manuscript paper used for the autograph of the "Great" Symphony verify that it dates back to as early as 1825.[15] That spring and early summer, largely in Gmunden, away from the pressures of Vienna, Schubert worked hard on his new piece and completed a great deal of it. This intense labor shows clearly on the manuscript; for this one contains more crossed-out notes and replaced pages than that of any other Schubert symphony. Whole sections of movements appear on noticeably different grains and colors of paper, datable to 1826. One sees that Schubert revised his work for several months, always in the hope of creating a brilliant piece of symphonic work worthy of a public performance. Furthermore, one learns from the official record of the Gesellschaft der Musikfreunde that between the 9th and 12th of October 1826 Schubert sent a symphony to the Gesellschaft for which, "as a token of the Society's gratitude," Schubert received a generous cash gift (*SDB* 559). The following message from Schubert to the Gesellschaft accompanied his present: "Convinced of the Austrian Musical Society's noble intention to support any artistic endeavour as far as possible, I venture, as a native artist, to dedicate to them this, my Symphony, and to commend it most politely to their protection. With all respect, Your devoted Frz. Schubert" (*SDB* 559).

Most likely, as that important day in October 1826 was approaching, Schubert was busy making last-minute revisions in the score. But the composer seemed pleased with his new symphony – he called it "This, my Symphony," in one breath erasing all his previous symphonic efforts from the record. Schubert was clearly proud of his "Symphony," and we know from extant payment receipts of two music copyists in the Gesellschaft der Musikfreunde that the Gesellschaft spent a good deal of money to have orchestral parts for this monumental piece prepared quickly after receiving the score. These receipts and the paper used to copy out the parts prove that the score and parts were in the Society's possession by the end of the summer of 1827. Moreover, in the writings of Leopold von Sonnleithner we read that at least once during Schubert's lifetime the Society's conservatory orchestra read through the piece at a rehearsal (*SMF* 431). Nonetheless, for as yet unknown reasons (although the difficulty of the piece is probably the explanation), an official public performance of the work was not scheduled by the Gesellschaft. It is just possible that Schubert became annoyed with the Gesellschaft because they were not quick to make plans for a performance, rescinded the score, revised it by perhaps simplifying a few treacherous passages, dated it March 1828 only at that point, and tried to sell it to a publisher.[16] Whatever may have happened, no publisher bought the work. Revisions notwithstanding, the Gesellschaft orchestra read through the symphony but apparently did not intend to perform it in concert.[17] Schubert settled for a planned performance of his other Symphony in C Major, the Sixth, instead. (Sadly, Schubert had died by the time this concert took place in December 1828.) It was not until March 21, 1839, that, upon Robert Schumann's instigation, Felix Mendelssohn conducted the first performance of the "Great" Symphony, in a cut version, at a Gewandhaus concert in Leipzig.

Even if the Gesellschaft failed to appreciate the value of Schubert's last symphony, the composer himself seems to have remained proud of this piece. In it he had matched Beethoven's symphonies in length, drive, weight, and freshness of form but had managed to inject the music with his special brand of expansiveness, leisureliness, lyricism, instrumental color, and harmonic finesse. In the first movement, the introduction's opening, germ motif, called out by the evocative and haunting French horns, gives rise to the trombones' epilogue (at m. 199) and ultimately serves as the movement's apotheosis in the coda (at m. 662). Tonal parentheses, subtle harmonizations, and exhaustive development also characterize this movement. Schubert's notion of development in 1825 points toward the future, especially to Bruckner. The materials are simple and lapidary enough to be combined easily, but the consecution of events is single-mindedly repetitive and sequential, although in an exciting and dynamic way.

The slow movement, typifying Schubert's love of melody, bears a resemblance to the corresponding movement of Beethoven's Seventh Symphony. Both of these A minor pieces are hypnotically enchanting with their inexorable processional motion and build-up of passion. The Scherzo has links to Beethoven's Ninth Symphony, for Schubert designs it as a sonata form in terms of tonal layout, sectionality, and thematic content. Furthermore, Schubert's finale, a gigantic but conventional sonata form with multipartite themes, includes a climactic figure (first heard at m. 277) that reminds one of Beethoven's "Freude" theme.

The highly Romantic traits of the "Great" Symphony, which also abound in the two completed movements of the "Unfinished" Symphony, would surely have infused Schubert's subsequent symphonies, had his life not ebbed away in November 1828. For just one short month earlier, in October, he set about sketching another symphony, D936A.

Here Schubert prepared piano sketches for three movements of a Symphony in D Major. There are sketches in two different versions for a first movement (145 and 71 measures long), an "Andante" (204 mm.), and two versions of a "Scherzo" (218 mm. – 124 for the scherzo and 94 for the trio – and 389 mm.). None of the movements is complete, although the second version of the Scherzo (without any trio) is sketched in its entirety. As in earlier piano sketches, Schubert entered some indications for the orchestration.

If one may regard Schubert's first six symphonies as vestiges of the Classical spirit and the "Unfinished" and the "Great" C Major as early Romantic updatings of the symphonic genre, then one may find in the sketches of 1828 the coming of a full-blooded Romanticism in the world of the symphony. A Lisztian transformation of theme, Brahmsian synthesis of gypsy tune and contrapuntal erudition, and Brucknerian pace, glowing brass texture, and build-up of sound breathe within the pages of these little-known sketches. Schubert was moving away from Classical form here. The first movement is large and sectional, replete with tempo changes and surprising switches of key. A somber dirge for a quartet of trombones in the key of B flat minor, marked "Andante," leads to a "Presto" in the tonic key of D major making use of the movement's first theme. An "Andante" in B minor follows; nearly complete as a sketch, its haunting theme is closely related to the trombone theme of the first movement. A wandering piece, close in spirit to the slow movement of

Mahler's Symphony No. 1 (six decades in the future), it seems to revolve around moments of bold modulation. The concluding movement, combining the functions of a scherzo and a finale, is strictly contrapuntal. At this time, Schubert was preparing to take lessons, presumably in counterpoint but perhaps actually in the writing of finales, with Simon Sechter, Vienna's foremost professor of music theory. Again one has to think that Schubert felt compelled to match Beethoven's contrapuntal achievements, especially remarkable in the Ninth Symphony, which Schubert must have heard at the work's premiere in May 1824 (although no proof exists); and it is also reasonable to suspect that by then Schubert believed that a good symphonic finale had to rest on an intricate contrapuntal scheme. This particular movement, however, was attempting to integrate the fugal approach with a gypsy tune, and the two do not seem to mix very well in this instance. This opinion notwithstanding, D936A promises a composition which might have become the fountainhead of the Romantic symphony. Alas, young Schubert died a month later and was denied the chance of taking the symphonic crown from Beethoven. Yet, Schubert's achievements in the field of the symphony, which he approached at first with youthful innocence, and then with nervous ambition, remain as evidence of his prodigious talent to compose large-scale instrumental music.

A note on the numbering of Schubert's symphonies

The first six symphonies pose no problem, as they are numbered in the order in which Schubert completed them. But then the confusion begins. When the Leipzig publishing firm of Breitkopf & Härtel issued the first edition (parts in 1840, score in 1849) of the "Great" Symphony in C Major, which Robert Schumann had discovered in 1839, it began to be known as Schubert's Symphony No. 7. The "Unfinished" Symphony, "rescued" from the home of Anselm Hüttenbrenner by Johann Herbeck in 1865, was first published in 1866 by C. A. Spina of Vienna. Because the big C Major Symphony had already come to be regarded as Schubert's Seventh, the "Unfinished" Symphony received the label of Symphony No. 8. This numbering was solidified by Breitkopf & Härtel when this firm published all the symphonies of Schubert in 1884–85 (with Brahms as editor) as part of its edition of Schubert's complete works. As time passed, those individuals whose sense of chronology was disturbed by assigning No. 8 to a work abandoned in 1822 and No. 7 to a work completed by 1828 decided to call the "Great" Symphony Schubert's Ninth, to leave the "Unfinished" as No. 8, and to fill in the seventh slot by assigning to it the

"Sketch" Symphony in E Major from the year 1821, a work completed by other musicians and, therefore, capable of orchestral performances.

Thus things remained until the publication of the 1978 edition of the thematic catalogue of Schubert's works. The editorial board of this German publication decided to renumber the "Unfinished" and "Great" symphonies in simple chronological order, as Schubert's Seventh and Eighth Symphonies, respectively. The two completed movements of the "Unfinished" Symphony, they felt, qualified it as a full-fledged Schubert symphony, albeit an incomplete one. On the other hand, Schubert's various sketched symphonies, including the enormous sketch in E Major of 1821, could not be counted among the composer's symphonic achievements. Therefore, in the 1978 catalogue the "Unfinished" became No. 7 and the "Great" was called No. 8. Many people, however, cling to the older numbering, especially since they grew up with it, so that nowadays one runs across the "Unfinished" listed as No. 7 or No. 8; the "Great" listed as No. 7, No. 8, or No. 9; and the "Sketch" listed as No. 7 or without any number.

11 Schubert's religious and choral music: toward a statement of faith

Glenn Stanley

They also wondered greatly at my piety, which I expressed in a hymn to the Holy Virgin and which, it appears, grips every soul and turns it to devotion. I think this is due to the fact that I have never forced devotion in myself and never compose hymns or prayers of that kind unless it overcomes me unawares; but then it is usually the right and true devotion.

Schubert, in a letter to his family (July 1825; SDB 434–35)[1]

Cre-do in u - num De - um!

Not you, I know well enough, but you will believe . . .

Ferdinand Walcher, in a letter to Schubert (January, 1827; SDB 597).

Although Schubert bitterly opposed the institution and dogma of the Catholic Church, in his short career he composed six complete Latin Masses, a German Mass, and numerous single Mass movements and other liturgical genres. Two large-scale non-liturgical pieces, a German-language *Stabat mater* (D383) and an unfinished oratorio, *Lazarus, oder: Die Feier der Auferstehung* (D689), as well as solo and choral settings of non-liturgical texts on Christian and pantheistic themes, express his devout belief in a divine presence unencumbered by confessional dogma. His setting of the Hebrew text of Psalm 92 (D953) for the Jewish community in Vienna indicates both his religious tolerance and Jewish efforts to integrate (or perhaps assimilate) into the general culture.

The Catholic liturgical music was composed for a society characterized as much by lack of faith as by continuing reverence for the public ceremonies of the Church.[2] The Mass retained its status as a preeminent musical genre, while oratorical works were highlights of Advent, Lent, and Holy Week. Regardless of his religious orientation, Schubert, like any Viennese composer in his day (but not long thereafter), was virtually compelled to compose religious music. Moreover, before he was sufficiently mature to form opinions about established religion, the choir boy Schubert received an introduction to the heritage of Catholic religious music, which he venerated, if only for its musical richness.

Scholarship on Schubert's religious music has focused on the six Masses, which are usually discussed as an early group of four composed between 1814 and 1816, and the single Masses composed in 1819–23 and 1828 that reflect Schubert's first maturity and final mastery.[3] In almost all of the literature on the Masses, the new style of the late Masses has been interpreted as the product of a conscious attempt by Schubert to distance himself from religious orthodoxy. The emphasis on the Masses has produced an unfair neglect of the *Stabat mater* and, to a lesser extent, *Lazarus*, which were composed in the years between the first four Masses and the last two. These works are highly significant: they were his free choice; they are not explicitly Catholic; their styles are remarkable for their time and place; their composition helped Schubert achieve the technical maturity that enriches the last two Masses; and they are the first large religious pieces in which Schubert consistently attempted to transcend convention in the expression of text. The late Masses may be better understood as the product of a heightened concern about text–musical relationships, as well as the refinement of his overall style, than as a denial of orthodoxy.

The early Masses

Two principal questions have motivated the research about the Masses: (1) how they adhere to and depart from Viennese traditions regarding form and style, and (2) the meaning of text Schubert omitted – in particular the significant phrase in the Credo, "Et unam sanctam catholicam et apostolicam ecclesiam" – in all the Masses.[4] For some scholars these questions have converged, because the increasing freedom from convention in the fourth and fifth Masses has been linked to the heretic's voice speaking through text that remains unsung.[5] Ultimately, the question is of greater relevance for Schubert's biographers and for church musicians concerned about the unsuitability of the Masses for liturgical performance. (In Schubert's life they were performed in church services, and, as Ronald Stringham notes, several posthumous attempts to make them liturgically correct necessitated considerable revisions of the music.[6])

The absence of small portions of text throughout the Masses has little import for the evaluation of the Masses as works of art; far more significant is the notion of a unified Austro-Viennese church style, often associated with the preferences of the Imperial Court, to which successful Mass composers had to conform. Hans Jaskulsky questions this view, and on the basis of stylistic comparisons identifies numerous traditional strands from which Schubert drew.[7] These encompass general styles according to

Mass genre (*Missa brevis, Missa longa, Missa solemnis*), as well as formal conventions that cut across the various genres, for example sonata-form Kyries, sectionalization practices and fugues in the Gloria and Credo,[8] prescriptions about length and against operatic tendencies,[9] and the personal styles of favored composers – Joseph and Michael Haydn, Mozart, and Beethoven. Certainly Schubert knew their Masses; there is, however, documentary evidence for only one performance that he conducted, Joseph Haydn's *Nelson Mass* on Easter Sunday 1820.

The first four Masses reflect Schubert's engagement with Mass conventions and stylistic debts within and external to the Mass repertory, but also contain some foreshadowings of his mature style. His first complete Mass, the *Missa solemnis* in F (D105) was performed in October 1814 for the centennial celebration of the dedication of the Schubert family's church in Lichtental, where Michael Holzer, his former teacher of voice, organ and figured bass, was the choir director.[10] (It is generally assumed that the Masses 2–4 [1815 and 1816], were also written for Holzer.) The Mass in F is competently executed but shows little originality in its design or style. Apart from the fugue at the end of the Gloria, choral homophony prevails. The solo parts are simple and non-virtuosic, although the high tessitura of the soprano part was evidently designed to showcase the soloist, Therese Grob.[11]

The large orchestra usually only accompanies – there is no attempt to imitate the symphonic style of Mozart's and Haydn's mature Mass writing. The influence of Mozart is, however, unmistakable in the setting of the "suscipe deprecationem nostram" from the Gloria, in which the minor harmonies, low registration and orchestration, notably the trombone parts, are reminiscent of both the second-act finale of *Don Giovanni* and sections of the Requiem. A post-Classical orchestral style is sometimes evident, as in the fanfares at the end of the first part of the Gloria, and in the prevalent lyrical woodwind part writing. Suggestions of Schubert's mature harmonic style appear in the occasional melodic and harmonic chromaticisms, the enrichment of the harmonic language through the integration of subsidiary diatonic harmonies, and the juxtaposition of major and minor chords on the same scale degree. While Schubert never violates the meaning of the text, with few exceptions (e.g. the "suscipe deprecationem"), he strikes a neutral and formal attitude toward it; aside from certain requisite brilliant passages such as the beginning of the Gloria the underlying *affect* is one of pastoral quiescence, a character common to much post-Classical Austrian church music.[12]

The Masses 2–4, *Missa brevis* Masses which were performed shortly after being composed, are primarily distinguished by their simplicity and modest technical demands. Choral homophony and non-virtuosic solo

Example 11.1 Mass No. 2 in G Major (D167), Credo, mm. 1–7

writing again prevail, the harmonic language does not significantly change, and concerns for textual expression are no more frequent than in the Mass in F. As in the first Mass, some of the solo parts (and their accompaniments) display a decidedly song-like character. Jaskulsky asserts a cyclical unity in Mass No. 2 in G, based on recurring harmonic progressions and a diatonic ascending linear melody that is later inverted and in the Sanctus chromaticized in the nature of a Baroque lament bass line.[13] The beginning of the Credo makes a clear reference to the prisoners' chorus from *Fidelio* (see Ex. 11.1). Once again Schubert turns to the world of opera in his search for expressive depth, and his reference implies an identification with *Fidelio* ideology just as the Austrian restoration began to assert itself.[14]

In Mass No. 3 in B flat (D324, 1815) a short canonic treatment of "cum sancto spiritu" replaces the more conventional fugue. The contrapuntal challenge is not of the highest order, but the passage demonstrates his interest in archaic styles years before his contrapuntal studies with the noted theorist Simon Sechter in 1828. This Mass has a larger orchestral apparatus than in the original instrumentation of Masses 2 and 4, and also includes more independent orchestral writing than any of the other early Masses. These features, as well as numerous musical details, have been attributed to Schubert's admiration for the *Nelson Mass*.[15]

Mass No. 4 in C (D452, 1816) was originally scored for chorus, soloists, and only two violins and a figured basso continuo part.[16] Its retrospective style, the so-called "Salzburger Kirchentrio," has led it to be dismissed as insignificant, but it may be understood in light of its musical references to Mozart's *Missae brevii* in the same scoring and verbal ones to Mozart in Schubert's diary during its composition.[17]

Pantheistic and Protestant impulses

Schubert stopped writing Masses for three years after 1816, perhaps because, when he failed to secure the position of music director in Laibach, he turned away from the kind of music that was required for such a job. In this period his interest in religious music shifted to non-Catholic texts and genres, a change that had already begun in 1815 with the setting for vocal quartet and piano of the Schiller text, *Hymne an den Unendlichen* (D232), and in 1816 intensified with the composition of the German *Stabat mater*, and two companion pieces to D232, *Gott im Ungewitter* (D985) and *Gott der Weltschöpfer* (D986).[18] Although Alfred Einstein finds the "musical and spiritual starting-point" of the three short choral pieces in Beethoven's solo setting of Gellert's text, "Die Ehre Gottes aus der Natur" (Op. 48 No. 4, before 1802),[19] their pantheism – the location and musical representation of a divinity in the sublimity of nature – owes as much to Haydn's oratorios *The Creation* and *The Seasons*. Despite their limited means, these works, along with the masterful settings of Goethe's *Gesang der Geister über den Wassern* (D538, for unaccompanied vocal quartet, in 1817; and D714, for eight male voice and strings, in 1821) bring an elevated, devotional element to the underlying Biedermeier nature of social (*gesellig*) secular choral music.

The depth of these compositions is also felt in the major religious works of this time, the German *Stabat mater* (1816, text by Friedrich Gottlieb Klopstock), and *Lazarus* (1820, text by August Hermann Niemeyer), of which Schubert completed the first and most of the second of the three acts.[20] For these works Schubert chose closely related Christian topics on texts written by mid-eighteenth-century north-German Protestant authors associated with the *Empfindsamkeit* movement. Both texts are replete with sentimental meditations on death and salvation and effusions of familial love. The highly personal emotionality of the poetry suited nineteenth-century tendencies toward an aestheticizing *Gefühlsreligion* and perhaps appealed to Schubert's Romanticism. Both texts, however, contain ideas and language surely antiquated when Schubert set them. Their stories are particularly appropriate for Lent and Holy Week, and the season of their composition suggests that they were so conceived, although neither work was performed during Schubert's lifetime.

Stabat mater

Klopstock heavily reworked the poetic content and form of the original Latin sequence; in setting up the movements, Schubert respected

Klopstock's transformation of the regular tercets of the sequence into free strophes of unequal length, but he omitted the last two quatrains entirely. The work falls into two large parts (movements 1–7 and 8–12), each crowned by a rigorous fugue with *colla parte* orchestral parts. This strategy is modeled on Pergolesi's popular Latin *Stabat mater* (1736), in which imitative duets in an archaic style occur at analogous places.[21] The lively fugues stand in sharp distinction to the prevailing lyricism of the arias, ensembles, and choruses. (There is no recitative.) Despite their uniformly slow or moderate tempos, these movements contain enough variety of styles, textures, and, especially, instrumentation to sustain interest. The orchestra is large, but most movements feature only several of the wind instruments, which are given sensitively crafted obbligato roles alone or in ensemble. The chamber-music quality of the orchestration contributes greatly to the contemplative nature of the work, represents a great advance in Schubert's orchestral technique, and, in its Romantic coloring, is very beautiful.

Within the general lyricism two contrasting characters emerge. In the elegiac first part, four of the six movements before the fugue discuss the pathos of the crucifixion. They all have minor keys (the fifth movement concludes in the major mode, see below) in which chromatic dissonances and Baroque figures such as *seufzer* motifs recall Pergolesi's setting as well as an equally popular *Stabat mater* composed by Haydn in 1767 that had been reorchestrated and published a decade earlier. (Another familiar composition by J. Haydn for the Lenten Season, *Die Sieben Wörter der Erlöser am Kreuze*, contains similar material.)

Apart from the eighth movement, whose harmonies gravitate between E minor and the concluding G major, and whose poetic character recalls that of the minor-mode movements in the first part, the entire second part and third and fourth movements in the first concern maternal and filial love and the joys of salvation and paradise. These tender movements are given major keys and breathe Romantic air. The conclusion of the fifth movement, on text about the anticipation of heaven, establishes with the aid of solo horns a serene pastoral quality reminiscent of secular choral music.

In the tenor aria, No. 6, "Ach, was hätten wir empfunden," the most deeply felt and stylistically interesting movement in the work, Schubert recreated the style of one of J. S. Bach's preferred aria textures, the trio-sonata, and captured the affective world of Baroque pathos (see Ex. 11.2).

The bass line is "realized" in the homophonic upper string parts, and the obbligato oboe part (a favorite Baroque choice for pathetic music) serves as a quasi-ritornello that is paraphrased in the first vocal entrance, and, as in Bach's arias, maintains its melodic independence when the voice part is active. Short phrases are interspersed with rests in both

Example 11.2 *Stabat mater* (D383), No. 6 mm. 1–10

upper parts; in the oboe, *Fortspinnung* technique is applied to the gradual lengthening of phrase following the short motivic statements at the beginning. Over a pedal bass (mm. 1–3 and periodically thereafter) harmonies change and dissonances arise through the voice leading in the string parts.[22] The highly compressed *ABA* form also harks back to Baroque models, but the *B* section ends in C minor (the key of *A*) rather than in its own tonic because the return of *A* coincides with the close of *B*. After the vocal part concludes in C minor, a final ritornello-like section moves to G major, the dominant of the C major fugue that follows.

A listener should not confuse this movement with an actual Baroque composition: there is no keyboard continuo part and in the *B* section the melodic and harmonic language reveals its nineteenth-century origins. Yet Schubert's debts to Bach are unmistakable, and his decision to imitate his style is all the more remarkable, because, although Handel's oratorios were heard in Schubert's Vienna, only a handful of professional musicians and amateurs with historical interests knew any of Bach's liturgical music.[23] Although aria movements 2 and 8 also have bass lines that move like true continuo parts, the vocal parts and the instrumental upper voices do not imitate Baroque idioms. Moreover, despite the undeniable Handelian character of portions (notably the beginning) of the cantata for chorus and piano, *Mirjams Siegesgesang* (D942, composed in 1828 on a Grillparzer text), there is no other example of such pervasive historicism in all of Schubert's religious music. Hence, we might best understand this composition, which preceded by a decade the north-German revival of the *St. Matthew Passion*, as a unique (and very pure) manifestation of his veneration for Bach's music, independent of a local performance tradition of Holy Week pieces or, as with Handel, popular acceptance of a foreign one.

One other aspect of the *Stabat mater* must intrigue the historically informed listener. In the autograph score of the third chorus, Schubert entered and then crossed out an exact citation of the last phrase of Haydn's patriotic hymn "Gott erhalte, Franz den Kaiser." Yet he substituted a close paraphrase (see Ex. 11.3), while several other movements include paraphrases of the hymn or material that can be readily associated with it.

Schubert surely intended some metaphorical comment with the references, but, lacking any extramusical evidence, we can only speculate about its meaning. Was Schubert trying to win favor with the court?[24] Or is Austria under the restoration being mourned? This view would interpret the references as a negative counterpart to the *Fidelio* citation in Mass No. 2. The last (and rather oblique) reference occurs in the subject of the final fugue, which paraphrases the descent from the sixth scale degree in the second phrase of Haydn's hymn. In the hymn the phrase ends on the fifth scale degree, but the fugue subject closes on B♮, the leading tone of the dominant of F and, in an awkward imitation of a Handelian–Haydnesque technique, is disproportionately sustained for an entire measure. Could Schubert, who had already written some competent fugues, in good faith compose a fugue subject that concludes as ungracefully as this one? Is the Empire being mocked? Such interpretations require a hermeneutic leap of faith; they cannot be proved, but they are tantalizing to entertain, and Schubert's cynicism about Austrian politics is historical fact.

Example 11.3 *Staber mater* (D383), No. 3 mm. 1–12

Lazarus

In the foreword to the first edition of the text of *Lazarus* (Leipzig, 1778) Niemeyer, a theologian in the Pietistic center of Halle, develops a theory of religious drama that emphasizes the expression of sentiment about the events of the story, rather than their depiction or the portrayal of characters. In a drama of this sort – and Niemeyer's text naturally exemplifies the theory – the lyric mode predominates while the dramatic and epic modes recede. Thus in *Lazarus* there is no narrator's role, although these were conventional even in non-liturgical German oratorios in the eighteenth century, and, despite his importance, Christ does not appear. He is evoked, and the miracle of Lazarus's resurrection is related by the friends and family who comfort Lazarus, bury him and rejoice at his resurrection.

Despite Niemeyer's theory, his text is dramatically realistic: rather than allowing characters to speak recitative-and-aria monologues as if they were alone, Niemeyer often has them express their feelings to each other in short, open-ended prose statements. When characters sing arias, they usually sing them to other characters. This dramatic technique, and the

Example 11.4 *Lazarus* (D689), mm. 68–92

contemplative Pietistic themes of familial love and communal religious feeling which it reinforces, motivated Schubert to compose in a style comparable to his opera *Alfonso und Estrella* (D732, 1821–22) but otherwise without precedent or contemporary counterpart in oratorio or opera. Particularly in the first act, the virtually seamless integration of lyrical accompanied recitative, arioso, and aria anticipates Wagner's musical dramaturgy in *Tannhäuser, Lohengrin* and even *Parsifal*, including the use of quasi-leitmotivic techniques in the orchestra, and also resembles Wagner's music for the expression of transcendental ideas.[25]

We can appreciate the subtlety of Schubert's work, including its harmonic dimension, by considering a passage at the beginning of Act I sung by Maria, Lazarus's sister, as she and her sister Martha attend to him in the garden of his house (see Ex.11.4).

Maria first speaks to Martha, but then she pauses for two measures before saying (in translation): "I fall silent before the wise council, kneel

Example 11.4 (*cont.*)

in dust and pray to the sublime one." Maria perceives and responds to a textually undefined divine communication represented by the instrumental music of measures 83–84, which develops and transforms a two-measure motif that unifies the entire section. It is introduced at the beginning of this section (mm. 68–69) in the upper voices and is fully harmonized; it is first stated in G major, then moves to A flat major. In measures 83–84 the motif consists of a recombination of the rhythm of the original first measure (the note values are doubled) and the descending thirds of both measures of the opening motif. Unaccompanied unison cellos and basses imply D flat minor in the lower register. The motivic concentration, and the changes in mode, register, and instrumentation, effectively evoke the gravity of the divine presence and "paint" the image of Maria kneeling in prayer. The transformation prepares the reascent into the upper register and the move to a resplendent D flat major for the word "Hocherhabenen" (mm. 89–91).

This and similar passages represent the most advanced style in the piece; the arias are more conventional with respect to their overall form, yet exhibit a similar fluidity in the text-motivated synthesis of lyrical and declamatory vocal writing that also anticipates Wagner. For a religious work, the music is strikingly secular. There is no oratorio-style *secco* recitative, and the arias lack the Baroque idioms that Schubert employed so effectively in the *Stabat mater*. The text of the third act contains a fair number of choruses (there is only one each in the first two acts), giving rise to the speculation that Schubert might have evoked religious genres such as chorales and fugues or imitated styles such as Handel's or Haydn's. But the libretto contains no chorales *per se* and the texts are too long for fugal setting. Moreover, references to oratorio styles would have clashed with the pervasive Romanticism of the music for solo voices and the choruses that Schubert did complete.

As in the *Stabat mater*, the orchestration contributes greatly to the pastoral mood of much of the music, which was occasioned by the specification in the text (unusual in an oratorio) of outdoor locales for all the dramatic action. The French horns and clarinets of the chorus "Sanft und still schläft unser Freund," sung while Lazarus's corpse is carried into a forest cemetery, enhance the voice parts reminiscent of a Romantic secular genre of choral songs on natural themes. The only readily identifiable religious element in the work depends on an instrumental technique, the use of unaccompanied trombones, which harks back to an older Austro-Italian tradition, the "Aequale," of trombone playing over an open grave. This reference reinforces the possibility of a performance during Holy Week, which in Austria had long featured the performance of "sepolcri," oratorios which often featured themes of death and graveyard scenes.[26]

Lazarus was first performed on Easter Sunday in 1830, but certainly in part due to its fragmentary nature remained obscure for decades thereafter. A Vienna performance in 1863 attracted positive response – Brahms copied parts of the first act and praised it in letters to Adolf Schubring and Joseph Joachim; a piano-vocal score appeared in the 1860s and the full score in the first complete edition. Its incomplete state represents a significant loss, but, even as a fragment, it is a masterpiece that deserves performance and critical recognition.

The late Masses

How naïve Schubert was to attach his final, vain hopes of an appointment at the Imperial Court to Mass No. 5 in A Flat (D678), a *Missa solem-*

nis composed over the years 1819–22. For this purpose, it is much too subjective and passionately religious, thus rivaling – though utterly different in its modes of expression – and representing an artistic effort uncannily similar to the great work composed contemporaneously, Beethoven's *Missa solemnis.* Yet Schubert felt that the work was "successful" and considered dedicating it to the imperial couple (*SDB* 248); Schubert's brother Ferdinand, however, was dissatisfied with the first performance, at which he conducted a predominantly amateur ensemble in late 1822 or early 1823. The comparative restraint of Mass No. 6 in E flat (D950, 1828), which was composed for Schubert's friend Michael Leitermayer, the choral director at the Alservorstädter Pfarrkirche in suburban Vienna, might have better qualified it for job-searching, but Schubert began to compose this Mass immediately after Josef Eybler, in 1827, denied Schubert's petition for a court performance of Mass No. 5 and thus blocked his application for the position of *Vizekapellmeister.* This incident dashed his last hopes for a significant post, but also demonstrates his commitment to the genre independent of any professional considerations. Mass No. 6 was the only Mass not to be performed during Schubert's lifetime. Ferdinand Schubert conducted its first performance in 1829. A review in the *Wiener Theaterzeitung* of October 22, 1829, noted its positive reception and praised its grandeur while discussing its technical difficulties, notably the vocal parts; a second Vienna performance in November 1829 moved a critic for the Leipzig *Allgemeine musikalische Zeitung* to criticize its length, its "dark style," which made it too much like a requiem, and its poor orchestration.[27] Although their lyricism still outshines their occasional monumentality, Schubert's late Masses are on a significantly larger scale than his earlier ones. They are symphonically conceived and display the fine instrumental solo and chamber writing first heard in the *Stabat mater* and *Lazarus.* The orchestration and the motivic work in the introduction to the Kyrie of Mass No. 5 imbues the pastoral tone with a new richness that ushers the listener into a world of religious sentiment hitherto absent from the Masses (see Ex. 11.5).

Compared to the earlier Masses, the solo vocal parts, which often retain a Lied character, are more thoroughly embedded in the symphonic texture; the solo ensembles and non-fugal choruses are more often polyphonic, and the textures, including double choruses and *a cappella* passages, are more differentiated with respect to voice groupings and register. All the vocal parts profit from the new expressive depth of the harmonic language, which is perhaps most immediately evident in the third-related keys that connect many sections of the Mass No. 5 and dramatize shifts in the text content. (See especially the moves from A flat in

Example 11.5 Mass No. 5 in A flat (D678), Kyrie, mm. 1–16

the Kyrie to E in the Gloria and F in the Sanctus to A flat in the Benedictus.)

The decisive difference between these Masses and the first four lies in the most basic compositional challenge: taking a musically interpretive stance to the words. Now, finally, Schubert sometimes endeavored to add meaning to the text by applying both the general technical advances that mark his mature style as well as the specific experience gained in composing the early Masses and the intervening dramatic music, both religious and secular. In view of the central problem of textual omissions, the most

Example 11.5 (*cont.*)

interesting instances may be found in passages that contain such liberties. Jaskulsky has persuasively argued that many of the omissions, conflations, and repetitions of text in all the Masses served formal ends – Schubert departed from sanctioned practice in order to shape movements or sections to his musical liking. The ritornello-like repetitions of the beginning of the Credo of Mass No. 5 are a well-known example of this technique, but, in view of its musical flaccidity, one which has been correctly viewed as detrimental to textual expression.

Several times in the late Masses Schubert repeated or deleted text in

Example 11.5 (*cont.*)

order to deepen expression or emphasize a particular aspect of meaning. One of the most discussed passages in Schubert's Masses, the "Et incarnatus est" in the Credo of Mass No. 5, has been celebrated for its archaic eight-voice part writing, *Grave* 3/2 meter and *colla parte* wind accompaniment.[28] Yet it is the repetition of the sentence that allows the varied second statement to intensify registerally and harmonically the already mystical character of the first one.

In the "Domine Deus" of the Gloria of Mass No. 6, Schubert created a miniature apocalyptic drama based on the opposition of two phrases built on only three lines of the entire text (given below as *A* and *B* in capital letters):

> Domine Deus, Rex coelestis!
> Deus Pater omnipotens!
> *A* DOMINE DEUS! AGNUS DEI! FILIUS PATRIS!
> QUI TOLLIS PECCATA MUNDI!
> *B* MISERERE NOBIS;
> suscipe deprecationem nostram.
> Qui sedes ad desteram Patris,
> miserere nobis.

The focus of the complete text is on the praise of God with which the Gloria begins. Schubert's text selection, but even more so his setting, shift the focus away from God onto man's fear of damnation (*A*) and hope for salvation (*B*): the pair of phrases is stated four times in a varied sequence – phrase *A* in the minor mode, *fortissimo*, declamatory vocal lines with an accompaniment featuring trombones and lower strings comparable to accompanied recitative; phrase *B* in the major mode, *pianissimo*, hymn-like, virtually unaccompanied. The four statements make a tonal arch in G: G–C–D–G, but the passage makes compellingly clear that form serves textual interpretation and expression. The master of Lied and religious drama has come to terms with the Catholic liturgy by writing personal, subjective music for those parts of the text that spoke to his own religious convictions.

12 Schubert's operas: "the judgment of history?"

Thomas A. Denny

When *Fierrabras* (D796), Schubert's last completed and best opera, received its Austrian premiere in 1988, the *Frankfurter Allgemeine Zeitung* proclaimed in its bold headline: "AGAINST THE JUDGMENT OF HISTORY: Schubert's 'Fierrabras' rescued triumphantly." Although not all critics agreed,[1] the headline succinctly captured the issues at stake in the Austrian premiere of *Fierrabras*, and indeed in any modern consideration of Schubert's operas in general. For "history" – some notable voices aside, such as Maurice J. E. Brown and Elizabeth Norman McKay – has generally judged Schubert a failure as an opera composer.[2] The Vienna *Fierrabras* revealed the risks of making such judgments without experiencing these works in the theater.

With the exception of three commissioned works, Schubert's theatrical works were neither performed during his lifetime, nor for a long time afterward. While some of his Singspiels have enjoyed intermittent exposure,[3] his "grand" operas have almost never been performed in their original form. For example, there have been performances of a work such as *Alfonso und Estrella* (D732) in abridged versions (Franz Liszt, Weimar, 1854), freely adapted versions (J. N. Fuchs, Vienna, 1882), bowdlerized versions (Kurt Honolka's *Die Wunderinsel*, 1958), and concert versions. Recently, there have even begun to be full performances, although *Alfonso*, unlike *Fierrabras*, has not yet made it to a major international opera house. In short, the generally negative body of received opinion about Schubert's operatic talent and accomplishment remains largely untested in the theater.[4]

The surprising power and richness which audiences and critics experienced on hearing Claudio Abbado's *Fierrabras* performances (and recording for Deutsche Grammophon) abruptly brought the discussion from the realm of conjecture to that of actual experience. There is no reason to expect that the impact of *Fierrabras* – written when Schubert's compositional powers were in the full bloom of his early maturity – would be widely replicated by professional staged productions of many of Schubert's other operas. Even outstanding performances would not rescue every early opera, every modest Singspiel and "farce with music." The lesson of the Vienna *Fierrabras* stems rather from the startling light it so vividly cast on the trajectory (with its 1823 highpoint) of Schubert's development as an operatic composer. In *Fierrabras*, Schubert proved himself capable of unleashing considerable dramatic power in the service of a serious chivalric subject. Shortly after *Fierrabras*, disillusioned with the circumstances and his prospects in the Viennese theaters, Schubert interrupted this promising trajectory. He had not yet produced any unquestionably great operas, and he may never have done so under any circumstances. But his achievement in *Fierrabras* nevertheless gives the lie to any categorical dismissal of his dramatic powers.

Of Metternich and Walter Scott, of Rossini and Beethoven: forces shaping the Viennese operatic world of Schubert

Many varied political, literary, and musical forces shaped Schubert's operatic output. It was the age of Metternich and his stifling censors. It was the age of Biedermeier sentimentality. It was the age of Sir Walter Scott's early fame, and an insatiable appetite for chivalric dramas (*Ritterdrama*). The fascination with magic dramas (*Zauberspiel*) had not yet faded. Melodramas – works employing orchestral accompaniment to spoken dialogue – appeared regularly in Viennese theaters. In opera specifically, it was the age of the Rossini craze, of sentimental bourgeois Singspiels in the attractive style of Josef Weigl, and of stillborn hopes for a more elevated, serious German opera. Some older repertories – the operas of Gluck, and operas from the French tradition by Méhul and Grétry – remained influential in Viennese circles. Lastly, it was the age of Beethoven.

During Schubert's lifetime, German opera still relied chiefly on dialogue rather than recitative. Singspiels with sentimental or comic plots predominated in this tradition. Composers such as Spohr, E. T. A. Hoffmann, Weber, and Schubert, however, sought to build on Mozart's and Beethoven's models by elevating the opera-with-dialogue medium to suit more powerful Romantic, heroic, and chivalric subjects. At the same time, some German composers were beginning to write through-composed operas, without dialogue. Scholars had often dated the origins of German through-composed opera to the early 1820s, with Schubert's *Alfonso und Estrella* (1821–22), Spohr's *Jessonda* (1823), and Weber's *Euryanthe* (1823). Recent research, however, has established that this wave of activity rests on a considerable tradition of through-composed operas by lesser-known composers, including two by Ignaz Mosel (*Salem*, 1813, and *Cyrus und Astyages*, 1816), and others dating back at least as far as Peter von Winter's *Marie von Montalban* of 1799.[5]

226 Thomas A. Denny

Rossini towered over the European operatic world around 1820. His sense of dramatic structure and pacing certainly found its way into Schubert's later operas. Particularly after 1820, most of Schubert's finest operatic ensembles and finales pay tribute to Rossini's example. Other aspects of the Italian composer's style, notably his sensuous and highly ornamented melodic style, influenced Schubert far less consistently. The French tradition – to some extent mediated by Beethoven's *Fidelio* – resonates in the fashionable "rescue" plots (complete with trumpet fanfares) and such musical devices as reminiscence motifs and passages of melodrama. Finally, Schubert knew many of Gluck's operas intimately, from score study with Salieri, from attendance at performances in Vienna, and no doubt from his contact with Johann Michael Vogl and Ignaz von Mosel, two great Gluckians. Orchestration aside, however, Gluck's style could offer no usable direct model for opera composition around 1820. (Schubert's only truly Gluckian work is *Lazarus* [D689], a beautiful, fragmentary oratorio. In *Lazarus*, Schubert developed a remarkably personal approach to accompanied recitative with lyrical interpolations, which strikes many listeners as a unique bridge between Gluck and Wagner.)

Schubert's compositions for the theater

Most musicians and music lovers are generally unaware of the surprisingly large quantity of music that Schubert composed for the theater. The surviving works, both finished and unfinished, number close to twenty and span his entire creative life.[6] Eight complete operas survive, ranging from short, modest "farces" to ambitious heroic dramas.

Schubert composed music for operas and other theater works during three principal periods of his life: during his teens (1811–1816); during the period of rapid artistic maturation sometimes known as the "years of crisis" (1819–1823); and during the last two years of his life, when he began drafting Eduard von Bauernfeld's *Der Graf von Gleichen* (D918).

The earliest period during which Schubert composed operas, 1811–16, is essentially a student period. Annotations and revisions in the early autograph scores (most notably in the two versions of *Des Teufels Lustschloß* [D84]) indicate that Schubert was responding to criticism, almost certainly that of his teacher, Salieri. Schubert proudly signed the score of this, his first completed opera, "Schubert, pupil of Mr. Salieri, principal Court Kapellmeister in Vienna."

Schubert never finished his first opera, *Der Spiegelritter* (D11). He began this work in December 1811, shortly before he commenced studying composition with Salieri. During the roughly four years Schubert studied with Salieri, he completed the two versions of the three-act *Des Teufels Lustschloß* (1813–15), two one-act Singspiels (Körner's *Der vierjährige Posten* [D190], and Albert Stadler's *Fernando* [D220], both in 1815), a two-act Singspiel (Mayrhofer's *Die Freunde von Salamanka* [D326]; 1815, perhaps into 1816), and most likely Goethe's three-act Singspiel *Claudine von Villa Bella* (D239; 1815) as well. His work on a three-act opera, *Die Bürgschaft* (D435; 1816), remained unfinished. One or more of these early Singspiels might have been destined for performance in a private *Haustheater*.[7] As for professional, public performances, however, Schubert seems to have had no contacts or prospects for performances in the professional theaters.

Some time in 1816, Schubert turned his energies to genres outside of the theater. During the next three years, many things changed in Schubert's life in general, and in his connection to the theatrical life of Vienna: he completed his formal compositional studies with Salieri; he abandoned the profession of school teaching and resolved to make his career as a professional composer; and he developed contacts with people associated with the court theaters (Vogl most notably, but also Leopold Sonnleithner and Ignaz Mosel). One external, but profoundly important, event of this period was the first Viennese performance of a Rossini opera, *L'inganno felice*, in November 1816.

It is significant that Schubert's first operatic project after this pause would be a commissioned work. No longer a young opera composer whose prospects for performance were largely fantasy, he had become a young man seriously building a career within the Austrian theater world. The Kärntnerthor Theater commissioned Schubert to compose *Die Zwillingsbrüder* (D647), a one-act "farce with music" in which his friend Vogl would play the roles of both twin brothers. Intrigues apparently delayed the performance for more than a year. As Schubert reported to Anselm Hüttenbrenner in May 1819: "In spite of Vogl, it is difficult to outwit such *canaille* as Weigl, Treitschke, etc." (*SDB* 117).

With the six performances of *Die Zwillingsbrüder* in 1820, Schubert had clearly entered the journeyman stage of his career in the theater. For the first time, he was able to hear his music performed in the Viennese theaters. The Viennese and foreign musical presses began to review these performances and even to report on his future theatrical projects. Schubert worked briefly in the theater as a coach. And he began to collaborate with theater-appointed librettists on other commissions. Although still inexperienced, he was now functioning as a professional.

Between 1819 and 1823 – that is, *after* as well as before Domenico Barbaja's arrival as impresario for the court theaters – Schubert received a series of commissions to compose various theatrical works. Viennese audiences and critics heard Schubert's music for Georg von Hofmann's melodrama, *Die Zauberharfe* (D644), in August 1820, his duet and aria composed for insertion into Herold's *Das Zauberglöckchen* (D723) in June 1821, and his incidental music for Helmina von Chézy's *Rosamunde* (D797) in December 1823. Unfortunately, the most important commission Schubert received during this period, that for *Fierrabras*, a three-act "heroic-romantic opera" which he composed between May 25 and October 2, 1823, never reached the stage during his lifetime.

Schubert's attempts to make inroads into German operatic life were not, moreover, limited to waiting for Viennese commissions. Between 1819 and 1823, Schubert began work on four operas he never finished: *Adrast* (D137), *Sakontala* (D701), one without name (D982), and *Rüdiger* (D791). Of greater significance are the two operas he did complete. He composed *Alfonso und Estrella* (1821–22), a three-act, through-composed opera, and *Die Verschworenen* (D787; 1823), a one-act Singspiel based on Aristophanes' *Lysistrata*, to a libretto by Ignaz von Castelli. Although neither of these operas appears to have been composed on commission, Schubert sought the help of singers such as Anna Milder and Vogl, the composer Carl Maria von Weber, and the poet Grillparzer in his attempts to arrange for performances in Germany. Schubert's efforts were not limited exclusively to new works. He paid to have the score of his early opera, *Des Teufels Lustschloß*, copied in 1822 and Josef Hüttenbrenner then made efforts to get it performed in Prague, Munich, and elsewhere.[8]

The expected 1823 performances of Schubert's *Fierrabras* never took place. Rossini's successes, especially after his triumphant 1822 visit to Vienna, and Weber's October 1823 failure with the much anticipated *Euryanthe*, caused Barbaja largely to lose interest in new German opera. From 1825 on, increasingly grave financial difficulties aggravated this tendency, causing intermittent, extended periods of theater closings, as well as a general shift to lighter and more popular theater genres than opera. Guest appearances at the court-run Kärntnerthor Theater by the popular Josephstädter-Theater company (1825) and by a French vaudeville troupe (1826) were symptomatic of the administration's efforts to attract the paying public and to trim costs.

Following the *Fierrabras* cancellation and the failed run of *Rosamunde* in December 1823, Schubert's discouragement with the theaters found palpable expression in the March 1824 letter to Leopold Kupelwieser: he complained that he has "composed two operas for nothing" (*SDB* 339). Schubert would compose no music for the theater for nearly four years. Although he apparently considered some libretti during 1824, he committed his energies to large-scale instrumental music. With Beethoven the clear role model, Schubert began paving the "path to a grand symphony" (*SDB* 339). Never again would Schubert have such tangible and realistic aspirations for performances in the Viennese theaters as he had from 1819 to 1823.

Schubert's final and unfinished operatic project was apparently a curious one. The Viennese censors had already rejected Bauernfeld's libretto for *Der Graf von Gleichen*, presumably because of its treatment of bigamy. Schubert's continuing work on the seemingly doomed project reflects either a defiant response to his despair with current Viennese theater life, or his pragmatic sense that the text would find acceptance as he turned inevitably to a wider German market.

In February 1828, Schubert sent to Schott's, the music publisher in Mainz, a "complete" list of individual works available for publication. Schubert only listed works in the most marketable types of domestic, social, and chamber music. In closing his letter, however, Schubert could not resist referring broadly to some compositions he had written for the public arena, "three operas, a mass, and a symphony." Knowing these would not be of immediate interest to Schott's, he added the disclaimer: "I mention these last compositions only in order to acquaint you with my strivings after the highest in art" (*SDB* 739–40).

Two things are noteworthy here – Schubert's selectiveness in the public works he offered and his invocation of distinctions between higher and lower aesthetic levels. Almost certainly, Schubert was selectively offering only the large-scale works of his early maturity, those operas, symphonies, and Masses completed since about 1820. (After 1820, Schubert repeatedly made clear that he was no longer promoting most of his early works.[9])

If Schubert's own selectivity gives us the license to focus on the operas of his maturity, his discussion of the "highest" in art gives us the license to focus on the operas with the expressive range, the expanded scale of musical-dramatic structure, and the serious subject appropriate to a "grand" heroic or Romantic opera. It was his "grand" operas, and not his Singspiels and other early operas, which were capable of standing alongside his "grand" symphony, representing the "highest" in Schubert's art. While one might profitably enfold other theatrical works of the 1820s into the discussion – the fragmentary *Lazarus* (although not an opera); the melodrama, *Die Zauberharfe*; the incidental music for *Rosamunde*; and the unfinished *Der Graf von Gleichen* – limitations of space require that we focus our discussion on the two "grand" Romantic or heroic German operas Schubert completed, *Alfonso und Estrella* and *Fierrabras*.

In turning our attention to these two operas, we will want to determine how successful Schubert was during his early maturity in finding a personal voice capable of projecting serious "grand" musical drama. In measuring his success, we will apply two principal criteria – first, Schubert's ability to project a wide range of emotional states with the intensity, the weight, and the tone appropriate to serious, "große" opera rather than to the lighter genre of Singspiel, and second, his ability to create extended, continuous, and coherent scenes (rather than shorter closed numbers).

Alfonso und Estrella

"such a miserable, stillborn concoction of a libretto that even such a genius
as Franz Schubert could not bring it to life"   *Franz Schober*[10]

Alfonso und Estrella is an important, but flawed work, which Schubert wrote at a particularly critical phase of his artistic maturation. In a period so littered with fragments as to be called the "years of crisis," *Alfonso* was the first large-scale work which Schubert had completed since the "Trout" Quintet (D667) of 1819. Schubert's choice to write this work as a through-composed opera reflects an ambitiousness and a seriousness of intent, even if we now know that its avoidance of dialogue was not a radical innovation.

Schubert composed most of the opera during a blissful working vacation in Upper Austria with the librettist Franz von Schober, an intimate and charismatic friend. Schober's extraordinarily weak libretto fuses plot action of the then fashionable chivalric mold (the story of Froila's son, Alfonso, coming of age, and the general reconciliation which results from his conquests in both love and war) with static pastoral elements (glorifying the idyllic life which the benign King Froila and his followers live in their mountain exile).[11] The most fatal of the libretto's weaknesses stems from Schober's failure to keep the static pastoral scenes subordinate to the more stageworthy action of the *Ritterdrama*. Too often the drama stands still through long cloying passages such as the ceremonial homage to Froila (Nos. 1–3). Even when Schubert's music for these idyllic moments is extraordinarily beautiful, it cannot invest such scenes with any real dramatic impact.

Not all the dramatic stagnation in this opera, however, can be blamed on an excess of pastoral elements. Even such a potential emotional highpoint as the first encounter between Alfonso and Estrella falls flat in Schober's and Schubert's hands. Estrella has lost her way during a hunting expedition in the mountains, and meets Alfonso, the son of her father's exiled arch-enemy. The two quickly fall in love. Schober provided some hundred lines of highly structured verse (mostly rhymed, metrically regular, and in regular stanzaic patterns). Schubert responded with a string of five closed numbers. None of the five rises substantially above the others in sensuousness or rapture. That, combined with the near total lack of recitative which could set off the lyrical effusions, results in a scene without dramatic shape or any clear lyrical climax. The music, unrelentingly tuneful in a Singspiel manner, comes across as square, the lovers as disappointingly chaste, and the whole scene as excessively long. (Andrew Porter's observation that this was "probably the longest love scene in opera before Act II of *Tristan*" may rest on objective measurements, but it reflects no doubt a subjective impression as well.[12])

Schubert's treatment of this love scene highlights two problems he would need to solve if he was going to write successful "große" operas. First, he needed to grasp the importance of recitative in shaping and pacing musical drama. Given that *Alfonso und Estrella* is a through-composed opera without spoken dialogue, it is astonishing, and highly problematic, that it contains so little recitative. Long stretches of the opera unfold with no break from, and no contrast to, the closed, lyrical numbers. Moreover, much of the recitative which Schubert did provide is unimpressive. (This is particularly surprising and disappointing when one looks at the remarkable recitatives he had composed for *Lazarus* not long before.)

Second, he needed to develop a more clearly defined sense of tone. In *Alfonso und Estrella*, Schubert still seemed unaware of the distinction between the sweet lyricism and small closed forms more characteristic of Singspiel and the emotional intensity and the larger dramatic forms appropriate for a "große" Romantic or heroic opera. The Act II love scene and numbers such as Alfonso's "Schon, wenn es beginnt zu tagen" (Act I, no. 5) jar the audience with a Singspiel-based songfulness (the Lied of Singspiel, rather than the piano Lied, is the influence here) which seems out of place in a "große" opera.

If their pastoral nature or their Singspiel tone weaken some parts of *Alfonso und Estrella*, other parts, notably Schober's chivalric episodes, called forth a different, and more successful, style of music and musical structure from Schubert. In composing the music to Adolfo's unwelcome suit for Estrella's hand (Act I, Nos. 9 and 10), for the vengeful ensemble led by the rejected Adolfo (Act II, No. 17), and for much of the denouement in the third act, Schubert revealed his growing capacity for writing operatic music of variety, emotional range, and dramatic pacing and shape. Only a few examples can be cited.

The finale to Act I ranks among the most effective numbers in the opera. A multi-tempo ensemble for soloists and chorus, its essential expressive and structural features demonstrate Schubert's understanding of Rossini's achievement. Following the opening triumphal entrance by

Adolfo and the warriors, Adolfo asks King Mauregato for the hand of Estrella, in recitative. Varied accompanimental motifs give shape to the recitative, highlighting key points in the drama, such as the moment Adolfo asks for Estrella's hand. An expressive cello interlude leads to the second tempo (Andantino), in which Estrella pleads with her father not to force her to marry Adolfo. The expressive and emotional climax of the finale, a marvelous Rossinian *pezzo concertato*, follows. Time stops during this F major Adagio while Mauregato grapples with his dilemma as King and as father, joined later by Estrella, then by Adolfo, and finally by the full chorus. This central, climactic ensemble projects an emotional richness and power which would be totally out of place in a Singspiel. The consternation continues in the ensuing Un poco più moto and Schubert then turns to recitative as Mauregato finally finds the loophole with which he can stall Adolfo's request.

To this point in the finale, we can observe the young Schubert in full command of the operatic language of the 1820s. He has shifted deftly between recitative and sections in tempo, and has risen to the lyrical demands of climactic moments and relaxed back appropriately into less heated declamation as needed. Schubert's dramatic instincts, however, now began to fail him. The homorhythmic singing between Adolfo and Estrella does not sufficiently differentiate their adversarial perspectives, or their quite uneven claims upon audience sympathy. Things only get worse. Schober (and Schubert failed to reject this) not only brought back the men's chorus for further celebration of the glories of battle but even brought back the women to extol the glories of the hunt. The result is dramatic nonsense, which deflates the considerable tension built up between Adolfo, Estrella, and Mauregato in the earlier sections of the finale.

The lengthy conspirators' ensemble of Act II (No. 17), another high point of the opera, provides a quite different example of Schubert's growing ability to respond to complex scenes with a coherent and dramatically paced structure. Despite the furtive Rossiniesque choral opening, the overall model for this ensemble does not seem to be Italian. Although Schubert did use different tempi, he moved continuously from one to the next without using sections of recitative to punctuate the form. The operative model here seems to be that of instrumental music. Extensive and apparently self-conscious motivic and thematic links between sections further reflect contemporary (German) instrumental practice far more than that of Italian opera. The rhetorically heightened dominant in the transitional passage during which Adolfo arrives at the hideaway would fit well into a symphonic modulation. The explicit use of the same rhythmic motif – aurally identical yet notated differently, initially as ¢ ♪♩.♪♩ and later in diminished form as c ♫♩♩ – to link the Allegro agitato to the Allegro assai seems to point forward to the famous motivic transition between the Andante introduction and the opening Allegro ma non troppo theme in the first movement of Schubert's "Great" C Major Symphony (D944).

Other effective dramatic moments which also reach beyond the tone and style of Singspiel include Mauregato's reaction to Estrella's disappearance, which reveals both the softer, fatherly aspects and the more despotic sides of his personality, and Schubert's flexible and expressive treatment of the various twists and turns of the plot during the third act, including Mauregato's anxious moment when he mistakes Froila for a ghost.

We might comment in passing on a few distinctive features of this work. Perhaps responding to the influence of French operas which were performed in Vienna, but no doubt to the general aesthetic of early nineteenth-century German organicism in music as well, Schubert employed a wide range of devices to produce audible, explicit unity, and coherence. He used motivic links, *attacca* transitions, reminiscence motifs (the French influence, most likely), and occasional quotation. The tonal arch which spans the last six numbers in Act II seems almost willfully schematic in its symmetry: No. 17 in the key of B; 18 in D; 19 in A; 20 (the mid-point) tonally open; 21 in A; 22 moves to D, and finally to B, where Schubert reuses the "Rache" motif from No. 17. This tonally closed musical complex corresponds to the dramatic span of Adolfo's uprising, from his plotting in No. 17 to his invasion in No. 22.

One final comment. The critical tradition which sees *Alfonso und Estrella* as an opera written under the strongest influence of Mosel's homage to Gluck seems far off base.[13] Despite its through-composed nature, many of the opera's most conspicuous features – its excessively complicated plot line, its near total avoidance of meaningful and interesting recitative, and the structure of its "scenes" – are quite remote from, even fundamentally at odds with, Gluck's aesthetic.

In conclusion, *Alfonso und Estrella* is an uneven work. Despite the weak libretto, the jarring disjuncture between the quite different styles appropriate to "grand" opera and the lighter pastoral and Singspiel sections, and some of his rather artificial attempts to achieve continuity and coherence, *Alfonso* contains some great moments which clearly demonstrate Schubert's maturing operatic talent. It still awaits a modern performance in a major international opera house.

Fierrabras

"I . . . work much at my opera and read Walter Scott"   *Franz Schubert*[14]

On first consideration, Schubert's composition of *Fierrabras* as an "opera with dialogue" might seem to indicate a stylistic regression back in the

direction of Singspiel. On the contrary, *Fierrabras* represents a major step
forward from *Alfonso und Estrella* in Schubert's mastery of the demands
of "grand" operatic writing. Josef Kupelwieser's libretto helped, for it is
far more competent than Schober's "concoction." Although the premise
and literary tone are as out of fashion today as the Walter Scott novels
Schubert read while working on the opera, Kupelwieser's text nevertheless contains some powerful situations, rich in conflict, and creates characters spanning a wide emotional range. Kupelwieser also provided
poetry and prose of sufficient variety and irregularity that it challenged
Schubert to write music of far greater dramatic flexibility than he had
written in any previous opera.

Kupelwieser's story centers around the loves, friendships, and aspirations of a group of young Franks and Moors caught in the middle of war
between their parents, Charlemagne (King Karl) of the Franks and
Boland of the Moors. Young Moors (Fierrabras and his sister Florinda)
have fallen in love with young Franks (Emma, daughter of King Karl, and
Roland, a great warrior). Roland returns Florinda's love but Emma loves
Eginhard, a Frank initially of rather unheroic cast, rather than Fierrabras.
Ultimately, the love and friendship among the young people overcomes
the political differences and the opera ends on a note of general reconcili-
ation.

Fierrabras is a far better opera than its tortured fate would suggest.
Admittedly, it contains a few weak, and even boring, numbers, including
the two at the end of Act II (Nos. 16 and 17), with an uninspired melodrama, and the opening chorus of Act III, in which the Frankish women
pass the time with a game. Other numbers are conventionally attractive,
such as the obligatory opening chorus of the women in Emma's quarters,
the opening duet between Eginhard and Emma, Eginhard's Lied with
Chorus (No. 7), and even the second, not-so-powerful aria (No. 21, with
chorus) of Florinda.

Balanced against these weaker moments, however, is a far larger quantity of potent musical and dramatic numbers, and several strong and
well-differentiated roles. Lyrical highpoints include: the sensuous duet
between the Moorish princess, Florinda, and her maidservant (No. 9);
Eginhard's "Romanze," joined by Emma, which opens the Act I finale; the
unaccompanied Singverein partsong of the Frankish knights (No. 14);
the Allegretto duet between Roland and Florinda within the melodrama,
No. 15. Effective moments involving action would include: the frantic
search for Eginhard by his comrades (No. 8); the ensemble in which King
Karl realizes Fierrabras' innocence; Eginhard's explosive arrival during
that ensemble; the melodrama in which Florinda storms the prison
tower. Schubert found a powerful voice with which to capture the raging

moods of both the Moorish leader, Boland (No. 12), and his strong willed daughter, Florinda, whose fearsome aria (No. 13) is a show-stopper.

Merely listing isolated strong and weak moments, however, cannot illuminate the signs evident in *Fierrabras* of Schubert's growing competence as an opera composer. For that, we must examine a few passages in detail.

Framed by a triumphal choral march (No. 3) and its reprise, King Karl greets his returning, victorious warriors in a large ensemble (No. 4). In this complex ensemble, Schubert moved fluidly between recitative, arioso, melodrama, and set pieces in tempo, traversing a wide range of emotion and effectively shaping the ebb and flow of dramatic tension into a coherent whole.

Particularly noteworthy in this number is Schubert's growing command and confidence in the various declamatory styles. King Karl, a character whose moods and manner shift as the complex situation evolves, can serve to illustrate this. For Karl's opening greeting, Schubert turned Kupelwieser's iambic, irregular lines of text into recitative which was simple and matter of fact. In the second section, as Karl acts with generosity toward the prisoners, Schubert set Kupelwieser's blank verse in tempo. Despite the melodic smoothness and harmonic sweetness, Schubert's irregular phrasing projects a speech-like quality. When Karl interrogates the sullen Fierrabras, a dotted rhythmic motif in the orchestra sharpens Karl's royal impatience. In Karl's final declamatory statement (midway through the women's chorus of praise for the soldiers [Andantino]), Schubert experiments with a non-recitative declamatory style, in tempo. Against the structured musical backdrop provided by an orchestral restatement of Emma's melody, Schubert allows Karl's commentary to slide freely between recitative-like patter and counter-melody.

In Roland's pivotal narration of his victory over Fierrabras, Schubert sets Kupelwieser's blank verse as a tonally closed unit in steady tempo, yet the range and freedom of declamatory and melodic treatments is remarkable. The lyrical choral section in which the Frankish maidens honor the soldiers ends with an orchestral postlude. This plays out underneath a brief but important conversation between Roland and Fierrabras. Schubert had the inspiration to set these few lines in spoken melodrama.

Schubertian lyricism pours forth abundantly in the final Allegretto, a *tour de force* exercise in varied vocal and orchestral textures. As the action stops for this "contemplative" ensemble, Schubert's music differentiates clearly among the contrasting viewpoints and moods of the three pairs of characters.

The effective finale to Act I also repays close examination. Viewed broadly, Kupelwieser's finale encompasses an opening section of lyricism, a tense and conflict-laden middle section of drama, and a concluding section of stage spectacle. Schubert succeeded in linking all 873 measures into a dramatic whole, and in giving appropriate musical expression to the three successive and contrasting modes. A full analysis would consume too much space; perhaps drawing attention to eight particularly distinctive moments within the finale will suffice to highlight the richness of Schubert's operatic control and invention. (1) Eginhard's opening "Romanze" in A minor (which Emma joins as it blossoms into A major for the third strophe) stands out as the luminous "hit" tune of the opera. (2) The length and expressive weight of the moody orchestral setting for Fierrabras's entrance (for his despairing monologue) looks ahead to Wagner's lengthy orchestral passages in which singers act out specific, yet untexted, emotional situations. (3) At the "Un poco più mosso," as the finale turns for the first time to action and the search for Emma ignites the entire palace, Schubert's music brings continuity, a crescendo of agitated activity, and musical order to Kupelwieser's irregular lines of text. Beginning at the entrance of the Chorus ("Wo ist sie?") and continuing more or less to the Allegro vivace, Schubert controls the motion with one of his characteristic textural webs of insistently repetitive accompanimental motifs. (This technique, which found apotheosis in the "Great" C Major Symphony, may reflect the influence of Rossini, but it might just as well reflect a natural extension of the type of motivic continuity Schubert had long practiced in his Lieder, including *Erlkönig* and *Gretchen am Spinnrade*.) (4) The Allegro vivace, where Fierrabras discovers the two lovers, marks the first moment of strong dramatic conflict. Fierrabras's motivation may strain credulity but Schubert flexibly controls the flow of the action in totally convincing fashion. In the opening confrontation, the vocal lines fit irregularly over a churning sextuplet continuity. Later, a stretto-like imitative section shapes the seething introspection. (5) Using recitative and various gradations of music in tempo for the brief scene between Emma and Fierrabras, Schubert liberates himself from Kupelwieser's structures, intensifying the mood at the line "Lass nichts den Vater wissen" (in the middle of Kupelwieser's stanza). (6) King Karl fully explodes out of the castle to discover amidst great agitation that his daughter is with the Moorish prisoner. (7) Revealing a perfect sense of pacing, Schubert froze the strong and clashing emotions into a thirty-one measure *pezzo concertato* trio in G of intensely expressive power. Eginhard's arrival bursts in on this moment. (8) King Karl's uncontrollable wrath erupts continuously throughout the agitated Allegro vivace in C minor. Interrupted by the bugle call, King Karl orders Eginhard to get to work on his peace mission, and a strong, if conventional, choral piece brings the finale to a conclusion.

Schubert's operatic powers in *Fierrabras* are clearly on the road to mastery. Given a competent libretto, he was already able to control large-scale musico-dramatic structures, to use recitative and the whole range of declamatory styles to complement and set off his lyrical strengths, and to create music which portrayed a broad spectrum of personalities, emotional states, and dramatic situations.

Schubert's music for the theater remains a problematic repertory. Many factors – the historic (and current) lack of performances, the quantity of fragmentary operas, and the difficulty in comparing such a wide range of popular and serious genres – impede a fully satisfactory assessment, and even a chronicling, of his achievements and failures.

We can nevertheless trace a striking development in Schubert's operatic compositions. His operas from the early 1820s stand clearly above his earlier efforts, both in their ambitions and their achievement. During that period of his life, Schubert was forging ahead with an astonishingly rapid transformation of his compositional style, affecting all the large-scale genres, opera included. Moreover, his operas no doubt benefited directly from his growing experience working in the Viennese theater. And it would seem that "serious" *Ritterdrama*, a genre to which he turned increasingly at this time, was more suited to his maturing style than either comic or sentimental Singspiel.[15]

The two completed serious "grand" operas of Schubert's maturity challenged Schubert to extend the emotional range of his operatic writing and to develop his control of large-scale structure in ways which the lighter Singspiels did not. In his serious operas, he sought to produce the "highest in art," music comparable in power to his mature symphonies and Masses. History appears to have underestimated the rapidity and the extent of his development in these last two completed works. A new level of achievement was already apparent in the more successful moments of *Alfonso und Estrella*, but Schubert proved himself even more in command just eighteen months later in *Fierrabras*. Although we still await the full revelations of *Alfonso* which only a first-rate performance might provide, the recent opportunity to experience *Fierrabras* in the theater made its power and effectiveness clear. It is unfortunate that the sketchiness of Schubert's last operatic project, *Der Graf von Gleichen*, makes it impossible to experience and assess his later development in any comparable fashion.[16]

Schubert wrote no unquestionably great opera. And we will gain little from indulging in speculation about how much further the trajectory of Schubert's operatic development might have carried him toward greatness, had he lived longer, or had the Viennese theater circumstances been more receptive to German opera during his lifetime. It is enough to note that by 1823 Schubert was writing opera of a remarkably high level. It is enough to acknowledge that *Fierrabras* deserves a spot on the periphery of the standard repertory. It is enough that we set aside the lingering generalizations that Schubert was an inept opera composer. With *Fierrabras*, and even with *Alfonso und Estrella*, Schubert had finally earned the descriptions one encounters in the periodicals of his day – he was indeed a "talented" and "greatly promising" ("talentvollen"; "vielver-sprechenden") young opera composer.[17]

PART III

Reception

13 German reception: Schubert's "journey to immortality"

Christopher H. Gibbs

Leopold von Sonnleithner, an early and ardent champion of Franz Schubert, remarked in 1857: "Without any doubt the description of how his compositions gradually gained recognition must also find a place in Schubert's biography; but this requires laborious study" (*SMF* 119). Robert Schumann had already sounded a similar theme nearly two decades earlier, warning that "he who is not yet acquainted with [the "Great" C Major] Symphony knows very little about Schubert."[1] Unpublished compositions should be immediately released, Schumann urged, so that "the world finally arrives at the full appreciation of Schubert" (*SMF* 405). The lack of a truly representative selection of Schubert's music prompted his biographer Heinrich Kreissle von Hellborn to write in 1865 that

> Schubert in his totality is only known and appreciated by a few. There are vocal works of all kinds, cantatas, overtures, orchestral, opera, and church music, of which until now not a single note has ever been heard. For forty years and more this music has remained unused, in some cases mere objects of painful solicitude, as though the composer had written his enchanting music only for himself, and not for ourselves and our children.[2]

These three concurring views of Schubert's problematic reception, expressed by his friend Sonnleithner, by his most passionate and articulate critical advocate, and by his first biographer, all point to the unusual difficulties caused by the posthumous release of so many extraordinary pieces. To borrow the phrase of another acquaintance, Josef Kenner, Schubert's "journey to immortality" encountered significant obstacles and detours (*SMF* 82). The history of Schubert's musical reception is thus largely the story of the gradual dissemination and increasing appreciation of his compositions.

Critical assessments reflect evolving tastes and cultural practices, and often reveal as much about the concerns and values of the historical period making the judgments as they do about the specific composer under consideration. The history of a composer's reception charts not only the changing evaluations and interpretations of his individual works, but also the broader revaluations of his overall artistic stature. In Schubert's case the sudden availability at mid century of so much of his greatest music confounded critical understanding and called for constant revision. As more than one nineteenth-century critic remarked in response to the steady stream of new publications, it was as if Schubert were still alive and composing.

This chapter explores Schubert's nineteenth- and early twentieth-century critical reception in German-speaking countries, and the following two chapters consider his reception in England and France. The German reception conveniently divides into three periods. The first, encompassing Schubert's lifetime, saw hundreds of his works performed and/or published, usually to popular and critical acclaim. The second, at mid century, saw the first appearance of masterpieces that expanded his reputation from a composer known primarily for songs and dances to one also esteemed for instrumental music. The third, beginning in the 1860s and lasting well into the twentieth century, saw Schubert achieve immortality, and was characterized by a curious juxtaposition of positivist scholarship and an increasing trivialization of his life and music in popular genres, such as novels, operettas, and musical arrangements.

Schubert in his own time: fame and neglect

The appearance of Franz von Schlechta's poem "An Herrn Franz Schubert" in the *Wiener allgemeine Theaterzeitung* on September 27, 1817, marked the first mention of Schubert in the press, a versified tribute that seems symbolically appropriate for a composer who made his reputation with the Lied. Only a limited group in Vienna then knew the music of the unpublished Schubert, aged twenty. During the next few years public and semi-public performances of individual Lieder, partsongs, overtures, as well as the cantata *Prometheus* (now lost) and two Singspiels (D647, D644), attracted some brief comment in the Viennese press, and occasionally in other German-language periodicals.

Usually laudatory, these notices are frustratingly superficial. Even though music criticism was still quite young, it already displayed the split between insight into musical compositions, which marks genuine criticism, and the chronicling of public events, which characterizes reviews. Viennese attention to Schubert's music first came from concert reviews (*Konzertberichte*) and from notices of published works, which amounted to consumer reports commenting on the level of technical difficulty that a player might expect, or remarking on the quality of the engraving.

Although of limited quantity and quality, the early criticism does point to some significant features of Schubert's initial reception. Most critics were supportive, and a few swiftly recognized his genius. They took serious note of his Lieder, and often remarked that although the genre did not, as a rule, warrant much consideration, Schubert's accomplishments justified extended treatment (e.g. *SDB* 353, 418). Schubert's startling innovations were thus quickly acknowledged; his eventual status as the composer who raised the Lied to full artistic status is prefigured in the enthusiastic initial 1821 reviews of *Erlkönig*, Op. 1, which would remain his preeminent work throughout the nineteenth century.[3] Viennese acclaim continued to the end, with a review of *Winterreise* just months before Schubert died: "Herein lies the nature of German Romantic being and art, and in this sense Schubert is a German composer through and through, who does honor to our fatherland and our time" (*SDB* 758).[4]

In contrast to the breadth of Beethoven criticism,[5] however, hardly more than a dozen substantial articles on Schubert appeared during his lifetime;[6] this scarcity was due in part to Viennese critical practices, to Schubert's youth, and, most importantly, to the unassuming genres for which he was best known – Lieder, partsongs, dances, and keyboard music. With the exception of a few notable Viennese articles, most of the significant criticism of Schubert's music appeared in foreign periodicals, and after 1824 primarily in Leipzig's *Allgemeine musikalische Zeitung*. This higher criticism weighed only published compositions, thereby sharply limiting discussion of Schubert's large-scale works, and further underscoring the importance of publication for the advancement of his fame.

The inaugural release, in 1821, of Schubert Lieder by the firm of Cappi & Diabelli triggered two articles that provide invaluable insights into Viennese views of the Lied, indicate Schubert's early stature in the genre, and offer an unusually high level of interpretive insight. The first article praised "the young composer with a rich lyrical gift" and "excellent talent," and applauded the sensitivity Schubert typically brought to the poems he set: "Not often has a composer had so large a share of the gift for making the poet's fancy so profoundly impressive to the receptive listener's heart."[7]

The second article, Friedrich von Hentl's "Blick auf Schuberts Lieder," also hailed Schubert's achievement: "Schubert's songs elevated themselves by ever undeniable excellent features to the rank of masterpieces of genius."[8] Hentl stressed "the spirit which unifies the whole, the poetry which animates it, and the organization which imparts expression to it" (*SDB* 214). Hentl immediately recognized those qualities that would most often win Schubert praise: the caliber of the poetry chosen and his understanding of it ("translation" is the word some commentators use), the extraordinary role accorded to the piano, and the originality of his imaginative conceptions. Although this was one of Schubert's first substantial reviews, Hentl seemed to make a preemptive strike against future complaints: "Whoever is inclined to doubt whether Schubert can write pure melody and to reproach him with relying for the effect of many of his songs on harmony and characteristic expression alone by means of excessive accompaniments, as in *Gretchen am Spinnrade*, has only to hear his lovely and extremely simple *Heidenröslein*, [among other songs]" (*SDB* 218).

In the coming years just such doubts were raised, especially in German journals. North-German critics tended to be more thorough than their Viennese counterparts, and also more conservative; having heard less of Schubert's music, they were more likely to harbor reservations about his compositional innovations. The most important and authoritative reviews appeared in Leipzig's *Allgemeine musikalische Zeitung*, which repeatedly mentioned Beethoven in its discussions of Schubert. As early as 1820 – thus before the publication of Schubert's *Erlkönig*, Op. 1 – one critic wrote: "In this first dramatic essay [the Singspiel *Die Zwillingsbrüder*, Schubert] seems to attempt to fly as high as Beethoven and not heed the warning example of Icarus" (*SDB* 139). Comparisons continued throughout the decade, sometimes to Schubert's benefit: the "freedom and originality" of Schubert's A Minor Sonata, Op. 42 (D845), can "probably be compared only with the greatest and freest of Beethoven's sonatas. We are indebted for this uncommonly attractive and also significant work to Herr Franz Schubert, who is, we hear, a still quite young artist of and in Vienna" (*SDB* 512). Reviewing the Sonata in G, Op. 78 (D894), some years later, a critic proclaimed: "The composer, who has made for himself a numerous following by not a few excellent songs, is capable of doing the same by means of pianoforte pieces." The same critic then promptly warned the young composer once again about the dangers of using a unique genius as a model: "Beethoven appears to us to be in a class by himself alone, as it were, especially as he showed himself in his middle and later period, so that in truth he should not by any means be chosen as an absolute model, since anyone who desired to be successful in that master's own line could only be he himself" (*SDB* 694).

An entrenched conception of the Lied genre is apparent in the *AmZ* reviews of Schubert's efforts. One critic commented that while Schubert had written "several very good, and a few excellent, pieces," he was less suited for "real song" (*das eigentliche Lied*, i.e. strophic settings) than for "continuously composed pieces, for four voices or for one voice with an independent, sometimes excessively full accompaniment."[9] Such excesses were found in *Erlkönig*, which "may be a highly overladen [*überladen*] piece of work, very difficult to perform; but it does contain spirit and vitality in general as well as a certain secret deviltry of expression" (*SDB* 543; cf. 690). In general, it was Schubert's unconventional harmonic adventures, not his melodies or formal structures, that most struck critics. Schubert's first big review in the *AmZ* was unusually negative, lamenting that he sought to compensate for the "want of inner unity, order and regularity by eccentricities which are hardly or not at all justified and by other rather wild goings-on" (*SDB* 353). Schubert's harmony might be praised as "original," chided as "excessive," or both: "original" was the word critics used most often, although it was sometimes coupled with "bizarre" or "eccentric."

Such ambivalence surfaced often in *AmZ* reviews: "he shows originality of invention and execution, sound knowledge of harmony and honest industry: on the other hand he often, sometimes very greatly, oversteps the species at hand [Lieder]... he likes to labor at the harmonies for the sake of being new and piquant; and he is inordinately addicted to giving too many notes to the piano part, either at once or in succession" (*SDB* 718). The year before, reviewing the Op. 59 Lieder, a critic wrote: "He modulates so often and often so very suddenly towards the remotest regions as no composer on earth has done... but it is equally true that ... he does not seek in vain, that he really conjures up something which had truly much to communicate to our fancy and feeling, and does it significantly" (*SDB* 636).

As serious criticism was limited to Schubert's published compositions, no reviews appeared of symphonies and only a few concerned his chamber music; large-scale keyboard pieces received most of the attention. Although Schubert's music was briefly mentioned in hundreds of reviews during his lifetime, critics rarely indicated what was new or special about his compositions. (Some published works, such as *Die schöne Müllerin*, were mysteriously ignored altogether.) Not until Robert Schumann began writing in the mid 1830s did Schubert enjoy concerted critical support and understanding that went much beyond grade assignments. The writings from the 1820s – brief or extended – were usually more evaluative than interpretive, their value and interest more historical than hermeneutic. A declaration from 1827 in Vienna's *Theaterzeitung* is illustrative: "The name 'Schubert' has a fair sound and his works, wholly enwrapped in the rosy veil of originality and feeling, stand high in public favor" (*SDB* 660). The information given here – that Schubert's music is both original and esteemed – is useful and consistent with other reports, but we learn nothing more substantive about the music itself.

Together with advertisements, reviews account for most of the published comment on Schubert in the 1820s. (After Schlechta's poem, a few

more poetic tributes appeared in Viennese journals [SDB 557, 838, 925].)
Although Schubert received ever-increasing attention during his lifetime,
he still went unmentioned in biographies, histories, and musical reference works.[10] The brevity of his career and its confinement primarily to
Vienna, the modest genres with which he first attracted public attention,
and the formidable amount of music that remained unpublished and
unknown – these factors limited criticism and account for the discrepancy between his stature then and in the decades that followed.[11]

Schubert in mid century: "working invisibly"

In his classic study of Viennese concert life (*Geschichte des Concertwesens
in Wien*, 1869), Eduard Hanslick succinctly captured Schubert's unusual
posthumous career: "If Schubert's contemporaries rightly gazed astonished at his creative power, what shall we, who come after him, say, as we
incessantly discover new works of his? For thirty years the master has
been dead, and in spite of this it seems as if he goes on working invisibly –
it is impossible to follow him."[12]

It may be inevitable that when a composer dies so young, with so
unrepresentative a portion of his music published, his artistic legacy will
be received with a sense both of revelation and of uncertainty. This phenomenon had curious repercussions for Schubert, occasionally prompting suspicions that such posthumous productivity could not be
authentic: "All Paris has been in a state of amazement at the posthumous
diligence of the song-writer Franz Schubert," commented *The Musical
World* in 1839, "who, while one would think his ashes repose in peace in
Vienna, is still making eternal new songs, and putting drawing-rooms in
commotion."[13]

Shortly after Schubert's death, the publisher Tobias Haslinger shrewdly
assembled his final fourteen songs, attached the title *Schwanengesang*
(D957), and marketed it as his *Letztes Werk*. The bulk of Schubert's
unpublished legacy went to his older brother Ferdinand, who valiantly
sought publication in the decades following. Throughout the 1830s and
1840s, hundreds of Lieder appeared for the first time, mostly released by
Schubert's first publisher, Anton Diabelli, as part of a series with the title
Franz Schuberts nachgelassene musikalische Dichtungen.

The fame of Schubert's Lieder also spread rapidly through an astounding number of reworkings, which included all manner of arrangements,
fantasies, and medleys. Piano transcriptions outnumbered the rest,
although nearly every domestic instrumentation was accommodated.[14]
Song orchestrations by Liszt, Berlioz, Brahms, and countless others facili-

tated the entrance of the Lied into public concerts and played a role in the creation of the orchestral Lied that flowered with Mahler, Strauss, and others at the end of the century.[15] Reworkings served a vital aesthetic and social function in nineteenth-century musical life. As recordings do today, they made music widely known and accessible. Arguably, commercial factors – which lay behind most nineteenth-century arrangements – are less significant in explaining the extensive reworkings of Schubert's music. For example, the already popular works of Rossini were the most often reworked in Vienna during the first half of the nineteenth century. In Schubert's case, during the same time, reworkings largely created his fame across Europe. In particular, Franz Liszt's reworkings, primarily dating from the 1830s and 1840s, spread Schubert's name far and wide.[16]

For all their importance in disseminating his music, albeit in altered form, the compositions attractive to arrangers were invariably already published; reworkings simply made available works much better known. Throughout the 1830s, however, an increasing number of outstanding instrumental pieces appeared for the first time. Diabelli published the Piano Trio in B flat, Op. 99 (D898), in 1836 and the Sonata in C, the "Grand Duo" (D812) dedicating it to Clara Wieck, in 1837.[17] Until published, compositions had little chance of public performance (although handwritten copies, primarily of Lieder and dances, circulated widely). Publication thus offered the chance for exposure beyond Vienna and for criticism as well.[18] Table 13.1 lists the posthumous publication and première dates of other significant works.

Some exceptional additions to the Schubert canon owed their discovery, publication, and promotion to Robert Schumann. After he learned of the "Great" C Major Symphony (D944) during a visit to Vienna, Schumann encouraged his friend Felix Mendelssohn to premiere the work in Leipzig (1839), and wrote one of the most famous of all his critical essays on the work – the occasion of his remark on the "heavenly length" of the symphony.[19] Schumann's criticism marked an interpretive high point in Schubert's reception. He recognized, valued, and extolled Schubert's genius as had no other critic to date; he repeatedly paired him with Beethoven and asserted that his music initiated a new era of Romanticism.[20] Moreover, his criticism probed keyboard and instrumental music, not Lieder, which mostly go unmentioned.[21]

Nineteenth-century commentary about Schubert can be informative and revealing; but the penetrating criticism of Schumann and, more importantly, the esteem and promotion of celebrated composers and performers, had a more lasting effect on Schubert's reception. The advocacy of Liszt was not limited to reworkings, but extended to his numerous performances as pianist and conductor and his activities as essayist and

Table 13.1. *Selected posthumous premières and publications*

1829	*Schwanengesang* (D957)
	Piano Sonata in A Minor (D664)
	Fantasy in F Minor, Op. Post. 103 (D940)
	Piano Quintet in A Major, "Trout," Op. Post. 114 (D667)
1831	Quartet in D Minor (D810)
1836	Piano Trio in B flat, Op. 99 (D898)
	Violin Sonatas, Op. Post. 137 (D384, 385, 408)
1837	Mass in B flat, Op. Post. 141 (D324)
	"Grand Duo," Op. Post. 140 (D812)
1839	Last three piano sonatas in C Minor, A Major, and B flat Major (D958–60)
	4 Impromptus, Op. Post. 142 (D935)
	Mendelssohn premieres "Great" C Major Symphony (D944), published the following year
1840	Allegro in A Minor, "Lebensstürme" (D947)
1846	Piano Sonata in B, Op. Post. 147 (D575)
	Mass in G (D167)
1850	Violin Fantasy in C Major, Op. Post. 159 (D934)
1851	Quartet in G (D887)
1853	Octet (D803) and String Quintet in C (D956)
1854	Liszt conducts première of *Alfonso und Estrella* (D732)
1856	Mass in F (D105)
1861	Premiere of *Die Verschworenen* (D787)
	Piano Sonata in C "Reliquie" (D840)
1865	Première of the "Unfinished" Symphony (D759, published 1867)
	Mass in E flat (D950)
1866	*Lazarus* (D689)
1870	*Quartettsatz* (D703)
1871	"Arpeggione" Sonata (D821)
1875	Mass in A flat (D678)
1884	Collected edition of Schubert's works begins to appear from Breitkopf und Härtel (*ASA*); first publication of symphonies nos. 1, 2, 3, 4, 5, 6; and of all of Schubert's dramatic works
1897	Schubert Centennial, collected edition is completed

editor.[22] Mendelssohn had played some of Schubert's music as early as 1827 (*SDB* 690), and later Brahms became an especially passionate advocate.[23] Many composers not only arranged Schubert's music, but also used it as a model for compositions of their own. While most commentators have emphasized Schubert's reliance on Beethoven, they have played down the ways in which later nineteenth-century composers looked to Schubert for inspiration.[24]

With so many prominent champions, important mid-century premières, the publication of so much music, glowing critical promotion by Schumann and others, and an ever-expanding amount of biographical information, Schubert's reputation grew steadily, even while a large amount of music awaited undiscovered, and both critical and biographical commentary remained meager. The first recognition of his historical significance came from the Lied, with the acknowledgment of Schubert as the composer whose works exemplified the genre.[25] The sites of Lieder performances changed as mixed programs, semi-private concerts by musical societies, and Schubertiades gradually expanded into more formal, public *Liederabende*, recitals, and symphonic concerts.[26] Julius Stockhausen's innovative concerts in the 1850s, especially those featuring the Müller song cycles, marked an important transition to the Lied recital as we know it today.

By the 1860s Schubert was more than just the foremost Lied composer. Beginning in the previous decade the Hellmesberger Quartet premièred string masterpieces such as the G Major Quartet (D887) and the C Major Quintet (D956) at Vienna's Musikverein, which led to their publication, together with the Octet (D803). Even dramatic works received some limited exposure, albeit in abridged, sometimes mangled, form. In 1854 Franz Liszt conducted the première of *Alfonso und Estrella* (D732) in Weimar; *Die Verschworenen* (D787) was given a concert performance in Vienna in 1861 (and staged in Frankfurt later that season); and the unfinished oratorio *Lazarus* (D689) was heard in 1863.

Most significantly, Johann Herbeck premiered the "Unfinished" Symphony in B Minor (D759, written in 1822) on December 17, 1865, in the Musikverein at the Gesellschaft der Musikfreunde. Hanslick, Vienna's leading critic, had previously warned of "over-zealous Schubert worship and adulation of Schubert relics," but he hailed this work and its performance, which "excited extraordinary enthusiasm" and "brought new life into our concert halls." According to Hanslick, after hearing only a few measures

> every child recognized the composer, and a muffled "Schubert" was
> whispered in the audience . . . every heart rejoiced, as if, after a long
> separation, the composer himself were among us in person. The whole
> movement is a melodic stream so crystal clear, despite its force and genius,
> that one can see every pebble on the bottom. And everywhere the same
> warmth, the same bright, life-giving sunshine![27]

Such significant premières, combined with the increased amount of publications, were both evidence of and catalyst for Schubert's growing stature. By mid century, lexicons, which serve as repositories of received opinion, placed Schubert among the elect for the first time. Eduard Bernsdorf's *Neues Universal-Lexikon der Tonkunst* (1856–61) is typical: "The famous master of song and generally one of the most god-gifted German composers" ("Der berühmte Liedermeister und überhaupt einer der gottbegnadetsten deutschen Tondichter").[28] A more symbolic gesture came in 1863 with the exhumation of Schubert's and Beethoven's bodies from Vienna's Währing Cemetery; they were submitted to a scientific process that measured, studied, and compared their skulls so as better to understand the mechanisms of genius.[29] (Twenty-five years later their bodies were moved to the "Grove of Honor" at the Central Cemetery.)

Serious biographical and scholarly investigation of Schubert only began in the second half of the century.[30] After the composer's death, several people failed in their attempts to write his biography.[31] In the late 1850s, Ferdinand Luib, former editor of the *Allgemeine Wiener Musik-Zeitung*, solicited accounts from Schubert's acquaintances in the hope, likewise never realized, of producing a substantial study of the composer. The watershed date for Schubert biography is 1865,[32] when Heinrich Kreissle von Hellborn published, in Vienna, the first full-scale work – *Franz Schubert*.[33] Using accounts from Schubert's friends, together with additional documents collected by Luib and others, Kreissle examined the composer's life and, albeit superficially and uncritically, his works. Scholars such as Philipp Spitta, Max Friedländer, and Hermann Kretzschmar were quick to point out that Kreissle's scholarship did not match the high caliber of such studies as Jahn's of Mozart (1856–59), Chrysander's of Handel (1858–67), Thayer's of Beethoven (1866–79), or Spitta's of Bach (1873–80). Although Kreissle drew heavily on anecdote and gossip, his book filled a void and decisively influenced writers and writings on Schubert until Otto Erich Deutsch began his far more comprehensive and reliable documentary compilations in the first decades of the next century.[34]

Positivism and kitsch

A third stage of Schubert's critical reception encompasses both the emergence of modern musical scholarship in Germany toward the end of the nineteenth century and popular celebrations of Schubert, exemplified by the 1897 centennial. Mixing scholarly positivism with popular trivialization of Schubert's life and works, this period featured unprecedented access to scores, catalogues, documents, and iconography.

Facts and verification preoccupied the newly defined discipline of *Musikwissenschaft*.[35] The move away from aesthetic concerns in favor of objective scientific approaches produced studies dealing more with form than content, with musical analysis rather than interpretation. The dominance of the critics, composers, and performers in the earlier periods of Schubert's reception now yielded to that of scholars, first to Sir George Grove and Gustav Nottebohm, then to the editors of the Schubert critical

edition, and later to Max Friedländer, Otto Erich Deutsch, and others –
those who catalogued and edited Schubert's music, and documented and
narrated his life.

Sir George Grove visited Vienna in 1867 and left with newly discovered
pieces – and with a heightened passion for Schubert. The catalogue of
works that he prepared formed an appendix to an English translation of
Kreissle's biography, and his own Schubert study appeared in an 1882
volume of the celebrated *Grove's Dictionary of Music and Musicians*. By
that date Nottebohm had already issued his impressive catalogue of
Schubert's published and unpublished music.[36] Friedländer, trained as a
singer under Stockhausen before beginning musicological studies under
Spitta, devoted himself primarily to investigating the German Lied. He
sought to establish authoritative texts in his collections of Lieder for
Edition Peters and to give in his dissertation a scholarly assessment of
available biographical information concerning Schubert.[37]

The *sine qua non* of positivist musicology is a critical edition of a composer's works, which the Berlin firm of Breitkopf und Härtel had already
undertaken for Bach, Handel, Mozart, Beethoven, Schumann, and
Chopin, among others. Finally, in 1884, such an edition was initiated for
Schubert (*ASA*). This ambitious project, commendably edited by
Eusebius Mandyczewski and others (including Brahms), drew upon
modern musical editorial practices and was finished in time for the centennial. Although relatively minor compositions continued to surface in
the next century, almost everything Schubert composed, including all the
multiple Lied variants, was at last available for performers to play and for
critics and scholars to assess.[38]

Beginning in the first decades of the twentieth century, Deutsch's pioneering collections of documents – letters, reviews, reminiscences, and
iconography – provided unusual entrance to primary materials.[39] His
later efforts to catalogue Schubert's oeuvre chronologically earned him
lasting citation through "Deutsch numbers." Generally avoiding explicit
interpretation, Deutsch concentrated on facts, figures, and bibliography,
even though his own perception of the man and the music inevitably
emerges in the way he assembled, presented, and annotated the documentation. The central importance of Deutsch's scholarship is readily
apparent in this *Companion*, as it is in nearly all twentieth-century
writing on Schubert.[40]

Even as scholarship delivered new access to music and documentation,
the celebration and marketing of Schubert's popularity was recasting the
man and his music for a mass audience. As his stature grew, so did public
tributes, along with other trappings of immortality. By the mid nineteenth century, Schubert's admirers had begun to erect statues, place

plaques on appropriate buildings, and rename streets in his honor. (In Vienna such activities were usually spearheaded by the Wiener Männergesang-Verein and the Wiener Schubertbund.[41])

Schubert's election to the musical pantheon is apparent in illustrations from the centennial year. In Otto Böhler's "Die Feier von Schubert's 100 Geburtstag im Himmel," he is crowned in heaven with a host of the greatest composers in attendance.[42] This popular assignment of Schubert to the immortals is consistent with the "scholarly" assessment found in Julius Fuchs's *Kritik der Tonwerke: Ein Nachschlagebuch für Freunde der Tonkunst* (Leipzig, 1897). The preface promises a "scientific and practical" work in which almost every imaginable composer since Bach, is ranked in order of achievement; specific works are also evaluated.[43] The positioning of composers (overwhelmingly German) according to "the lasting worth of their creations" gives Schubert an extraordinarily high position; he is literally in a class by himself:

I.1	I.2	I.3
Bach	Schubert	Gluck
Beethoven		Haydn
Handel		
Mozart		

II.1
Brahms
Mendelssohn
Schumann
Wagner
Weber

The trivializing features in Schubert's *fin-de-siècle* reception only accelerated in the years between the centennial *Schubertjahre* of 1897 and 1928. Poems, short stories, and novels offered distorted, sentimental visions of his life and loves, and cast Schubert as the "Liederfürst," a melodic genius who spontaneously composed immortal songs. As mentioned in chapter 2, legends also spread extensively through operettas, and eventually through films. These trivializations influenced not only which of his pieces were most often performed and published, but also must have certainly affected how the music was heard.

Schubert's popular and serious reception attests to his "journey to immortality." Scholarship made available almost all of his music and brought to light essential biographical documentation.[44] Along with all the kitsch, more dignified biographies appeared (such as those by Richard Heuberger and Walter Dahms),[45] the opera *Fierrabras* received its belated

Otto Böhler, "Die Feier von Schubert's 100 Geburtstag im Himmel"

première, and extraordinary performers such as Artur Schnabel promoted virtually unknown masterpieces in concert halls and on early
recordings. By the first decades of the twentieth century the nature of
musical culture had undergone profound changes, with audiences that
listened to music in different ways. One became more likely to "play"
Schubert on the phonograph than on the piano with a friend or family
member. What may be most remarkable is how easily Schubert's music
could adapt, and be adapted, to serve new times and new audiences.

14 Schubert's reception history in nineteenth-century England

John Reed

The songs

During his lifetime Schubert was known almost solely as a composer of *Hausmusik* – songs, dances, marches, and other characteristic pieces for the piano. So much is clear from the fact that of the 478 compositions published before his death (*SDB* 946), 209 were solo songs or partsongs with piano accompaniment, and 249 were keyboard pieces. It was as a song composer that he first made his name in Vienna, and inevitably when his name first began to be heard abroad it was for his songs. In London the pioneer was a German from Bremen called Christian Wessell, who came to London in the 1820s and founded the publishing firm of Stodart and Wessell.

The sequence of events as reflected in the *Harmonicon*, a musical monthly which managed to survive for eleven years (1822–32), was as follows. In December 1830 the London firm of Johanning and Whatmore published a Christmas and New Year annual which included as one of its items Schubert's F Minor *Moment musical* (D780, 3) under its original published title of *Air Russe*. The annual, called the *Cadeau*, also appeared a year later, and this time included Schubert's *Erlkönig* (D328), using Sir Walter Scott's translation of the text. In the summer of 1832 the famous dramatic soprano Wilhelmine Schröder-Devrient came to London to take the prima donna role in the first London production of Beethoven's *Fidelio*, and took the opportunity to introduce *Erlkönig* to a London audience, whereupon Wessell and Stodart decided to publish the song with Scott's words "as sung by Madame Schröder-Devrient."[1]

Wessell himself continued to publish Schubert songs till he retired in 1860. Where he led, others were not slow to follow. In the 1840s for instance, Cramer, Addison and Beale of London brought out a series of song volumes with the texts "imitated from the German by Thomas Oliphant." It was not till 1871 that Ernst Pauer, a pianist and critic of German origin, attempted anything like a representative collection of Schubert songs with the original texts. This was in four volumes, containing eighty-two songs, with original German texts and English translations. The 1870s saw a veritable flood of Schubert editions, culminating in 1885 with the earliest of Max Friedländer's edition of the songs (for the *Edition Peters*), enthusiastically welcomed by Federick Niecks as a revelation in a three-page essay in the *Monthly Musical Record* of March 1885.

Pauer's inclusion of the two complete song cycles in his four-volume edition is significant. Individual songs from them had been sung as interludes in orchestral concerts since the 1830s, and many were favorites with audiences, though usually with bland and sometimes banal English words. Julius Stockhausen had sung *Die schöne Müllerin* (D795) complete in Vienna in May 1856, but there is no evidence of a complete performance in England before 1904, when Raimund von zur Mühlen sang the complete cycle at the newly built Bechstein Hall, now the Wigmore Hall.[2]

Until the 1860s Schubert and Schumann were both regarded as "modern," indeed as avant-garde composers, and underrated, much as Mahler, Schoenberg, and Berg were underrated in the first half of the twentieth century. In London, as in Vienna, the new mercantile and professional aristocracy of talent was slowly but surely assuming the reins of power from the old aristocracy of birth, but it was more concerned to defend the music of the great Classical masters than to promote the "new music" of the early Romantics. The only progressive organization in the London musical world in the 1830s was the Society of British Musicians, founded in 1834 to promote the music of contemporary native composers. It was little more than a small group of young enthusiasts, with the critic James William Davison as their leader, who looked to William Sterndale Bennett to revitalize English music. Davison, who took over as chief critic of *The Times* in 1846 and remained as a sort of unofficial chairman of the London corps of music critics until his death in 1885, had no use for the "new music" and must be held partly responsible for the tone of acrimonious depreciation which appears in some Schubert notices in the press. In 1844 for instance, Mendelssohn came to London at the invitation of the Philharmonic Society to conduct their annual series of concerts, and brought with him the orchestral parts of two Schubert works, the Overture to *Fierrabras* (D796) and the "Great" C Major Symphony (D944), intending to perform them in London. But the orchestra refused to rehearse the symphony, and Mendelssohn was so angry that he withdrew his own overture to *Ruy Blas* from the program and insisted on playing Schubert's overture instead. This performance, on June 10, 1844, was the first Schubert orchestral work played in England. Davison's notice in the *Musical World* dismissed it as "literally beneath criticism" and added:

> Perhaps a more overrated man than this Schubert never existed. He has
> certainly written a few good songs. But what then? Has not every composer
> who ever composed written a few good songs? And out of the thousand and
> one with which Schubert deluged the musical world it would indeed be hard
> if some half-dozen were not tolerable. And when that is said, all is said that
> can justly be said about Schubert.[3]

At which point all that needs to be said surely is that Davison himself had
written, and published, a few (not so good) songs, and fulsome notices of
two of them appeared in this same issue of the *Musical World*.

The publication of Schubert Lieder, as we have seen, owed much to the
enterprise of German-speaking foreign nationals who made their homes
in London, and the performance of them probably owes even more. Josef
Kroff, the Bohemian singer and composer who arrived in London in
1835, sang *Der Wanderer* (D489) at a Classical quartet concert in 1836,
presumably in German. The Austrian bass, Josef Staudigl, spent much of
his time during the 1840s in London, and was much admired for his
Schubert Lieder. It comes as something of a surprise however to find
English artists noted in the musical press for what must surely have been
the first public performance of *Der Hirt auf dem Felsen* (D965) in
England. "Mrs. Bishop sang 'The Swiss Peasant on the Rock,' a cantata by
Schubert, at the Hanover Square Rooms. Thomas Willman played the
clarinet obbligato."[4]

The reception history of Schubert's instrumental music in England,
however, can be satisfactorily covered only as an account of the careers of
two German musicians who made England their permanent home, and
were devoted to his music: Charles Hallé (1819–95) and August Manns
(1825–1907). To complete the picture, we shall have to include George
Grove (1820–1900), the English publicist, polymath, biographer and
critic, but his contribution was essentially supportive, as he would have
been the first to acknowledge. Hallé and Manns were the key figures.

Piano music

Sir Charles Hallé was born plain Karl Halle in April 1819 at Hagen in
Westphalia, the son of the local church organist. The acute accent on the E
came later, probably in 1836, when he went to Paris intending to study
piano under Friedrich Kalkbrenner. He is usually remembered nowadays
as the founder of the orchestra which bears his name, and his achievement as a pianist has been largely forgotten. Yet he made his name as a
pianist, and from 1850 always reserved the months of May and June for
keyboard recitals either in London or elsewhere. He was among the first

to make the piano sonata *Konzertfähig*, and the very first to play all thirty-two Beethoven sonatas from memory in a single series of recitals. In Paris he met Liszt, Chopin, Berlioz, the young Wagner, and the galaxy of creative genius which made Paris at that time the artistic capital of the world. The revolution of 1848 brought him and his family, along with many other musicians, to London, and coincidental circumstances led to his accepting an invitation to move to Manchester, then known only as the financial and industrial capital of north England, and "take the musical life of the city in hand," as he put it in his memoirs.[5]

In January 1849 he initiated a series of chamber concerts with internationally known artists, taking the financial risk on his own shoulders. At the end of the year, he made his own terms and accepted the conductorship of the "Gentlemen's Concerts." He also started an amateur choir, which became the forerunner of the Hallé Choir. Nothing daunted by the fact that only three single tickets and a handful of others were sold for the first of his chamber music concerts, Hallé's optimism in the end was fully justified. Within two years the series had to be extended from six to eight concerts. He seized the opportunity to give the first performances in England of Schubert's two piano trios. The E flat Piano Trio, Op. 100 (D929), was played on October 31, 1850, and repeated a month later, twice again in Manchester, and once in London. On this last occasion the artists were Hallé (piano), W. B. Molique (violin), and Alfredo Piatti (cello). The first performance of the B flat Piano Trio, Op. 99 (D898), was given by the same artists on November 10, 1853, and repeated first in Manchester and then in London.

In 1859 the "Monday Popular Concerts" began at the new St. James's Hall in London, with a consciously educational motivation. The aim was to meet the growing demand for chamber music at prices which would attract the vast population of potential but unattached music lovers. Hallé, with Arabella Goddard and Clara Schumann, became a regular performer at these concerts, and took the opportunity to introduce audiences to Schubert's piano music. Moreover, from 1861 on he mounted a regular series of solo piano recitals in May and June each year in London. This became a feature of the London musical scene until the 1890s. It has to be remembered that the solo "recital" – even the word was regarded with suspicion – was unknown until Liszt experimented with it in the 1840s. Hallé did more than anyone to familiarize the musical public with it in England. In 1861 he played all Beethoven's piano sonatas in chronological order in a series of eight recitals. (This feat was repeated in 1862, 1866, and finally in 1891.) In 1867 he turned his attention to the Schubert piano sonatas, having already introduced five of them at the "Monday Pops," and played nine of them. An even more ambitious program followed in 1868, when Hallé played all eleven Schubert sonatas then available in print, together with all the shorter keyboard works of Beethoven. Here is a sample program:

Part I	Grand Sonata in A Minor, Op. 164	Schubert
	Song *The Violet*	Mozart
	Twenty four Variations on a theme in D	Beethoven
Part II	Fantasia Sonata in G Major, Op. 78	Schubert
	Song *Marie*	Schubert
	Bagatelles, Op. 126 Nos. 1–2–3–4	Beethoven
	Suites de Valse Allemagne, Op. 33	Schubert

Pianoforte: Mr. Charles Hallé
Vocalist: Miss Anna Jewell

In thus juxtaposing the work of Schubert and Beethoven, Hallé was consciously challenging the orthodox nineteenth-century view that Schubert did not belong among the great composers, because his music lacked the unity of form, continuity of theme and architectonic power of a Beethoven. The point was not lost on the critics. The *Musical World* observed: "In associating Schubert with Beethoven and dividing his program between the two, Mr. Hallé has imparted quite a new interest to his recitals." And the *Musical Times*: "The ten grand sonatas of Schubert, the one Fantasia Sonata in G, and the Fantaisie in C are all on a grand scale of form and development worthy of Beethoven, and approach nearer to that grand model than any similar work by any other composer." To complete this comprehensive demonstration of Schubert's keyboard works, in 1867–68 Hallé edited for Chappell and Co. the first English edition of the eleven "grand sonatas" of Schubert, followed by the Impromptus, Op. 90 (D899), the *Moments musicaux*, the "Wanderer" Fantasy, Op. 15 (D760), and other minor works.[6] Between May 1859 and June 1868 Hallé was responsible for the premières in England of all these works except one. The single exception was the A Minor Sonata of 1825 (D845) which was first performed by Walter Macfarren in May 1865.

What, one wonders, would we make of Hallé's pianism if we could hear him today? Writing at the turn of the century, Hermann Klein remembers him as "coldly correct and scholastic," and so he may well have seemed in comparison with lions of the keyboard like Paderewski and Anton Rubinstein. A. M. Diehl (Alice Mangold) says that "he was essentially an artist devoted to the interpretation of the musical classics, rather than the executant using them to express his own individual emotions." Perhaps the most convincing account of his keyboard manner, however, comes from Joseph Bennett, the critic of the *Daily Telegraph*:

He exemplified a school that was fast passing away – the school in which it was taught that the pianoforte rightly claimed to be a distinctive instrument, and not a sort of parlor orchestra. His playing was all refinement, precision and neatness. He struck no wrong notes, and dropped no right ones; nevertheless there were moments when one could have wished him less rigidly correct. He would have been more human, and in consequence more interesting. In rendering Schubert, however, he was unapproachable.[7]

The chamber music

The publication of the chamber music proceeded more slowly. Performances began in London in May 1852, when a quartet led by Joachim played the D Minor Quartet, "Death and the Maiden" (D810), at one of John Ella's "Musical Union" concerts. But it was naturally to the "Monday Pops" (which became the "Monday and Saturday" Pops in 1865) that music-lovers looked for performances of Schubert's string quartets and major chamber works by international artists from 1859 onward. The "Trout" Quintet (D667) was first played in 1867. The first performance of the great C Major String Quintet (D956) was given on January 19, 1863, and fourteen performances followed over the next twenty years. The artists in the first performance were Sainton, Ries, Webb, Paque, and Piatti. Joseph Bennett in the *Daily Telegraph* found it "gloriously overflowing in original, striking and beautiful ideas."[8]

In February 1869 Joachim, Blagrove, and Piatti achieved a world première at St. James's Hall with Schubert's early (1817) String Trio (D581). The Octet for Wind and Strings (D803) was played for the first time in England in March 1867 in the abridged version (omitting the Variations and the Menuetto and Trio). The firm of Peters in Leipzig published the full score in 1872, and it rapidly became a favorite; over twenty performances were given at St. James's Hall over the next fifteen years.

Orchestral works

August Friedrich Manns was born at Stolzenberg in Stettin on March 12, 1825, the fifth son of a glass-blower with a talent for playing the fiddle. At home he learned to play the cello and the horn as well as the violin. At fifteen he was apprenticed to the town musician at Elbing, and later volunteered for the army as a bandsman, in this way gaining a working knowledge of the instruments of the orchestra which was to stand him in good stead later. He came to England in May 1854 as E flat clarinettist and assistant conductor of the newly founded Crystal Palace orchestra, and in October 1855, after an unpleasant passage at arms with the conductor and a spell as freelance, took over as conductor and director of that orchestra at the invitation of George Grove, the recently appointed secretary to the Crystal Palace Company. Thus began the alliance between Grove and Manns which was to set new standards of orchestral playing in England, and reveal for the first time the greatness of Schubert's symphonic works.

Their talents and experience were complementary. Grove was the musical amateur in his many and diverse enthusiasms, literary skill and administrative ability, also perhaps in his occasional errors of judgment. Manns was the professional, with a wide-ranging knowledge of the orchestra and the repertory which made him, in Stanford's judgment, the best conductor in England. Together they were able to bring about a revolution in public taste in the second half of the century by means of the regular Saturday concerts at the Crystal Palace. This revolution led to the revaluation of Schubert's orchestral music which coincides in the 1860s with Hallé's advocacy of the piano sonatas so as to make this decade a sort of *Wunderjahrzehnt* for Schubert lovers. It also coincided with the first attempts to put together a coherent story of Schubert's life and work. Heinrich Kreissle von Hellborn's biography, published in German in 1865, was released in an English translation by Arthur Duke Coleridge in 1869.[9] Kreissle's study made a strong impression on George Grove, and led indirectly to his famous visit to Vienna in 1867.

In 1865 also the fantastic story of the "Unfinished" Symphony broke on an unsuspecting world. In October 1866 Spina, Diabelli's successor, sent the score of the symphony to Grove, and Manns gave the first performance at the Crystal Palace on April 6, 1867. Later in the year this was followed by performances by the Philharmonic in London (May 20) and by Hallé in Manchester (December 5).

In the meantime Grove had decided to go to Vienna, taking the young composer Arthur Sullivan with him. Grove himself tells the story in the appendix to Coleridge's translation of Kreissle's biography. They returned with copies of the score of the "Tragic" Symphony (D417) and the C Major Symphony of 1817 (D589), the missing parts of the *Rosamunde* music, retrieved at the last moment from a dusty pile of music in the cupboard of Dr. Schneider, the nephew and heir to Schubert's brother Ferdinand, and a promise from Dr. Schneider to send them copies of anything else that might turn up!

In his book *Forty Years of Music* Joseph Bennett, the critic of the *Daily*

Telegraph, gives an evocative account of what it was like to be a devotee of the Saturday concerts in the 1860s: "All that was great," he writes,

> . . . in the London musical world might have been seen at Victoria Station on the winter Saturdays, as the special trains were backing to the departure platforms. It was a goodly crowd, however looked at [e] but they talked music, and in 1867–68 principally Schubert, who then was, for the first time, shining in all the glory of his heaven-descended art. It was not a company of many opinions, but a band of worshippers, having one faith and one soul. And it was good to be among and of them.[10]

The story of the "Great" C Major Symphony is well known and needs only to be briefly recounted. It was first performed, without the repeats in the first and last movements, by Mendelssohn at the Leipzig *Gewandhaus* in March 1839. The parts were published in 1840, and also a four-hand piano arrangement. When Manns, who was anxious to perform it at the Crystal Palace, planned to include it in his plans for 1856, Grove was at first unwilling to agree, because of its length and reputation for being unplayable. Manns wisely invited him to attend a rehearsal, and from then on Grove became the work's most enthusiastic supporter. As a precaution, however, the first performance was divided into two; the first three movements were played on Saturday, March 5, 1856, and the last three a week later. The first complete performance took place a year later, on July 11, 1857.[11] But for many years it remained a problematic work to perform. When first performed at the new St. James's Hall in March 1859 it prompted a lively correspondence in the musical press, and when Hallé gave the first performance in Manchester, the critic of the *Manchester Guardian* wrote: "There are ideas enough in it to make up half a dozen symphonies, and beautiful and striking ideas too, but sown broadcast as it were, with little coherence and presenting scarcely a trace of that consistency of design which is one of the great charms in the symphonies of Haydn, Mozart, Beethoven and Mendelssohn."

Grove and Manns, like Hallé, were firm believers in the doctrine that if you count yourself an enthusiast for the music of a great composer, you must be interested in everything he wrote. They set out to present Schubert whole, all his compositions, preferably in chronological order, so that the development of his genius could be effectively studied. Manns's astonishing record of first performances was sustained by this belief, even though it was made possible by the special relationship between Grove in Sydenham and Spina in Vienna. The list of Schubert symphonies, with dates when they were first performed at the Crystal Palace, speaks for itself. All performances were conducted by Manns except the realization of the incomplete E Major sketch in 1883, conducted by the orchestrator, J. F. Barnett.

No. 1 in D Major	Feb. 5, 1881	World première
No. 2 in B flat Major	Oct. 20, 1877	World première
No. 3 in D Major	Feb. 19, 1881	World première
No. 4 in C Minor	Feb. 29, 1868	First performance in England
No. 5 in B flat Major	Feb. 1, 1873	First performance in England
No. 6 in C Major	Nov. 21, 1868	First performance in England
No. 7 sketch in E	May 5, 1883	World première
No. 8 in B Minor	April 6, 1867	First performance in England
No. 9 in C Major	April 5/12, 1856	First performance in England

In February and March 1881 Manns played the complete symphonies of Schubert in chronological order, and on this occasion (March 19) the B Minor *Entr'acte* from *Rosamunde* was used as the finale of the "Unfinished." Joseph Joachim's orchestration of the "Grand Duo" (D812) was played at the Crystal Palace on March 4, 1876.

The phenomenon of Schubert's popularity with the public in the late 1860s was so sudden and so marked that it was called the "Schubert episode" in Frederick Shinn's short history of the Saturday concerts.[12] The Queen honored all the principal actors in this story with a knighthood: Grove in 1883, Hallé in 1888, and Manns in 1903. In the 1890s the musical scene changed. New executants and new composers occupied the center of the stage, and Schubert was largely forgotten. So much so that when in the 1920s Artur Schnabel took up the piano sonatas once again it seemed to some critics that they had never been played in public before. Grove was remembered for his dictionary, Hallé for his orchestra, and Manns for his association with the Crystal Palace, but their claim to be remembered as the champions of Schubert's genius and the architects of his place among the great composers has been largely forgotten.

15 Schubert's reception in France: a chronology (1828–1928)

Xavier Hascher

At the same time as Schubert's fame started to spread across Europe during the late 1820s and 1830s, Paris rose to unprecedented heights as the Continent's foremost and busiest musical center. In spite of King Louis-Philippe's overt lack of interest in music (manifested in a complete absence of governmental support) the French capital became, more than it ever was, a place of intense rivalry between composers and performers from many different countries. Rossini and Meyerbeer (who had settled there before the July Revolution), Chopin, Liszt, and Wagner – to name but a few – bear witness to this extraordinary attraction. Particularly illustrative is the career of one of Schubert's champions, the Bohemian violin virtuoso Josef Slawjk (1806–33), who, unable to withstand such a competitive atmosphere, had to retreat to Vienna, obviously a less strenuous city.

Success in Paris could make the difference between international glory and recognition on a purely local level. The establishment of Schubert's fame, therefore, even though posthumous, necessitated the acknowledgment of the Parisian public. Hence the importance of retracing the history of Schubert's reception in France, more perhaps than in any other non-German country.

The historical process of discovering Schubert's musical output in France during the nineteenth century and up to the centenary of his death, falls roughly into four uneven periods.

1827–35: From the first edition of a work by Schubert to Nourrit's performance of *la Jeune Religieuse*

That France, particularly Paris, represented a potential market for Schubert's music, we learn from a letter of October 1828 from the German publisher Schott to Schubert, where the former deplores the "uselessness" of the Impromptus (D935) for sale to the French public (*SDB* 817). Even before Schubert's death, however, a work of his had been published in this country – the *Rondeau brillant* for Violin and Piano, Op. 70 (D895), written for Slawik and released by Artaria in Vienna in 1827, appeared the same year from the Parisian publisher Simon Richault (1780–1866). This piece was followed in 1829 by the Piano Trio in E flat, Op. 100 (D929), and by the two string quartets, Op. 125 Nos. 1 and 2 (D87, in E flat, and D353, in E), in 1831.

Despite a commonly held opinion, it was thus not Schubert's Lieder, but rather his chamber music that first penetrated Gallic soil. The earliest public performance recorded is also that of a chamber work, the Piano Trio in E flat, played by Mlle Malzel at one of the Colbert *matinées* of the Tilmant brothers at the end of 1833 or the beginning of 1834.[1]

In the meantime, the publication of other instrumental pieces included the following:

1831   *Les Viennoises. Walses autrichiennes pour le piano* Op. 9
       (D365) and Op. 18 (D145)
1832   *Walzes allemandes et deux Ecossaises pour violon et piano,*
       Op. 33 (D783)
       Marche funèbre à l'occasion de la mort d'Alexandre pour
       le piano à quatre mains, Op. 55 (D859)
1832–33   String Quartet in A Minor, Op. 29 (D804)
       String Quartet in D Minor (D810)
       Impromptus, Op. 90 Nos. 1 and 2 (D899)
       Piano Sonata in A Major, Op. 120 (D664)
1834   *Variations à 4 mains*, Op. 10 (D624)
       Quatre Polonaises pour le piano à quatre mains, Op. 75
       (D599)

During this time Schubert's songs were only known through a few sets of variations by Carl Czerny,[2] until the publication by Richault – in a French translation by Bélanger – of the *Six Mélodies célèbres* in 1833 or 1834.[3] According to various sources, some of the Lieder had already appeared before certain members of the capital's élite. As early as 1832, Franz Liszt played them in the salons of Alexis-François Rio or of his own mistress, the countess Marie d'Agoult. It is at the home of the Czech banker-composer Josef Dessauer (1798–1876) that the celebrated singer Adolphe Nourrit (1802–39) heard him play *Erlkönig* in 1834.[4] Nourrit was obviously conquered and in December sang *Ave Maria* (D839) in the salon of the then successful *romance* composer Louise (or "Loïsa") Puget (1810–89). In January 1835, Nourrit interpreted an orchestral version of *la Religieuse* (*Die junge Nonne* D828) at the Conservatoire, which met immediate approbation, notably from Berlioz.[5] Two days after the concert, the critic Joseph d'Ortigue wrote with a mixture of perspicacity and over-optimism:

> It is sad, for an enlightened nation, that it should be necessary to teach the public, and even some artists, the name of a man who, when he is better appreciated, will take his place between Beethoven and Weber. The *Société des concerts* would claim new rights to the gratitude of the friends of the art if . . . it did for Schubert's orchestral music, what in more modest meetings, MM. Urhan, Liszt, Hiller, Nourrit, Tilmant, etc., etc., did for the songs, trios and quartets of this great master.[6]

1835–50: Schubert's rise to fame as a Lied composer

Even though d'Ortigue implies that some of the chamber works had already been performed in private circles before Nourrit's concert, and despite public performances of the slow movement of the D Minor Quartet by Chrétien Urhan in 1836,[7] of the Piano Trio in E flat (with the young César Franck taking up the piano part) the following year, and of the "Trout" Quintet (D667) with Doehler and Tilmant in 1839, it is the songs which brought Schubert into the limelight. Meanwhile, his instrumental pieces, not meeting with such success, seemed relegated to comparative obscurity. Besides Nourrit, who introduced a handful of songs to the audiences in Marseilles, Lyon (performing with Liszt), and perhaps Bordeaux – but committed suicide in 1839 – the great exponent of Schubert's Lieder was François-Pierre Wartel (1806–82). A pupil of Nourrit's, he became so identified with the composer that he was bestowed with the nickname "Wartel-Schubert." Like Nourrit, he traveled around the country, singing in Amiens in 1846 and in Nancy in 1849. Rouen had been initiated to *Ave Maria* at least in 1840, with the singer Mme Nathan-Treilhet. Other singers who promoted Schubert's Lieder include Jean-Antoine-Just Géraldy, Kathinka and Sabine Heinefetter, Cornélie Falcon, Sophie Bodin, Pauline Viardot, and Mlles Méquillet and Unald.

In the meantime, publication of the songs progressed steadily, so that by 1845 Richault offered no less than 336 distributed among fifteen series and four volumes. Maurice Schlesinger (1798–1871), the editor of the *Revue et Gazette musicale de Paris* whose catalogue also included various dances and transcriptions, became Richault's main competitor. Starting with the Three Italian Songs, Op. 83 (D902) in 1837,[8] he advertised a collection of twenty-six songs in 1839 (in a translation by Emile Deschamps) which expanded to fifty-two the following year. Besides independent songs such as *Tu es le repos* (*Du bist die Ruh* D776) and *Sois toujours mes seules amours* (*Sei mir gegrüßt* D741), this collection included many Lieder from the song cycles, particularly *Die schöne Müllerin* (D795).

The most striking feature of the period, however, is the vogue of the Lied transformations, from straightforward transcriptions to variations, fantasies, and elaborate paraphrases. After Czerny's example from the early 1830s, an army of arrangers ensued – although not all were entirely bereft of artistic dignity, notably Liszt and Stephen Heller (1813–88).[9] Besides those already quoted, transcriptions for the piano reveal the names of innumerable, more or less famous, virtuosos such as Heinrich Herz, César Franck, Charles Mayer, Alphonse Thys, Theodor von Doehler, Emile Prudent, Savart, Joseph Czerny, Victor Delacour, Edouard Wolff, Sir Charles Hallé. Other instrumental arrangements included cello (Elise Christiani, Félix Battanchon, Alexandre Batta, Joseph Merk), violin (Alexey Fyodorovtich L'vov, Nicolas Louis, C. Pfeiffer and Charles de Kontsky), cornet à pistons (P. Gatterman), and horn (Eugène Vivier). Some songs were also available with guitar accompaniment (by Napoléon Coste), while the most famous were even orchestrated by Liszt, Berlioz, and others.[10]

In the wake of Schubert's success, Dessauer, Berlioz, Meyerbeer, and Heinrich Proch tried their hand at the Lieder or at the newly born *mélodie*. The demand was such that in the early 1840s, when the fame of the composer was about to reach its peak, it was justly feared that the German Lied would kill the old French *romance* for good – as the following little scene amusingly bears witness:[11]

> THE ROMANCE: I am eminently French, and I've come to beg you to protect me and take sides with me.
>
> 1841: Against whom?
>
> THE LIED: Mein Gott! Against me, who come to take herr place. I am feiporrous like she, and morre dan she; I haffe morre naiffety dan she. I vos de feifforite tchilt of Schubert and I am now dat of Proch ant Dessauer. . . .[12]

1850 to 1870s–80s: Schubert's chamber music becomes standard repertory

Shortly before the next decade, though, the novelty of the Lied had waned, and interest shifted to figures such as Wagner, Verdi, Johann Strauss, and even Félicien David. Yet the second half of the century saw the accession of some of the chamber compositions to quasi-repertory status. If performances of these works seem rather infrequent during the

1840s (one of the trios was played at some Parisian *soirée* in 1847), they became almost weekly occurrences in the 1870s and the 1880s. The favorite items were the E Flat Piano Trio, the *Rondo brillant,* and the "Wanderer" Fantasy Op. 15 (D760) – most often heard in Liszt's orchestration (Saint-Saëns regularly performed the solo part with Edouard Colonne conducting), albeit sometimes played on two pianos. The D Minor Quartet was only known through its slow movement, occasionally performed in a version for string orchestra (again under Colonne's direction), while Girard orchestrated one of the most popular *Moment musical,* in F Minor (D780), for the other great concert-organizer of the time, Jules Pasdeloup. Among the other pieces to receive increasing exposure were the "Trout" Quintet, the *Divertissement hongrois* (D818) – which Eduard Reményi transcribed for violin – the Piano Trio in B flat, Op. 99 (D898), and the "Trockne Blumen" variations for flute and piano (D802). Although some of the piano sonatas had long been in print, documentation of public performances is scarce. Charles-Valentin Alkan, who had already played some pieces by Schubert in the 1830s, played the G Major Sonata, Op. 78 (D894), in March 1875, and Gustave Pradeau the B flat Sonata (D960) in April 1876. The violinist Jules Armingaud and his *Société classique,* whose names are recurrently linked with the performance of Schubert's chamber music, gave the first performances of a movement from the G Major Quartet (D887) in March 1859 and of the Andante of the *Quatrième Quatuor* [?] in March 1865, yet with no further apparent consequence.

1870s–80s to 1928: From the discovery of Schubert the symphonist to the centenary of the composer's death

Although Schubert's religious music remained unknown in France throughout the century, with the possible exception of a Mass performed at Saint-Eustache in Paris on Ascension Day of 1836, a fragment from his unfinished oratorio *Lazarus* (D689) was sung by Pauline Viardot and her daughter Marianne in their Paris *hôtel particulier* in February 1878. In contrast, the first performance of the "Great" C Major Symphony (D944) took place relatively early, in November 1851, at the *Société philharmonique* under François Seghers's baton. Although the reviewer of the *Ménestrel* praised the slow movement, "written in a masterly manner," he condemned the "prolixity and the too many repetitions" of the other movements, especially finding fault with the extreme length of the finale.[13] The symphony was not played again until Pasdeloup conducted it at the *Cirque d'hiver* in February 1873, repeating the venture at the end of 1875. The *Société des Concerts* only approached the work in January 1897 for the centenary of Schubert's birth, although they had rehearsed the first movement in 1841.[14] The first movement of the "Unfinished" Symphony (D759) was premiered in November 1878 by Pasdeloup, whose "role as a pioneer, an international mediator" was acknowledged by the *Gazette musicale*.[15] Both movements were then performed in October 1881 with Colonne at the Châtelet, and repeated the following year. The favorable, although not overwhelming, reception incited Emile Deldevez, the conductor of the *Société des concerts*, to take up the work with the Conservatoire orchestra. He conducted it twice in January 1883;[16] once again – especially in the light of the future popularity of the work – the reception was rather lukewarm:

> The Allegro and Andante of an unfinished symphony by Schubert, which the *Société* allowed us to hear for the first time, are charming pieces. They are both in a pleasant style, but for that very reason stand in each other's way; we believe that the Andante could be reproduced to the best effect on its own.[17]

The only other orchestral piece revealed to the French public during the century seems to have been the overture to the opera *Fierrabras* (D796), which was played at the *Cirque Fernando* in November and December 1875 (and perhaps sometime before, in 1874). Of Schubert's stage works, the Singspiel *Die Verschworenen* (D787) appeared in a French adaptation by Victor Wilder under the title *la Croisade des dames* in February 1868, and was followed by a run of at least twenty nights.

Thus the panorama of Schubert's music offered to the French public in the nineteenth century remained, as elsewhere, largely incomplete. The Lied was well represented, and to a far lesser extent, the chamber music – although we remain uncertain about complete public performances of those works which we now regard as Schubert's most important contribution to this genre such as the late string quartets and piano sonatas. The only orchestral work to enjoy true popularity by 1928, however, was the B Minor Symphony. Schubert remained unrecognized as a composer of opera and religious music.

Yet we should refrain from condemning French audiences and critics altogether for their one-sided view and their failure to acknowledge the full range of Schubert's greatness. First, because this seems to have been the case in almost every other country; and second, because the French did not fail to rate Schubert as a musical genius of the very first order and let him enjoy considerable recognition, while the Romantic generation – George Sand, Alfred de Musset, Gérard de Nerval – who never confused him with the cheap *romance*-makers of the day, indeed felt deep sympathy for his music.

This recognition took time and needed cultivation. Early French writings on Schubert from the 1830s and 1840s abound in erroneous biographical details and tend to overemphasize the importance of the Lied, whilst taking for granted Schubert's inferiority to Mozart, Beethoven, and Weber in the other fields of composition.[18] They regularly stress the presence of a poetic side to his songs, comparing the composer to Heine, or even Byron. The first books on Schubert, by Barbedette and Audley,[19] date from the last third of the century, following Heinrich Kreissle von Hellborn's first German biography. The centenary of Schubert's death in 1928 saw the publication of a number of articles (including a special number of the *Revue musicale* devoted to the composer) as well as new books, among which must be distinguished Jacques-Gabriel Prod' homme's *Schubert raconté par ceux qui l'ont vu* (Paris, 1928), which remains to this day the only attempt at translating the documents collected by Deutsch into French.

16 Franz Schubert's music in performance: a brief history of people, events, and issues

David Montgomery

The history of music in performance relies on a variety of resources: studies in the evolution of instruments, ensembles, and voices; the evidence of autographs, editions, proofs, marginalia, parts, books, diaries, and letters; tutors and related writings by teachers and performers over the years; and the documentation of concert life in programs and reviews. And since the 1890s, modern performance history has been revealed through a massive archive of recordings.

Schubert research, however, is somewhat disadvantaged in all of these areas except the last. Although we know much about the instruments and ensembles of his day, that information is not specific to Schubert. And of the hundreds of performance tutors published during or since Schubert's time (and now seldom read), few even mention his name.[1] Until the first critical edition (*ASA*) began to appear in the 1880s his works were published piecemeal and poorly, and many autographs and other source materials went missing. During Schubert's lifetime, and for many years after his death, his music – especially his instrumental music – was championed by a mere handful of performers. For this reason, few pedagogical lines or performance traditions accumulated until late in the nineteenth century.

The only reliable body of evidence we have concerning Schubert in performance is the recordings. Somewhere around 1900 the recording industry discovered the saleability of certain pieces in the Schubert repertory: short works were tailored to match the capacity of the disc (*Ave Maria, Erlkönig*, etc.), then longer ones (*Der Hirt auf dem Felsen*, piano character pieces), and finally large-scale instrumental pieces (chamber works and the last two symphonies). But while recordings promoted Schubert's music, they also stultified it. Performers fixed their interpretations in wax, whereupon the power and breadth of commercial distribution and broadcasting began its awesome work. With each advance in sound carriers – rolls, 78 discs, LPs, tapes, and, most recently, CDs – a rather standard "Schubert style" has been passed down to successive generations. A few musicians have stood gallantly apart from these influ-

Example 16.1a and 16.1b C Major String Quintet (D956), mm. 42–51

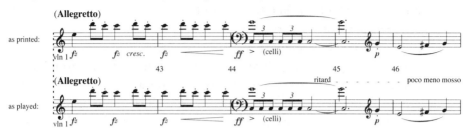

ences, but most performers have been enticed in one way or the other. For example, in the C Major String Quintet (D956), how many ensembles, even today, can eschew the now traditional *Schrammelmusik* ritard, slide and "lift" in the passage given in Ex. 16.1?

I first heard this mannerism in my student days, and being young and thirsty for highly "musical" performances, I was convinced that such gestures represented the essence of Schubert's style. I even borrowed the mannerism for use in his piano music, blissfully unaware that it arose in late nineteenth century Austro-Hungarian cafés and had little to do with Franz Schubert.

Among the tasks of the "historically informed" performance movement, now that it has begun to treat seriously the music of the nineteenth century, is the clarification of such anomalies and anachronisms.[2] In the case of Beethoven, it has attempted to do just that; but Beethoven has always been taken a bit more seriously than Schubert in this regard. Schubert's own documented thoughts and observations about performance are few. Reports by his friends exist, but they are not specific. Moritz von Schwind tells us that "Schubert's quartet was performed, a little slowly in his opinion, but very purely and tenderly."[3] But how slow is "a little slowly"? What exactly did he mean by "very purely" ("sehr rein")? Did he mean that the overall sound was pleasant, that the intonation was good, or perhaps even that Ignaz Schuppanzigh's ensemble played the work with no added ornaments?

Since Schubert counted for his success mostly on the loyalty, integrity, competence, and reputation of those musicians who played and sang his music, I have built the first two parts of this chapter around preeminent Schubert performers. Part I is dominated by singers, which fact seems to reflect history. No attempt at comprehensiveness could succeed here, and many Schubertians will go unmentioned. Within a loosely chronological context of performance genres, I have singled out a few musicians who represent important lines of thinking, or whose approaches suggest certain issues. The third part of this chapter is a closer consideration of Schubert problems in the context of today's historical performance consciousness.

Schubert and Schubertians in the nineteenth century

Schubert's first great champion among singers was the leading male singer of the Kärntnerthor Theater and Hofoper, Johann Michael Vogl (1768–1840), whom the composer often accompanied. On tour of Upper Austria with Vogl, Schubert described the musical rapport he felt: "the manner and means with which Vogl sings and I accompany him, *the way we seem to be one single being in these moments,* is for these people really new, really unexperienced [italics mine]."[4] Schubert took many of his songs to Vogl before final drafting, and we do not know how many compositional choices were influenced by the singer. Vogl may have been interested chiefly in the music, but he could not have been averse to casting a bit more light upon himself as well.[5] Apparently he treated Schubert's music quite freely in performance, and he may have exercised a heavy editorial hand in posthumous publications of the songs. He is suspected of authoring the substantial changes to the second edition of *Die schöne Müllerin* (D795), brought out by Diabelli after Schubert's death. Some of these alterations are minor but mindlessly frequent additions of grace notes (see Ex. 16.2). Other changes involve outright pitch alterations (see Ex. 16.3).

Example 16.4 – again from *Die schöne Müllerin* – is taken not from the Diabelli edition, but from the private Lieder album of Franziska Tremier, née Pratobevera. Here the embellishments change the rhythmic shape of the line, as well as its pitch content. The song is also transposed down a major third for an alto voice. The author of the changes has not been positively identified.

Simple ornamentation, as in Example 16.2, was probably a common aspect of performance in that day. But altered rhythms, pitches, and harmonies are more serious matters (Examples 16.3 and 16.4), particularly if they find their way into printed editions.[6]

Example 16.2a and 16.2b
Original version of *Mein!* (D795, 11), mm. 9–15
Diabelli version of *Mein!* (D795, 11), mm. 9–15

Example 16.3a and 16.3b
Original version of *Mit dem grünen Lautenbande* (D795, 13), mm. 4–7
Diabelli version of *Mit dem grünen Lautenbande* (D795, 13), mm. 4–7

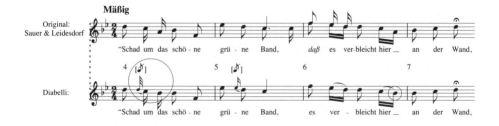

Transpositions, of course, were often necessary to suit a singer's range. Printed collections in various ranges, such as we rely upon today, did not exist, and singers often kept private copies in suitable keys for players who could not transpose. Schubert himself probably transposed in performance to suit the singer. Leopold von Sonnleithner maintains, however, that Vogl transposed songs into difficult and unusual keys and registers in order to create or force extraordinary effects through pitchless and whispered delivery, falsetto, or sudden outcries.[7] Whether he devised these tricks to cover for an aging voice, or whether he was simply an actor

Example 16.4a and 16.4b
Original version of *Trockne Blumen* (D795, 18), mm. 6–12
Tremier version of *Trockne Blumen* (D795, 18), mm. 6–12

at heart is difficult to know. Sonnleithner also mentions another interesting aspect of Vogl's later style: "Vogl certainly overstepped the written boundaries the more his voice deserted him – but he always sang strictly in tempo."[8]

Several years after Vogl's death, Ignaz von Mosel wrote that it was a loss "even more lamentable because he failed to heed my urgent and repeated exhortations to publish a guide to declamation and dramatic singing – one that only he was truly capable of writing."[9] Vogl had been aware of the need, and had written in his diary: "Nothing has so often revealed the lack of a useful singing method as Schubert's songs."[10] He began work on a method shortly before he died, but this fragment has been lost.

One of Vogl's most celebrated operatic colleagues was Anna Milder (1785–1838), who, in addition to her fame as the creator of the role of Leonore in *Fidelio*, was also an unwavering Schubert supporter. From the *Berlinische Zeitung* we have a critical report of a public concert in 1825 by Milder, who sang *Suleika* II (D717) and *Erlkönig* to a full audience and great acclaim:

> The great voice of this singer pleases one best in the noble style of singing –
> as in the two Goethe songs, *Suleika* and *Erlkönig* – which Mme. Milder
> echoed masterfully from her own heart to our hearts. . . . The tender melody
> [*Suleika*], sung with intimate feeling by Mme. Milder, was enhanced
> throughout by bright colors in the quite singular piano accompaniment –
> played with polish by the singer's sister, Mme. Bürde, née Milder. The
> sighing of the westwind, and the longing of tender love were effectively
> represented in these tones. *Der Erlkönig*. . . also was splendidly presented.[11]

Milder seems to have sung with great warmth, but without Vogl's theatricality. The word "noble" in the review, plus her status as the leading Gluck heroine of the day, seems to set the right tone.

The third great Schubert song interpreter in the composer's lifetime was Carl Freiherr von Schönstein (1797–1876). Schubert dedicated *Die schöne Müllerin* to him, and Schönstein became the foremost champion of this work. Whereas Vogl's general singing style was declamatory and theatrical, Milder's perhaps expressive but patrician, Schönstein's style was smooth and non-ornamental.[12] In him we recognize the spiritual ancestor of such lyrical singers as Dietrich Fischer-Dieskau, Hermann Prey, Håkon Hagegård, Olaf Bär, or Boje Skovhus. Sonnleithner believed Schönstein was "one of the best, perhaps the best, Schubert singer, of his time. . . . This friend of the arts was distinguished by a beautiful, nobly sonorous high-baritone voice, sufficient training, aesthetical and scholarly education, and sensitive, lively feeling."[13] Schubert, in one of his last letters (September 25, 1828) responded to an invitation, saying: "I accept . . . with pleasure, for I always like to hear Baron Schönstein sing."[14]

The Schubert singer of greatest historical interest, Franz Schubert himself, probably also had a clear, uncomplicated voice.[15] Anton Ottenwalt writes on November 27, 1825, that Schubert sang "quite beautifully" at Schober's;[16] and Franz von Hartmann writes on December 17, 1826, that "Schubert sang magnificently, particularly *Der Einsame* and *Dürre* [*Trockne*] *Blumen*."[17]

Two singers whose careers began during Schubert's lifetime, but who championed his music mostly after his death were Wilhelmine Schröder-Devrient (1804–60) and Joseph Staudigl (1807–61). Schröder-Devrient lived, after 1823, in Dresden. In 1836 the *Wiener Zeitschrift* acknowledged "with what wonderfully gripping, thoroughly dramatic vividness" she sang Schubert's Lieder.[18] Otto Brusatti writes that Joseph Staudigl was the "legitimate successor of Vogl and Schönstein," singing *Der Wanderer* (D489) and *Erlkönig* over 300 times in public.[19] Reacting to his performance of *Der Wanderer*, the *Humorist* reported: "Just such mediums are sought by the ossianic spirit that wafts through Schubert's airs. That is Poetry in Performance."[20]

The most professional pianist in Schubert's circle was Karl Maria von Bocklet (1801–81).[21] Schubert's report of Bocklet's premiere of the Piano Trio in E flat, Op. 100 (D929), with Schuppanzigh and Josef Linke (December 26, 1827) indicates sincere approval (*SDB* 714). Bocklet also premiered two other difficult works, the C Major Violin Fantasy (D934) and the "Wanderer" Fantasy, Op. 15 (D760), and Schubert dedicated the Piano Sonata in D Major, Op. 53 (D850), to him. The Leipzig *Allgemeine musikalische Zeitung* wrote that in Bocklet's hands "every composition gains new color, renewed life, and an exotic, hitherto unexperienced form through his magical performance style."[22]

About Schubert's own playing, one must read between the lines of the occasional report, for example:

> . . . In Upper Austria. . . I played [the variations from my new two-hand sonata, Op. 42] myself, and apparently not without an angel over my shoulder, because a few people assured me that under my hands the keys became like voices. If this is true I am really pleased, because I can't stand this damnable chopping that even quite advanced pianists indulge in. It pleases neither the ear nor the spirit. [23]

Not much of specific value can be learned from this report, but at least we know (as if we didn't know already) that Schubert stood on the side of lyricism in performance. Albert Stadler confirmed that Schubert had "a beautiful touch, a quiet hand – [his was] nice, clear playing, full of soul and expression. He belonged to the old school of good pianists, where the fingers did not attack the poor keys like birds of prey."[24] Sonnleithner made another important point:

> More than a hundred times I heard him rehearse and accompany his own songs. Above all, he kept strict time, except in those few instances where he had specifically marked a ritardando, morendo, accelerando, etc. Furthermore, he permitted no excessive expression. . . . The Lied singer . . . himself does not represent the person whose feelings he portrays; [thus] poet, composer and singer must conceive the song as *lyrical*, not *dramatic*.[25]

Of the major European pianists active during Schubert's last years and after his death, Felix Mendelssohn was probably best equipped to promote that controlled lyricism. If the general reports of his style are accurate, he was an expressive player within the dictates of the written score. Mendelssohn's 1839 premiere of the "Great" C Major Symphony (D944) in Leipzig is one of the milestones in performance history. But in fact, as a pianist he had played Schubert's music in public even during the latter's lifetime. In Berlin he accompanied Karl Bader in a performance of

Erlkönig in November of 1827, and the Leipzig *Allgemeine musikalische Zeitung* described his playing as "finished and powerful."[26] Mendelssohn was later active as a Schubert accompanist in Leipzig, where his singing partner was Henriette Grabau (1805–52). She first gained recognition when she sang *Die Forelle* (D550) at one of the *Extraconcerte* in the Gewandhaus on October 20, 1828, about a month before Schubert died. Charming and gracious, Grabau was a favorite with Leipzig audiences. The *AmZ* reviewed her often, but gave no musical details; when she sang *Erlkönig* (March 6, 1837) the report merely read: "in solo songs she excels, with a highly trained and cultivated voice that gains strength ever anew."[27]

At the 1828 concert where Grabau first sang *Die Forelle*, Clara Wieck made her public debut with Emilie Reichold in a four-hand performance.[28] Wieck, like her future husband Robert Schumann, was attracted to Lieder, and in particular, to Schubert's. She often performed Liszt's Schubert transcriptions, and later in her career she gave Lied concerts with the baritone and conductor Julius Stockhausen (1826–1906). Stockhausen had been a pupil of Manuel Garcia *fils,* and was an intimate friend of Brahms. He believed strongly that Schubert's works should be presented in their entirety, and he stressed the cyclical unity of the major song groups. Richard Heuberger relates that Brahms regarded Stockhausen's zeal in this respect misguided where *Schwanengesang* (D957) was concerned.

> Brahms was rude with [Julius] Röntgen in the morning, because with
> [Johannes] Messchaert he had [played] a number of songs from Schubert's
> *Schwanengesang*. Brahms maintained that they didn't all belong together and
> that it was silly to sing them as a group. To Röntgen's argument that
> Stockhausen also sang them as a group, Brahms replied, "Well, I never had
> much influence on Stockhausen, and I was always against that sort of thing.
> But if you know better, then that's just fine!"[29]

In Vienna in 1856, Stockhausen became the first artist to sing *Die schöne Müllerin* as a complete cycle. From Hamburg in 1864, Fritz Brahms wrote to Johannes that Stockhausen had recently sung *Winterreise* to a "bursting full house," that he intended to sing it again at discount price tickets, and then later *Die schöne Müllerin* as well.[30] Hanslick wrote of Stockhausen in 1854 that he was "equipped with an unusually well schooled voice in an era when screaming is more popular."[31] Stockhausen published a comprehensive singing manual, dedicated to vocal style in song, oratorio and opera from Bach to Wagner; but strangely, Schubert's name does not appear even once.[32]

Brahms was an avid Schubert player, as a soloist and as an accompanist to Joseph Joachim, Julius Stockhausen, Joseph Hellmesberger, Gustav

Walter, George Henschel, and others.[33] When someone remarked that Schubert's technical demands were not so high – an attitude that has pervaded conservatories and competitions until the present – Brahms replied, "Don't say that! His music is so often eternally perfect! I believe that most people doubt the difficulty of Schubert's music, because it is known how easily he composed. Well, for one person it's hard, and for the next it's easy! And even Schubert often had his problems."[34] Brahms's playing, like Mendelssohn's, is said to have been well-structured and musically responsible; his approach to Schubert's piano music was probably similar.

During Schubert's lifetime his chamber music had fared better than his other instrumental works. Bocklet and Josef Slawjk had premiered the B Minor Rondo for Violin and Piano (D895), plus the C Major Fantasy (D934).[35] Schuppanzigh's quartet had premiered the A Minor Quartet, Op. 29 (D804) in March 1824, and later the Octet (D803).[36] By the time of Schubert's "Composition Concert" (March 26, 1828), when the ensemble played the first movement of the G Major Quartet (D887), Schuppanzigh had been replaced by Joseph Böhm (1795–1876), who also played with Bocklet and Linke in a further performance of the Piano Trio in E flat.

After Schubert's death public performances of his chamber music declined until the 1850s, when the Hellmesberger Quartet presented the later quartets in the Musikvereinssaal in Vienna.[37] The quartet had been founded in 1849 by its first violinist, Joseph Hellmesberger (1828–93), the son and pupil of Schubert's school friend, the violinist Georg Hellmesberger (who also taught Joachim, Auer, Hauser, and Ernst). The Hellmesberger Quartet's performances of Schubert's works led the way to some important first publications, including the G Major Quartet, the C Major Quintet, and the Octet. The other major ensemble to take Schubert's music seriously was the Joachim Quartet (founded in the 1860s), also famous for its commitment to the works of Brahms and Beethoven.

Among nineteenth-century conductors, the list of major Schubert supporters begins with his friend Johann Baptist Schmiedel and continues with Mendelssohn, Wilhelm Grund, Georg Schmidt, Johann Herbeck, A. F. Riccius, August Manns, William Cusins, Julius Stockhausen, Brahms, and George Henschel. Schmiedel and Brahms were more involved with Schubert's vocal works, whereas the others were responsible for the symphonic premieres. Mendelssohn's premiere of the "Great" C Major Symphony in Leipzig had been followed in 1841 by performances in Halle,[38] Bremen,[39] Potsdam[40] and Hamburg.[41] By 1850 it had been played in New York,[42] but years went by before it was premiered in London or Paris.[43] Stockhausen was possibly the first conductor to perform it without cuts (Hamburg, 1863).[44] In Stockhausen's view, Schubert's difficulties and challenges could not be avoided or edited, but were best presented for what they were.

Schubert and the recording age

The first Schubert "performances" on record date from the last years of the nineteenth century: among them are a recording of *Ave Maria* made by Edith Clegg in England in 1898 and a group of Lied recordings by anonymous singers (in French) released by the Pathé brothers in 1899. With some notable exceptions (Elena Gerhardt, Harry Plunket Greene, George Henschel, Rita Gingster, Therese Behr) the early recordings were made by famous opera singers.

The general style on these recordings is familiar: pronounced vocal slides and lifts, close vibrato (or sometimes none at all), extended holds in places where today we are accustomed only to localized rubatos, some extreme tempo variations, etc. From these practices can we learn anything about an even earlier period? Minnie Nast's "pure tone" and lack of a continuous vibrato (*Heidenröslein*, 1902) are echoed by other sopranos, and suggest a lingering tradition among high voices of the period. But Gustav Walter's deeply moving performance of *Am Meer* (1904) reveals a continuous, modern vibrato, albeit slim and perfectly controlled. Walter – a clear, high tenor – was forty years older than Nast; he was born in 1834, only six years after Schubert died. Knowing, as we do, that singers rarely rebuild their basic techniques as they grow older, we might assume that Walter learned that vibrato sometime in the late 1840s or early 1850s.

Walter probably chose his pianist carefully for these recordings (he made three), for he once had been accompanied by no less an artist than Johannes Brahms. But in general, the accompanists on these early recordings rarely aspired to artistic greatness. A comic example is provided by Paul Knüpfer's 1901 recording of *Ungeduld* (which title more or less suited the occasion), wherein his unfortunate pianist (mercifully unnamed) is first coaxed and finally dragged along by his musical collar to the end of the performance. Fortunately, notable exceptions existed. Much can be learned about interactive Lied accompaniment through the recordings of George Henschel (1850–1934), who played for himself, and Arthur Nikisch (1855–1922), who was the regular partner of Elena Gerhardt (1883–1961). Nikisch's beautiful playing on their recording of *An die Musik* (1911) might well replicate Schubert's own close manner of accompanying Vogl. And the occasional pianist aspired even to brilliance, as on Lilli Lehmann's 1906 recording of *Erlkönig* or Harry Plunket Greene's 1904 recording of *Abschied* (pianists unnamed).[45] Later in the century the ideal Lied accompanist was to emerge in the person of Gerald Moore (1899–1987), who played for the greatest singers of the modern age – from Feodor Chaliapin to Hermann Prey. He and Dietrich Fischer-Dieskau probably recorded more Schubert songs, together and separately, than any pianist and singer in history. Moore's book on the cycles is a revealing performance document.[46]

Actually, all great Schubert pianists have had a common interest in Lied accompaniment; for example, Benjamin Britten (whose Schubert performances with Peter Pears gave rise to heated discussion about the assimilation of dotted rhythms to triplets),[47] Edwin Fischer (who recorded Lieder with Schwarzkopf and taught a group of pianists who also became great Schubert accompanists), and Artur Schnabel (1882–1951). Schnabel and his wife Therese Behr (1876–1959) "spread the word" among a devoted new generation of pupils and Schubert listeners. Their six program Berlin cycle of 1928 featured the two Müller cycles and *Schwanengesang*, plus a number of individual songs (in addition to the eight last sonatas and the "Wanderer" Fantasy).[48] They reintroduced a number of forgotten songs, and attempted to rid the known ones of unworthy performance traditions.

Schnabel and his son Karl Ulrich Schnabel made recordings of Schubert four-hand works, as did Benjamin Britten and Svjatoslav Richter, and several other celebrated "teams." But the first duo to explore Schubert's four-hand literature comprehensively was formed by two Fischer pupils – Jörg Demus and Paul Badura-Skoda – who also collected period pianos and reintroduced them to the public as the proper instruments for playing Schubert.

Schubert's chamber music with piano – the violin–piano duos, the piano trios, and "Trout" Quintet – was recorded copiously in the first half of the century. Ensembles with piano tended to be made up of soloists – Casals–Thibaud–Cortot, Kreisler–Rachmaninoff, Heifetz–Piatigorsky–Rubinstein – and the industry has continued to promote such groupings. The commercial reasoning behind this practice is obvious, but from the beginning the resultant performances were often marked by the highly distinguishable habits of the individual players rather than by the ensemble thinking that arises, for example, from constant quartet playing. Schubert's string quartets, on the other hand, were played and recorded by permanent chamber ensembles – the Flonzaley, the Kneisel, the Léner, the Busch, the (1st) Pro Arte, the (2nd) Budapest and the Kolisch Quartets. They concentrated mostly on the *Quartettsatz*, (D703), the late quartets (D804, 810, and 887), and the C Major Quintet. In terms of historical perspective, the Kolisch Quartet was especially important. Rudolf Kolisch (1896–1978) developed techniques that allowed modern players to re-create the performance practices of the late eighteenth and early nineteenth centuries. He devised bowings, bow strokes, and fingerings that would approximate the proper sounds; he researched tempos of the earlier period and insisted upon proper sonic balances (i.e., the first violinist does not always have the tune!).

The conductors of the early twentieth century recorded only a handful of Schubert's orchestral works: the ballet music to *Rosamunde* (D797), the "Unfinished" Symphony (D759), and the "Great" C Major Symphony. Most of these recordings reflect the performance styles of the last century: cuts (mostly in matters of repeats, but not entirely), ponderous tempos, wide tempo fluctuations and rubatos, large forces, reorchestrations, and more. In the late 1950s René Leibowitz (1913–72) began to remove some of these layers of tradition, most successfully in terms of phrasing and structure, but also through more serious consideration of internal tempo relationships.[49] His goal was to replace tradition with objective performance criteria, and his trailblazing recording of Schubert's "Great" C Major Symphony (RCA GL 32533, no date) obviated a number of mannerisms of the past. The next advances in the performance of this work were made by Carlo Maria Giulini (DG, 2530 882, 1977) and Charles Mackerras (Virgin, 7596692 3, 1988), whose readings of the autograph (where the opening is marked ¢ instead of c as in many editions) led them to the 2:1 tempo relationship between the opening and the Allegro of the first movement. In 1990, Roger Norrington (EMI 7 49949 2) went the final step by finding not only the proper relationship between these two sections, but the proper basic tempo as well.[50]

Schubert issues in the context of the historical performance movement

Given that most Schubert lovers are now familiar with the sound of period-style instruments (but not solo voices), to offer a description here seems unnecessary.[51] But the performer who is interested in more than just the sonic aspect of historical performance *vis à vis* Schubert has a number of other issues to consider.

Style

Example 16.1 showed a practice of the "Viennese style"; further characteristics include comfortable tempos, *gemütlicher Humor* (represented by exaggerated string slides, rhythmic hesitations, etc.) and related mannerisms. This style is said to have arisen from Biedermeier dance traditions, but seems indistinguishable from that of late nineteenth century Viennese *Unterhaltungsmusik* – typified in the playing of the Schrammel Brothers Quartet and the conducting of Eduard Strauss. Strauss, notably, learned his rubatos not from his family, but from the school of Liszt, Wagner, and Bülow.[52] One can see how the flexibility of the gesture in Example 16.1 might have been useful to a dance accompanist whose primary job was to unite music and motion, and who, having coordinated his upbeat with the ascending figure on the dance floor, was then obliged to hesitate slightly until Newton's law took effect. But in the context of Schubert's music – especially the serious works – such gestures become kitsch. Can a more historical approach to Schubert's style gradually wean us and our audiences from such popular misrepresentations?

Structure

The main issue here concerns repeats in dance forms: does the "one time only" rule for the repeat – now so ingrained in our collective consciousness – apply to Schubert? For Mozart and Haydn the practice is not binding, but no authoritative studies exist for the early nineteenth century. Special cases raise questions about such issues as the proper place for the final repeat in the Scherzo of the C Major Quintet.[53]

Notation

Four highly volatile issues are involved. (1) Articulation: the meaning of dots and wedges, and Schubert's shorthand for repeating articulated passages. These two questions have been treated (not solved) for earlier composers, but for Schubert they remain relatively unexplored. Norrington's notes to his recording of the C Major Symphony express the problem succinctly. (2) Rhythmic alteration: does one assimilate Schubert's dotted notes with his triplets where they coincide? This issue has raged throughout the twentieth century, and although it has been shown to be a simple question of compromise for technical accommodation, many scholars continue to see it as a notational problem.[54] Some musicians sidestep the problem by overseparating the component rhythms (double and even triple dotting against the triplets), as in most performances of the first movement of the Piano Trio in B flat, Op. 99 (D898).[55] But Schubert calls purposefully for the conflict as the dominant affect of such movements. Overdotting was indeed an expressive device for soloists in the galant period; it is mentioned in sources as late as Schubert's period, but it is not appropriate for ensemble playing. (3) Expressive marks: here the question concerns such problems as elongated accents vs diminuendos. Some performers believe the answer to be a simple matter of placement: over the note or under it.[56] A highly disputed case is the last chord of the C Major Quintet, often printed (and played) with a diminuendo. Martin Chusid lets it read firmly and sensibly as an accent in the *Neue Schubert-Ausgabe*, although in other contexts the intent of the hairpin sign is not so clear.[57] Nevertheless, Jaap Schröder's assertion that Schubert's intention "has in many cases to be decided upon by the interpreter's taste and sense of style" reveals one of the central weaknesses of the historical movement to date – the tendency, when in doubt, to revert to intuition instead of renewed research.[58] (4) Texts: what is an Urtext? Does one choose the 1825 or 1827 published text of *Der Einsame* (D800)? Does one reject Brahms's finishing touches to Schubert's C Minor Symphony, even though that decision demands a return to the incomplete state of Schubert's score? Where do the limits of "authenticity" clash with those of common sense?[59]

Tempo

This issue is twofold. In a controversial but brilliant article of 1943, Rudolf Kolisch derived a set of basic tempi for Beethoven's entire works from his known metronome markings – matching movements by character.[60] A similar project is possible for Schubert: known metronome marks, for example, include those for his first published twenty songs (Opp. 1–7), the individual pieces of an entire opera (*Alfonso und Estrella*), and the parts of the Deutsche Messe (D872).[61] A related consideration concerns the instrumental movements based on songs (*Der Wanderer* [♩ = MM 63], *Der Tod und das Mädchen* [♩ = MM 63], *Die Forelle, Sei mir gegrüßt*, etc.) in relationship to the tempi of those songs. Second is tempo alteration. In traditional performances, unmarked tempo swings between given sections sometimes range as much as 5–20 metronome marks. Menuet and scherzo trios are particularly susceptible to tempo shifts, but also variation movements, minor key sections within major key movements, and second thematic groups in general.[62]

These are only the most pressing issues that await closer attention by those who take Schubert's music as serious art. A complete list might occupy us for years. Once the reading and research is done, we will probably find that much of what we have taken to be instinct about how to perform Schubert has been, in reality, deep conditioning. With some effort, we can replace this conditioning with a search for ideals. After all, Franz Schubert was concerned not with clay, but with ether.

> *Follow the heavenly sounds*
> *And there shall we find Schubert again.*
>
> after Franz von Schober's *An Franz Schubert's Sarge*

Notes

Introduction

1 Another epitaph is: HE BADE POETRY RESOUND AND MUSIC SPEAK, and the sketchier: HE GAVE TO POESY (ART OF POETRY) TONES (SOUNDS) AND LANGUAGE (SPEECH) TO MUSIC. NEITHER SPOUSE NOR MAIDEN, IT IS AS SISTERS THAT THE TWO EMBRACE ABOVE SCHUBERT'S HEAD (GRAVE) (*SDB* 899).

2 "Aus Franz Schubert's Nachlass," *Neue Zeitschrift für Musik* 8 (1838), 179; my translation.

3 Heinrich Kreissle von Hellborn, *Franz Schubert* (Vienna, 1865), 463–64; translation modified from Arthur Duke Coleridge, *The Life of Franz Schubert* (London, 1869; rpt. New York, 1972), II: 150.

4 See, for example, *SDB* 698, 723; this was the phrase used in the English journal the *Harmonicon* as well (*SDB* 602).

5 See John Reed's appendix, "How Many Schubert Songs?" in *The Schubert Song Companion* (Manchester, 1985), 483–84. The question might be more precisely phrased as "How many Schubert songs survive?" since some are known to be lost, and songs have continued to surface in this century. See also Maurice J. E. Brown, "The Therese Grob Collection of Songs by Schubert," *Music and Letters* 49 (1968), 122–34; and his "The Posthumous Publication of the Songs," in *Essays on Schubert* (London, 1966), 267–90.

6 *SDB* lists most of the contemporaneous performances and publications, and gives many of the reviews that appeared during Schubert's lifetime. See also the informative articles by Otto Biba, archivist of the Gesellschaft der Musikfreunde in Vienna: "Schubert's Position in Viennese Musical Life," *19th-Century Music* 3 (1979), 106–13; "Franz Schubert in den musikalischen Abendunterhaltungen der Gesellschaft der Musikfreunde," in *Schubert-Studien: Festgabe der Österreichischen Akademie der Wissenschaften zum Schubert-Jahr 1978*, ed. Franz Grasberger and Othmar Wessely (Vienna, 1978), 7–31; and "Franz Schubert und die Gesellschaft der Musikfreunde in Wien," in *Schubert-Kongreß: Wien 1978: Bericht,* ed. Otto Brusatti (Graz, 1979), 23–36.

7 Attempts to salvage some of Schubert's four-hand masterpieces came from arrangers, such as Liszt for dances, Joseph Joachim for the "Grand Duo" (D812), and Felix Mottl for the F Minor Fantasy (D940).

8 Although over a hundred opus numbers were published during Schubert's lifetime (or shortly afterward with numbers assigned by him), many more works than this appeared because Lieder, partsongs, and dances were often issued in sets. (Moreover, some works, mainly songs and dances, were published without opus numbers.) Otto Erich Deutsch places the total

number of contemporaneously published works at 472 (*Schubert: Die Dokumente seines Lebens* in NSA [Kassel, 1964], VIII/5, 601), but that figure depends on what he decided constitutes an individual piece. Is equal weight to be given to a one-page dance as to a multi-movement sonata? Does *Winterreise* count as one work or twenty-four? As Deutsch considers each individual variation an individual work, three of Schubert's four-hand compositions (D624, 813, 908) therefore count as twenty-four pieces among the total of 472.

9 For a fascinating discussion of small-scale forms, their generic designations, and relationships to a hierarchy of genres, see Jeffrey Kallberg, "Small Forms: In Defence of the Prelude," in *The Cambridge Companion to Chopin*, ed. Jim Samson (Cambridge, 1992), 124–44.

10 The mixture of genres is a hallmark of early Romanticism; see Jeffrey Kallberg, "The Rhetoric of Genre: Chopin's Nocturne in G Minor," *19th-Century Music* 11 (1988), 238–61.

11 Schubert's self-borrowing is well known, but the obvious examples of instrumental works based on Lieder – the "Trout" Quintet, the "Death and the Maiden" Quartet – are only a small sample of a far more extensive and significant network of stylistic and thematic interconnections, cross-references, allusions, and reworkings in his work; many examples are listed in Appendix 3 "Thematic and stylistic links between the songs and the instrumental works," in Reed, *The Schubert Song Companion*, 494–98.

12 *The Classical Style: Haydn, Mozart, and Beethoven* (New York, 1971), 460.

13 *Geschichte der europäisch-abendländischen oder unserer heutigen Musik* (Leipzig, 1834).

14 See Herfrid Kier, *Raphael Georg Kiesewetter (1773–1850): Wegbereiter des musikalischen Historismus* (Regensburg, 1968), 91–95.

15 *Geschichte des Concertwesens in Wien* (Vienna, 1869), 139ff.

16 In a more recent discussion of the eventful first decades of the nineteenth century, the German music historian Carl Dahlhaus explicitly takes up Kiesewetter's historiography that pairs Beethoven and Rossini and argues that in the "twin styles" of instrumental and operatic music, Beethoven claimed a new role for the art of music. Beethoven's compositions are texts requiring exegesis; a performer must plumb their depths in order to interpret their riches. A listener may not understand the work at first; appreciation comes with time and study. The Italian opera tradition, epitomized by Rossini, represents a different kind of relation between music as "text" and its actualization. Rossini's scores were more a recipe realized in the opera house, where performance "forms the crucial aesthetic arbiter as the realization of a draft rather than an exegesis of a text"; see *Nineteenth-Century Music,* trans. J. Bradford Robinson (Berkeley, 1989), 8–15.

17 *The Frontiers of Meaning: Three Informal Lectures on Music* (New York, 1994), 56; Scott Burnham explores how the musical values associated with Beethoven have informed ways of looking at music in *Beethoven Hero* (Princeton, 1995).

18 Dahlhaus, *Nineteenth-Century Music,* 79.

19 Inconsistent and confusing categorizing of these works further indicates the

state of flux in the Lied repertory at the turn of the century: although Mozart called *Das Veilchen* a "Lied," it was published by Artaria in 1789 as one of "two arias"; *Adelaide* first appeared in 1797 as a "cantata."

20 The editor, theorist, and critic Johann Christian Lobe wrote, "High above all composers who have come after Beethoven stands the original healthy creative power of Franz Schubert, who, like Mozart, went to his grave so early. While Beethoven was still alive and holding the position of master in the greatest brilliance of his fame, the younger composer not merely competed with him, but even won a victory over him. In his Lieder he surpassed everyone, even Beethoven"; see *Musikalische Briefe: Wahrheit über Tonkunst und Tonkünstler von einem Wohlbekannten* (Leipzig, 1852), II: 73; my translation.

21 C. D., "Die Lied- und Gesangskomposition: Das Schubertsche Lied," *Signale für die musikalische Welt* 17 (1859), 33; my translation.

22 Solomon first raised the issue in "Franz Schubert's 'Mein Traum'," *American Imago* 38 (1981), 137–54. His case only achieved wide notoriety with public lectures and the article "Franz Schubert and the Peacocks of Benvenuto Cellini," *19th-Century Music* 12 (1989), 193–206; see also "Schubert: Music, Sexuality, Culture," *19th-Century Music* 17 (1993), a special issue devoted to Schubert.

23 James Webster discusses some recent examples of criticism that place Schubert "under the sign of neurosis" by relating his life to his music (see "Music, Pathology, Sexuality, Beethoven, Schubert," *19th-Century Music* 17 [1993], 89–93).

24 The "double" transcendence of works of art is explored by Charles Rosen in his elucidation of Walter Benjamin's conception of a work's "afterlife"; see "The Ruins of Walter Benjamin," in *On Walter Benjamin: Critical Essays and Recollections*, ed. Gary Smith (Cambridge, Mass., 1988), 129–75.

1 Franz Schubert and Vienna

This essay draws upon two lectures given at two *Schubertiades* sponsored by the 92nd Street Y of New York City in 1992 and 1994. I am particularly grateful to Christopher Gibbs for excellent substantive and editorial suggestions.

1 Adalbert Stifter, *Aus dem alten Wien: Zwölf Studien*, ed. Otto Erich Deutsch (Leipzig, 1909), 111.

2 Friedrich Schreyvogel, "Ferdinand Raimund Leben und Werk," in *Ferdinand Raimund: Sämtliche Werke* (Munich, 1960), 721. Schubert certainly knew of this play, performed with music by Joseph Drechsler (1782–1852). The fifteen-year-old Schubert used a textbook by Drechsler (*SDB* 24 and 580).

3 See Robert Waissenberger, "Adalbert Stifters Ethik des Biedermeier," in *Bürgersinn und Aufbegehren: Biedermeiers und Vormärz in Wien 1815–1848* (hereafter cited as *BuA*) (Vienna, 1988), 442–45.

4 See Maynard Solomon, "Franz Schubert and the Peacocks of Benvenuto Cellini," *19th-Century Music* 12 (1989), 193–206; and a special issue of the same journal (17 [1993]), edited by Lawrence Kramer, entitled "Schubert: Music, Sexuality, Culture."

5   These two terms refer to the era 1815–48. "Pre-March" (*Vormärz*) is used to identify the years before the March Revolution of 1848, often back to 1815. *Biedermeier* refers to the same period, but more specifically to the emergence of a distinct middle-class urban style. Both terms are used here merely to refer to the general time period, not to evoke any specific generalizations about the era. In the case of Schubert, only the first fifteen years are relevant, making the use of either term somewhat irrelevant.

6   The reader is encouraged to examine *BuA*, whose extensive materials and commentary covering the wide range of life and culture during this period are excellent. See also a slightly different version, Robert Waissenberger, ed., *Wien 1815–1848. Bürgersinn und Aufbegehren: Die Zeit des Biedermeier und Vormärz* (Vienna, 1986).

7   See Robert Schumann, "Franz Schuberts letzte Kompositionen," in *Gesammelte Schriften,* 2 vols. (Leipzig, 1914), I: 327–31.

8   See the two volumes of *Neue Dokumente zum Schubert-Kreis,* ed. Walburga Litschauer (Vienna, 1986 and 1993), and the publications of the Internationales Franz Schubert Institut, especially its journal *Schubert durch die Brille.*

9   Anton Weiss, ed., *Fünfzig Jahre Schubertbund* (Vienna, 1913).

10   The Society began raising money for the monument in the early 1860s; a plaque had already been put on his birthplace in 1858. The Society even traveled to Stuttgart to help dedicate a Schubert monument there in 1878.

11   Two ideal sources for both the Männergesangverein's attitude and the late nineteenth- and early twentieth-century right-wing political appropriation are: Karl Adametz, *Franz Schubert in der Geschichte des Wiener Männergesangvereines* (Vienna, 1938), and Anton Weiss, *Jahresbericht des Schubertbundes in Wien 1896–1897* (Vienna, 1897).

12   See for example Alfred Orel, "Musikstadt Wien," in *Wien: Geschichte, Kunst, Leben,* ed. Anton Haasbauer (Vienna, 1942), 57. See also Leon Botstein, *Music and its Public* (PhD diss., Harvard University, 1985) and the liner notes to *Schubert Orchestrated* (Koch Schwann CD, 3 7307 2 [1995]). An interesting Viennese effort to merge the universal and the local was Robert Lach's *Das Ethos in der Musik Schuberts* (Vienna, 1928), a lecture held at the university centenary celebration.

13   See Otto Brusatti, ed., *Schubert im Wiener Vormärz: Dokumente 1829–1848* (Graz, 1978); and Otto Erich Deutsch, ed., *Schubert: Die Erinnerungen seiner Freunde* (Wiesbaden, 1983).

14   The protagonist – Jakob – of the story (first begun by Grillparzer in 1831) can be seen as a mixture of Grillparzer's images of Beethoven and Schubert. What is crucial in this context is the close detailed connection created between the music–making and the life and culture of the city.

15   See Ernst Hilmar, *Franz Schubert in his Time* (Portland, Oreg., 1988). I am referring, of course, to the work of Clifford Geertz in his two books *The Interpretation of Cultures* (New York, 1973) and *Local Knowledge* (New York, 1983).

16   La Mara, *Musikalische Studienköpfe Vol I: Romantiker,* 7th edn. (Leipzig,

1896), 71–136. This volume went into at least twelve editions.

17   See Richard Traubner, *Operetta: A Theatrical History* (New York, 1983), 424–26.

18   The exception from this paradigm now being made in Schubert's case concerns sexuality, construed perhaps a bit too ahistorically. See the suggestive works by Niklas Luhmann, *Die Ausbreitung des Kunstsystems* (Bern, 1994), 7–55; and *Unbeobachtbare Welt: Über Kunst und Architektur* (Bielefeld, 1990), 7–45.

19   See the sections on design in *BuA* and Paul and Stefan Asenbaum, eds., *Moderne Vergangenheit 1800–1900* (Vienna, 1981).

20   A nearly contemporary view of Nussdorf, from where Stifter looked out onto the city, can be seen in Jakob Alt's 1822 watercolor (*BuA* 481).

21   As Bruno Grimschitz observed in 1927, from the early nineteenth century on it was understood that the aesthetic greatness of Austria had culminated in the Baroque. Through Baroque architecture, the Austrian had become "European" (see *Die österreichische Zeichnung im 19. Jahrhundert* [Zurich, 1928], 3–5). In turn, for Schwind and Stifter's contemporaries throughout the Habsburg Empire, the Baroque represented the Austrian. The representational public architecture built in Vienna during Schubert's lifetime, in its adaptation of neoclassicism, never shed its evident debt to the Viennese Baroque architecture of the eighteenth century that dominated the city's landscape; see the section "Baukunst" in *BuA*, 498–531.

22   Karl Kobald, *Franz Schubert und seine Zeit* (Zurich, 1935), 247–65; also his *Schubert und Schwind* (Vienna, 1921).

23   See Peter Gülke, *Franz Schubert und seine Zeit* (Laaber, 1991), 47–64.

24   For example, the significance of the medieval was mirrored in lithographs from 1823 and an 1826 oil painting *Das Käthchen von Heilbronn*, all by Schwind. Schwind's 1823 sketches on death and graves possess clear allusions to the Gothic. Religious art in the 1820s was as much an evocation of history as a matter of piety. See Otto Weigmann, ed., *Schwind: Des Meisters Werke* (Stuttgart, 1906); see also Friedrich Haack, *Moritz von Schwind* (Bielefeld, 1923).

25   See Charles Sealsfield-Karl Postl, *Austria as it is*, ed. Primus Heinz Kucher (Vienna, 1994).

26   Eduard von Bauernfeld, *Erinnerungen aus Alt Wien* (Vienna, 1923), 371.

27   He was arrested, spent fourteen months in jail, then was released and exiled to the Tyrol. His career was destroyed, however (*SDB* 128–30). See also John Reed, *The Schubert Song Companion* (Manchester, 1985), 479.

28   Reed, *The Schubert Song Companion*, 470.

29   Following Bauernfeld's cue, one might say that the modern reader must refer to the pre-1989 states of Eastern Europe, to Romania for example, to appreciate the political and psychic costs of autocracies with extensive secret police networks and censorship authority. Steblin makes a similar point. See below, note 33.

30 See the outstanding monograph by Waltraud Heindl, *Gehorsame Rebellen: Bürokratie und Beamte in Österreich 1780 bis 1848* (Vienna, 1991). One clear link between this sector of society and Schubert was the Pratobevera family.

31 See Schubert's observation about a bad performance in the Theater an der Wien in May 1826 (*SBD* 528).

32 Johann Nestroy, who had made his theatrical debut in 1822 at the Kärntnertor Theater as Sarastro, used *The Magic Flute* overtly and indirectly in two farces that focused not only on the external politics but on the consequences of the many forms of rationalized adaptation developed by the Viennese. *Der Zerrissene* from 1844 and the 1845 *Das Gewürzkrämerkleeblatt oder Der unschuldigen Schuldigen* take apart the conceits and habits of the full range of the Viennese middle class, particularly its civil servants and men of commerce.

33 Rita Steblin, "The Peacock's Tale: Schubert's Sexuality Reconsidered," *19th-Century Music* 17 (1993), 11.

34 In this satire, Sarastro has become a discontent middle-class civil servant who longs for the past and calls in sick on his birthday. Tamino has lost the magic flute and goes daily to the office. Pamina cooks breakfast, bringing in soup instead of the milk and coffee of bygone times. Papageno has been bribed. Monastatos, now the lover of the Queen of the Night, has become the Director of the "Bureau of Light Extinguishing." He is about to be ennobled as "Edler von Schneeweiss" (Earl of White Snow). He is upset that Tamino fails to doff his hat when he sees him on the street. The Queen of the Night is in charge. She has taken the light of wisdom and turned it into an artificial means of lighting tobacco. She is obsessed with cologne, her upset stomach, and making sure that she walks in public affecting a proper and respectable style. The three boys have been sent as apprentices to a cabinet maker. The Queen admonishes Monastatos to make sure that her civil servants remain too busy to read; Franz Grillparzer, *Sämtliche Werke*, ed. August Sauer, vol. XIII (Stuttgart, n.d.), 121–29.

35 See Alice M. Hanson, *Musical Life in Biedermeier Vienna* (Cambridge, 1985); the German edition of this book contains many minor but crucial corrections, see *Die zensurierte Muse: Musikleben im Wiener Biedermeier* (Vienna, 1987).

36 Consider the recurrent uses of the image of the knight in the work of Schwind and comparable subject matter in Schubert. See Weigmann, ed., *Schwind*, 8 and 34; and Schubert's early Romanze D114, and late Sir Walter Scott songs (e.g. D837 from 1825).

37 Much of the discussion owes a debt to three seminal works on the public realm in the late eighteenth century and the early nineteenth century: Jürgen Habermas, *Strukturwandel der Öffentlichkeit: Untersuchungen zu einer Kategorie der bürgerlichen Gesellschaft* (Darmstadt, 1962); Reinhart Koselleck, *Critique and Crisis: Enlightenment and the Pathogenesis of Modern Society* (Cambridge, Mass., 1988); and Peter Uwe Hohendahl, *Literarische Kultur im Zeitalter des Liberalismus 1830–1870* (Munich, 1985).

38   On the aristocracy see Hannes Stekl, *Österreichs Aristokratie im Vormärz* (Vienna, 1973); the memoirs of J. F. Castelli and Karoline Pichler are indispensable sources for this period in Vienna.

39   So did fashion and style. The new Viennese middle-class public embraced a freer and distinct and expressive clothes style for both men and women. See Max von Boehn, *Die Mode im XIX. Jahrhundert* (Munich, 1907), plate 28.

40   Genre painting became popular in part as a reaction. It rivaled landscape painting as the emblematic visual medium of the era. Genre scenes sought to depict the individual in a realistic and naturalistic setting, as if to assert that the simple person, betraying no lineage, placed in ordinary circumstances, and engaged in daily life, was sufficient as an image to communicate unique worth and humanity. The direct and often sentimentalized depiction of the everyday, inside and outside the home, was an act of self-assertion that only seemed innocent, politically speaking; see the section on "Bildend Kunst" in *BuA*.

41   See Weigmann, ed., *Schwind*, 2–4.

42   In this regard, the case of the poet Nikolaus Lenau is most instructive. Lenau, like Stifter, came to Vienna to study. He lived there, with some interruptions, from 1823 to 1830. After inheriting a small fortune from his grandmother he emigrated to America in the early 1830s, only to return later in the decade. In his early poems, the theme of the conflict between reality and hope is central. In his 1826 "Die Jugendträume," the human comes of age sensing that he himself is a God; his expectations are bolstered by a pristine nature. The reality of human existence, of societal facts in the man-made world (e.g. the city), dash these sensibilities and inspire the individual to flee away from the world further and further, to retain the capacity for fantasy and to escape. In the longer "allegorical dream" entitled "Glauben, Wissen, Handeln" from 1830, Lenau uses the idea of memory to express the sense of life as a labyrinth, a hopeless and pointless experience without respite. What is remarkable in this longer poem are the explicit references to Greece, Rome, and the "Germania" of a past age. Psychic despair is deepened by historical nostalgia and pessimism. "Forgetting," the creation of art, and the capacity to dream become associated with one another as sources of solace; see Nikolaus Lenau, *Sämtliche Werke*, ed. Eduard Castle (Leipzig), 22 and 43.

43   See Dagmar C. G. Lorenz, *Grillparzer: Dichter des sozialen Konflikts* (Vienna, 1986).

44   This essay does not discuss Schubert's efforts to write for the Viennese stage. Clearly he recognized the unique character and significance of theater in Vienna after 1815. On the Viennese theater see Roger Bauer, *La Réalité Royaume de Dieu: Études sur l'originalité du théâtre viennois dans la première moitiá du XIXe siècle* (Munich, 1965); and Josef Mayerhofer, ed., *Wiener Theater des Biedermeier und Vormärz* (Vienna, 1978). See also the more systematic chronicle account of all the theaters in Schubert's day in Franz Hadamowsky, *Wien: Theater Geschichte* (Vienna and Munich, 1988).

45   Consider the 1820 series of sixteen erotic scenes done by Peter Fendi (1796–1824), an artist best known for his portraits of the aristocracy and his

sentimental genre paintings. The Vienna of Schubert's day produced such items as pornographic meerschaum pipes depicting females masturbating. Pornography from Paris made its way east to German-speaking cities. One example that reached southern Germany linked the rage for music-making with sexual exploits by depicting the black and white keys of the piano as a series of legs and vaginas; see Hans Ottomeyer and Ulrike Laufer, eds., *Biedermeiers Glück und Ende. . . . die gestörte Idylle 1815–1848* (Munich, 1987), 594–96; see also *BuA* 618. A far more respectable and less lurid vehicle for private fantasy was reading. Moritz von Schwind completed a successful and popular set of illustrations for an 1825 edition of *A Thousand and One Nights*. In Vienna, the mundane and externally conventional holders of such fantasies were themselves ripe for satire. The more fantastic one's mental life, the more grotesque ordinary existence and the docile acceptance of lack of freedom seemed. Nestroy exploited this. So did Schwind. In 1826, he executed his satirical drawings of "Gotham" life, termed *Krähwinkeliaden* (a parallel to Schubertiades). Here the pretensions, idiocies, and hypocrisy of the educated Viennese come into full view. Likewise, Schwind's 1824 series "Embarrassment," the subjects of which are seduction and deceit, focus on the corruption of language and manners in Vienna, the clash between the claims of overt speech and behavior and actual meaning (Weigmann, ed., *Schwind*, 27–31, 45–47, and 52–53).

46   D. Z. Wertheim, *Versuch einer medicinischen Topographie von Wien* (Vienna, 1810), 72, quoted in Wolfgang Pircher and Andreas Pribersky, "Die Gesundheit, die Polizei und die Cholera" in the collection *Wien im Vormärz* by Renate B. Banitz-Schweizer, Andreas B. Baryli, *et al.* (Vienna, 1980) (hereafter cited as *WiV*), 203.

47   *WiV,* 209.

48   In this discussion Vienna is defined by the greater Vienna to the line around the suburban districts outside the inner city. The sources for this section include A. Hickmann, *Wien im XIX Jahrhundert* (Vienna, 1903), Maren Seliger and Karl Ucakar, *Wien: Politische Geschichte Vol. I 1740–1895* (Vienna, 1985), and *BuA.*

49   Hickmann, *Wien im XIX Jahrhundert,* Chart Nos. 20 and 21.

50   The statistical material comes in part from Maren Seliger and Karl Ucakar, *Wien: Politische Geschichte Vol. 1 1740–1895,* 125–64.

51   See *BuA,* 460–545.

52   See B. R. Mitchell, *European Historical Statistics 1750–1975,* 2nd edn (New York, 1980) and Hickmann, *Wien im XIX Jahrhundert.*

53   See also the articles by Andreas B. Baryli, Wolfgang Häusler, Peter F. Feldbauer, and Renate B. Banik-Schweizer in *WiV*; and Gustav Otruba, "Entstehung und soziale Entwicklung der Arbeiterschaft und der Angestellten bis zum Ersten Weltkrieg," in *Österreichs Sozialstrukturen in historischer Sicht,* ed. Erich Zöllner (Vienna, 1980), 128–30.

54   Roman Sandgruber's article in *BuA,* 596, and his "Indikatoren des Lebensstandards in Wien in der ersten Hälfte des 19. Jahrhunderts," in *WiV,* 57–74.

55 See Hickmann, *Wien im XIX Jahrhundert*, Tables 32–33 and *BuA*, 568–72; see also Eugen Guglia, *Das Theresianum in Wien: Vergangenheit und Gegenwart* (Vienna, 1912), 96–132, for a sense of the character and role of education beyond the elementary level.

56 See Pirchler and Pribersky, "Die Gesundheit," in *WiV*, 205–06; and Felix Czeike, *Historisches Lexikon Wien* (Vienna, 1993), II: 355.

57 Stifter, *Aus dem alten Wien*, 283–87.

58 This section is intended to be speculative and does not pretend to serve as a surrogate for close analysis of specific works by Schubert.

59 It should be noted that the Viennese world in which Schubert lived was decidedly distinct from the Vienna inhabited by Beethoven during the 1820s. The difference was generational, compounded by the fact that Beethoven was isolated by deafness and fame. There has been a consistent effort to link Beethoven and Schubert, but the gulf remained, made more complicated by Beethoven's dependence on and association with a milieu of aristocrats to whom Schubert had limited access. See Leon Botstein, "The Patrons and Publics of the Quartets: Music, Culture and Society in Beethoven's Vienna," in *The Beethoven Quartet Companion*, ed. Robert Martin and Robert Winter, (Berkeley, 1994), 77–110.

60 Here was music-making alone, primarily at the piano. See Leo Grunstein, *Das Alt-Wiener Antlitz: Bildnisse und Menschen aus der ersten Hälfte des XIX Jahrhunderts*, 2 vols. (Gilhofer and Ranschburg, 1931), Plate 71. The image is of the composer and pianist Leopoldine Blahetka (1809–85) whose path first crossed with Schubert when she was a child, in 1818, when she played in a concert that also contained the first public performance of a work by Schubert (*SBD* 87). Deutsch says she was seven but she was really just over eight years old.

61 See Franz Mailer, "Die Walzer des Biedermeier," and Reingard Witzmann, "Wiener Walzer und Wiener Ballkultur: Von der Tanzekstase zum Walzertraum," in *BuA*, 126–37.

62 See David Brodbeck, "Dance Music as High Art: Schubert's Twelve Ländler, Op. 171 (D790)," in *Schubert: Critical and Analytical Studies*, ed. Walter Frisch (Lincoln, Nebr., 1986), 31–47.

63 Leo Strauss, *Persecution and the Art of Writing* (Chicago, 1952).

64 The great cycles of Wilhelm Müller's settings of *Die schöne Müllerin* and *Winterreise* would make plausible objects for this analysis. The settings in three of Schubert's most famous songs – Schiller's *Gruppe aus dem Tartarus* (D583); Goethe's *Geheimes* (D719); and *Du bist die Ruh* (D776) – are other potential cases in point. So too is his early and popular Goethe setting *Gretchen am Spinnrade* (D118). See for example the analysis in a recent textbook dealing with *Der Wanderer* (D489) in Walter Dürr, *Sprache und Musik* (Kassel, 1994), 216–39.

65 See Arnold Feil, *Franz Schubert: Die schöne Müllerin. Winterreise* (Portland, Oreg., 1988), 11–28; and Susan Youens, *Retracing a Winter's Journey: Schubert's Winterreise* (Ithaca, 1991). One might also read *An mein Klavier* (D342) in this manner.

66 On the guitar in the early nineteenth century in Vienna, see Lenau's "An meine Guitarre" from 1832 in Lenau, *Sämtliche Werke*, 24; "Schubert's Guitar" in *BuA*, 108; and *SDB* 177, 225, 291, 509. Many of Schubert's songs and his partsongs were first published with guitar accompaniments by Cappi & Diabelli.

67 See, for example, the Dresden *Abendzeitung* (*SDB* 418). Robert Schumann referred to Schubert's mastery in "genre painting" in his review of Berlioz's *Symphonie fantastique* in Schumann, *Gesammelte Schriften*, I: 85.

68 See *SDB* 352–55 (June 25, 1824).

69 See, for example, Friedrich von Hentl's 1822 review in the *Wiener Zeitschrift für Kunst* (*SDB* 214–19).

70 See the Leipzig *Allgemeine musikalische Zeitung*, March 1, 1827 (*SDB* 512–15); see also Leo Balet, *Die Verbürgerlichung der Deutschen Kunst, Literatur und Musik im 18. Jahrhundert* (Strassburg and Leiden, 1936), 498–508.

71 *SDB* 269, and also the review from the Vienna *Allgemeine musikalische Zeitung*, *SDB* 277.

72 *SDB* 151 and 121. See the text of Schober's *An die Musik* (D547).

73 Nowhere is this awareness more clear than in Franz von Schober's New Year's Eve poem from 1823 (*SDB* 257–79; and 257, 279, and 336–37).

74 From a text dedicated to Schubert by Mayrhofer (*SDB* 190–91).

2 Images and legends of the composer

1 The phrase "armer Schubert" was often used by his friends; see, for example, *SMF* 14, 116, 132, 139, 202, 229, 233, 252, 254.

2 See, for example, *SDB* 441, 828; *SMF* 24, 34, 35, 62, 69, 185, 314, 319; Gerhard von Breuning even refers to "our poor Schubert" (*unser armer Schubert*) (*SMF* 254).

3 The best iconographical sources for Schubert are: Otto Erich Deutsch, *Sein Leben in Bildern* (Munich and Leipzig, 1913); Ernst Hilmar and Otto Brusatti, *Franz Schubert: Ausstellung der Wiener Stadt- und Landesbibliothek zum 150. Todestag der Komponisten* (Vienna, 1978); and Ernst Hilmar, *Schubert* (Graz, 1990).

4 In 1825 the Cappi & Co. publishing house advertised a copper engraving of Rieder's portrait as "the extremely good likeness of the composer Franz Schubert" (*SDB* 477–78; cf. 417).

5 Schubert referred to "my littleness" (*SDB* 433 and 435). A military conscription form places Schubert's height at 157 centimeters (*SDB* 83–84; cf. 926).

6 Almost all are included in *SDB*; for a different translation see *Franz Schubert Letters and Other Writings*, ed. Otto Erich Deutsch, trans. Venetia Savile (London, 1928).

7 Because of the enormous fame of *Erlkönig*, there were many stories about its fate: the difficulty Schubert encountered getting it published; how one publisher returned it to the wrong Franz Schubert (another composer of the same name working in Dresden) who pronounced it trash; how Schubert

played it on a comb, and so forth; see Christopher H. Gibbs, *The Presence of* Erlkönig: *Reception and Reworkings of a Schubert Lied* (PhD diss., Columbia University, New York, 1992), 86–159.

8   See Carl Dahlhaus, *Ludwig van Beethoven: Approaches to his Music*, trans. Mary Whittall (Oxford, 1991), 1.

9   Although the story is found in most biographies of the two composers, Maynard Solomon has provided good reasons to be skeptical, see "Schubert and Beethoven," *19th-Century Music* 3 (1979), 114–25.

10   The bodies of Schubert and Beethoven were exhumed twice, in 1863 and 1888.

11   Although *Erlkönig* was Schubert's official Op. 1, three Lieder – *Erlafsee* (D586), *Widerschein* (D639), and *Die Forelle* (D550) – were released in the less-assuming venues of periodicals and almanacs; see *NSA*, IV/1a/xv-xvi; and Ewan West, "The Musenalmanach and Viennese Song, 1770–1830," *Music and Letters* 67 (1986), 37–49.

12   Josef von Spaun was later (1858) to recount a similar astonished benediction dating from Schubert's school days. He says that after only two lessons, the teacher and organist Wenzel Ruzicka told him: "I can teach him nothing, he has learnt it from God himself" (*SMF* 128, cf. 35, 145, 362).

13   Most of the reviews are found in *Franz Schubert: Dokumente 1817–1830*, ed. Till Gerrit Waidelich, vol. I, (Tutzing, 1993), and many are translated in *SDB*.

14   In addition to David Gramit's chapter in this volume, see his *The Intellectual and Aesthetic Tenets of Franz Schubert's Circle* (PhD diss., Duke University, 1987).

15   *Franz Schubert: Jahre der Krise 1818–1823*, ed. Werner Aderhold, Walther Dürr, and Walburga Litschauer (Kassel, 1985).

16   The same rigorous self-criticism emerged shortly before his death when, informing the influential publisher Schott about his compositions, Schubert did not acknowledge most of his symphonies, dramatic music, and chamber works (*SDB* 739–40).

17   For a discussion of Schubert's illness see Eric Sams, "Schubert's Illness Re-examined," *Musical Times* 121 (1980), 15–22.

18   See *SDB* 824–925; as this collection contains only a few reviews written after Schubert's death, the best source for documents from the 1830s and 1840s is Otto Brusatti, ed. *Schubert im Wiener Vormärz: Dokumente 1829–1848* (Graz, 1978).

19   Schubert left a large number of unfinished works that date from all stages of his career. Not many projects were unfinished because of his early death.

20   See Hans Lenneberg, "The Myth of the Unappreciated (Musical) Genius," *Musical Quarterly* 66 (1980), 222–24.

21   *Geschichte des Concertwesens in Wien* (Vienna, 1869), I: 283; my translation.

22   Otto Biba, "Schubert's Position in Viennese Musical Life," *19th-Century Music* 3 (1979), 106–13.

23   Gustav Nottebohm, *Thematisches Verzeichniss der im Druck erschienenen Werke von Franz Schubert* (Vienna, 1874); the complete edition, admirably edited by Eusebius Mandyczewski, was not really complete, and not only

because some pieces turned up later. Largely, it seems, at the urging of Johannes Brahms, who edited the volume of symphonies, various early works were omitted entirely; see Otto Erich Deutsch, "Schubert: the Collected Works," *Music and Letters* 32 (1951), 226–34.

24 See Alice M. Hanson, *Musical Life in Biedermeier Vienna* (Cambridge, 1985).

25 A question recently posed by the critic David Cairns in fact demonstrates what it declares: "Is there a comparable case of a great composer – one that many would unhesitatingly place among the half-dozen supreme creators, a junior member [*sic*] of the company of Mozart, Beethoven, Bach, Handel, and Haydn – whom commentators feel so free to patronize: a master who is so often approached in the expectation of finding weaknesses, whether for censure or indulgent forgiveness?" *Responses: Musical Essays and Reviews* (New York, 1973), 195.

26 "Schubert chose scarcely a single musical artist for his closest and most intimate relationships, but for the most part only artist practitioners in other branches, who could indeed pay homage to his genius, but were incapable of leading it. An excellent, experienced composer would probably have guided Schubert towards even more works of the larger kind and have stood by him as adviser in matters of outward form, well-planned disposition and large-scale effect" (*SDB* 856). Compare Sonnleithner's later statement (1857) that Schubert "had no friend who stood to him in the relation of master, who might have been able to guide him in such undertakings [i.e. large-scale works] by advising, warning, and correcting him" (*SMF* 112).

27 *Conversation-Lexicon der neuesten Zeit und Literatur* (1834); my translation.

28 *Musikalisches Conversations-Lexicon, Encyklopädie der gesammten Musik-Wissenschaft* (Leipzig, 1835), 300, my translation; see Christopher H. Gibbs, "Schubert in deutschsprachigen Lexica nach 1830," *Schubert durch die Brille* 13 (June 1994), 70–78.

29 See *SMF* 10, 13; later comments include *SDB* 853, 858–59.

30 Albert Stadler quoted this letter from Vogl, and commented on it, in 1858 (*SMF* 146); Vogl's ideas, expressed in a lost diary, were also quoted in Bauernfeld's obituary for Vogl in 1841 (*SMF* 226). A particularly revealing observation is found in a letter to Spaun from his brother-in-law Anton Ottenwalt when Schubert visited Linz in 1825. Ottenwalt's defense of Schubert's intellect and his insistence on Schubert's personal convictions seem both to confirm and contradict Vogl's notion of the composer's unmediated inspirations: "Of Schubert – I might almost say of our Schubert – there is much I should like to tell you. . . . He talked of art, of poetry, of his youth, of friends and other people who matter, of the relationship of ideals to life, and so forth. I was more and more amazed at such a mind, of which it has been said that its artistic achievement is so unconscious [*seine Kunstleistung sei so unbewusst*], hardly revealed to and understood by himself, and so on. Yet how simple was all this! – I cannot tell you of the extent and the unity of his convictions – but there were glimpses of a world-view that is not merely acquired, and the share which worthy friends may have in it by no means distracts from the individuality shown by all this" (*SDB* 442). Four years later,

Ottenwalt added a similar passage to Spaun's Schubert obituary (*SDB* 878). Eduard Bauernfeld made a similar observation (and tellingly invokes Mozart as a comparable phenomenon): "There are people who regarded the author of such songs, who was at the same time able to deliver them so tenderly and feelingly, as a kind of musical machine that had only to be wound up to grind out the most beautiful Mozartian (or Schubertian) melodies without itself feeling anything" (*SMF* 33).

31   The depiction of an effeminate Schubert in nineteenth-century English writings is examined by David Gramit in a fascinating article, "Constructing a Victorian Schubert: Music, Biography, and Cultural Values," *19th-Century Music* 17 (1993), 65–78.

32   *Schumann on Music: A Selection from his Writings*, ed. and trans. Henry Pleasants (New York, 1988), 142.

33   The comparisons were duly published as *Actenmässige Darstellung der Ausgrabung und Wiederbeisetzung der irdischen Reste von Beethoven und Schubert* (Vienna, 1863).

34   *Memories of Beethoven: From the House of the Black-Robed Spaniards*, ed. Maynard Solomon, trans. Henry Mins and Maynard Solomon (Cambridge, 1992), 116.

35   Heinrich Kreissle von Hellborn, *Franz Schubert* (Vienna 1865), 466; translated by Arthur Coleridge as *The Life of Franz Schubert* (London, 1869), II: 152.

36   *Franz Schubert*, 260; *The Life of Franz Schubert*, I: 262.

37   Best known is Leopold Kupelwieser's *Party Game of the Schubertians* which shows the Schubert circle at play. Painted for Franz von Schober in 1821, it depicts a scene at the Atzenbrugg Castle, owned by an uncle of Schober's, where Schubert and his friends gathered every year from 1817 to 1823. The friends play charades, while Schubert sits at the piano, which may suggest that he provided improvised incidental music; see *SMF* 214.

38   Schwind made sketches, an unfinished oil painting, and a sepia drawing; see Hilmar, *Schubert*, 55, 61–62; and *SDB* 784.

39   Maurice J. E. Brown, *Essays on Schubert* (London, 1966, rpt. 1978), 161; a key to the individuals is given in *SDB* 784.

40   Brown speculates that this was the song, *Essays on Schubert*, 161.

41   See *SMF* 7–39; Ferdinand Schubert's valuable essay was written around this time and consulted by Spaun and Bauernfeld, but only appeared when Schumann published it in the *Neue Zeitschrift für Musik* in 1839 (*SMF* 34–39).

42   An early Schubert story by Elise Polko is in her extremely popular *Musikalische Märchen, Phantasien und Skizzen* (Leipzig, 1852), a book that had many editions and was translated into a number of languages; two English translations appeared, one by Fanny Fuller (Philadelphia and New York, 1864) and another by Mary P. Maudslay (London, 1876). See also Ottfried (i.e. Gottfried Jolsdorf), *Schubert-Novellen: Sechs Blätter aus dem Liederkranze des unsterblichen Meistersängers* (Innsbruck, 1862).

43   The incorporation of Schubert's music into theater pieces began as early as 1834 with Adolf Müller's *Der Erlenkönig*. Franz von Suppé's one-act operetta *Franz Schubert* (1864) tells the story of Schubert's flight from Vienna to the

suburbs where he encounters the "schöne Müllerin" who inspires his song cycle. The most famous Schubert operetta was Heinrich Berté's *Das Dreimäderlhaus*, discussed below; see Gibbs, *The Presence of* Erlkönig, 337–43.

44 There are four film versions alone of *Das Dreimäderlhaus* (see *Gänzl's Book of the Musical Theatre*, ed. Kurt Gänzl and Andrew Lamb [London, 1988], 1045), as well as other movies about Schubert's life; see Robert Werba, *Schubert und die Wiener: Der volkstümliche Unbekannte* (Vienna, 1978).

45 According to Ernst Hilmar, *Das Dreimäderlhaus* has been translated into some twenty languages and there have been over 100,000 performances in at least sixty countries (Hilmar, "The Trivialized Schubert," lecture presented at the fourth *Schubertiade* symposium at the 92nd Street Y in New York City, February 2, 1992). It was known in French as *Chanson d'amour*, in Italian as *La Casa delle Tre Ragazze*, and in English as *Lilac Time* (arranged by G. H. Clutsam for the Lyric Theatre, London, in 1922) and *Blossom Time* (arranged by Sigmund Romberg for the Ambassador Theater in New York in 1921); see Richard Traubner, *Operetta: A Theatrical History* (New York, 1983), 425.

46 *Ein unbekanntes frühes Schubert-Porträt? Franz Schubert und der Maler Josef Abel* (Tutzing, 1992); see also Elmar Worgull, "Ein repräsentives Jugendbildnis Schuberts," *Schubert durch die Brille* 12 (1994), 54–89.

47 See Albi Rosenthal, "Zum 'Schubert-Porträt' von Abel," *Schubert durch die Brille* 12 (1994), 90–91.

48 The portrait is included at the beginning of the chapter on Schubert in *The Romantic Era*, vol. II of the *Heritage of Music*, ed. Michael Raeburn and Alan Kendall (Oxford, 1989), 74; and in Yehudi Menuhin and Curtis W. Davis, *The Music of Man* (New York, 1979), 157.

49 The film was released in theater and television versions, the former under the title "Notturno." See Walburga Litschauer, "Zu Fritz Lehners Schubert-Film *Notturno*," *Schubert durch die Brille* 2 (1989), 26–29.

50 See Solomon, "Franz Schubert's 'Mein Traum,'" *American Imago* 38 (1981), 137–54; "Franz Schubert and the Peacocks of Benvenuto Cellini," *19th-Century Music* 12 (1989), 193–206; and "Schubert: Some Consequences of Nostalgia," *19th-Century Music* 17 (1993), 34–46.

51 See the special issue of *19th-Century Music*: "Schubert: Music, Sexuality, Culture," 17 (Summer 1993). The final commentary is by Robert Winter ("Whose Schubert?"), and traces various appropriations of "our Schubert" over the course of the nineteenth and twentieth centuries.

3 *Music, cultivation, and identity in Schubert's circle*

1 To name only two relatively recent such publications, see Appendix C, "Personalia," in John Reed, *Schubert* (London, 1987), 268–86, and Ernst Hilmar's richly illustrated *Franz Schubert* (Graz, 1989), 49–86.

2 The title of Peter Clive, *Mozart and his Circle: A Biographical Dictionary* (London, 1993), is a case in point: not only is the formulation unusual in the field, it refers not to a particular group of close friends, but to everyone with whom Mozart had significant contact during his life.

3   Newman Flower, *Franz Schubert: The Man and his Circle* (New York, 1928), 50.

4   Stadler's memoirs were written in response to biographical inquiries by Ferdinand Luib, and are cited and translated in *SMF* 144–45. Deutsch's own more extensive list of Schubert's friends (*SME*, 1–5) is similar in nature. Note that the orchestra composed primarily of officials-in-training supplemented with a few choirboy-students (Schubert and Randhartinger) is a youthful parallel to the typical orchestra of the time consisting primarily of gentleman amateurs supplemented by a few professional musicians. On this structure and its subsequent professionalization, see William Weber, "Mass Culture and the Reshaping of European Musical Taste, 1770–1870," *International Review of the Aesthetics and the Sociology of Music* 8 (1977), 5–21.

5   See the discussion by Leon Botstein in "The Patrons and Public of the Quartets: Music, Culture, and Society in Beethoven's Vienna," in *The Beethoven Quartet Companion*, ed. Robert Winter and Robert Martin (Berkeley and Los Angeles, 1994), 77–109, esp. 83–93. For further discussion of the demographic, social, and musical context, see Alice M. Hanson, *Musical Life in Biedermeier Vienna* (Cambridge, 1985).

6   From a document written by Humboldt in 1809; cited in Wilhelm Dilthey and Alfred Heubaum, "Ein Gutachten Wilhelm von Humboldts über die Staatsprüfung des höheren Verwaltungsbeamten," *Jahrbuch für Gesetzgebung, Verwaltung und Volkswirtschaft im Deutschen Reich* 23 (1899), 253; translation from Friedrich A. Kittler, *Discourse Networks 1800/1900*, trans. Michael Metteer, with Chris Cullens (Stanford, 1990), 59. For a more extensive discussion of this culture in relation to the Lied in particular, see David Gramit, "Schubert's Wanderers and the Autonomous Lied," *Journal of Musicological Research* 14 (1995), 147–68.

7   Heinrich Kreissle von Hellborn, *Franz Schubert* (Vienna, 1865; rpt. Hildesheim and New York, 1978).

8   Flower, *Franz Schubert*, 115.

9   For the complete German text of this 1849 document (excerpted in *SMF*), see David Gramit, *The Intellectual and Aesthetic Tenets of Franz Schubert's Circle* (PhD diss., Duke University, 1987), 381–82.

10 From "On Franz Schubert," Bauernfeld's obituary article of 1829 (*SMF* 32).

11 For a closer examination of this relationship, see David Gramit, "Schubert and the Biedermeier: the Aesthetics of Johann Mayrhofer's 'Heliopolis'," *Music and Letters* 74 (1993), 355–82.

12 For a more detailed account of this group, see Helga Prosl, *Der Freundeskreis um Anton von Spaun: Ein Beitrag zur Geistesgeschichte von Linz in der Biedermeierzeit (1811–1827)* (PhD diss., Leopold Franzens Universität, Innsbruck, 1951).

13 On the Austrian school curriculum, see Georg Jäger, "Zur literarischen Gymnasialbildung in Österreich von der Aufklärung bis zum Vormärz," in *Die österreichische Literatur: Ihr Profil an der Wende vom 18. bis zum 19. Jahrhundert (1750–1830)*, ed. Herbert Zeman, 2 vols. (Graz, 1979), I: 85–118.

14 From undated letters in the manuscript collection of the Stadt- und

Landesbibliothek, Vienna, Inventory Nos. 36662 and 36659, respectively. The context of the letters and their content date them to the second decade of the century. For the German texts, see Gramit, *Intellectual and Aesthetic Tenets*, 376–78.

15   From a letter on the nature of poetry written by Anton von Spaun to Franz von Schober, February 16, 1813, Stadtbibliothek Inv. No. 36272. For the German text, see Gramit, *Intellectual and Aesthetic Tenets*, 383–84.

16   Mayrhofer's comments appear in a dialogue, "Raphael," that he contributed to the second volume of the *Beyträge* (Vienna, 1818), 305–06; he wrote of the "Verzeichnungen und Verirrungen der deutschen Schule" and the "Canon des Schönen und Wahrhaften, mit einem Worte des Classischen." On Mayrhofer's authorship of the article, see Gramit, *Intellectual and Aesthetic Tenets*, 71n. Spaun's letter to Schober of May 15, 1817, is Stadtbibliothek Inv. No. 36654: "die völlig unbestimmte, chaotische Sehnsucht des Herzens." Ottenwalt wrote to Schober on July 28, 1817 (Stadtbibliothek Inv. No. 36529): "führen häufig ein kleines, vielleicht verkehrtes Leben, lassen Geschichte nichts gelten, wissen von nichts als öder Nacht der absoluten All-und-Nichts Lehre, über der die Irrlichter und Gespenster der Romantik schweben."

17   Walther Dürr, "Der Linzer Schubert-Kreis und seine 'Beiträge zur Bildung für Jünglinge,'" *Historisches Jahrbuch der Stadt Linz* (1985), 51–59, argues that the Linz circle around Spaun had a fundamentally more political, action-oriented stance than the later, aestheticizing circle around Schubert. While the differences between the two groups should not be overlooked, to summarize them in this way not only minimizes a significant overlap of personnel, but also undervalues the level of aesthetic interest in the earlier group and the political awareness of the later; as the quotation from Spaun's letter given above suggests (p. 61), in neither group did political awareness carry with it expectations of political activity.

18   For further discussion of literary taste, see Gramit, *Intellectual and Aesthetic Tenets*, 170–85 and 253–60.

19   See, for example, Josef von Spaun's letter to Bauernfeld of early 1829: "In spite of the admiration I have felt for my dear friend, for years, I am of the opinion that, in the field of instrumental and church music, we shall never make a Mozart or a Haydn out of him . . ." (*SMF* 30).

20   On Vogl, see Andreas Liess, *Johann Michael Vogl: Hofoperist und Schubertsänger* (Graz and Cologne, 1954).

21   (*SDB* 248); translation slightly emended.

22   For further discussion of elite culture in this context, see Kittler, *Discourse Networks*, esp. 143–44; Wolfgang Kaschuba, "Deutsche Bürgerlichkeit nach 1800: Kultur als symbolische Praxis," in *Bürgertum im 19. Jahrhundert: Deutschland im europäischen Vergleich*, ed. Jürgen Kocka, 3 vols. (Munich, 1988), III: 9–44; and Martha Woodmansee, "The Interest in Disinterestedness: Karl Philipp Moritz and the Emergence of the Theory of Aesthetic Autonomy in Eighteenth-Century Germany," *Modern Language Quarterly* 45 (1984), 22–47. In relation to music, my ideas have been influenced by Andreas Maier, who was kind enough to share his paper, "'Gluck'sches Gestöhn' und 'welsches

Larifari': Anna Milder, Franz Schubert und der deutsch-italienische Opernkrieg," *Archiv für Musikwissenschaft* 52 (1995), 171–204, before its publication.

23 Cited in Paul Bornstein, ed., *Der Briefwechsel des Grafen August von Platen*, 4 vols. (Munich and Leipzig, 1914), III: 101.

24 The first quotation is from Spaun's "On Schubert" (1829), the second from his "Notes on my Association with Franz Schubert" (1858) (*SMF* 24 and 140).

25 Maynard Solomon, "Franz Schubert's 'Mein Traum,'" *American Imago* 38 (1981), 137–54; and "Franz Schubert and the Peacocks of Benvenuto Cellini," *19th-Century Music* 12 (1989), 193–206. For an overview of public responses to Solomon's work, as well as scholarly debate over it, see "Schubert: Music, Sexuality, Culture," *19th-Century Music* 17 (1993).

26 Solomon, "Peacocks," 202.

27 For a rebuttal, see Rita Steblin, "The Peacock's Tale: Schubert's Sexuality Reconsidered," *19th-Century Music* 17 (1993), 5–33. For responses, see Solomon, "Schubert: Some Consequences of Nostalgia," *ibid.*, 34–46; Kristina Muxfeldt, "Political Crimes and Liberty, or Why Would Schubert eat a Peacock?" *ibid.*, 47–64; and Robert S. Winter, "Whose Schubert?" *ibid.*, 94–101.

28 Mayer, who later visited Vienna and met Schubert and other members of the circle, was writing from Breslau, where Schober had lived from 1823 to 1825. Stadt- und Landesbibliothek Inv. No. 36477: "Ich bin der glücklichste der Menschen . . . – ich habe einen dreifarbigen Katz! . . . Ich habe mich seitdem du weg bist noch viel mehr auf die Katzen gelegt; es ist immer besser als wenn ich auf den Hund gekommen wäre. – Ich habe mit zwei schlanken, einem imposanten, einem schnurrigen, und zwei fleißigen Katzen Bekanntschaft gemacht. Ich könnte dir viel darüber erzählen, da ich aber nicht weiß ob meine Freunde auch die deinigen sind, so wäre es doppelt indiskret davon zu reden, erstens weil es dich ennuyiren könnte u zweitens weil ich meine Katzen compromittiren könnte."

Another association – Franz von Bruchmann's close relationship to the poet August, Graf von Platen, whose homosexuality has long been common knowledge among literary scholars, and whose ideals of intense male friendship have much in common with those of Schubert's friends – has also been overlooked in the controversy.

29 Kenner's remarks are discussed in Solomon, "Peacocks," 194 and 197.

30 Stadtbibliothek Inv. No. 36525: "Anton saß am Clavier im Zimmer der Fr. v. Brandt, und spielte während der einbrechenden Dämmerung, seine Variationen über das Almerlied, die neuen über das russische Volkslied, wovon ich das Thema schon so liebe, weil es in Moll ist – und den schwermüthigen Traunerlieder, und noch einiges. Die Töne zogen mich mit sich fort. . . . Auf einmal besann ich mich, daß die Kremsmünsterer morgen fort müssen, es zog mich zu ihnen. . . . Dann blieb ich dort zwischen ihnen stehen, gab dem freundlichen Kahl die rechte Hand und legte die linke um unsern guten Ferdinand, der Arm in Arm mit Kenner dasaß. Er zog mich mit seinem rechten Arm näher an sich, und wie so die Töne recht in die Seele

redeten, fühlte ich den leisen, innigen Druck ihrer Hände, und ich musste ihnen wechselweise ins Gesicht schauen und in die lieben Augen. Wie sie still da sassen, angenehm bewegt von der Musik, und doch so friedlich und heiter, und ich sie so ansah, da dacht' ich: Ihr Guten, Ihr seid wohl glücklich in eurer Unschuld. Euch macht die Musik weicher, aber nicht traurig, nicht unruhig; was euer Herz verlangt, das faßt Ihr in der Hand eines Freundes, und andere Wünsche kennt Ihr nicht, denen die Melodie nur höhere Wellen gibt."

31   Prosl, *Freundeskreis*, 47.

32   The correspondence of Kupelwieser and Lutz is preserved in a twentieth-century manuscript copy in the Niederösterreichisches Landesmuseum in Vienna. Some of the letters are excerpted in *SDB*, and more extensively in Rupert Feuchtmüller, *Leopold Kupelwieser und die Kunst der österreichischen Spätromantik* (Vienna, 1970); Feuchtmüller also includes an index to the letters.

33   The concept of homosocial bonding as crucial to nineteenth-century society is developed by Eve Kosofsky Sedgwick, *Between Men: English Literature and Male Homosocial Desire* (New York, 1985).

34   Solomon, "Peacocks," 205.

35   Muxfeldt, "Political Crimes," 61–64.

36   Reed, *Schubert*, 81.

37   Virgil Nemoianu, *The Taming of Romanticism: European Literature and the Age of Biedermeier* (Harvard Studies in Comparative Literature, XXXVII) (Cambridge, Mass., and London, 1984), 40. Compare Schubert's own poem, "Klage an das Volk!", from his letter to Schober of September 21, 1824, which, after bemoaning the inactive and powerless present, concludes, "only to you, O sacred art, is it still granted to depict in images the time of power and deeds, to soften a little the great pain that can never reconcile that time with our fate." My translation. For the German text, see Deutsch, ed., *Schubert: Die Dokumente seines Lebens* in *NSA* (Kassel, 1964), VIII/5, 258–59. For a comprehensive survey of the Biedermeier and the associated literature, see Friedrich Sengle, *Biedermeierzeit: deutsche Literatur im Spannungsfeld zwischen Restauration und Revolution, 1815–1848*, 3 vols. (Stuttgart, 1971–80).

38   For further discussion of the Biedermeier in relation to Schubert, see Gramit, "Schubert and the Biedermeier" and the literature cited there.

39   See Gramit, *Intellectual and Aesthetic Tenets*, 151–54.

40   For the German text, see Walburga Litschauer, ed., *Neue Dokumente zum Schubert-Kreis: Aus Briefen und Tagebüchern seiner Freunde* (Vienna, 1986), 54.

41   This interpretation draws on the ideas of Michel de Certeau, *The Practice of Everyday Life*, trans. Steven F. Rendall (Berkeley and Los Angeles, 1984), see, in particular, pp. 37–38 on the tactical use of wit.

4   *Schubert's inflections of Classical form*

1   In fact, the poet Johann Chrysostomus Senn, known for his liberal views, was arrested along with Schubert two years before Schubert set his text. Senn was

deported after fourteen months' imprisonment. See John Reed, *The Schubert Song Companion* (Manchester, 1985), 384 and 479.

2   See my *Sonata Forms* (New York, 2nd edn 1988), 256–57.

3   For discussion of this development section see *ibid.*, 360–62. The second subject of this movement also begins with two phrases of five bars, but only by prolonging the last chord of each phrase for a full bar: this functions not like a five-bar rhythm, but like four bars with a fermata or pause.

4   I have given other examples in *The Frontiers of Meaning: Three Informal Lectures on Music* (New York, 1994).

5   Schubert and his poets

1   See Dietrich Berke, "Zu einigen anonymen Texten Schubertscher Lieder," *Die Musikforschung* 22 (1969), 485–89; Walther Dürr, "Schubert's Songs and their Poetry: Reflections on the Poetic Aspects of Song Composition," in *Schubert Studies: Problems of Style and Chronology*, ed. Eva Badura-Skoda and Peter Branscombe (Cambridge, 1982), 1–24; Hans Joachim Kreutzer, "Schubert und die literarische Situation seiner Zeit," in *Franz Schubert: Jahre der Krise 1818–1823 (Arnold Feil zum 60. Geburtstag)*, ed. Werner Aderhold, Walther Dürr, and Walburga Litschauer (Kassel, 1985), 29–38; and Herbert Zeman, "Franz Schuberts Teilhabe an der österreichischen literarischen Kultur seiner Zeit," in *Schubert-Kongreß Wien 1978: Bericht*, ed. Otto Brusatti (Graz, 1979).

2   Heinrich Kreissle von Hellborn, *Franz Schubert* (Vienna, 1865), 496.

3   See the fourth and final chapter of my *Schubert's Poets and the Making of Lieder* (Cambridge, 1996) for more on the Schulze songs.

4   Schubert would surely have known of Heinrich Josef Edler von Collin's (1722–1811) connection to Beethoven, who admired Heinrich's verse-tragedies on classical themes and wrote an overture (Op. 62) for the poet's drama *Corialan* in 1807.

5   Ewan West, *Schubert's Lieder in Context: Aspects of Song in Vienna 1778–1828* (PhD diss., Oxford University, 1989), 262.

6   There is considerable useful information about Schubert's poets (and much else pertaining to his Lieder), albeit necessarily presented in capsule form, in section II, "The authors," of John Reed's *The Schubert Song Companion* (Manchester, 1985), 461–81.

7   See Helena Jansen, *Karoline Pichlers Schaffen und Weltanschauung im Rahmen ihrer Zeit* (Graz, 1936), and Gertrude Prohaska, *Der literarische Salon der Karoline Pichler* (PhD diss., University of Vienna, 1946).

8   *SMF* 182–83. See also Ludwig Landshoff, *Johann Rudolph Zumsteeg (1750–1802): Ein Beitrag zur Geschichte des Liedes und der Ballade* (Berlin 1902); Günther Maier, *Die Lieder Johann Rudolf Zumsteegs und ihr Verhältnis zu Schubert* (Göppingen, 1971); Franz Szymichowski, *Johann Rudolf Zumsteeg als Komponist von Balladen und Monodien* (PhD diss., University of Frankfurt am Main, 1932); Jürgen Mainka, *Das Liedschaffen Franz Schuberts in den Jahren 1815 und 1816: Auseinandersetzung mit der Liedtradition des 18. Jahrhunderts* (PhD diss., Berlin Technische Universität, 1958); Edith

Schnapper, *Die Gesänge des jungen Schubert vor dem Durchbruch des romantischen Liedprinzips* (Bern and Leipzig, 1937); and Willy Spilling, *Die Problematik des Schubertschen Liedes um das Jahr 1815* (PhD diss., University of Prague, 1931). See also Herbert Zeman, "Dichtung und Musik: Zur Entwicklung des österreichischen Kunstliedes vom 18. bis zum 19. Jahrhundert," in *Musik und Dichtung: Festschrift Anton Dermota zum 70. Geburtstag,* ed. H. Zeman (Vienna, 1980), 20–34, and the same author's *Die Österreichische Literatur: Ihr Profil an der Wende von 18. zum 19. Jahrhundert (1750–1830)* (Graz, 1979).

9   See my "Memory, Identity, and the Uses of the Past: Schubert and Luciano Berio's Recital I (for Cathy)," in *Franz Schubert – Der Fortschrittliche? Analysen–Perspektiven–Fakten,* ed. Erich Wolfgang Partsch (Tutzing, 1989), 231–48. Berio quotes *Der Jüngling an der Quelle,* and both Salis-Seewis's poem and Schubert's setting are discussed in this article.

10   See Barbara Kinsey, "Schubert and the Poems of Ossian," *Music Review* 34 (1973), 22–29.

11   David Gramit, *The Intellectual and Aesthetic Tenets of Franz Schubert's Circle* (PhD diss., Duke University, 1987), 54–55.

12   See Richard Kramer, "Der Jüngling am Bache: Schubert at the Source," in *Distant Cycles: Schubert and the Conceiving of Song* (Chicago, 1994), 25–46.

13   An early example of Schubert's discomfiture with Schiller's "Denk-Poesie," or "thought poetry" (versified philosophy), and the reasons for that discomfiture can be found in the setting of *Hoffnung* (D251), composed on August 7, 1815. The poem is a miniature philosophical meditation to the effect that the world waxes old and then young, while humanity is born to strive for betterment. Hope, Youth, the World, Mankind, etc. appear in this tiny didactic work, but no "I," no one poetic speaker. Schubert strives for some sort of profundity by setting the tiny song in the unusual key of G flat major, but that is hardly sufficient to create by itself a musical analogue to philosophical musings. Schubert returned to the same poem, possibly in 1817, and adopted an entirely different approach (D637).

14   The two most recent biographical studies of Goethe are Nicholas Boyle, *Goethe: The Poet and the Age,* vol. I, *The Poetry of Desire (1749–1790)* (Oxford, 1991), and Karl Otto Conrady, *Goethe: Leben und Werk* (Frankfurt am Main, 1987). The second volume of Boyle's biography, entitled *The Age of Renunciation 1790–1832,* is forthcoming.

15   The existing bibliography on Schubert and Goethe includes: Friedrich Blume, "Goethes *Mondlied* in Schuberts Kompositionen," *Der Bär: Jahrbuch von Breitkopf & Härtel* (1928), 31–58, reprinted in *Syntagma Musicologicum,* ed. Martin Ruhnke (Kassel, 1963), 813–33; Marius Flothuis, "Franz Schubert's Compositions to Poems from Goethe's 'Wilhelm Meister's Lehrjahre'," in *Notes on Notes: Selected Essays by Marius Flothuis,* ed. Sylvia Broere-Moore (Amsterdam, 1974), 87–138; Walter Frisch, "Schubert's *Nähe des Geliebten* (D162): Transformation of the *Volkston,*" in *Schubert: Critical and Analytical Studies,* ed. Walter Frisch (Lincoln, Nebr., 1986), 175–99; Joseph Müller-Blattau, "Franz Schubert, der Sänger Goethes," in *Goethe und die Meister der*

Musik (Stuttgart, 1969), 62–80; Walther Dürr, "Aus Schuberts erstem Publikationsplan: Zwei Hefte mit Liedern von Goethe," in *Schubert-Studien: Festgabe der Österreichischen Akademie der Wissenschaften zum Schubert-Jahr 1978*, ed. Franz Grasberger and Othmar Wesseley (Vienna, 1978), 43–56.

16 Robert S. Winter makes this observation in "Whose Schubert?", *19th-Century Music* 17 (1993), 101.

17 Rita Steblin, "Wilhelm Müllers Aufenthalt in Wien im Jahre 1817: Eine Verbindung zu Schubert durch Schlechta," *Vom Pasqualatihaus: Musikwissenschaftliche Perspektiven aus Wien* 4 (Fall 1994), 19–26. Steblin observes that Müller and Schubert might have been in the same place at the same time on at least one occasion: a performance of Müller's poem "Der Glockenguß zu Breslau" on December 22, 1817, at the Leopoldstadt theatre along with the tale "Der Gang zum Hochgerichte" by Schubert's friend Franz von Schlechta, whose "Auf einen Kirchhof" Schubert had already set to music (D151). See also my *Retracing a Winter's Journey: Schubert's Winterreise* (Ithaca, 1991) and *Schubert: Die schöne Müllerin* (Cambridge, 1992) for more on Müller.

18 *Musen-Almanach für das Jahr 1814* (Vienna), 244.

19 Kristina Muxfeldt, *Schubert Song Studies* (PhD diss., State University of New York at Stony Brook, 1991), chapter 3, "Interpretation and Revision of the Poetic Model," 75–126; see her chapter in the present volume in which she offers a detailed discussion of the alterations to *Nachtviolen*.

20 See chapter 4 of my *Schubert, Müller and Die schöne Müllerin* (Cambridge, forthcoming) for a more complete discussion of these omissions.

21 Maurice J. E. Brown, *Essays on Schubert*, (New York, 1966), 268. The *NSA* similarly distinguishes between "Fassung" and "Bearbeitung."

22 Marius Flothuis, "Schubert Revises Schubert," in *Schubert Studies*, 61–84, and Hans Holländer, "Franz Schubert's Repeated Settings of the Same Song-Texts," *Musical Quarterly* 14 (1928), 563–74.

23 See my forthcoming study "Cupid Revised: an erotic borrowing in Schubert's Early Songs."

6 *Schubert's songs*

1 The importance of these arrangements is suggested by Joseph Kerman "*An die ferne Geliebte*," in *Beethoven Studies* 1, ed. Alan Tyson (New York, 1973), 133.

2 Robert Schumann, *Gesammelte Schriften über Musik und Musiker*, ed. Martin Kreissig, 2 vols. (Leipzig, 1914), II: 147.

3 The phenomenon is discussed, among other places, in Susan Youens's *Schubert: Die schöne Müllerin* (Cambridge, 1992), 22–30.

4 As valuable as the *NSA* is in many other respects, the editorial decision to abandon any effort at refining the chronology of the songs in favor of highlighting their publication groupings ensures that the *ASA* will remain an indispensable tool for scholars for a long time to come. The new edition reserves the first five volumes for songs that Schubert saw through to

publication, relegating the remaining songs (in what is left of the chronologically based order of their presentation in the new Deutsch *Verzeichnis*) to nine subsequent volumes. With the roughly two hundred published songs pulled out of any chronology, it is extremely difficult to gain a sense of compositional context for any of them by referring only to the new edition.

5   The remarkably close relationship between the tight motivic development in *Dass sie hier gewesen* and the development of images in the poem has been admired by various critics. In Charles Rosen's recent account of this and several other Schubert songs in a lecture entitled "Explaining the Obvious," the method by which this is accomplished is recognized as one instance of a more general mode of developing the contour and range of the motivic material found with great frequency in Schubert. See Charles Rosen's *The Frontiers of Meaning: Three Informal Lectures on Music* (New York, 1994), 72–126.

6   Richard Kramer offers a compelling rehearing of the harmonic underpinning of the opening measures of *Nähe des Geliebten* (and much else in the song, including provocative speculations on the significance of G flat as its key) in his *Distant Cycles: Schubert and the Conceiving of Song* (Chicago, 1994), 13–16. An earlier essay by Walter Frisch, "Schubert's 'Nähe des Geliebten' (D162): Transformation of the *Volkston*," in *Schubert: Critical and Analytical Studies*, ed. Walter Frisch (Lincoln, Nebr., 1986), 175–99, offers much insight into Schubert's relation to earlier traditions.

7   In Reichardt's music these rarely go beyond mechanical accompanimental figurations which establish a general mood (as in his *Musensohn*, or *Euphrosyne*). Schubert uses such figures as a stable "identity" which can be made to undergo change and development to stimulate an analogy with the physical or mental motions suggested by the poem.

8   The review in the Leipzig *Allgemeine musikalische Zeitung* of June 24, 1824 is among the most damning (*SDB* 478–79).

9   Donald Francis Tovey, "Franz Schubert," in *The Main Stream of Music and Other Essays* (New York, 1959), 109–10.

10   In his diary on June 13, 1816, Schubert modestly ascribed the success of *Rastlose Liebe* to the musicality of Goethe's poetic genius (*SDB* 86). "Musical poetry" is defined by Schiller in the essay "On Naïve and Sentimental Poetry" (1795–96) as poetry which, like music, produces a given state of mind without relying on the imitation of a specific object, as do the plastic arts. This resonates well with the abstract imagery Goethe's poetic persona conjures in "Rastlose Liebe." Musical poetry, according to Schiller, "does not refer principally to the actual and material elements of music in poetry, but more generally, to all those effects which poetry is able to produce without subordinating the imagination to a specific object." The remark arises in a note on Klopstock; see Friedrich Schiller, *"Naive and Sentimental Poetry" and "On the Sublime". Two Essays*, Trans. with introduction and notes by Julius A. Elias (New York, 1966), 133.

11   A comparison with settings of the same text by other composers is instructive. The settings by Zelter and Reichardt – conveniently reprinted and discussed in Thrasybulos Georgiades's *Musik und Lyrik* (Göttingen, 1967), 63–69 – are both much more concerned with matching each change in poetic voice with a comparable musical articulation. An incomplete, but substantial, draft by Beethoven also survives. A comparison of Schubert's treatment of a small detail, the fleeting, but powerful, harmonic inflection on the "eigen" of "Ach, wie so eigen schaffet es Schmerzen," with Beethoven's protracted stress of the same word through multiple repetition is immensely revealing of the radical difference in their approaches. The best published transcription of the sketch is in Douglas Johnson's *Beethoven's Early Sketches in the Fischoff Miscellany* (PhD diss., Berkeley, 1977), 456–59.

12   The manuscript is today split in two and housed half in the University library in Oslo, and half at the Austrian National Library. Together with *Nachtviolen*, which is divided between the two halves of the manuscript, the autograph originally contained at least two other Mayrhofer songs, *Heliopolis I* and *Heliopolis II*, of which only the former was published while Schubert was still alive.

13   The manuscript of the poems is currently housed in the *Handschriftensammlung* of the Vienna Stadtbibliothek.

14   David Gramit offers a more explicit biographical interpretation of the textual alterations in his "Schubert and the Biedermeier: the Aesthetics of Johann Mayrhofer's *Heliopolis*," *Music and Letters* 74 (1993), 355–82. I too have discussed this and other similar revisions before both in my dissertation (*Schubert Song Studies*, State University of New York at Stony Brook, 1991) and in a paper entitled "Schubert's Poetic Revisions," delivered at the American Musicological Society meeting in Pittsburgh in 1992. Among the most impressive additional examples are the revisions to *Versunken* (D715), on a poem by Goethe, and the Rückert song *Greisengesang* (D778).

7   Schubert's social music

I would like to thank Bryan Gilliam for many helpful comments on an earlier draft of this chapter.

1   Alfred Einstein, *Schubert: A Musical Portrait* (New York, 1951), 29.

2   For a discussion of this abstract hierarchy, see Carl Dahlhaus, "Was ist eine musikalische Gattung?", *Neue Zeitschrift für Musik* 135 (1974), 620–25.

3   Einstein, *Schubert*, 254 and 246.

4   Alice M. Hanson, *Musical Life in Biedermeier Vienna* (Cambridge, 1985), 121.

5   *Ibid.* In other words, Schubert's audiences were for the most part not connoisseurs but rather discriminating amateurs.

6   *Ibid.*, 86.

7   Otto Biba, "Franz Schubert in den musikalischen Abendunterhaltungen der Gesellschaft der Musikfreunde," in *Schubert-Studien: Festgabe der Österreichischen Akademie der Wissenschaften zum Schubert-Jahr 1978*, ed. Franz Grasberger and Othmar Wessely (Vienna, 1978), 8.

8   The other published collections were *Walzer, Ländler und Ecossaisen*, Op. 18
     (1823); *Deutsche Tänze und Ecossaisen*, Op. 33 (1825); *Galoppe [sic] et
     Ecossaises*, Op. 49 (1825); *Valses sentimentales*, Op. 50 (1825); *Hommage aux
     belles Viennoises. Wiener Damen-Ländler (und Ecossaisen)*, Op. 67 (1826);
     Valses nobles, Op. 77 (1827); *Grätzer Walzer*, Op. 91 (1828). For a discussion
     of the anthologies, see Walburga Litschauer, *NSA* (Kassel, 1990), VII/ii/6,
     Vorwort.

9   Maurice J. E. Brown, "The Dance-Music Manuscripts," in his *Essays on
     Schubert* (New York, 1966), 242. Walburga Litschauer notes that Schubert's
     friends made no distinction between the German dance and the waltz. See
     Litschauer, *NSA* VII/ii/6, *Vorwort*.

10 Walburga Litschauer, "Franz Schuberts Tänze – zwischen Improvisation und
     Werk," *Musiktheorie* 10 (1995), 3–9.

11 Brown, "The Story of the 'Trauerwalzer'," in *Essays on Schubert*, 291.

12 Brown, *Schubert: A Critical Biography* (New York, 1978), 229–30.

13 Brown, "The Dance-Music Manuscripts." Litschauer identifies the
     composition of "chains" of dances, especially Ländler, in the same key as a folk
     practice. See Litschauer, "Franz Schuberts Tänze," 6.

14 Schubert thus wrote them down the day after the first public performance of
     his works. Did he perhaps improvise them at a party after the concert?

15 A number of dances seem to begin in one key, only to have the second section
     open and close in its relative major or minor. See, for example, the following
     écossaises from MS 37: D977, numbers 5 and 8; and D145 (Op. 18), number
     2.

16 For discussions of periods and sentences, see Arnold Schoenberg,
     Fundamentals of Musical Composition, ed. Gerald Strang and Leonard Stein
     (London, 1967), and Erwin Ratz, *Einführung in die musikalische Formenlehre*
     (Vienna, 1973).

17 Litschauer, "Franz Schuberts Tänze," 6.

18 David Brodbeck, "Dance Music as High Art: Schubert's Twelve Ländler, Op.
     171 (D790)," in *Schubert: Critical and Analytical Studies*, ed. Walter Frisch
     (Lincoln, Nebr., 1986), 44.

19 Einstein, *Schubert*, 199 and 216. Brown uses these Ländler several times in his
     biography to illustrate fine points of Schubert's style. See Brown, *Schubert*,
     129, 213, and 221.

20 David Brodbeck, "Brahms's Edition of Twenty Schubert Ländler: an Essay in
     Criticism," in *Brahms Studies: Analytical and Historical Perspectives. Papers
     Delivered at the International Brahms Conference, Washington, D.C., 5–8 May
     1983*, ed. George S. Bozarth (London, 1990), 229–50.

21 Robert Schumann, *On Music and Musicians*, ed. Konrad Wolff, trans. Paul
     Rosenfeld (New York, 1969), 125.

22 Hanson, *Musical Life*, 118.

23 Dahlhaus, "Was ist eine musikalische Gattung?", 620–21.

24 Einstein, *Schubert*, 241. For discussions of the "Grand Duo" and the great F
     Minor Fantasy (D940) in the present volume, see the chapters by Charles
     Rosen and William Kinderman, respectively.

25   Einstein, *Schubert*, 282.

26   The marches appeared as Opp. 27 (D602), 40 (D819), 51 (D733), 55 (D859), 63 No. 1 (D823), 66 (D885); the variations as Opp. 10 (D624), 35 (D813), 82 No. 1 (D908), and 84 No. 1 (D823); the polonaises as Opp. 61 (D824) and 75 (D599). The remaining works are the *Rondeau brillant* (Op. 84 No. 2, D823), the Rondo in A (Op. 107, D951), the Overture in F (Op. 34, D675), and the *Divertissement à l'hongroise* (Op. 54, D818).

27   Jonathan Bellman, "Toward a Lexicon for the *Style hongrois*," *Journal of Musicology* 9 (1991), 214–37.

28   Einstein, *Schubert*, 77, 133, 244–45, 280.

29   Schubert modeled his "Trout" Quintet on Hummel's arrangement for the same ensemble of his own Septet. See Basil Smallman, *The Piano Quartet and Quintet: Style, Structure, and Scoring* (Oxford, 1994), 29. Hummel's quintet, however, makes almost no use of the texture characteristic of Schubert's work.

30   Dietrich Berke, *NSA* (Kassel, 1974), III/4, *Vorwort*.

31   The one female partsong to appear in print during Schubert's lifetime was *Coronach* (Op. 52 No. 4, D836); see below.

32   Biba, "Schubert in den musikalischen Abendunterhaltungen," 10.

33   Berke, *NSA*, III/4, *Vorwort*.

34   Schubert had first attempted to set Goethe's poem as a Lied in September 1816, but he did not complete that setting. His work with the text culminated in the final partsong version discussed below.

35   Lawrence Kramer writes of the "sudden extravagance of Mignon's rhetoric" at these lines in "Decadence and Desire: The *Wilhelm Meister* Songs of Wolf and Schubert," *19th-Century Music* 10 (1987), 239.

36   Schubert composed *Gott in der Natur* (D757), *Ständchen* (D920), and *Mirjams Siegesgesang* (D942) for Anna Fröhlich.

37   For an account of the male partsongs, see Maurice J. E. Brown, "The Part-Songs for Male Voices," in his *Essays on Schubert*, 59–84.

38   Walter Dürr, "Zwischen Liedertafel und Männergesang-Verein: Schuberts mehrstimmige Gesänge," in *Logos Musicae: Festschrift für Albert Palm*, ed. Rüdiger Görner (Wiesbaden, 1982), 36–54; Dietrich Berke, "'Gesang der Geister über den Wassern': Die mehrstimmigen Gesänge," in *Franz Schubert: Jahre der Krise 1818–1823 (Arnold Feil zum 60. Geburtstag)*, ed. Werner Aderhold, Walther Dürr, and Walburga Litschauer (Kassel, 1985), 39–47.

39   These partsongs were Opp. 11 (*Das Dörfchen, Die Nachtigall*, and *Geist der Liebe*), 16 (*Frühlingsgesang* and *Naturgenuss*), and 17 (*Jünglingswonne, Liebe, Zum Rundetanz*, and *Die Nacht*).

40   Not all of the partsongs described here as being in three sections, however, are ternary forms.

8 *Schubert's piano music*

1   See Theodor W. Adorno, "Schubert," in *Moments musicaux* (Frankfurt, 1964), 18–36. This essay originally dates from 1928.

2   For recent discussions of the problems of assessing Schubert's total output of

sonatas, including fragmentary works, see Eva Badura-Skoda, "The Piano Works of Schubert," in *Nineteenth-Century Piano Music*, ed. R. Larry Todd (New York, 1990), 100–02; and Andreas Krause, *Die Klaviersonaten Franz Schuberts: Form – Gattung – Ästhetik* (Kassel and New York, 1992), 13–15.

3   *Franz Schubert: Klaviersonaten Band III. Frühe und unvollendete Sonaten*, ed. Paul Badura-Skoda (Munich, 1976). See also the edition prepared by Howard Ferguson of the complete piano sonatas including the unfinished works, 3 vols. (London, 1979).

4   Krause, for instance, has questioned the association of the A major movement (D604) with the F sharp Minor Sonata (D571/570), as well as the inclusion of four movements in the F Minor Sonata fragment (D625), arguing that the D flat Adagio (D505) is replaced by the scherzo, and that the work exists in two different, three-movement versions.

5   "Playing Schubert's Piano Sonatas," liner notes to the 1994 recording of the sonatas in A flat Major (D557), B flat Major (D575) and G Major (D894); London 440 307–2.

6   Peter Szondi, "Friedrich Schlegel und die romantische Ironie," in *Friedrich Schlegel und die Kunsttheorie seiner Zeit*, ed. Helmut Schanze (Darmstadt, 1985), 151, cited in Krause, *Die Klaviersonaten Franz Schuberts*, 114.

7   See in this regard the chapter "Unvollendetes," in Hans Gal, *Franz Schubert oder Die Melodie* (Frankfurt, 1970), 184–215; Eng. trans. as *Franz Schubert and the Essence of Melody* (London, 1974), 152–77.

8   See Schnebel, "Klangräume – Zeitklänge: Zweiter Versuch über Schubert," in *Musik-Konzepte Franz Schubert*, ed. Heinz-Klaus Metzger and Rainer Riehn (Munich, 1979), 95–96.

9   This relationship has been noted by various authors, including Hans Költzsch, *Franz Schubert in seinen Klaviersonaten* (Leipzig, 1927; rpt. Hildesheim and New York, 1976), 95; and Krause, *Die Klaviersonaten*, 131, 138. Geoffrey Saba has recorded the F Minor Sonata in a four-movement version completed by the late Prussian/Australian scholar W. A. Dullo: *Schubert Recital*, Innovative Music Productions Ltd. (1991), PCD 950. Wilhelm Kempff and many others played Erwin Ratz's completion of the F Minor Sonata (Universal Edition).

10   *Schubert*, trans. David Ascoli (London, 1951), 245.

11   *Schubert* (London, 1987), 137.

12   See *On Music and Musicians*, ed. Konrad Wolff, trans. Paul Rosenfeld (New York, 1969), 113.

13   Tobias Haslinger published the sonata in 1827 with the title "Fantasie, Andante, Menuetto und Allegretto"; critics responded to this title in the first reviews (*SDB* 674, 685, 693–94).

14   "Schubert's Last Sonatas," in *Music Sounded Out* (New York, 1990), 72–141. Brendel's most recent recordings of the later sonatas and other piano works have appeared with Philips Classics Productions.

15   Hans-Joachim Hinrichsen, *Untersuchungen zur Entwicklung der Sonatenform in der Instrumentalmusik Franz Schuberts* (Tutzing, 1994), 323–25.

16   Edward T. Cone, "Schubert's Beethoven," *The Musical Quarterly* 56 (1970), 779–93; Charles Rosen, *The Classical Style* (New York, 1971), 456–58.

17 Charles Fisk, "Schubert's Last Finales," unpublished paper presented at the annual meeting of the American Musicological Society, Oakland, 1990.

18 Tovey, "Schubert," in *Essays and Lectures on Music* (London, 1949), 119.

19 See Thomas Kabisch, *Liszt und Schubert* (Munich, 1984).

20 Einstein, *Schubert*, 324.

21 *On Music and Musicians*, 118–19.

22 *Schubert: The Final Years* (New York, 1972), 228.

23 For a more detailed discussion of the form of this work see Arthur Godel, "Zum Eigengesetz der Schubertschen Fantasien," in *Schubert-Kongreß: Wien 1978: Bericht*, ed. Otto Brusatti (Graz, 1979), 202–04; and my essay, "Schubert's Tragic Perspective," in *Schubert: Critical and Analytical Studies*, ed. Walter Frisch (Lincoln, Nebr., 1986), 75–82, from which some of the present discussion is drawn.

24 "Schubert's Piano Duets," *Musical Times* 117 (1976), 121.

9   *Schubert's chamber music*

1 Exceptions that prove the rule include the Variations for Flute and Piano on *Trockne Blumen* (D802), written for the flute virtuoso Ferdinand Bognar, and both the Rondo for Violin and Piano (D895) and the Fantasy for Violin and Piano (D934), written for the violinist Josef Slavjk. All three compositions, though composed late in his life, are among the least successful works of their period.

2 See "From Franz Schubert's Life" by his brother Ferdinand (*SDB* 912–13).

3 *SDB* 91, notes about Josef Doppler, and "On the Musical Evenings at Schubert's and his Father's Homes" by Leopold Sonnleithner, *SMF* 342.

4 Verbal communication in February 1974.

5 I have photocopies of parts for two overtures. Neither has a title, but I recognized one as the overture to Salieri's opera *Palmyra*.

6 See Martin Chusid, "Schubert's Overture for String Quintet and Cherubini's Overture to *Faniska*," *Journal of the American Musicological Society* 15 (1961), 78–84.

7 "Revisionsbericht," *ASA* 52.

8 Martin Chusid, *The Chamber Music of Schubert* (PhD diss., Univ. of California, Berkeley, 1961), 303–05 and 320–21. See also my article "Concerning Orchestral Style in Schubert's Earliest Chamber Music for Strings," in *Music in Performance and Society: Essays in Honor of Roland Jackson* (Warren, Mich., 1996).

9 Alfred Orel, *Der junge Schubert* (Vienna and Leipzig, 1941), 18.

10 According to Orel the fragmentary manuscript of a string quartet first movement in C minor (D103) was probably complete at one time. He completed the movement and it was published (score by Philharmonia of Vienna, 1939; parts by Robitschek, also of Vienna and the same year).

11 The sketching as a string trio allowed Schubert to compose the first movement of the quartet version in the incredibly short time of four and a half hours, as he noted on the autograph.

12   Carl Czerny, *School of Practical Composition* (London, 1848), I: 33. According to William Newman, *The Sonata Since Beethoven* (Chapel Hill, 1969), 787, the English translation was made from a German version dating from *c.* 1840. He points out, however, that the first German edition of this book was published by Simrock of Bonn in 1849–50, after the English edition.

13   *Franz Schubert: Jahre der Krise 1818–1823*, ed. Werner Aderhold, Walther Dürr, and Walburga Litschauer (Kassel, 1985).

14   "Revisionsbericht," *ASA* 82.

15   See Martin Chusid, "Schubert's Cyclic Compositions of 1824," *Acta Musicologica* 36 (1964), 37–45.

16   For more on Schubert's variations, see Maurice J. E. Brown, *Schubert's Variations* (London, 1954).

17   See note 15.

18   Schubert was to use the theme again for a set of variations, the Impromptu for Piano in B flat (D935, Op. 142 No. 3). As justification for multiple usage of a well-known theme of his own, Schubert may have had in mind Beethoven's employment of his Orchestral Contredanse No. 7 in the *Prometheus* music, as well as for two sets of themes and variations, Op. 35 for Piano, and the finale of the "Eroica" Symphony.

19   See also the beginning of the second part of the Ländler, mm. 9–16, and the beginning of the second part of the Scherzo, mm. 23–32.

20   Martin Chusid, *The Chamber Music of Schubert*, 293.

21   See the letter to his brother Ferdinand in *SDB* 363.

22   See Martin Chusid, "A Suggested Redating for the E-flat Piano Sonata," in *Schubert-Kongreß: Wien 1978: Bericht*, ed. Otto Brusatti (Graz, 1979), 37–44.

23   Schubert's early String Quartet in C Major (D32) and Haydn's String Quartet in C Major (Op. 76 No. 3, the "Emperor") also have minor finales. This is not a common phenomenon and it is of some interest that all three pieces mentioned are in the same key.

24   There are several "Tutti" and "Solo" indications in the autograph and a number of measures of the cello part have either noteheads with two stems or additional notes calling for a second part. Schubert seems to have had in mind performances with contrabass added, as in the "Trout" Quintet, or small string orchestra. See Arnold Feil, "Preface" to *NSA* VI/7, xiv.

25   The title no doubt refers to the origin of the piano trio from the accompanied piano sonata in which the cello part in particular tended to duplicate the bass of the keyboard part. See, for example, the piano trios of Haydn.

26   See Robert Winter, "Paper Studies and Schubert Research," in *Schubert Studies: Problems of Style and Chronology*, ed. Eva Badura-Skoda and Peter Branscombe (Cambridge, 1982), 248–49.

27   With rare exception, the many piano trios by Haydn are in two or three movements; those by Mozart are all in three. Only Beethoven wrote his piano trios most often in four movements.

28   Schuppanzigh had played with Beethoven at the keyboard for the first performance of the "Archduke" Trio on April 11, 1814. See Anton Schindler, *Beethoven as I Knew Him* (Chapel Hill, *c.* 1968), 171. He also led the group

performing one or both of Schubert's piano trios at their first performances. See *SDB* 698 (E flat Trio) and *SDB* 724–25 (B flat Trio?).

29   The premiere took place April 2, 1800. Elliot Forbes, ed. *Thayer's Life of Beethoven* (Princeton, rev. edn. 1967), 255.

30   The clarinettist in 1827 may have been George Klein (*SDB* 628).

31   Schubert also wrote an Octet for Winds in F Major (D72, 1813) of which a fragment of the first movement as well as the Minuet and finale survive.

32   Chusid, *The Chamber Music of Schubert*, 234–41.

33   As he was to do later in the first movement of the Piano Sonata in the same key (D960), also with tonal consequences later in the movement.

34   See diagram no. 8 in Chusid, "A Suggested Redating," 44.

10 *Schubert's orchestral music*

This essay is based on an article I wrote for *Thesis*, the magazine of the Graduate School and University Center of the City University of New York. "The Symphonies of Schubert: Pieces of a Puzzle" appeared in *Thesis* 3/2 (Fall 1989), 22–29. I should like to thank Jim Holt, editor, and Jerry Kisslinger, managing editor, for permission to draw from that article in this essay.

1   See Leonard Michael Griffel, *Schubert's Approach to the Symphony* (PhD diss., Columbia University, 1975), 11–13.

2   For a discussion of this issue, see Mi-Sook Han Hur, *Irregular Recapitulation in Schubert's Instrumental Works* (PhD diss., The City University of New York, 1992), 18–20, 26–28. On the related issue of the influence of overture style on Schubert's large-scale instrumental works, see two articles by Martin Chusid: "Schubert's Overture for String Quintet and Cherubini's Overture to *Faniska*," *Journal of the American Musicological Society* 15 (1962), 78–84; and "Das 'Orchestermässige' in Schuberts früher Streicherkammermusik," in *Zur Aufführungspraxis der Werke Franz Schuberts*, ed. Vera Schwarz (Munich, 1981), 77–86.

3   See an excellent discussion of Schubert's choice of D major in Brian Newbould, *Schubert and the Symphony: A New Perspective* (London and Exeter, 1992), 33–34.

4   Young Schubert would have known symphonies by not only the Viennese masters but also by a number of lesser composers in or near Vienna around the turn of the century, such as Ignaz Umlauf (1746–96), Franz Süssmayr (1766–1803), Anton Eberl (1765–1807), Joseph Wölfl (1773–1812), Leopold Kozeluch (1747–1818), Anton Wranitzky (1761–1820), Andreas Romberg (1767–1821), Franz Krommer (1759–1831), Friedrich Witt (1770–1836), Bernhard Romberg (1767–1841), and Adalbert Gyrowetz (1763–1850). Stylistic traits of the symphonies of the time include irregular phrasing, bold modulations, syncopated rhythms, episodes in minor keys, chromaticism, folk melodies, sudden changes of harmony, and lyrical passages – all of which became an integral part of Schubert's symphonic style.

5   See Josef von Spaun's obituary of Schubert, as revised by Anton Ottenwalt, *SDB* 866.

6   See Griffel, *Schubert's Approach*, 25–30.

7   For example, Schubert himself deleted twenty-four highly repetitious measures from the closing section of the exposition of the First Symphony's opening movement. Would that he had revised the Sixth Symphony's first development section, a boring series of statements of the exposition's closing material.

8   Leopold von Sonnleithner (1797–1873), author of several accounts of the history of music in Vienna during the first half of the nineteenth century, was an ardent admirer of Schubert's music. His recollections of both the Frischling and Hatwig orchestras are presented in "Musikalische Skizzen aus Alt-Wien," *Recensionen und Mittheilungen über Theater, Musik und bildende Kunst* (March 23, 1862), 177–80.

9   A facsimile edition of these sketches (and also D708A and D936A, discussed below) was published by Bärenreiter in 1978; the German conductor and musicologist Peter Gülke published both a transcription of these sketches and his own orchestral completions of them in 1982 (Edition Peters). These fragments were orchestrated also by the British scholar Brian Newbould in 1979–81. Recorded in London in 1982 and 1983, Newbould's versions may be heard in the complete set of Schubert symphonies issued by Philips in 1984: 412 176–2.

10 Gerald Abraham suggested that the *entr'acte* in B minor from the *Rosamunde* music (D797, 1823) is actually the finale to the "Unfinished" and should be performed as such. See "Finishing the Unfinished," *Musical Times* 112 (June 1971), 547–48. I remain unconvinced.

11 Program notes for the Crystal Palace Season, 1880–81, 576.

12 Maynard Solomon, "Schubert and Beethoven," *19th-Century Music* 3 (1979), 115.

13 We know very well how Brahms much later put off completing a first symphony for at least fifteen years because he felt oppressed by the shadow of Beethoven. And we may also recall that Beethoven himself was not up to finishing his first symphony until the year 1800, when he was almost thirty, conceivably because he, too, feared comparison with the master who had preceded him, Joseph Haydn, whose last London Symphonies had been completed in 1795. (Probably for the same reason, Beethoven had not allowed the publication of any of his string quartets until 1801.)

14 Newbould, *Schubert and the Symphony*, 298–99, suggests that the D936A sketches represent the "Last" (and, therefore, the "Lost") Symphony of Schubert, the one that Eduard von Bauernfeld had in mind when he spoke of an 1828 symphony.

15 See Robert Winter, "Paper Studies and the Future of Schubert Research," in *Schubert Studies: Problems of Style and Chronology*, ed. Eva Badura-Skoda and Peter Branscombe (Cambridge, 1982), 209–75.

16 There is no clear record of an attempt by Schubert to sell this work to a publisher, but only his reference to "a symphony" in the letter to B. Schott's Söhne cited above (see *SDB* 739–40).

314 Notes to pages 203–08

17 See Otto Biba, "Schubert's Position in Viennese Musical Life," *19th-Century Music* 3 (1979), 107–08.

11 *Schubert's religious and choral music*

1 The hymn is certainly *Ellens Gesang III*, "Hymne an die Jungfrau" (D839), better known as *Ave Maria*. Schubert composed songs on religious texts throughout his career; among them are masterpieces such as the four "Hymns" on Novalis texts (D659–62). They do not constitute an independent sub-genre within the entire corpus of Schubert's songs, but rather draw on various song styles. For this reason, as well as for limitations of space, they cannot be considered in this essay.

2 See Alice M. Hanson, *Musical Life in Biedermeier Vienna* (Cambridge, 1985), 127ff., for a description of the cynical attitudes toward the clergy and quotations from contemporary observers about the misuse of church services for social interaction and display of fashionable clothing.

3 The principal study in English is Ronald Stringham's unpublished PhD dissertation, *The Masses of Franz Schubert* (Cornell University, 1964). It has been largely superseded by Hans Jaskulsky's book, *Die lateinischen Messen Franz Schuberts* (Mainz, 1986). Significant topical essays which are not later cited include Kurt von Fischer, "Bemerkungen zu Schuberts As-dur-Messe," in *Franz Schubert: Jahre der Krise 1818–1823*, ed. Werner Aderhold, Walther Dürr, and Walburga Litschauer (Kassel, 1985), 121–29; and Hans Jancik, "Franz Schubert und die Wiener Kirchenmusik seiner Zeit," in *Franz Schubert und die Pfarrkirche Lichtental* (Vienna, 1978), 28–31.

4 See Jaskulsky, *Messen*, 52–73, for a review of the literature and his own view that the omissions were not coincidental; were not undertaken for purely musical reasons; nor are they attributable only to a faulty copy of the Mass text, an argument advanced by Paul Badura-Skoda in his essay "On Schubert's Mass Texts," *American Choral Review* 32 (Winter–Spring 1990), 5–7. See also Leopold Nowak, "Franz Schuberts Kirchennmusik," in *Bericht über den Internationalen Kongress für Schubertforschung Wien 25. bis 29. November 1928* (Augsburg, 1929), 183–87; and Reinhard van Hoorickx, "Textänderungen in Schuberts Messen," in *Schubert-Kongreß: Wien 1978: Bericht*, ed. Otto Brusatti (Graz, 1979), 249–54.

5 See Talia Pecker Berio in the foreword to the first volume of the Masses: *Messen I* in *NSA* (Kassel, 1990), I/1, ix, who views Mass No. 6 as a "confrontation with faith and with the liturgical text as well as an opening to new [musical] paths, which death abruptly ended."

6 Stringham, *Masses*, 89–91.

7 See Jaskulsky, *Messen*, 20–31. In 1827 the Hofkapellmeister Joseph Eybler justified his denial of Schubert's request for a court performance of the Mass in A flat with the argument that it is not in the style that the Kaiser "loves," but Jaskulsky contends that Eybler invented this reason because he favored the court composer Josef Weigl and wanted to avoid paying the honorarium due Schubert if his Mass was accepted for performance.

8   There is a wealth of material on formal organization. Important English-language contributions include Stringham's dissertation (see n. 3) and Bruce MacIntyre's book, *The Viennese Concerted Mass of the Early Classic Period* (Ann Arbor, 1986). Among German authors, Jaskulsky treats formal problems in Schubert's Masses against the backdrop of Austrian convention, and, in her recent dissertation (*Das Gloria in Beethovens Missa Solemnis* [University of Munich, 1994], 9–27), Birgit Lodes presents an in-depth discussion of the tradition of Gloria settings.

9   A decree of the Hofkanzlei of December 19, 1806, forbade women singing in church unless they were related to the choir director or teacher of the school associated with the church at which they were to sing. The decree was intended to prevent operatic styles in liturgical music and thus ensure that the music preserved a "contemplative" rather than "entertaining" character; see Otto Biba, "Besetzungsverhältnisse in der Wiener Kirchenmusik," in *Zur Aufführungspraxis der Werke Franz Schuberts*, ed. Vera Schwarz (Munich, 1978), 180–87. In 1833 Archbishop Mulde, the highest officer of the Austrian Catholic church, forbade the performance of any non-liturgical works in churches, even including oratorios; see Frank Frederick Mueller Jr., *The Austrian Mass between Schubert and Bruckner* (DMA thesis, University of Illinois at Urbana-Champaign, 1973), 8.

10 The Mass in F was first performed in October 1814; Schubert conducted and friends and members of his family participated, as they did for later religious music. It is likely that the church hired additional players (and perhaps singers) for the performance, for the ensemble requirements exceeded the normal resources of a small suburban church. Salieri, with whom Schubert had studied at the Stadtkonvikt, attended the Mass and probably helped to arrange a performance in Vienna shortly thereafter. These performances were the first public hearings of Schubert's music.

11 See Otto Biba, "Kirchenmusikalische Praxis zu Schuberts Zeit," in *Franz Schubert: Jahre der Krise 1818–1823*, 113–21, and "Besetzungsverhältnisse," 180–87. According to Biba, the consistently high solo and choral soprano parts in Schubert's Masses represent a departure from the practice forbidding women singers in liturgical performance (see n. 9). Biba has not provided documentary evidence that women sang in the choruses performing Schubert's Masses in his lifetime.

12 See Leopold M. Kantner, "Franz Schuberts Kirchenmusik auf dem Hintergrund stilistischer Zusammenhänge und persönlicher Einstellung," in *Schubert-Studien: Festgabe der Österreichischen Akademie der Wissenschaften zum Schubert-Jahr 1978*, ed. Franz Grasberger and Othmar Wessely (Vienna, 1978), 131–41.

13 Jaskulsky, *Messen*, 117.

14 The canon for solo voices in the Benedictus is clearly modeled after the quintet in the first act of *Fidelio*, but no ideological implications are evident here. Other references to Beethoven's works include Nathanael's aria in the second act of *Lazarus*, whose heroism is reminiscent of Florestan's in *Fidelio*, Maria's first aria in the first act of the same work that cites the first song in *An*

die ferne Geliebte, and the "Dona nobis pacem" of the Mass in A Flat, which owes a debt to the first movement of the violin concerto.

15 Jaskulsky, *Messen,* 140.

16 For the publication of the Mass in 1825 (with a dedication to Holzer) Schubert composed two oboe (or clarinet) parts, two trumpet parts and a timpani part for the first edition by Diabelli in 1825. It appears in this form in both editions of the complete works. Ferdinand Schubert composed parts for trumpets and timpani to the Mass in G while his brother still lived and in 1847 added oboes and bassoons, at which time he published the Mass under his own name. These additions were doubtlessly undertaken as a concession to contemporary preference for large orchestral ensembles. Schubert recomposed movements in several Masses: a more monumental "Dona nobis pacem" for the Mass in F (1815), a Benedictus with a much simpler soprano solo part for the Mass in G (1828? the original part had been composed for Therese Grob), and made numerous revisions to the Credo of the Mass in A flat including a new, much stricter fugue for "cum sancto spiritu."

17 Jaskulsky, *Messen,* 117.

18 Schubert planned to publish the three choral works as a group; this plan was realized by Carl Czerny in 1829.

19 See Einstein, *Schubert: A Musical Portrait* (New York, 1951), p. 91.

20 The libretto of 1778, when the original setting by Rolle was performed, designates the three parts as "Handlungen," the German equivalent of act.

21 Schubert might also have taken the underlying key scheme, F minor moving to F major, from Pergolesi's setting.

22 While the models for the overall ensemble and the melodic style could only be found in Bach's sacred music, Schubert might well have encountered this technique – one of Bach's most idiosyncratic and powerful – in his keyboard music, for example the B flat Minor Prelude from the second book of the *Well-Tempered Clavier.* See Einstein (*Schubert,* 298) for borrowings in Mass No. 6 from both books of the *Well-Tempered Clavier.*

23 Schubert attended private concerts of historical music at the home of Raphael Georg Kiesewetter, at which Bach's motet *Jesu meine Freude* was sung in 1818 and 1823 and the *Magnificat* setting was regularly performed. The *Magnificat* contains several arias with an obbligato instrumental part; the oboe part and the chromatic, minor-mode pathos of No. 3 "Quia respexit humilitatem," place it in a close stylistic and expressive relationship to "Ach was hätten wir empfunden." Whether the former served as a direct model for the latter cannot be determined on the basis of the available evidence. See Herfrid Kier, *Raphael Georg Kiesewetter, 1773–1850: Wegbereiter des musikalischen Historismus* (Regensburg, 1968), 57–73.

24 Maynard Solomon holds this view and in a personal communication to the author pointed out that such a motivation would be consistent with the pattern of work dedications to members of the Austrian nobility.

25 On the vocal style see Kubik, "Die Ambivalenz als Gestaltungsprinzip. Untersuchungen zur Deklamation in Schubert's *Lazarus,*" and for the

orchestral writing see Maurice J. E. Brown, *The New Grove Schubert* (New York and London, 1983), 85.

26   See Kubik, foreword to *Lazarus oder die Feier der Auferstehung, NSA* (Kassel, 1987), II/2, ix-xiii.

27   These reviews represent the only significant critical response to the Masses when first performed, after which they remained obscure for decades. Mass No. 4 was the only one published while Schubert lived, and the others awaited decades for performance and publication. Schumann briefly mentioned the Masses in the *Neue Zeitschrift für Musik* (1839); in 1874 Brahms performed parts of Mass No. 4. By the middle of the century Mass No. 2 had gained wide currency for liturgical use, and the late Masses were (and remain) acknowledged as among the finest of their time.

28   With the exception of this Mass, Schubert observes convention and follows Michael Haydn and other Austrian composers in setting "Et incarnatus est" for solo voices. Jaskulsky finds precedents for the historicisms in Antonio Caldara's *Missa dolorosa* and J. J. Fux's *Missa Purificationis*.

12 *Schubert's operas*

1   The review by Gerhard R. Koch, dated May 10, appeared on May 14, 1988. Enthusiastic reviews greeted the opera in numerous papers throughout Germany and Austria. Even the opera's detractors, notably Wilhelm Sinkovicz, who wrote the negative reviews in Vienna's *Die Presse* for both the 1988 and 1990 performances, acknowledged implicitly in his reviews that the audience and other critics found the work convincing.

2   Reinhard van Hoorickx, in his sympathetic "Les Opéras de Schubert," *Revue Belge de Musicologie* 28–30 (1974–76), 238–59, summarized the general view: "Certes, on ne cesse de répéter que Schubert n'avait pas un tempérament dramatique, qu'il avait mal choisi ses livrets, etc. . . . C'est partiellement vrai, mais ce n'est pas toute la vérité" (p. 238). Brown argued in many places of the need to experience Schubert's operas in the theater, most concentratedly in his "Schubert's Two Major Operas: a consideration of the Possibility of Actual Stage Production", *Music Review* 20 (1959), 104–18. McKay has devoted much of her career to the study of Schubert's operas (see her "Schubert as a Composer of Operas," in *Schubert Studies: Problems of Style and Chronology*, ed. Eva Badura-Skoda and Peter Branscombe [Cambridge, 1982], 85–104; and *Schubert's Music for the Theater* [Tutzing, 1991]).

3   *Die Verschworenen* (1823), sometimes known as *Der häusliche Krieg*, the title the censors gave it, became Schubert's most popular Singspiel. Although it was not performed during Schubert's lifetime, *Die Verschworenen* became somewhat of a repertory piece in late nineteenth-century Vienna, with runs during the seasons of 1861–62, 1872–73, 1877–81 inclusive, and 1897 (see Franz Hadamowsky, *Die Wiener Hoftheater [Staatstheater] 1776–1966*, 2 vols. [Vienna, 1966]).

4   In February 1977, the Reading University Opera Club (England) gave the first

fully staged performance, albeit in English translation, of the complete *Alfonso und Estrella*. The first performance of the complete opera in its original language took place in Graz on September 28, 1991.

Felix Mottl conducted a shortened version of *Fierrabras* in its stage production at Karlsruhe in 1897. This same version, in French translation, was staged in Brussels in 1928. Several concert presentations of the opera occurred during the 1970s. Around 1980, interest in staging *Fierrabras* increased, with staged performances taking place in Philadelphia (1980), at Hermance Castle in Geneva (1981), in Augsburg (1982), and in a semi-professional production at Oxford (1986). Claudio Abbado conducted the May 1988 Theater an der Wien performances as well as the June 1990 Staatsoper performances of the same production. More recently, Wuppertal has mounted a production.

5   See Till Gerrit Waidelich, *Franz Schubert: Alfonso und Estrella* (Tutzing, 1991), esp. 55–71, for a discussion of the early history of the through-composed German opera.

6   For the complete texts of Schubert's operas, see Christian Pollack, *Franz Schubert: Bühnenwerke: Kritische Gesamtausgabe der Texte* (Tutzing, 1988). For scores of Schubert's operas, we must rely chiefly on the new complete works edition (*NSA*), although not all the operas have been published at this time, and on the old complete works edition (*ASA*), a project whose usefulness has always been limited by J. N. Fuchs' editorial decision to retain the old vocal clefs.

7   Otto Biba, "Schubert's Position in Viennese Musical Life," *19th-Century Music* 3 (1979), 112.

8   For Hüttenbrenner's accounting, see *SDB* 260. For the correspondence regarding possible performances, see *SDB* 238, 240, and 273.

9   See the undated letter to Bäutel (*SDB* 264–65) regarding orchestral works, the July 1824 letter to Ferdinand stating that "there is nothing about" his early quartets (*SDB* 362), and even the recycling and salvaging of sections or movements from early piano works in later works such as D568 in E flat and D958/IV.

10   Franz Schober writing to Heinrich Schubert on November 2, 1876 (*SMF* 208).

11   For further discussion of this unsuccessful mixture, see Waidelich, *Alfonso und Estrella*, 28, and Thomas A. Denny, "Archaic and Contemporary Aspects of Schubert's *Alfonso und Estrella*: Issues of Influence, Originality, and Maturation," in *Eighteenth-Century Music in Theory and Practice: Essays in Honor of Alfred Mann*, ed. Mary Ann Parker (New York, 1994), 241–61.

12   *The New Yorker*, December 11, 1978, 65.

13   See George R. Cunningham's dissertation, *Franz Schubert als Theaterkomponist* (Freiburg, 1974) for the most extended presentation of this line of thinking. Conjecture regarding Mosel's role reached a wider audience through record liner notes written by Walther Dürr, including those for *Alfonso und Estrella* (Angel record SCL-3878 [1978]) and *Lazarus* (Orfeo, C011101A).

14   Letter to Schober, August 14, 1823 (*SDB* 286).

15 More than one reviewer and observer of Schubert's comic *Die Zwillingsbrüder* had already suggested that the tragic, or heroic, mode seemed more suited to Schubert than the farcical (*SDB* 134–141, esp. 134, 136, 139).

16 For a photographic reproduction of the autograph draft of this opera, see Ernst Hilmar, ed., *Franz Schubert: Der Graf von Gleichen* (Tutzing, 1988). Richard Kramer provided a quite detailed review of this publication, including considerable summary of the nature of the composition itself, in *19th-Century Music* 14 (1990), 197–216.

17 See notices in the *Zeitung für die elegante Welt* (Leipzig), No. 95, col. 760, May 16, 1822 and the *Wiener allgemeine Theaterzeitung*, No. 122, p. 488, October 11, 1823 (*SDB* 219 and 291, respectively).

13 German reception

1 *On Music and Musicians*, ed. Konrad Wolff, trans. Paul Rosenfeld (New York, 1969), 108.

2 Heinrich Kreissle von Hellborn, *Franz Schubert* (Vienna, 1865), 580; translation modified from Arthur Duke Coleridge, *The Life of Franz Schubert* (London, 1869; rpt. New York, 1972), II: 255.

3 See Christopher H. Gibbs, *The Presence of* Erlkönig: *Reception and Reworkings of a Schubert Lied* (PhD diss., Columbia University, 1992).

4 Of the initial reviews of part one of *Winterreise*, two were unqualified raves (*SDB* 758, 781) and two more cautious (786, 795).

5 A study of Schubert criticism, comparable to Robin Wallace's *Beethoven's Critics: Aesthetic Dilemmas and Resolutions During the Composer's Lifetime* (Cambridge, 1986), would not yield much because of the paucity of reviews; a collection of reviews of Schubert's music would have little to offer in comparison with Stefan Kunze's *Beethoven im Spiegel seiner Zeit* (Laaber, 1987).

6 There has been relatively little study of Schubert's critical reception; see Herbert Biehle, *Schuberts Lieder: In Kritik und Literatur* (Berlin, 1928); and Christoph-Hellmut Mahling, "Zur Rezeption von Werken Franz Schuberts," in *Zur Aufführungspraxis der Werke Franz Schuberts*, ed. Vera Schwarz (Munich, 1981), 12–33.

7 January 19, 1822, in the Vienna *AmZ* (*SDB* 206–8). Although unsigned, the critique was probably the impressive Friedrich August Kanne, himself a composer, friend, and champion of Beethoven; the article refers to the earlier review (May 12) of *Erlkönig* in the same journal (*Schubert: Die Dokumente seines Lebens* in *NSA* [Kassel, 1964], VIII/5, 126–27).

8 March 23, 1822, in the *Wiener Zeitschrift für Kunst, Literatur, Theater und Mode*. For background on Hentl, see Clemens Höslinger, "Ein Vergessener aus Schuberts Umkreis: Friedrich v. Hentl," *Schubert durch die Brille* 4 (1990), 13–16.

9 *SDB* 543; cf. 353, 603; *SMF* 23. The critic may have been Gottfried Wilhelm Fink, who eventually became the journal's editor and often wrote about Schubert; see Reinhold Schmitt-Thomas, *Die Entwicklung der deutschen*

Konzertkritik im Spiegel der Leipziger Allgemeinen Musikalischen Zeitung (1798–1848) (Frankfurt, 1969), 97–101.

10   See Christopher H. Gibbs, "Schubert in deutschsprachigen Lexica nach 1830," *Schubert durch die Brille* 13 (June 1994), 70–78.

11   See the section "The neglected Schubert?" in chapter 2 pp. 46–48.

12   Quoted by Otto Erich Deutsch in "The Reception of Schubert's Works in England," *Monthly Musical Record* 81 (1951), 202–03. Compare Carl Engel's remark: "So far as new works were concerned, Schubert did not die in 1828 at the age of 31, but lived to be well over eighty" in *Musical Quarterly* 14 (1928), 470.

13   Deutsch, "The Reception of Schubert's Works," 202.

14   See Gibbs, *The Presence of* Erlkönig, chapters 4, 5, and 6.

15   See Edward Kravitt, "The Orchestral Lied: an Inquiry into its Style and Unexpected Flowering around 1900," *Music Review* 37 (1976), 209–26; Hermann Danuser, "Der Orchestergesang des Fin de siècle: Eine historische and ästhetische Skizze," *Die Musikforschung* 30 (1977), 425–52.

16   See Alan Walker, "Liszt and the Schubert Song Transcriptions," *Musical Quarterly* 67 (1981), 50–63; Thomas Kabisch, *Liszt und Schubert* (Munich, 1984); and Gibbs, *The Presence of* Erlkönig, chapter 4. The popular critical reception of his reworkings is also found in Dezső Legány, ed., *Franz Liszt: Unbekannte Presse und Briefe aus Wien 1822–1886* (Vienna, 1984); and Otto Brusatti, *Schubert im Wiener Vormärz* (Graz, 1978).

17   For their 1839 release, Diabelli dedicated the final three piano sonatas to Robert Schumann (D958–60).

18   A fascinating selection of the Viennese criticism from these years is found in Brusatti, *Schubert im Wiener Vormärz*; other sources are listed in Willi Kahl, *Verzeichnis des Schrifttums über Franz Schubert 1828–1928* (Regensburg, 1938).

19   *On Music and Musicians*, 107–12.

20   See Leon B. Plantinga, *Schumann as Critic* (New Haven, 1967).

21   See Ares Rolf, "Schubert in der *Neuen Zeitschrift für Musik* (1834–1844)," *Schubert durch die Brille* 15 (June 1995), 75–94.

22   See Kabisch, *Liszt und Schubert*, and Gibbs, *The Presence of* Erlkönig, 212–18.

23   See Robert Pascall, "Brahms and Schubert," *Musical Times* 124 (1983), 289; James Webster, "Brahms First Maturity," *19th-Century Music* 2 (1978), 18–35, and 3 (1979), 52–71; David Brodbeck, "Dance Music as High Art: Schubert's Twelve Ländler, Op. 171 (D. 790)," in *Schubert: Critical and Analytical Studies*, ed. Walter Frisch (Lincoln, Nebr., 1986), 31–47; and Brodbeck, "Brahms's Edition of Twenty Schubert Ländler: an Essay in Criticism," in *Brahms Studies: Analytical and Historical Perspectives. Papers Delivered at the International Brahms Conference, Washington, D.C., 5–8 May 1983*, ed. George S. Bozarth (Oxford, 1990), 229–50.

24   This topic has not received the attention it merits. In addition to Webster's article cited in the previous note, see Eugen Schmitz, *Schuberts Auswirkung auf die deutsche Musik bis zu Hugo Wolf und Bruckner* (Leipzig, 1954).

25   See the Introduction, pages 8–9.

26   See Edward F. Kravitt, "The Lied in 19th-Century Concert Life," *Journal of the American Musicological Society* 18 (1965), 207–18.

27   *Hanslick's Musical Criticisms*, ed. and trans. Henry Pleasants (New York, 1978), 102.

28   Vol. III, p. 513; see Gibbs, "Schubert in deutschsprachigen Lexica."

29   *Actenmässige Darstellung der Ausgrabung und Wiederbeisetzung der irdischen Reste von Beethoven und Schubert* (Vienna, 1863).

30   See Willi Kahl, "Wege des Schubert Schrifttums," *Zeitschrift für Musikwissenschaft* 11 (1928), 79–95.

31   The longest tribute came from Schubert's oldest friend, Josef von Spaun (1788–1865). The length of the article necessitated its abridgement when three installments were published anonymously in the Linz periodical *Oesterreichisches Bürgerblatt für Verstand, Herz und gute Laune* (March and April 1829; *SDB* 865–79). It was abridged by the editor Anton Ottenwalt, Spaun's brother-in-law. (For the original version, see Georg Schünemann, ed., *Erinnerungen an Schubert: Josef von Spauns erste Lebensbeschreibung* [Berlin and Zurich, 1936] and partly translated in *SMF* 18–29.) Schubert's older brother Ferdinand apparently wrote his tribute in the late 1820s, although it remained unpublished until 1839, when Robert Schumann printed it in the *Neue Zeitschrift für Musik* (*SDB* 912–25).

32   The book actually appeared in Vienna late in 1864 (the preface is signed November 7), but is dated 1865; for information about Kreissle's life and his biographical work on Schubert, see Maurice J. E. Brown, *Essays on Schubert* (London, 1966), 170–76.

33   This work was preceded in 1861 by his much shorter *Franz Schubert: Eine biografische Skizze*, also published in Vienna.

34   Not only was Kreissle's book serialized in the *Niederrheinische Musik-Zeitung für Kunstfreunde und Künstler* and *Signale für die musikalische Welt*, twice translated into English and reworked into French, but it also served as the primary basis for numerous shorter biographies, essays, and articles. Edward Wilberforce's reworked condensation (London, 1866) was superseded by Arthur Duke Coleridge's complete translation (London, 1869), which also included a useful catalogue of works by Sir George Grove. Other early studies rely primarily on Kreissle: George Lowell Austin's *The Life of Franz Schubert* (Boston, 1873); Agathe Audley, *Franz Schubert: sa vie et ses œuvres* (Paris, 1871); and the chapter in Félix Clément, *Les Musiciens célèbres* (Paris, 1868), 455–67. There were a few relatively independent biographical studies, such as Hippolyte Barbedette, *Franz Schubert: sa vie, ses œuvres, son temps* (Paris, 1865). August Reissmann's book *Franz Schubert: Sein Leben und seine Werke* (Berlin, 1873) concentrated more on Schubert's music than his biography. Another valuable source, Constant von Wurzbach's monumental *Biographisches Lexikon des Kaiserthums Oesterreich*, provided information about many crucial individuals in Schubert's life and included an eighty-page entry on Schubert (1876) with detailed catalogues and appendices (vol. xxxii: 30–110).

35   Guido Adler's 1885 article "Umfang, Methode und Ziel der

Musikwissenschaft" in the inaugural issue of the *Vierteljahrsschrift für Musikwissenschaft* 1 (1885), 5–20, is widely viewed as having set the program for modern musicology.

36   *Thematisches Verzeichniss der im Druck erschienenen Werke von Franz Schubert* (Vienna, 1874).

37   *Beiträge zur Biographie Franz Schubert's* (Berlin, 1889).

38   Otto Erich Deutsch, "Schubert: the Collected Works," *Music and Letters* 32 (1951), 226–34.

39   Deutsch's original plan was to release the documentation of Schubert's life in four parts (*SDB* xiv): a revised and translated edition of Grove's biography, together with a Schubert bibliography (later done by Willi Kahl); documents of Schubert's life (*Franz Schubert: Die Dokumente seines Lebens und Schaffens* vol. II/1 [Munich and Leipzig, 1914]), and a second part, not released, devoted to obituaries and reminiscences; an iconography volume (*Franz Schubert: Sein Leben in Bildern*, vol. III ([Munich and Leipzig, 1913])); and a thematic catalogue. Before the war only the two volumes appeared. The former was revised, augmented, and translated as *Schubert: A Documentary Biography*, trans. Eric Blom (London, 1946) and most recently revised as *Schubert: Die Dokumente seines Lebens* in *NSA* (Kassel, 1964), VIII/5. The reminiscences by those who knew Schubert are collected in *Schubert: Die Erinnerungen seiner Freunde*, 3rd edn (Leipzig, 1974) and translated by Rosamond Ley and John Nowell as *Schubert: Memoirs by His Friends* (London, 1958). Deutsch's thematic catalogue first appeared in English as *Schubert: Thematic Catalogue of All His Works* (London, 1951), and was revised as *Franz Schubert: Thematisches Verzeichniss seiner Werke in chronologischer Floge* in *NSA* (Kassel, 1978), VIII/4.

40   Willi Kahl's remarkably comprehensive, if inevitably incomplete, *Verzeichnis des Schrifttums über Franz Schubert 1828–1928* (published in 1938), lists 3,122 items he had identified concerning Schubert and his music. More recently, Otto Brusatti assembled a valuable collection of Viennese reviews written between 1829 and 1848, see *Schubert im Wiener Vormärz*.

41   See Anton Weiss, *Fünfzig Jahre Schubertbund* (Vienna, 1913); Karl Adametz, *Franz Schubert in der Geschichte des Wiener Männergesang-Vereines* (Vienna, n.d. [1939?]). Viennese Schubert celebrations are complicated by the nationalist and political motivations behind much of the promotion of Schubert by the Wiener Männergesangverein and the Schubertbund; see Leon Botstein, *Music and its Public: Habits of Listening and the Crisis of Musical Modernism in Vienna, 1870–1914* (PhD diss., Harvard University, 1985), 361–82; as well as his chapter in the present volume.

42   Another image, "Schubertfeier im Elysium," shows Schubert accompanying Mozart and Haydn in a celestial performance of the "Trout" Quintet before an audience that includes Beethoven.

43   The foreword to the book promises the "purpose is twofold: one scholarly, the other practical."

44   For a discussion of Schubert research since 1928 see Ernst Hilmar, "Die Schubert-Forschung seit 1978," in *Schubert durch die Brille* 16/17 (1996), 5–19.

45   Heuberger, *Franz Schubert* (Berlin, 1902); and Dahms, *Schubert* (Leipzig, 1912).

14 Schubert's reception history in nineteenth-century England

1 *Harmonicon*, 10 (1832), 14 and 280; 9 (1831), 40. Deutsch mistakenly gives 1831 as the date of Schröder-Devrient's visit to London ("The Reception of Schubert's Works in England," *Monthly Musical Record* 81 [1951], 202).

2 For the discovery of this important first public performance, and for much other help in researching this essay, I am indebted to Patricia Troop, of the Schubert Institute (UK). The original program of the von zur Mühlen recital on June 17, 1904, survives in the Wigmore Hall archive.

3 *Musical World*, June 13, 1844. On the supposed performance of the C Major Symphony by the Queen's Band at Windsor Castle at the instigation of the Prince Consort, see my article "The Prince Consort and the 'Great' C Major: a Dubious Scenario Examined," *Music and Letters* 74 (1993), 558–61.

4 See *Musical World*, June 3, 1836; and the *Times*, May 29, 1836.

5 See *Life and Letters of Sir Charles Hallé* (London, 1896), 107ff.

6 The eleven sonatas played by Hallé in his 1868 series of recitals and published by Chappell 1867–68 were as follows: in order of publication: (1) Grand Sonata in A Minor, Op. 42 (D845); (2) Grand Sonata in D Major, Op. 53 (D850); (3) Fantasia Sonata in G Major, Op. 78 (D894); (4) Grand Sonata in A Major, Op. 120 (D664); (5) Grand Sonata in E flat, Op. 122 (D568); (6) Grand Sonata in A Minor, Op. 143 (D784); (7) Grand Sonata in B Major, Op. 147 (D575); (8) Grand Sonata in A Minor, Op. 164 (D537); (9) Grand Sonata in C Minor (D958); (10) Grand Sonata in A Major (D959); (11) Grand Sonata in B flat (D960). Hallé also included in his 1868 series the C Major unfinished sonata (D840), the "Reliquie," and the so-called "Five Pieces" (D459/459A) of 1816.

7 See Hermann Klein, *Thirty Years of Musical Life in London* (London, 1903), 305; A. M. Diehl (Alice Mangold), *Musical Memories* (London, 1897), 109; Joseph Bennett, *Forty Years of Music 1865–1905* (London, 1908), 170.

8 *Daily Telegraph*, January 20, 1863.

9 Edward Wilberforce's abridged English translation had appeared a few years earlier; see *Franz Schubert: A Musical Biography* (London, 1866).

10 Bennett, *Forty Years of Music*, 337.

11 There is no evidence to support the supposition of Deutsch ("The Reception of Schubert's Music," 237) that the "Great" C Major was played by the Queen's Band at Buckingham Palace; see note 3 above.

12 See F. G. Shinn, *Forty Seasons of Saturday Concerts* (Crystal Palace Co., Sydenham, 1896), 11–13.

15 Schubert's reception in France: a chronology (1828–1928)

1 Théophile-Alexandre, violinist (1789–1878), and Alexandre, cellist (1808–80). "Mlle Malzel" refers perhaps to Hélène Robert-Mazel.

2 One is based on the songs *Ständchen* (D889) and *Das Wandern* (D795, 1). Jacques-Gabriel Prod'homme ("Schubert's Works in France," *Musical Quarterly* 14 [1928], 494–95) claims that in 1829 the *Bibliographie de [la] France* had registered the publication, by Richault, of "two favorite melodies, Op. 62, nos. 1 and 2, for piano, by Czerny."

3   *La Poste* (*Die Post* D911, 13); *la Sérénade* (*Ständchen* D957, 4); *Au bord de la*
    mer (*Am Meer* D957, 12); *la Fille du pûcheur* (*Das Fischermädchen* D957, 10);
    la Jeune Fille et la Mort (*Der Tod und das Mädchen* D531); *Berceuse* (*Schlaflied*
    D527).

4   This oft-quoted story is told by Louis Quicherat in his *Adolphe Nourrit, sa vie,*
    son talent, son caractère (Paris, 1867), II: 30.

5   "Société des Concerts du conservatoire: Premier concert," *Journal des Débats*
    politiques et littéraires (January 25, 1835), 2. This excerpt, as well as the
    following, are reproduced in the *Cahiers F. Schubert* 1, 2, 6 (October 1992,
    April 1993–95), 27–46, 49–67, and 25–70.

6   "Feuilleton. – 20 janvier 1835: Variétés musicales," *Le Temps: Journal des*
    Progrès 1920 (January 20, 1835), 1–2.

7   The violinist-violist Chrétien Urhan [Auerhan] (1790–1845) played a
    prominent role in the revelation of Schubert's music to the French public. He
    wrote a certain number of transcriptions after Schubert, notably a "Quintet
    for three violas, cello, double-bass and timpani *ad lib*."

8   It is somehow revealing that Schlesinger began precisely with Schubert's
    Italian songs rather than German Lieder.

9   See Christopher H. Gibbs, *The Presence of* Erlkönig: *Reception and Reworkings*
    of a Schubert Lied (PhD diss., Columbia University, 1992), chapters 4 and 6.

10 *Ibid.*, 221; 327–36.

11 It has to be remembered that, in French, the word "romance" is feminine,
    whereas "Lied" is masculine.

12 La Romance
    Je suis éminemment française, et je viens vous prier de me protéger, de
    prendre mon parti.
    1841
    Contre qui?
    Le Lied
        Parplé! contre moi qui fiens prendre sa blace. Ché suis faporeux comme elle
    et plis qu'elle; ché plis te naifeté qu'elle. Ché été le Binchamin de Schubert et
    ché lé suis à présent té Proch et té Dessauer.
        "Le premier de l'an musical," *Revue et Gazette musicale de Paris* 77
    (December 31, 1840), 648.

13 "Nouvelles diverses," *Le Ménestrel* 53 (November 30, 1851), 3.

14 The "Great" C Major was not to be heard again until it was played in 1908 by
    Charles Lamoureux.

15 Charles Bannelier, "Revue musicale de l'année 1879," *Revue et Gazette*
    musicale de Paris 1 (January 4, 1880), 3.

16 And not 1873, as it is wrongly assumed by Prod'homme (see n. 2).

17 Gaston Dubreuilh, "Concerts et soirées," *Le Ménestrel* 7 (January 14, 1883), 54.

18 See notably: G. Olivier de la Marche, "Archives musicales: Etat actuel de la
    musique en Allemagne et en Italie," *Le Pianiste* 6 (January 20, 1835), 44–45;
    Joseph d'Ortigue, *Le Temps* (1835), and "Revue du monde musical: Schubert,"
    Revue de Paris 30 (June 1836), 271–75; Ernest Legouvé, "Revue critique:
    Mélodies de Schubert," *Revue et Gazette musicale de Paris* 3 (January 15,

1837), 26–27; Léon Escudier, "Mélodies de François Schubert," *La France musicale* 12 (March 18, 1838), 3–4; and Henri Panofka, "Biographie: François Schubert," *Revue et Gazette musicale de Paris* 41 (October 14, 1838), 406–09.

19   Hippolyte Barbedette, *Franz Schubert: Sa vie, ses œuvres, son temps* (Paris, 1866), originally issued in *Le Ménestrel* (1864–65); Agathe (Périer) Audley, *Franz Schubert, Sa vie et ses œuvres* (Paris, 1871); also worth mentioning is Félix Clément, *Les Musiciens célèbres* (Paris, 1868), 455–67.

16 *Franz Schubert's music in performance*

1   David Montgomery, *Historical Information for Musicians: Sourcebooks for the Study of Performance Practices in European Classical music. Vol. I, Musical Tutors, Methods and Related Sources: c.1650–1995* (Huntingdon: 1997) (Hamburg, forthcoming).

2   To date it has not achieved this goal. For example, on the only "historically informed" recording of the Quintet available at the time of this writing (L'Archibudelli & Smithsonian Players, Vivarte SK 46669, 1991) such gestures, including the one above, have merely been transferred to period instruments.

3   Schwind to Schober, March 14, 1824, *Schubert, Die Dokumente seines Lebens*, ed. Otto Erich Deutsch, *NSA* (Kassel, 1964), VIII/ 5, 230 (translation by Jean R. Dane).

4   September 12, 1825. *Dokumente*, 314. This and further translations mine.

5   See Walter Dürr, "Schubert and Johann Michael Vogl: a Reappraisal," *19th-Century Music* 3 (1979), 126–40.

6   See *NSA* IV/2a/2b (Kassel, 1975) for full versions of these examples. *Franz Schuberts Werke in Abschriften* (Kassel, 1975), (under "Volume 80") lists five other songs altered by Vogl: *Antigone und Oedip* (D542), *Der Fischer* (D225), *An Emma* (D113), *Jägers Abendlied* (D215), and *Gebet während der Schlacht* (D171). Echoing Kreissle von Hellborn, John Reed lists two others, *Wer sich der Einsamkeit ergibt* (D478) and *Blondel zu Marien* (D626), whose embellishments may have come from Vogl; see *The Schubert Song Companion* (Manchester, 1985), 68, 434. Also see Robert Schollum, "Die Diabelli Ausgabe der 'Schönen Müllerin'," in *Zur Aufführungspraxis der Werke Franz Schuberts*, ed. Vera Schwarz (Munich and Salzburg, 1981), 140–61. For further examples in Schubert's music, see Walter Dürr's article in the same volume, "'Manier' und 'Veränderung' in Kompositionen Franz Schuberts," 124–39.

7   Andreas Liess, *Johann Michael Vogl: Hofoperist und Schubertsänger* (Graz and Cologne, 1954), 135–36; see *SMF* 112.

8   Otto Erich Deutsch, ed., *Schubert: Die Erinnerungen seiner Freunde* (Leipzig, 1957), 98.

9   "Die Tonkunst in Wien während der letzten fünf Decennien," *Allgemeine Wiener Musik-Zeitung* (1843), 566; cited in Liess, *Vogl*, 129.

10   *Tagebücher*, chapter XIV, no. 2, cited in Liess, *Vogl*, 129.

11   *Dokumente*, 289.

12   See Liess, *Vogl*, chapter XI ("Vogl, der Schubertinterpret").

13   Deutsch, ed., *Erinnerungen*, 117.

14   *Dokumente,* 537–38.

15   Deutsch's unflattering remark that Schubert's "voix de compositeur" was not suited to performance was a commentary on a letter from Anton von Doblhoff to Franz von Schober of April 2, 1824 (*Dokumente,* 237). Dobloff's report reads, "Schubert himself cannot sing," which meant only that Schubert was not feeling well. See successive entries by Schwind.

16   *Dokumente,* 326.

17   *Ibid.,* 390. These two songs are among the most discussed of the "embellished and altered" publications; Heinrich Kreissle von Hellborn suggests that the changes in *Der Einsame* are the worst of all, probably in reference to the high G's added in the 1827 Diabelli edition; *Franz Schubert* (Vienna, 1865), 121n. But one would like to know, as Agatha Christie might have put it, if any crime was committed in the first place. Schubert was still alive in 1827 and might even have approved this publication.

18   Otto Brusatti suggests that she sang Schubert's songs far more often than the sources report, see *Schubert im Wiener Vormärz: Dokumente 1829–1848* (Graz, 1978), 71. Her most celebrated contribution to Schubert's recognition was to convince the aging Goethe (in a private concert, April 1830) of the greatness of Schubert's *Erlkönig* setting. In 1832, Schröder-Devrient sang "Erlkönig" in London with great success, prompting the firm of Wessell & Co. to publish a "Series of German Songs," including, by 1839, thirty-eight Schubert songs.

19   Brusatti, *Schubert im Wiener Vormärz,* 85.

20   *Ibid.,* 85.

21   Sophie Müller mentions, in addition to Bocklet and Schubert, Leopoldine Blahetka (pupil of Joseph Czerny) and Antonie Oster (a prodigy who died in 1828 at the age of seventeen) as "our most outstanding pianists," *Dokumente,* 508; *SDB* 761. Of the major pianists active in Vienna, Carl Czerny, Johann Nepomuk Hummel, Ferdinand Hiller, and Ignaz Moscheles met Schubert, but to what extent they played his music has not been researched. See Vera Schwarz, "Die ersten Interpreten Schubertscher Klaviermusik," in *Aufführungspraxis,* 105–10.

22   5 (February 1836), col. 76.

23   Letter to his parents, July 25, 1825; *Dokumente,* 299; *SDB* 436.

24   Deutsch, ed., *Erinnerungen,* 124.

25   *Ibid.,* 98. On the subject of personae, read Stadler's account of the *Erlkönig* experiment with multiple voices (*Erinnerungen,* 130), plus Edward Cone's thoughts in *The Composer's Voice* (Berkeley, 1974); and compare George Thill's 1930 recording (rereleased on EMI RLS 766), on which Thill sings the narrator and the Erlking, Henri Etcheverry sings the father, and a boy soprano named C. Pascal sings the child.

26   *AmZ* 30/3 (January 16, 1828), col. 42.

27   *AmZ* 39/14 (April 1837), col. 226.

28   Reichold gave the German premiere of the "Trout" Quintet in Leipzig on November 23, 1829, shortly after its initial publication.

29   Richard Heuberger, *Erinnerungen an Johannes Brahms,* ed. Kurt Hofmann (Tutzing, 1971), 115.

30   *Johannes Brahms in seiner Familie: Der Briefwechsel*, ed. Kurt Stephenson (Hamburg, 1973), 99.

31   Kurt Stephenson, *Hundert Jahre Philharmonische Gesellschaft in Hamburg* (Hamburg, 1928), 120.

32   *Gesangstechnik* (Leipzig, 1884).

33   See Renate and Kurt Hofmann, *Johannes Brahms: Zeittafel zu Leben und Werk* (Tutzing, 1983), *passim*. Among the works Brahms played in public are the F Minor Impromptu (D935, 1), *Die schöne Müllerin*, the C Major Violin Fantasy, and the "Trout" Quintet.

34   Heuberger, *Erinnerungen an Johannes Brahms*, 120.

35   See Marianne Kroemer, "Geiger der Schubertzeit in Wien," in *Aufführungspraxis*, 97–104.

36   This was the second "Schuppanzigh Quartet," with Karl Holz, Franz Weiß, and Josef Linke.

37   The original quartet consisted of Joseph Hellmesberger, Sr., M. Durst, C. Heissler, and C. Schlesinger. A few years later, Brahms made his Viennese debut with this ensemble.

38   *AmZ* 43.6 (February 1841), col. 142. Also see *Der Courier*, 4 (1841), 4 and 4/7 (1841), 3, cited in Walter Serauky, *Musikgeschichte der Stadt Halle, Beiträge zur Musikforschung*, vol. III (Halle, 1939; rpt. Hildesheim, 1971).

39   *AmZ* 43/13 (March 1841), col. 278.

40   *Ibid.*

41   See *Der Freischütz* XIV, 222ff.

42   Kate Mueller, *Twenty Seven Major American Symphony Orchestras* (Bloomington, 1973). Also see "Schubert in America: First Publications and Performances," *Inter American Music Review* 1 (1978/79), 5–28.

43   See Christoph Hellmut Mahling, "Zur Rezeption von Werken Franz Schuberts," in *Aufführungspraxis*, 12–23.

44   See Stephenson, *Hundert Jahre*, 143.

45   All of the recordings mentioned above have been rereleased on an EMI collection entitled *Schubert Lieder on Record* (EMI RLS 766).

46   *The Schubert Song Cycles, with Thoughts on Performance* (London, 1975).

47   See Desmond Shawe-Tayler, "Schubert as Written and Played," *London Sunday Times* (June 30, 1963); continued as "Schubert as Written and As Performed: a Symposium," *Musical Times*, 104, (1963), 626–28.

48   Schnabel is often credited with the first complete cyclic programs of Schubert's sonatas, but that distinction actually goes to Johann Ernst Perabo, a pupil of Moscheles who was active in Boston in the 1860s and 1870s.

49   "Tempo et caractère dans les symphonies de Schubert," in *Le Compositeur et son double: essais sur l'interprétation musicale* (Paris, 1971), 140.

50   Giulini and Mackerras retain the traditional opening tempo, forcing the 2:1 ratio to be expressed through laboriously slow tempos for the Allegro – a case, proportionally speaking, of the tail wagging the dog. For the history of this problem, see Jürgen Neubacher, "Zur Interpretationsgeschichte der Andante Einleitung aus Schuberts großer C Dur Sinfonie (D944)," *Neue Zeitschrift für Musik* 150 (1989), 15–21.

51 For details about period instruments, voices, and overall sound, the reader may wish to consult the Norton Handbooks, where proper space has been allotted to the subject: *Performance Practice: Vol. II, Music after 1600,* ed. H. M. Brown and Stanley Sadie (New York, 1989).

52 See the article "Eduard Strauss" by Mosco Carner and Max Schönherr in *The New Grove Dictionary of Music and Musicians,* ed. S. Sadie (London, 1980), xviii: 215.

53 See Roger Fiske, preface to the 1981 reprint of the Eulenburg score (E.E. 1115), ed. Max Hochkofler (London, 1970).

54 See David Montgomery, "Triplet Assimilation in Schubert: Challenging the Ideal," *Historical Performance* 4 (1993), 79.

55 For example, the Stern–Rose–Istomin recording (CBS, MPK 45697, 1965).

56 See Claudio Abbado/Stefano Mollo, recording notes to Symphonies 3 and 4 (DG 423 653 2, 1988). Review by Denis Stevens, "How to do the Right Thing Musically," *New York Times* (Sunday, January 13, 1991).

57 VI:2 (BA 5508).

58 Notes to Schubert's Octet on period instruments (Virgin 7 91120 2).

59 Abbado/Mollo, recording notes; see note 56 above.

60 "Tempo and Character in Beethoven's Music," *Musical Quarterly* 24 (1943), 169ff. and 291ff.

61 Hartmut Krones began this work, but limited his findings to *Winterreise*. See ". . .Nicht die leiseste Abweichung im Zeitmasse," *Österreichesche Musikzeitschrift* 45 (1990), 680–90.

62 See William Newman, "Freedom of Tempo in Schubert's Instrumental Music," *Musical Quarterly* 61 (1975), 528–45.

Index of Schubert's works cited

329

Chamber Music

Index of names